The Legacy of the Siege of Leningrad, 1941–1995
Myth, Memories, and Monuments

The siege of Leningrad constituted one of the most dramatic episodes of World War II, one that individuals and the state began to commemorate almost immediately. Official representations of "heroic Leningrad" omitted and distorted a great deal. Nonetheless, survivors struggling to cope with painful memories often internalized, even if they did not completely accept, the state's myths, and they often found their own uses for the state's monuments. Tracing the overlap and interplay of individual memories and fifty years of Soviet mythmaking, this book contributes to understandings of both the power of Soviet identities and the delegitimizing potential of the Soviet Union's chief legitimizing myths. Because besieged Leningrad blurred the boundaries between the largely male battlefront and the predominantly female home front, it offers a unique vantage point for a study of the gendered dimensions of the war experience, urban space, individual memory, and public commemoration.

Lisa A. Kirschenbaum is a professor of history at West Chester University of Pennsylvania. She is the author of *Small Comrades: Revolutionizing Childhood in Soviet Russia, 1917–1932* (2001). She is the recipient of a fellowship from the National Endowment for the Humanities and grants from the Kennan Institute for Advanced Russian Studies of the Woodrow Wilson Center. She has published articles in *Slavic Review* and *Nationalities Papers*, and she has contributed to the *Women's Review of Books*.

The Legacy of the Siege of Leningrad, 1941–1995

Myth, Memories, and Monuments

LISA A. KIRSCHENBAUM

West Chester University of Pennsylvania

CAMBRIDGE
UNIVERSITY PRESS

CAMBRIDGE UNIVERSITY PRESS
Cambridge, New York, Melbourne, Madrid, Cape Town,
Singapore, São Paulo, Delhi, Mexico City

Cambridge University Press
32 Avenue of the Americas, New York, NY 10013-2473, USA

www.cambridge.org
Information on this title: www.cambridge.org/9780521123556

First published 2006
First paperback edition 2009
Reprinted 2012

A catalog record for this publication is available from the British Library.

Library of Congress Cataloging in Publication Data

Kirschenbaum, Lisa A.
The legacy of the Siege of Leningrad, 1941–1995 : myth, memories,
and monuments / Lisa A. Kirschenbaum.
    p. cm.
Includes bibliographical references and index.
ISBN 0-521-86326-0 (hardback)
1. Saint Petersburg (Russia) – History – Siege, 1941–1944. I. Title.
D764.3.L4.K548 2006
940.54′21721–dc22   2005031818

ISBN 978-0-521-86326-1 Hardback
ISBN 978-0-521-12355-6 Paperback

To my parents, Diane and M. Barry Kirschenbaum,
and to the memory of Reginald E. Zelnik (1936–2004)

Contents

Illustrations

Preface

In August 1991, a small group of Communist diehards launched a coup against Soviet President Mikhail Gorbachev. I happened to be in Moscow at the time, and I learned of the coup when a neighbor, who had been listening to the radio, banged on my door and let me know that we were now living in a state of emergency. Over the next three days, I was an eyewitness to the opposition to the coup that centered on the White House, the headquarters of the government of the Russian Federation, and its newly elected president, Boris Yeltsin. I read the broadsides and leaflets produced to fill the gap left by the absence of regular newspapers. I watched the plotters' televised press conference. I listened to a parade of dignitaries – including Yeltsin, Elena Bonner, and Evgenii Evtushenko – make speeches from the balcony of the White House. I saw an elderly woman admonishing young soldiers perched on armored vehicles along Kalinin Prospekt. I lent a hand in efforts to build a barricade on Manezh Square.

It was during those three days that the seeds of this project were planted. The sense that we were living through and, in a small but not unimportant way, making history was ubiquitous, largely unquestioned, and a bit unnerving. Events looked more threatening, more dramatic, and especially more coherent on CNN than they had on the steps of the Russian White House. All the same, what I read and saw on television immediately became part of my memory of those days. I left Moscow the day after the coup ended, fascinated by how people come to represent and understand their life stories as part of history. Eventually my interest in this process led to the Great Fatherland War, a formative moment in the nation's history and in the life histories of the people who fought and suffered in it.

Acknowledgments

From inspiration to realization is, of course, a long road. I would like to express my gratitude to the people who contributed to this book in all sorts of ways. I have benefited enormously from the advice and questions of friends and colleagues who read all or part of the book in its various forms: Eliza Ablavotski, Carol Avins, Jeffrey Brooks, Maria Bucur, Barbara Engel, Sibelan Forrester, Karin Gedge, Helena Goscilo, Peter Gray, Michael Hickey, Katherine Jolluck, Adele Lindenmeyr, Karl Loewenstein, Lynn Mally, Louise McReynolds, Benjamin Nathans, Claire Nolte, Kendrick Oliver, Cynthia Paces, Rochelle Ruthchild, Roshanna Sylvester, Barbara Walker, Robert Weinberg, and Elizabeth Wood. I extend my thanks to Steven Maddox for his generous help with photographs. Nancy Wingfield happily read and reread everything I sent her, offered invaluable suggestions and support, and helped me hunt down a very difficult-to-find reference.

Conversations with Susan Gans on the nature of trauma and memory helped me to refine my thinking on these issues. In the early, indeed formative, stages of this project, I was fortunate to have the opportunity to participate in Susan Suleiman's National Endowment for the Humanities (NEH) seminar on representations of the occupation and World War II in French literature, history, and film. The seminar's lively, interdisciplinary discussion had a profound impact on the overall shape and approach of this book. I am happy to thank the seminar's participants, as well as the other groups that have responded to papers and presentations over the years, including the American Association for the Advancement of Slavic Studies, the Center for Gender Studies at the European Humanities University (Minsk), the Women's Studies Center at the University of Łódź, and the Centre for Metropolitan History at the University of London.

I am indebted to the librarians and archival staff at the Central State Archive of St. Petersburg, the Central State Archive of Literature and Art of St. Petersburg, Harvard University, the Hoover Institution, the Library of Congress, the National Archives and Records Administration, the Russian National Library, and West Chester University. I gratefully acknowledge the financial support of the National Endowment for the Humanities, the Kennan Institute for Advanced Russian Studies, and West Chester University.

This book incorporates, in modified form, parts of the following previously published material, with the publishers' permissions: "Wartime Commemorations of the Siege of Leningrad: Catastrophe in Myth and

Memory," in Peter Gray and Kendrick Oliver, eds., *The Memory of Catastrophe* (Manchester: Manchester University Press, 2004), 106–17; "Gender, Memory, and National Myths: Ol'ga Berggol'ts and the Siege of Leningrad," *Nationalities Papers* (http://www.tandf.co.uk), 28 (September 2000): 551–64.

Finally, I need to thank the people whose contributions are more profound and more difficult to list. To my parents, Diane and Barry Kirschenbaum, I owe my love of books and of unusual travel opportunities. Their enjoyment and encouragement of my work have been an enormous gift. My other great teacher, Reggie Zelnik, did not live to see the publication of this book. I hope that it reflects something of his light and humane touch.

To John Conway, my husband, who has never known me not to be working on this book, goes the greatest thanks of all – for his love, friendship, insight, and dinner table conversation.

A Note on Transliteration and Translation

I have used the Library of Congress system of transliteration, except in the cases of a few very well-known names, such as Yeltsin. Following Joseph Brodsky's lead, I have transliterated the city's nickname as "Peter." All translations are my own, except where noted.

The Legacy of the Siege of Leningrad, 1941–1995

Myth, Memories, and Monuments

Introduction

Nothing but a legend, you say? You want nothing but facts? Facts are perishable, believe me, only legends remain, like the soul after the body, or perfume in the wake of a woman.

Amin Maalouf[1]

The almost nine-hundred-day siege of Leningrad constituted one of the most dramatic and tragic episodes of World War II. Even before it ended, the siege became one of the war's most widely told stories. Both the Soviet and the Allied press transformed besieged Leningrad into legend, a compelling story of steadfastness and heroism. Inside the blockaded city, Leningraders undertook a startling array of commemorative projects, ranging from keeping diaries to producing documentary films. Perhaps the best known of these contemporary commemorations is Dmitrii Shostakovich's monumental *Leningrad Symphony*. Begun in blockaded Leningrad, the piece had more than fifty international premiers in 1942 and became an emblem of the city's suffering and its strength. In the summer of 1942, the remnants of the Leningrad Philharmonic, supplemented by musicians stationed at the Leningrad front, performed the symphony in Leningrad itself. Broadcast by radio throughout the city, the concert immediately became part of the epic story of the blockade. One of the violins played that evening became a museum piece.

---

[1] Amin Maalouf, *The Rock of Tanios*, trans. Dorothy S. Blair (New York: George Braziller, 1994), 261. Cited in Ellen L. Fleischmann, "Selective Memory, Gender, and Nationalism: Palestinian Women Leaders of the Mandate Period," *History Workshop Journal*, no. 47 (Spring 1999): 142.

The extraordinary and unexpected plight of blockaded Leningrad easily lent itself to mythmaking. Just weeks after the surprise invasion of 22 June 1941, rapidly advancing German troops threatened the city. By the end of August, the local newspapers and radio were exhorting Leningraders to become "heroic defenders" on the "city front." Thus, the epic terms in which the state media would narrate the siege were set quite early. Of course, not all Leningraders responded as the authorities hoped. A minority blamed the military disasters on the Communists and called for Leningrad to be declared an open city. Still, the extent of defeatist sentiment in Leningrad should not be exaggerated. As the historian Andrei Dzeniskevich concludes, "The overwhelming majority of workers maintained loyalty to the party and the Soviet state."[2] Indeed, thousands of Leningraders became involved in local defense, working overtime in the war industry and standing watch on rooftops to extinguish incendiary bombs in buckets of sand.

The first air raids came in early September. The blockade began shortly thereafter. On 8 September 1941, German forces occupied the southern shore of Lake Ladoga (east of the city) and, together with Finnish troops north of the city, severed all land routes in and out of Leningrad. Facing determined resistance from the Soviet Army, the Germans failed to capture the city. They decided to rely instead on siege and starvation. The front lines stabilized within four kilometers of the city, and Leningraders found themselves cut off from what they began to call the mainland.

During the late fall and throughout the winter of 1941–42, the city's population – predominantly women, children, and the elderly – faced conditions that defy imagination. Temperatures in January 1942 reached forty degrees below zero centigrade (minus forty degrees Fahrenheit). Leningraders suffered the bitter cold in a city without heat, electricity, running water, or public transportation. Between 20 November and 25 December, the daily bread ration for dependents fell to a low of 125 grams (not quite 4.5 ounces, perhaps fifteen or twenty small bites of bread). Thousands died of starvation every day, and corpses piled up in streets and courtyards.

The situation within the city improved somewhat in early 1942, when an ice road across frozen Lake Ladoga, dubbed the "Road of Life" by the media, began to carry convoys of food into the city and to transport

---

[2] Andrei Dzeniskevich, "The Social and Political Situation in Leningrad in the First Months of the German Invasion: The Psychology of the Workers," in Robert W. Thurston and Bernd Bonwetsch, eds., *The People's War: Responses to World War II in the Soviet Union* (Urbana: University of Illinois Press, 2000), 77.

the sick and starving to the mainland. With the arrival of spring, the worst period of the blockade came to an end. The evacuation of civilians continued during the summer as flotillas replaced the ice road across Lake Ladoga.

The city remained within easy reach of German artillery, but something like normalcy returned. During the winter of 1942–43, the city's population was far smaller than it had been a year earlier, and better prepared for a winter under siege. Now German artillery fire took more lives than starvation. In January 1943, a Soviet offensive opened a narrow corridor that allowed the reestablishment of a rail connection to the mainland, albeit under heavy fire. A year later, fireworks – which some Leningraders mistook for artillery fire – marked the victorious lifting of the blockade. The human losses were staggering. Conservative postwar estimates put the number of dead at 670,000. More recently, historians have suggested a figure of one million deaths due to starvation as a reasonable approximation. No city in modern times has withstood greater losses.[3]

Since the war, and particularly since the early 1960s, the remarkable story of the blockade has been retold in countless memoirs, interviews, previously unpublished diaries, histories, films, monuments, poems, and museum exhibits. This book tells the story of these stories. Rather than attempting to reconstruct the experience of the blockade, the book aims to trace how, in the half century between the beginning of the Soviet-German war and the end of the Soviet Union, both the people who survived the siege and the state that claimed it as evidence of its own legitimacy remembered and recounted it.

At first glance, the story of the story of the blockade appears to be a relatively straightforward tale of the shifting tactics of the propaganda state. Desperate to mobilize the population, the wartime state extolled the resourcefulness, self-sacrifice, and self-reliance of heroic Leningrad. Shostakovich won the Stalin Prize for his symphony, and Leningrad won the designation "Hero City." Once the war had been won, Josef Stalin, eager to claim responsibility for the overall victory, suppressed the story. The blockade museum, opened during the war, was shuttered. Work on

---

[3] A. R. Dzeniskevich, *Blokada i politika: Oborona Leningrada v politicheskoi kon"iunkture* (St. Petersburg: Nestor, 1998), 45–68. V. M. Koval'chuk, "Tragicheskie tsifry blokady (K voprosu ob ustanovlenii chisla zhertv blokirovannogo Leningrada)," in A. A. Fursenko, ed., *Rossiia v XIX-XX vv: Sbornik statei k 70-letiiu so dnia rozhdeniia Rafaila Sholomovicha Ganelina* (St. Petersburg: Dmitrii Bulanin, 1998), 357–69. David M. Glantz, *The Siege of Leningrad, 1941–1944: 900 Days of Terror* (Osceola, WI: MBI Publishing, 2001), 180.

building war memorials ceased. After Stalin's death in 1953, his political heirs, in search of their own legitimizing myths, revived the story of the blockade, building new monuments and museums and staging elaborate rituals of remembrance.

What complicates this picture of a memory fabricated by and for the state is the fact that long after the Soviet collapse, the images, tropes, and stories of the state-sanctioned cult of the war continued to show up in the oral and written testimonies of blockade survivors – even survivors who were generally unsparing in their attacks on the Soviet state. The freer atmosphere created by the era of glasnost in the late 1980s and the dissolution of the Soviet Union in 1991 undoubtedly expanded the limits of the speakable. It became possible, for example, for survivors to condemn Stalin's refusal to declare Leningrad an open city. Nonetheless, the stories told by the survivors of the blockade, the *blokadniki*, remained remarkably stable. Few, for example, were eager to claim that they themselves had advocated surrender. The so-called Leningrad epic, like the myth of the people's war more generally, outlived the state that sponsored it.[4] Apparently, Leningraders (now Petersburgers) had at some point made the story of heroic Leningrad their own.

The wartime ubiquity of blockade stories and the degree to which the blockade was "commemorated in advance" help to explain this paradoxical outcome.[5] Many contemporary accounts of the blockade aimed to transform the overwhelming, painful, and confusing experiences of the city front into a coherent narrative of historic events. These narratives often appeared in the official media and were told in state-approved terms. However, because the tellers, whether "ordinary" Leningraders or well-known contributors to the Soviet media, were people who had experienced the air raids, shelling, and starvation firsthand, individual memories often shaped official narratives, even as official narratives worked to sanitize, co-opt, and contain memory. Entangled from the outset, official

---

[4] Amir Weiner, *Making Sense of War: The Second World War and the Fate of the Bolshevik Revolution* (Princeton, NJ: Princeton University Press, 2001), 384. Catherine Merridale, *Night of Stone: Death and Memory in Twentieth-Century Russia* (New York: Viking, 2000), 16–17, 213, 238–39, 329. Nina Tumarkin, "The Great Patriotic War as Myth and Memory," *European Review* 11 (2003): 595, 609–10. Benjamin Forest and Juliet Johnson, "Unraveling the Threads of History: Soviet-Era Monuments and Post-Soviet National Identity in Moscow," *Annals of the Association of American Geographers* 92 (September 2002): 531–32.

[5] Pierre Nora, "General Introduction: Between Memory and History," in Lawrence D. Kritzman, ed., *Realms of Memory: Rethinking the French Past*, trans. Arthur Goldhammer (New York: Columbia University Press, 1996), 1: 18.

representations and individual recollections could not be easily distinguished and separated, even by survivors critical of the Soviet state.

Tracing the complicated interweaving of the political and the personal in stories of the blockade requires an approach that is at once chronological and thematic. The first part of this book (Chapters 1–3) focuses on the prewar and wartime narratives and commemorations that provided the framework for later memories and monuments. The second part explores immediate postwar efforts to rebuild the city and efface the memory of the blockade (Chapter 4) and the return of stories and monuments dedicated to the blockade in the 1960s and 1970s (Chapters 5 and 6). The book's final part, which analyzes how and whether blockade stories shifted in late– and post–Soviet Russia, as well as the return of the city's prerevolutionary name (Chapters 7 and 8), brings the story up to 1995. Each part is also organized thematically around the interactions of individual memories with state-sanctioned myths, urban space, and efforts to construct monuments and rituals of remembrance. The Epilogue addresses the question of the meanings of memories, myths, and monuments as fewer and fewer people who lived through the blockade remain to tell the tale.

Memories and Myth

Blockade stories are at once deeply personal and profoundly political. The state's "memory created from above" often distorted or omitted a great deal, but it also deftly appropriated the "everyday" memory of survivors.[6] The power of blockade stories lay precisely in their complicated fusion of mythologized versions of individual life histories and of the nation's history. Struggling to cope with painful memories and to endow tragedy with meaning, survivors often internalized, even if they did not completely accept, the state's myths, and they often found their own uses for the state's monuments. Thus, the book does not attempt to draw sharp distinctions between the allegedly "raw," "unvarnished," "real" memories of survivors and the presumptively politicized myths – or lies – created by the state.[7] Instead, I view "myth" as deeply connected to

---

[6] Alon Confino, "Collective Memory and Cultural History: Problems of Method," *American Historical Review* 102 (December 1997): 1394, 1402.

[7] Nina Tumarkin emphasizes the disjuncture between the survivors' "raw" memory and the state's "myth." Tumarkin, *The Living and the Dead: The Rise and Fall of the Cult of World War II in Russia* (New York: Basic Books, 1994), 188. Cynthia Simmons and Nina Perlina argue that "only with the advent of glasnost" could "unvarnished" accounts

memory. While it may not have been absolutely true, the myth of heroic Leningrad nonetheless offered a real and indispensable means of turning the "muddle of images" that people collected in wartime into meaningful and memorable narratives.[8]

War, as the psychiatrist Derek Summerfield has pointed out, "is a public and collective experience, leaving memories which can be described as social as much as personal."[9] I use "memory" to designate the elements in this amalgam that are primarily personal or autobiographical: the stories told by individual survivors to themselves or others that describe what Ol'ga Grechina called, in her 1994 memoir, "the blockade that I suffered, the one that is mine."[10] Such stories constitute a vital constituent of individual identity, the "scaffolding upon which all mental life is constructed."[11] Often, but not always, they maintain a personal, intimate tone, and insist, as Grechina's does, that "it is all the honest truth."

"appear in print in the USSR." Simmons and Perlina, *Writing the Siege of Leningrad: Women's Diaries, Memoirs, and Documentary Prose* (Pittsburgh: University of Pittsburgh Press, 2002), xxxi. Geoffrey Hosking contrasts "real memory" and "the mythologized substitute." Hosking, "Memory in a Totalitarian Society: The Case of the Soviet Union," in Thomas Butler, ed., *Memory: History, Culture, and Mind* (Oxford: Blackwell, 1989), 118. Éléonora Martino-Fristot contrasts "tragic" individual memory and "epic" public memory, while also tracing their interactions. Martino-Fristot, "La mémoire du blocus de Léningrad, 1945–1999" (Ph.D. diss., Ecole des hautes etudes en sciences sociales, 2002).

[8] The term "muddle of images" is from Samuel Hynes, "Personal Narratives and Commemoration," in Jay Winter and Emmanuel Sivan, eds., *War and Remembrance in the Twentieth Century* (New York: Cambridge University Press, 1999), 207. Studies of memory that have influenced my approach include Susan Crane, "Writing the Individual Back into Collective Memory," *American Historical Review* 102 (December 1997): 1372–85; Andrew Lass, "From Memory to History: The Events of 17 December Dis/membered," in Rubie S. Watson, ed., *Memory, History, and Opposition under State Socialism* (Santa Fe, NM: School of American Research Press, 1994), 87–104; Paula Hamilton, "Memory Remains: Ferry Disaster, Sydney, 1938," *History Workshop Journal*, no. 47 (Spring 1999): 192–210; Daniel J Sherman, *The Construction of Memory in Interwar France* (Chicago: University of Chicago Press, 1999).

[9] Derek Summerfield, "The Social Experience of War and Some Issues for the Humanitarian Field," in Patrick J. Bracken and Celia Petty, eds., *Rethinking the Trauma of War* (London: Free Association Books, 1998), 22. See also Jennifer Cole, "Painful Memories: Ritual and the Transformation of Community Trauma," *Culture, Medicine, and Psychiatry* 28 (March 2004): 87–105.

[10] I have used the translation in Simmons and Perlina, *Writing the Siege*, 106. Ol'ga Grechina, "Spasaius' spasaia: Chast' I: Pogibel'naia zima (1941–1942 gg.)," *Neva*, 1994, no. 1: 212.

[11] Gerald D. Fischbach and Joseph T. Coyle, "Preface," in Daniel L. Schacter, ed., *Memory Distortion: How Minds, Brains, and Societies Reconstruct the Past* (Cambridge, MA: Harvard University Press, 1995), ix. The anthropologist Jonathan Boyarin proposes that "identity and memory are virtually the same concept." Boyarin, "Space, Time, and the

Personal narratives, in short, often claim to be purely personal and thus to provide privileged access to the truth of the blockade and the individual. Such claims are easily and often taken at face value.[12] By contrast, pairing "memory" with "myth" offers a means of calling attention to the ways in which personal memories – especially personal memories of the social trauma of war – are shaped by what Summerfield calls "social memory" and what I call myth.

"Myth" in this context is not meant as a synonym for state-manu-factured falsehood, a tendentious account of the blockade in need of debunking. Neither is it meant to evoke the common understanding of myth as a fictitious, even fantastic narrative used to explain the unknown.[13] Instead, the term is meant to suggest the shared narratives that give form and meaning to the recall of past experience. In "its original sense," as Stuart Charmé points out in his study of biography, "'myth' [*mythos*] refers to plot." In any individual life, this plot is "not apparent in the immediate quality of experience." On the contrary, it must be imaginatively constructed.[14]

The necessity of constructing meaningfully plotted memory may be especially acute in the case of chaotic, painful, unmanageable recollections of war. Examining personal narratives from World War I, Samuel Hynes emphasizes that "myth here, it scarcely needs saying, is not a synonym for falsehood; rather, it is a term to identify the simplified, dramatized story that has evolved...to contain the meanings of the war that we [or survivors] can tolerate, and so make sense of its incoherencies and contra-dictions." This simplified, dramatized narrative can, Hynes argues, both "confirm, but also perhaps construct" the "memories of men who fought but did not write about their wars" because it endows the "incoherence of war" with "order and meaning."[15] It is precisely this sense of a tolera-ble narrative distilled from and, in turn, shaping personal memories that I mean to evoke with the term myth. My interest is not in ascertaining the accuracy of myths, but in emphasizing, as Malcolm Smith does in his

---

Politics of Memory," in Jonathan Boyarin, ed., *Remapping Memory: The Politics of TimeSpace* (Minneapolis: University of Minnesota Press, 1994), 23.

[12] Joan Scott, "The Evidence of Experience," *Critical Inquiry* 17 (Summer 1991): 777.

[13] Fleischmann, "Selective Memory," 143–44.

[14] Stuart L. Charmé, *Meaning and Myth in the Study of Lives: A Sartrean Perspective* (Philadelphia: University of Pennsylvania Press, 1984), 151.

[15] Hynes, "Personal Narratives," 207. See also George Mosse's concept of the "Myth of the War Experience," "which looked back on the war as a meaningful and sacred event" but was not "entirely fictitious." George L. Mosse, *Fallen Soldiers: Reshaping the Memory of the World Wars* (New York: Oxford University Press, 1990), 7.

study of the London Blitz, that myths "are important historical events in their own right."[16]

Like the myth of the London Blitz, which may be its nearest analogue, the simplified, dramatized story of the Leningrad blockade grew out of the state's effort to mobilize an urban population under attack. In both cases, the media worked to persuade individuals that their personal sorrows, along with their seemingly small contributions to the war effort, carried historic, if not epic, importance. Stories of remarkable fortitude and courage, authenticated by images of Londoners singing in shelters or of young women standing watch on Leningrad's rooftops while the bombs fell, transformed the everyday horrors of urban war into heroic legend. Both myths drew on experiences remembered by individuals while providing those who lived through the war with compelling and uplifting frameworks for narrating – and therefore remembering – their own experiences. Both proved exceptionally durable.[17]

Such durable myths are sometimes identified as "collective memory" or "social memory." I have avoided these terms primarily because they lack the emphasis on narrative provided by myth. Other scholars have criticized these terms because they create the misleading impression that collectives somehow "remember" just as individuals do, and have suggested "collective remembrance" and "collected memory" as alternatives.[18] While these terms convey the process by which individuals participate in the construction of public remembrances and monuments, they are less effective than myth in underlining the centrality of shared narratives in the construction of individual memories. Moreover, myth, unlike terms that emphasize retrospective "remembrance," leaves open the possibility that the experience remembered and the act of "collecting" memory may be simultaneous. This was certainly the case in wartime Leningrad, where the process of planning and constructing museums, memorials, and archives began long before the blockade ended.

---

[16] Malcolm Smith, *Britain and 1940: History, Myth, and Popular Memory* (New York: Routledge, 2000), 6.

[17] Angus Calder, *The Myth of the Blitz* (London: Jonathan Cape, 1991), 1–3. Jean R. Freedman, *Whistling in the Dark: Memory and Culture in Wartime London* (Lexington: University of Kentucky Press, 1999), 1–2, 14. Smith, *Britain and 1940*, 2–9.

[18] Maurice Halbwachs, *On Collective Memory*, trans. Lewis A. Coser (Chicago: University of Chicago Press, 1992). On "collective remembrance," see Jay Winter and Emmanuel Sivan, "Setting the Framework," in *War and Remembrance*, 9–10. On "collected memory," see James E. Young, *The Texture of Memory: Holocaust Memorials and Meaning* (New Haven, CT: Yale University Press, 1993), xi–xii. See also Hynes, "Personal Narratives," 206; Boyarin, "Space, Time," 23.

In the Soviet case, where the "evolution" of simplified, dramatized stories involved a great deal of state intervention, ideology might provide a workable substitute for myth. However, it too lacks a clear emphasis on narrative. Myth may be understood as ideology turned into a story – by both the state seeking legitimacy and individuals seeking meaning in traumatic events. Richer in local detail and more dynamic than ideology, myth may also be more readily internalized.[19] Focusing on the construction of mythical narratives provides a powerful means of exploring ideology and memory as, in the words of the historian Michael David-Fox, "mutually interactive phenomena that can mold one another in powerful ways."[20]

The idea that individual memories cannot be cleanly separated from myth – in the sense outlined here of shared, simplified narratives – draws on recent studies in cognitive psychology and on work in psychiatry that emphasizes the social dimensions of memory. Such work critiques the "current discourse on trauma," which views abnormal, so-called traumatic memory as the universal result of traumatic events, with perhaps some variation across cultures. The emphasis on the universality of traumatic memory leads to the conclusion that post-traumatic stress disorder (PTSD) may affect victims of traumas that range, as the title of an important book on treating trauma has it, from domestic abuse to political terror.[21] The concept of the "unrepresentablity" of trauma, the difficulty if not impossibility of assimilating it into "normal" memory, has been particularly influential and contested in studies of the memory of the Holocaust.[22] However, recent work in cognitive psychology has called

[19] Lars T. Lih, "*Vlast'* from the Past: Stories Told by Bolsheviks," *Left History* 6, no. 2 (Fall 1999): 29.

[20] Michael David-Fox, "Cultural Memory in the Century of Upheaval: Big Pictures and Snapshots," *Kritika: Explorations in Russian and Eurasian History* 2 (Summer 2001): 612.

[21] The phrase "current discourse on trauma" comes from Patrick J. Bracken, "Hidden Agendas: Deconstructing Post Traumatic Stress Disorder," in *Rethinking the Trauma of War*, 38. Judith Herman, *Trauma and Recovery: The Aftermath of Violence – from Domestic Abuse to Political Terror* (New York: Basic Books, 1997). On cross-cultural variations, see Selma Leydesdorff et al., "Introduction: Trauma and Life Stories," in Kim Lacy Rogers, Selma Leydesdorff, and Graham Davis, eds., *Trauma and Life Stories: International Approaches* (London: Routledge, 1999), 1–26. On the history of the concept of trauma, see Paul Lerner and Mark S. Micale, eds., *Traumatic Pasts: History, Psychiatry, and Trauma in the Modern Age, 1870–1930* (New York: Cambridge University Press, 2001); Ruth Leys, *Trauma: A Genealogy* (Chicago: University of Chicago Press, 2000). On the history of PTSD, see Allan Young, *The Harmony of Illusions: Inventing Post Traumatic Stress Disorder* (Princeton, NJ: Princeton University Press, 1995).

[22] Shoshana Felman and Dori Laub, eds., *Testimony: Crises of Witnessing in Literature, Psychoanalysis, and History* (New York: Routledge, 1992). Cathy Caruth, *Unclaimed*

into question the "special," abnormal status of traumatic memory. It is by no means a settled proposition that the cognitive processes involved in remembering extremely happy events differ appreciably from those involved in remembering traumatic ones.[23] At the same time, psychiatrists involved in treating traumatized individuals in war zones from Rwanda to Bosnia argue that the discourse on trauma "has systematically sidelined the social dimensions of suffering; instead it promotes a strongly individualistic focus, presenting trauma as something that happens inside individual minds." Questioning the universality of PTSD, they emphasize that the meanings individuals attach or come to attach to their own suffering shape their perceptions and memories of the war experience.[24]

This critique of the discourse on trauma is relevant to a study of the memory of blockaded Leningrad, where, as in the more recent conflicts that have stimulated the critique, the trauma in question involved an attack on an entire community, and responses were necessarily both individual and social. The belief that sacrifices served a just and worthwhile cause, the ability to "draw on social or political values, and on cooperative effort and solidarity" made it possible for those experiencing war to view themselves not as "passive victims" of trauma but as "active citizens." None of which is to deny that such experiences often produce lasting damage. Rather, the central point, for humanitarian aid organizations and historians, is that "war-affected populations are largely directing their attention not inwards, to 'trauma,' but outwards, to their devastated social world."[25] The damage that they see is in the world, not in themselves. From this point of view, the finding that the Soviet veterans and survivors of the war interviewed in the 1990s "do not remember trauma" is not so surprising, and does not necessarily require an explanation grounded

---

Experience: Trauma, Narrative, and History (Baltimore: Johns Hopkins University Press, 1995). Saul Friedlander, ed., *Probing the Limits of Representation: Nazism and the "Final Solution"* (Cambridge, MA: Harvard University Press, 1992). Dominick LaCapra, *Representing the Holocaust: History, Theory, Trauma* (Ithaca, NY: Cornell University Press, 1994). Y. Zerubavel, "The 'Mythological Sabra' and Jewish Past: Trauma, Memory and Contested Identities," *Israel Studies* 7 (2002): 115–44.

[23] J. D. Read, "Introduction to the Special Issue: Trauma, Stress, and Autobiographical Memory," *Applied Cognitive Psychology* 15 (December 2001): S1–S5. Stephan Porter and Angela Birt, "Is Traumatic Memory *Special*? A Comparison of Traumatic Memory Characteristics with Memory for Other Emotional Life Experiences," in ibid., S101–17. Dorthe Bernsten, "Involuntary Memories of Emotional Events: Do Memories of Traumas and Extremely Happy Events Differ?" in ibid., S135–58.

[24] Bracken, "Hidden Agendas," 38.

[25] Summerfield, "The Social Experience," 23, 34.

in the peculiarities of the "Russian way of thinking about life, death, and individual need" that make "notions of psychological trauma...as foreign as the imported machinery that seizes up and fails in a Siberian winter."[26]

The Leningrad case emerges as a particularly clear example of the centrality of social connection and shared values in surviving and remembering war. Chapter 2 documents how, from the first days of the war, the local media infused Leningrad's wartime experience with mythic narratives and images, encouraging Leningraders to understand themselves as "heroic defenders" of a moral and civilized community. Later chapters turn to memoirs, diaries, and oral histories to demonstrate how Leningraders, struggling to cope with the painful realities of the blockade, to make sense of tragedy, and to rebuild their lives, often internalized state myths and incorporated the media's images and slogans into their own memories (Chapters 5 and 7). The myth, whatever its objective truth, offered a means of endowing losses with meaning as the necessary and terrible price of victory. It also raised expectations that the victory would somehow redeem the losses.

Myth, Legitimacy, and Disillusionment

A central theme of the book's story about blockade stories is the role of myth in the construction and eventual delegitimization of Soviet identities. Recent work on Soviet identities has challenged not only the totalitarian model that represented Soviet people as coerced and terrorized but also the so-called revisionist interpretation that insisted on the agency of Soviet citizens actively pursuing their individual self-interests. Studies focusing on Soviet identities have emphasized instead the "mechanisms by which individuals became enmeshed...in the broad agendas and language of the regime."[27] Focusing on the 1920s and 1930s, these studies trace how

---

[26] Merridale, *Night of Stone,* 251, 16.

[27] Stephen Kotkin, "The State – Is It Us? Memoirs, Archives, and Kremlinologists," *Russian Review* 61 (January 2002): 50. Work in this vein includes Kotkin's *Magnetic Mountain: Stalinism as Civilization* (Berkeley: University of California Press, 1995); Jochen Hellbeck, "Fashioning the Stalinist Soul: The Diary of Stepan Podlubnyi (1931–1939)," *Jahrbücher für Geschichte Osteuropas* 44 (1996): 344–73; Hellbeck, "Working, Struggling, Becoming: Stalin-Era Autobiographical Texts," *Russian Review* 60 (July 2001): 340–59; Igal Halfin, *Terror in My Soul: Communist Autobiographies on Trial* (Cambridge, MA: Harvard University Press, 2003); Anna Krylova, "Soviet Modernity in Life

individuals developed Soviet identities by learning to "speak Bolshevik" or by constructing their own "personal Bolshevism" in autobiographies and diaries.[28]

From this perspective, disillusionment emerged not as a result of subversive or dissident ideas but as the consequence of previous illusions. Believing (or suspending disbelief) too well and too long in the face of too much adverse evidence, Soviet people somehow reached a "moment of repudiation." Stephen Kotkin's list of such possible moments includes

one of the famines, one's arrest or that of a relative, the Hitler-Stalin pact, first-hand contact with capitalist societies as a result of World War II, the 'welcome back' from the war with the Gulag, the postwar reimposition of the kolkhoz [collective farm], the Secret Speech, 1956 in Hungary, 1968 in Prague, the shock from the first tourist or business trip to the postwar West.

Unable to account for the new data, belief, like the exhausted regime itself, simply collapsed, and Soviet people, figuratively and literally, left the Soviet experience behind.[29] Problematizing the categories of "collaboration" and "resistance," studies that focus on Soviet identities point to the conclusion that not dissent but circumstances, particularly the increasingly undeniable fact that Soviet socialism would never bury the consumerist economies of the West, subverted the regime. Nonetheless, the fundamental question remains: What made it possible for people "enmeshed" in the regime's language to conclude in a single moment of clarity that their efforts to write themselves into the state's story had been disastrously misplaced?

A study of the construction, repression, reinvigoration, and reconfiguration of the myth of the blockade helps to explain the tsunami of disillusionment that eventually overwhelmed the Soviet state by calling attention to the delegitimizing potential of the Soviet Union's chief legitimizing myths. In the 1960s, when the state established a veritable

and Fiction: The Generation of the 'New Soviet Person' in the 1930s" (Ph.D. diss., Johns Hopkins University, 2001).

[28] On "speaking Bolshevik" see Kotkin, *Magnetic Mountain*, 198–237. Hellbeck calls the diarist Stepan Podlubnyi's "appropriation of public norms" his "personal Bolshevism." Hellbeck, "Fashioning," 361.

[29] Kotkin, "The State," 49–50. See also Kotkin, *Armageddon Averted: The Soviet Collapse, 1970–2000* (New York: Oxford University Press, 2001), 31–34, 42–48, 67–73; Martin Malia, *The Soviet Tragedy: A History of Socialism in Russia, 1917–1991* (New York: Free Press, 1995), 436; Alexei Yurchak, "The Cynical Reason of Late Socialism: Language, Ideology, and Culture of the Last Soviet Generation" (Ph.D. diss., Duke University, 1997); Paul Hollander, *Political Will and Personal Belief: The Decline and Fall of Soviet Communism* (New Haven, CT: Yale University Press, 1999).

cult of the Great Fatherland War – the war that had saved European civilization from fascism and established the Soviet Union as a super-power – it revived wartime language and myths that recalled the mood of unity and shared purpose that it hoped to reestablish.[30] The language and myths of wartime, which differed in substantial ways from the state's prewar language, also contained reminders of the unfulfilled expectations raised by the war. As Boris Pasternak observed in the epilogue to *Doctor Zhivago*, the war raised brittle hopes that the "reign of the lie" had finally ended.[31] Ludmilla Alexeyeva, who was fifteen in 1941, remembered the war as providing a similar sense of the possibility of taking "real" action. The German invasion persuaded her that "I had to act. I had to act as an individual. All of us had to. Our leaders were wrong. They needed us. They needed the public. By realizing that, we became citizens." The conviction that "our leaders were wrong" did not necessarily entail a rejection of Soviet myth. On the contrary, Alexeyeva credited the official media's account of the murder of the partisan Zoia Kosmodem'ianskaia with providing a deeply influential model of individual action and citi-zenship.[32] The war cult had the unintended consequence of perpetuating such (unrealized) visions of Soviet citizenship and the Soviet person.

A comparison with the equally persistent myth of the London Blitz underscores the potential for disillusionment contained in memories of the blockade. The Blitz was widely perceived (how accurately is another question) as a moment of profound national renewal. As Malcolm Smith notes, not only the war generation but also the "generation of the 1950s and 1960s" looked back on 1940 with nostalgia as "the turning point of

---

[30] Tumarkin, *The Living and the Dead*. Amir Weiner, "The Making of a Dominant Myth: The Second World War and the Construction of Political Identities within the Soviet Polity," *Russian Review* 55 (October 1996): 638–60. Kotkin, *Armageddon*, 44–45.

[31] Boris Pasternak, *Doctor Zhivago*, trans. Max Hayward and Manya Harari (New York: Pantheon, 1958), 507. See also Bernd Bonwetsch, "War as a 'Breathing Space': Soviet Intellectuals and the 'Great Patriotic War,'" in *The People's War*, 137–53. I discuss the wartime shift in official language more fully in "'Our City, Our Hearths, Our Families': Local Loyalties and Private Life in Soviet World War II Propaganda," *Slavic Review* 59 (Winter 2000): 825–47.

[32] Ludmilla Alexeyeva and Paul Goldberg, *The Thaw Generation: Coming of Age in the Post-Stalin Era* (Boston: Little, Brown, 1990), 19, 20–21. On the Zoia myth, recently debunked as largely a creation of the press, see E. S. Seniavskaia, "Geroicheskie simvoly: Real'nost' i mifologiia voiny," *Otechestvennaia istoriia*, 1995, no. 5: 38–39; translated as "Heroic Symbols: The Reality and Mythology of War," *Russian Studies in History* 37 (Summer 1998): 61–87. See also Rosalinde Sartorti, "On the Making of Heroes, Heroines, and Saints," in Richard Stites, ed., *Culture and Entertainment in Wartime Russia* (Bloomington: Indiana University Press, 1995), 176–93.

British history," when "the war against fascism produced a war for the New Jerusalem of the welfare state and Keynesian economics."[33] Soviet veterans and blokadniki also often bathed war memories in nostalgia. But theirs was a nostalgia for wartime élan and what might have been, not for the dawn of a new world.[34] In Leningrad, where the myth of the blockade became connected to the long literary tradition of mythologizing the city, its history, and its inhabitants, war stories proved an especially rich source of alternative identities rooted in, but also potentially moving beyond, the Soviet experience and the language of the Soviet state.

The City of Memory

> The city, however, does not tell its past, but contains it like the lines of a hand, written in the corners of the streets, the gratings of the windows, the banisters of the steps.
>
> Italo Calvino[35]

Leningraders lived simultaneously in the real city – the city of communal apartments, queues, and crowded trams – and the city of memory. By "city of memory" I mean the imagined city that city dwellers carry in their minds. Indeed, for those who love and know a city intimately, the memories mapped onto urban places may be more real than the "real" city. It is the reality of this city of memory that makes it possible to claim, as Brian Ladd does in his study of twentieth-century Berlin, that "Berlin is a haunted city."[36] But it is not the city's buildings and streets that "tell its past." Its ghosts live in the minds of its inhabitants, who see the city's spaces as animated by memory, who navigate the real city by remembering where a certain bakery or a friend's apartment used to be.[37]

The centrality of the written word in both Russian and Soviet culture and the importance of Petersburg for Russian literature added an important and pervasive element of myth – shared, dramatized narratives – to the city of memory. As Katerina Clark has noted, what in literary studies

---

[33] Smith, *Britain and 1940*, 4.

[34] E. S. Seniavskaia, *Frontovoe pokolenie, 1941–1945: Istoriko-psikhologicheskoe issle-dovanie* (Moscow: Institut rossiiskoi istorii RAN, 1995). Bonwetsch, "War as a 'Breathing Space,'" 137–39.

[35] Italo Calvino, *Invisible Cities*, trans. William Weaver (New York: Harvest Books/HBJ, 1978), 11.

[36] Brian Ladd, *The Ghosts of Berlin: Confronting German History in the Urban Landscape* (Chicago: University of Chicago Press, 1997), 1.

[37] Michel de Certeau, *The Practice of Everyday Life*, trans. Steven Rendall (Berkeley: University of California Press, 1984), 108.

is conventionally called the Petersburg myth or theme or text "has been an obsession of Russian intellectual life since at least the beginning of the nineteenth century." The myth of the city sometimes threatened to overshadow the city itself, as writers often expressed the "sense that Petersburg at some level 'exists' only as the focus of a myth of Petersburg, that is, only in books."[38] The architects who built the much-reviled high-rise apartment complexes on the outskirts of Leningrad after the war underscored the importance of the myth of the "older more 'real' Leningrad (which is Petersburg)" when they argued that "writers need to come and inhabit this hinterland of mute giants – people it with human characters before the people that live here will feel that they themselves really exist."[39] The stories, images, and themes – particularly the theme of destruction and redemption – that characterized the Petersburg myth provided a frame for individual experiences and memories of the city that largely ignored Soviet categories and the Soviet state's efforts to transform urban space.

That war invaded a city steeped in myth and memory meant that the ghosts of the blockade inhabited an already haunted landscape. Thus, the interaction of the myths and memories constructed around the blockade with the dense texture of myth and memory that Leningraders associated with familiar urban places constitutes a second important theme of the book. Chapter 1 explores the prewar terrain of the city as a landscape of memory. It traces how the Soviet state's efforts to impose its own meanings on the cityscape, coupled with the city dwellers' practice of imagining the city as a complex web of personal and mythical stories, facilitated the construction of wartime myths, which drew on the themes of apocalypse and spiritual purification central to the older Petersburg myth. Chapter 3 returns to the question of place and memory, exploring the role played in wartime commemorations by images of the uncanny city, where familiar neighborhoods became war zones and the housewife's

---

[38] Katerina Clark, *Petersburg, Crucible of Cultural Revolution* (Cambridge, MA: Harvard University Press, 1995), 4, 3. On the Petersburg theme, see Vladimir Toporov, "Peterburg i 'Peterburgskii tekst russkoi literatury' (Vvedenie v temu)," in *Mif. Ritual. Simvol. Obraz: Issledovanie v oblasti mifopoeticheskogo* (Moscow: Progress, 1995), 259–367; Jennifer Jean Day, "Memory as Space: The Created Petersburg of Vladimir Nabokov and Iosif Brodskji" (Ph.D. diss., Indiana University, 2001), 3–39.

[39] Geoffrey Barraclough, "Late Socialist Housing: Prefabricated Housing in Leningrad from Khrushchev to Gorbachev" (Ph.D. diss., University of California, Santa Barbara, 1997), 82, 92. Olga Sezneva finds a similar need for urban myth in post-Soviet Kaliningrad. Sezneva, "Living in the Russian Present with a German Past: The Problems of Identity in the City of Kaliningrad," in David Crowley and Susan E. Reid, eds., *Socialist Spaces: Sites of Everyday Life in the Eastern Bloc* (Oxford: Berg, 2002), 47–64.

daily tasks became heroic. Chapter 4 focuses on the immediate postwar efforts – some embraced by Leningraders, some forced upon them – to erase the physical traces of the blockade and on the marks left by the blockade in the city of memory.

Chapter 8 analyzes the 1991 debates surrounding the decision to return the name St. Petersburg to the map. This process, I argue, illustrates how the myth of the blockade and the Petersburg myth framed Leningraders' memories and allowed them to defend, rework, or renounce Soviet identities. The local dimensions of the city's myths became paramount, as Leningrad's democrats attempted to forge what Svetlana Boym has described as "an identity on the basis of a local antinationalist tradition, one that was determined not by ethnicity but by urban culture – a kind of provincial cosmopolitanism."[40] From this point of view, the blockade demonstrated not that Leningraders were Soviet people but that they were Petersburgers.

Myth, Memories, and Monuments

The Soviet media had long predicted a war with the capitalist West, but had utterly failed to prepare Soviet citizens for the devastation wrought by the German invasion. Under these circumsntances, the wartime ascription of "historic" if not "epic" status to current events lent new significance to a long-standing Soviet practice. In the wake of the October Revolution, the state had sponsored a massive memory project aimed at collecting oral and written reminiscences of participants as a means of giving "individuals opportunities to see themselves as members of October's cast."[41] During the industrialization drive of the early 1930s, the impulse to record world-historical events in the making produced numerous commemorative projects.[42] As in the case of the histories of October, the proposed histories of the Soviet Union's new industrial enterprises were to be built on the individual memories of "ordinary" participants. More broadly, the Soviet state encouraged Soviet citizens, including the newly literate, to keep diaries and write autobiographies as a means of tracing and enacting the Revolution in their everyday lives. Such self-writing emerged as a key Bolshevik practice among all levels of the population.[43]

---

[40] Svetlana Boym, *The Future of Nostalgia* (New York: Basic Books, 2001), 123.
[41] Frederick C. Corney, *Telling October: Memory and the Making of the Bolshevik Revolution* (Ithaca, NY: Cornell University Press, 2004), 82.
[42] Kotkin, *Magnetic Mountain*, 371–73.
[43] Hellbeck, "Working, Struggling," 241.

This tendency to link individual subjectivities and large-scale events produced immediate and often spontaneous efforts to commemorate the blockade. Thus, the book's third important theme is the coalescence of myths and memories into monuments. Here, "monument" functions as a synonym for "memorial," a generic term that covers a wide variety of remembrances: war memorials, films, photo albums, anniversary celebrations, archives, museums, poetry collections, and oral history projects.[44] This broad definition has the advantage of putting the handmade album constructed by schoolchildren who lived through the blockade on a par with the Monument to the Heroic Defenders of Leningrad with its forty-eight-meter obelisk. Both, in different ways and to varying degrees, involve the overlap and interplay of personal stories and public myths. The wartime commemorations examined in Chapter 3 illustrate the ways in which Leningraders' individual monuments to the blockade appropriated the formulas and images of the wartime media. Chapter 6 demonstrates how, in the somewhat more open political climate that followed Stalin's death, designers – many of whom were blokadniki or veterans – worked to include spaces for quiet reflection and mourning, for individual memory, in the state's monuments. Myth structured memory, but it also relied on memory to lend it moral and emotional authenticity.

The Epilogue turns to the mix of nostalgia, disillusionment, Russian nationalism, Petersburg pomp, and Soviet kitsch that characterized the city's post-Soviet commemorations of the fiftieth anniversary of the end of the blockade (1994) and of the end of the war (1995). These eclectic commemorations, often adopting and adapting Soviet-era rituals and monuments, suggest that Soviet identity was never singular or unambiguous, even when it drew on seemingly unambiguous claims regarding the victory over fascism. Rather, Soviet myths and the "blockade that I suffered" were deeply and fundamentally entwined. The individual memories that Leningraders brought to Soviet sites of memory – that in part structured those sites – complicated, without necessarily rejecting, the closure and cant of official myths. Focusing on the interactions of Soviet myth and local memory, the book explores how Leningraders used official narratives to validate loss and to fill in the gaps that they (adaptively) allowed to form in their own recall. It seeks to explain how the story of heroic Leningrad managed to legitimize, outlast, and ultimately discredit the Soviet state.

---

[44] On the distinction between monument and memorial, see Young, *The Texture of Memory*, 3–4.

PART I

MAKING MEMORY IN WARTIME

I

Mapping Memory in
St. Petersburg–Petrograd–Leningrad

> I saw how the city was dying. . . . Petersburg, created by Peter, and immortalized by Pushkin, the dear, strict, and dreadful city – was dying.
>
> Zinaida Gippius, 1920[1]

From the moment of its founding, Petersburg was both a city and a symbol, a city where history veered into myth. That the city existed at all was largely the result of the will of a single, larger-than-life personality, the reforming tsar Peter I. In 1703 – in what subsequent historians and social commentators have understood as an act of enlightenment and of hubris, of inspired creation, ruthless vision, and poor planning – Peter decreed the foundation of a new imperial city on territory recently won from Sweden in the Great Northern War. Turning his back on what he regarded as backward and parochial Moscow, Peter, the first tsar to visit the West, built in the westernmost reaches of his empire, on the sea, where the Neva River empties into the Gulf of Finland. It was a remote and inhospitable site. The chill wind that blows in from the gulf intensifies the harsh winters and dismal autumns to be expected a mere six degrees of latitude south of the Arctic Circle. Under Peter's watch, the almost inaccessible swamps of the Neva delta claimed the lives of thousands of forced laborers, a fact that turned into the myth of a "city built on bones and tears." Peter's first wife, Eudoxia, whom he forced to become a nun in 1698 because she opposed what she regarded as his sacrilegious rejection of the traditions

---

[1] Zinaida Gippius, *Peterburgskii dnevnik* (1929; reprint, Tel Aviv: Izdatel'stvo "Arkhivy," 1980), 13.

of old Muscovy, allegedly issued the prophecy – or perhaps it was a curse – that "the city will be empty."[2]

The city that Peter founded, with its straight and orderly avenues and neoclassical façades – largely the legacy of Catherine II – also became a symbol of rational, enlightened, European modernity, a visible rejection of the tangled alleys and onion domes of Moscow. In his 1905 novel *Petersburg,* Andrei Belyi drolly noted that the capital's central boulevard, Nevskii Prospekt, "is rectilinear (speaking among ourselves), because it is a European prospect; every European prospect is not simply a prospect, but (as I have already pointed out) a prospect is European, because, h'm...yes..." In any event, Belyi concluded, Nevskii Prospekt, like the city itself, "is not altogether Russian."[3] Dubbed by its proponents the northern Palmyra, the Venice of the North, Russia's "window on Europe," Petersburg was at once the emblem of a new Russia and "not altogether Russian," a symbol of European reason and of Russian autocracy. The myth of the city, as Katerina Clark points out in her study *Petersburg, Crucible of Cultural Revolution,* is "Russia's main myth of national identity."[4]

A whole literary tradition – known as the Petersburg theme or text or myth – grew up around the contradictions and oppositions the city embodied. Petersburg's climatic extremes became vital and expressive elements in its myth. Always prone to flooding, despite the system of canals that was meant to tame the waters, the city suffered catastrophic floods in 1772, 1777, 1824, 1903, and 1924. The 1824 flood provided the setting for the emblematic literary representation of the city, Aleksandr Pushkin's long poem *The Bronze Horseman* (Mednyi vsadnik, 1833), in which Étienne-Maurice Falconet's sculpture of the emperor on a rearing horse

---

[2] Iu. M. Lotman, "Simvolika Peterburga i problemy semiotiki goroda," in *Izbrannye stat'i v trekh tomakh* (Tallinn: Aleksandra, 1992), 2: 14. Solomon Volkov, *St. Petersburg: A Cultural History,* trans. Antonina W. Bouis (New York: Free Press, 1995), 1–14. Katerina Clark, *Petersburg, Crucible of Cultural Revolution* (Cambridge, MA: Harvard University Press, 1995), 3–5. Blair A. Ruble, *Leningrad: Shaping a Soviet City* (Berkeley: University of California Press, 1990), 23–35. Nicholas Riasanovsky, *The Image of Peter the Great in Russian History and Thought* (New York: Oxford University Press, 1985). W. Bruce Lincoln, *Sunlight at Midnight: St. Petersburg and the Rise of Modern Russia* (New York: Basic Books, 2002), 1–4.

[3] Andrei Belyi, *St. Petersburg,* trans. John Cournos (New York: Grove Press, 1959), xxii.

[4] Clark, *Petersburg,* 3. See also Rolf Hellebust, "The Real St. Petersburg," *Russian Review* 62 (October 2003): 495–507; Renate Lachmann, *Memory and Literature: Intertextuality in Russian Modernism,* trans. Roy Sellars and Anthony Wall (Minneapolis: University of Minnesota Press, 1997), 51; Sidney Monas, "St. Petersburg and Moscow as Cultural Symbols," in Theofanis George Stavrou, ed., *Art and Culture in Nineteenth-Century Russia* (Bloomington: Indiana University Press, 1983), 26.

1. The Bronze Horseman, symbol of the city. The dome of St. Isaac's Cathedral is visible in the background. Photo by author.

came to life, terrorizing a clerk, who, having lost his beloved to the flood, cursed the city and its founder. The 1924 flood, coming exactly one hundred years after the most mythologized flood in the city's history, appeared to Petersburgers not only as a natural disaster but also as an inauspicious portent somehow connected to the decision in the same year to rename the city Leningrad.[5] Yet if nature often threatened to destroy the city, it also magnified its grandeur. During the spectacular white nights around the summer solstice, the eerie and ethereal midnight light makes Petersburg's granite embankments and stuccoed façades appear almost weightless, pink stone floating above a shimmering river, a fairy-tale city. In his introduction to *The Bronze Horseman*, Pushkin celebrated this mood of the city as well, proclaiming his love for the "limpid dusk and moonless radiance of nights so full of thought."[6] (See Illustration 1.)

Central to the Petersburg theme was the notion of constant and free interchange between the city and its literary doubles. Having come

[5] Ruble, *Leningrad*, 23. Volkov, *St. Petersburg*, 339–40. Clark, *Petersburg*, 5.
[6] Marshall Berman, *All That Is Solid Melts into Air: The Experience of Modernity* (New York: Penguin Books, 1982), 181–89; quotation from *The Bronze Horseman*, 183. Grigorii Kaganov, *Images of Space: St. Petersburg in the Visual and Verbal Arts*, trans. Sidney Monas (Stanford, CA: Stanford University Press, 1997).

alive in Pushkin's poem, Falconet's sculpture itself became what Nikolai Antsiferov, one of the great connoisseurs of the city's literary representations, called the city's *genius loci,* a real landmark that marked a symbolic center.[7] Fedor Dostoevskii's tales of the underbelly of St. Petersburg not only reflected the neighborhood around Haymarket Square but also, as Antsiferov noted, created real attitudes, expectations, and understandings of the lived experience of the city. Thus, Antsiferov remembered that his reading of Dostoevskii had made his student poverty easier to bear: "All the adversities of Petersburg life are accepted beforehand: literature had made them attractive. . . . I even liked the danger and prospect of hunger . . . I looked at life through the prism of literature."[8] In this same vein, the cultural historian Vladimir Toporov has argued that "in the most complex, and perhaps key cases, it is equally difficult to decide conclusively what in the text is from the city, and – more often – what in the city is from the text."[9]

By the time Antsiferov published his *Soul of Petersburg* (Dusha Peterburga) in 1922, the city was no longer Petersburg and no longer the capital, but the Petersburg myth lived on. In a burst of the same sort of patriotism that brought Americans "French" (as opposed to German) toast, Nicholas II in 1914 decided that Sankt-Peterburg sounded too German, and renamed the city Petrograd. (The original name was actually Dutch, as Peter had hoped to produce an Amsterdam on the Neva.) Three years later, with German armies threatening to take Petrograd, the embattled Bolsheviks moved the capital back to Moscow, where it has remained ever since.[10] Despite these changes, the layers of myth and memory – both personal and public, real, fictive, and imagined – connected to the cityscape worked to reshape, and thereby maintain, the symbolic power of Petersburg–Petrograd–Leningrad. The city may be understood, to borrow a portion of Pierre Nora's definition of a "realm of memory," as "a circle within which everything counts, everything is symbolic, everything is

---

[7] Nikolai Antsiferov, *Dusha Peterburga* (1922; reprint, Paris: YMCA Press, 1978), 27. Emily Johnson, "Transcendence and the City: Nikolai Antsiferov's *The Soul of Petersburg* as an Aesthetic Utopia," in Ian Lilly, ed., *Moscow and Petersburg: The City in Russian Culture* (Nottingham: Astra Press, 2002), 103–16. I thank the author for sharing an advance copy of this work.

[8] Quoted, with ellipses, in Jennifer Jean Day, "Memory as Space: The Created Petersburg of Vladimir Nabokov and Iosif Brodskji" (Ph.D. diss., Indiana University, 2001), 21.

[9] Vladimir Toporov, "Peterburg i 'Peterburgskii tekst russkoi literatury' (Vvedenie v temu)," in *Mif. Ritual. Simvol. Obraz: Issledovanie v oblasti mifopoeticheskogo* (Moscow: Progress, 1995), 282.

[10] Volkov, *St. Petersburg,* 195–96. Anatolii Sobchak, *Iz Leningrada v Peterburg: Puteshestvie vo vremeni i prostranstve* (St. Petersburg: Kontrfors, 1999), 14.

significant." At the same time, the symbolic power of the city depended on the "ability to resurrect old meanings and generate new ones along with new and unforeseeable connections."[11]

The tendency of Petersburg authors and readers to "look at life through the prism of literature," coupled with the themes of both apocalypse and fantastic, macabre beauty central to the Petersburg myth, make what Clark calls its "clichés" an essential starting point for the consideration of how the city's inhabitants perceived and narrated their memories of revolution and war.[12] Accounts of the famine years of the Civil War – which in many ways prefigured the blockade and famine of World War II – were shaped, as the introduction to Zinaida Gippius's diary quoted in the epigraph illustrates, by the terms and images of the Petersburg myth. During World War II, the complicated connections between the myth of the city and national identity played themselves out in the streets of Leningrad, as some of the most resonant prerevolutionary place names returned. The relationship of places, names, and memory – between the locations where events occurred and the sites of commemoration created in individual memories and in the cityscape – is particularly complicated in a city like present-day St. Petersburg, where multiple memories and monuments often occupy the same space. The tendency of memories of the nine-hundred-day siege to move toward myth – toward "the sacrificial, the prophetic, the sacramental, and the universally significant" – owed much to the already enchanted landscape invaded by the war.[13]

Through the Prism of Memory and Literature

Rimma Neratova, who was a medical student in the city at the time of the Nazi invasion in 1941, remembered how the memory of the famine that had gripped Petrograd during the Civil War helped to save her family during World War II:

Since time immemorial, Aunt Matia's light yellow cloth suitcase had been stored on a large black shelf in our front hall.... Ancient rusks were stored in it. In the early and mid-1920s, all Petrogaders stored up reserves of rusks, in case there was a new famine. The rusks were older than I was.

---

[11] Pierre Nora, "General Introduction: Between Memory and History," in Lawrence D. Kritzman, ed., *Realms of Memory: Rethinking the French Past*, trans. Arthur Goldhammer (New York: Columbia University Press, 1996), 20, 15.

[12] Clark, *Petersburg*, 6.

[13] Paul Fussell, *The Great War and Modern Memory* (New York: Oxford University Press, 1975), 131.

During the blockade, the suitcase full of dried biscuits, an unassuming and, as it turned out, quite practical site of memory, had "unheard of value."[14]

Throughout the fall of 1941, Neratova's father, who, "having been through two wars, revolution, prison, and famine, justly considered himself experienced," directed everyone in the family to join any line they happened across and to buy whatever they found to add to the family's "food reserves" and "barter fund." He put special stock in tomato juice. As early as September, her father issued the "order" to buy a children's sled. In hindsight, his explanation was prophetic, if overoptimistic. Anticipating the breakdown of public transportation and the cessation of snow removal, he predicted, "During the winter, this may be our salvation – you can carry firewood and whatever you please.... During the winter, it will be worth its weight in gold!" Thus, Neratova and her sister went to the Passazh department store and bought "two gold children's sleds." "Two months later," Neratova concluded, the sleds proved useful, "but for death, not life."[15] The family survived the starvation winter and was evacuated in March 1942.

Neratova's father likely remembered that during the catastrophic winter of 1918–19, famine conditions prevailed, and children's sleds became – as they did again during the winter of 1941–42 – a primary means of transporting the dead to the cemeteries.[16] Indeed, accounts of the "dying city" that came out of the Civil War often bear an extraordinary resemblance to those that came out of World War II. Not only did the survival strategies and the obsessions of the hungry remain remarkably stable – they were expressed in remarkably similar ways. The darkly ironic image of the child's sled used to haul corpses constituted a vivid memory for survivors of both wars.

During the Civil War, Petrograders lived through a period of famine that began before the Bolshevik Revolution, became catastrophic in late 1918, and persisted into the following fall, when White forces under General Nikolai Iudenich briefly blockaded the city. They shared with survivors of the shorter but more intense period of starvation during the

---

[14] Rimma Neratova, *V dni voiny: Semeinaia khronika* (St. Petersburg: Zhurnal "Zvezda," 1996), 42.

[15] Ibid., 42–43.

[16] On conditions in Petrograd, see Mary McAuley, *Bread and Justice: State and Society in Petrograd, 1917–1922* (New York: Oxford University Press, 1991), 263–88; V. I. Musaev, "Byt gorozhan," in V. A. Shishkin, ed., *Petrograd na perelome epokh: Gorod i ego zhiteli v gody revoliutsii i grazhdanskoi voiny* (St. Petersburg: Dmitrii Bulanin, 2000), 61–74.

Leningrad blockade the impulse to document even the least-appetizing meal in often loving detail and to note their innovations and skill in preparing whatever came to hand. In his Civil War reminiscences, the literary critic Viktor Shklovskii noted, with a combination of irony and pride, "We used rye flour and horsemeat to make beef stroganoff."[17] During the Civil War, the poet Nikolai Tikhonov, who also lived through the World War II blockade, wrote a poem celebrating the foul-smelling salt-fish (*vobla*) that constituted an important, and often maligned, part of the average Petrograder's diet.[18] In a similar poetic vein, the literary critic Lidiia Ginzburg remembered that in besieged Leningrad, "both the millet and the sprats were – beautiful."[19]

If some similarities between memories of the two famines can be attributed to the similarities between the two experiences, some memories – of the civilized city transformed into a wasteland of snow and ice and of the spirit of the besieged city – suggest not only shared experiences but also a shared fund of stories, images, and myths through which experience was perceived, interpreted, narrated, and remembered. The artist Vladimir Milashevskii's memoirs of the Civil War, written at a distance of fifty years, self-consciously drew on the myth of the city as a precarious European outpost. As the snow that no one bothered to clear piled up, it seemed to Milashevskii that "Europe was being conquered by Scythia! The architectural clarity of right angles and parallels in the buildings of the capital [which, of course, Petrograd no longer was] was lost! . . . Everything seemed to take the form of icebergs and icicles, as in the frame of a village well in January!"[20] To understand the hungry, grim winter in terms of the disappearance of rectilinear prospects and the transformation of the imperial capital into a vassal of Scythia, indistinguishable from "other Russian cities" that, in Belyi's words, "offer little more than piles of little wooden houses," was to recast personal observation in the terms of myth.[21] Survivors of the Civil War famine connected the snowbound winter of 1918–19 to recurrent mythical visions of the

---

[17] Viktor Shklovskii, *A Sentimental Journey, Memoirs, 1917–1922*, trans. Richard Sheldon (Ithaca, NY: Cornell University Press, 1970), 180.

[18] Compared to the rations on which Leningraders starved in 1941 and 1942, the Civil War rations were relatively generous. Ekaterina L. Yudina, "Metropolis to Necropolis: The St. Petersburg Myth and Its Cultural Extension in the Late 1910s and 1920s" (Ph.D. diss., University of Southern California, 1999), 44. Shklovskii, *Sentimental*, 234.

[19] Lidiia Ginzburg, *Blockade Diary*, trans. Alan Myers (London: Harvill Press, 1995), 63.

[20] Vladimir Milashevskii, *Vchera, pozavchera . . . Vospominaniia khudozhnika* (Moscow: Kniga, 1989), 196. Yudina, "Metropolis," 37.

[21] Belyi, *St. Petersburg*, xxii.

city destroyed – whether by flood, as in Pushkin, or by a terrorist bomb, as in Belyi.[22] Survivors of the Leningrad blockade followed their lead as once again Eudoxia's curse – "the city will be empty" – seemed on the verge of fulfillment.

As in the Petersburg myth, images of doom and destruction coexisted in survivors' accounts with promises of rebirth and redemption. The cultural historian Toporov's definition of the Petersburg text as tracing "the path to moral salvation and spiritual rebirth in conditions where life perishes in the kingdom of death" effectively describes many reminiscences of both the Civil War and World War II.[23] Shklovskii connected the famine experience to the moral and spiritual values of Christianity and antiquity – albeit with no small measure of irony – when he proclaimed, "How much greed for fat runs through the Bible and Homer! Now the writers and scholars of Petrograd understand that greed."[24] The poet Osip Mandelstam associated the Civil War famine with a quasi-religious ecstasy: "At last we found inner freedom, real inner merriment. . . . Apples, bread, potatoes – they sate not only physical but spiritual hunger."[25] The poet Ol'ga Berggol'ts described a similar state of clarity and liberation in one of her best-known poems from the blockade, "February Diary": In the midst of cold, filth, and hunger, "we breathed such stormy freedom,/ that our grandchildren might envy us."[26] The at once utopian and eschatological myth of Petersburg provided a framework for understanding starving Petrograd – and later starving Leningrad – as both spiritual community and martyr city, both heroic and tragic.

None of which is to suggest that everyone who survived the famine years or the blockade told their stories in terms borrowed from the Petersburg myth. Rather, the relevant point is that the preexisting myth – already associated with the famine of the Civil War – offered a powerful and well-known template for the interrelated tasks of coping with, understanding, narrating, and commemorating the traumatic events of the blockade. As the cultural historian Solomon Volkov has asserted, with the Civil War,

[22] Toporov, "Peterburg," 295–300. Americans have a similar tradition of imagining the destruction of New York. Max Page, "Creatively Destroying New York: Fantasies, Premonitions, and Realities in the Provisional City," in Joan Ockman, ed., *Out of Ground Zero: Case Studies in Urban Reinvention* (Munich: Prestel, 2002), 166–83.

[23] Toporov, "Peterburg," 279. Lotman, "Simvolika," 13.

[24] Shklovskii, *Sentimental*, 234.

[25] Cited in Volkov, *St. Petersburg*, 224. See also Sharon Leiter, *Akhmatova's Petersburg* (Philadelphia: University of Pennsylvania Press, 1983), 69.

[26] Ol'ga Berggol'ts, "Fevral'skii dnevnik," in *Sobranie sochinenii v trekh tomakh* (Leningrad: Khudozhestvennaia literatura, 1989), 2: 38.

"to suffer together with Petersburg became a ritual."[27] While poets, novelists, and critics were those most likely to borrow established literary formulas, during the blockade their narratives reached a wider public via books, newspapers, and radio. Berggol'ts, who during the blockade was the beloved voice of Leningrad radio, wrote "February Diary" for broadcast on Red Army Day in February 1942 and conceived of the poem "as a lyrical conversation with Leningraders."[28] Such cultural productions suggested compelling ways of dealing with and talking about unimaginable times.

Soviet officials and Western historians alike have often characterized the blockade of Leningrad during World War II as unique, unprecedented, or incomparable.[29] Of course, in many ways it was – almost three years long and claiming perhaps a million or more lives, the blockade, like the total and brutal war of which it was a part, had no ready analogues. Nonetheless, it is essential to keep in mind that people who found themselves in the midst of "unprecedented" events had a habit of searching for precedents, for frameworks of understanding.[30] They turned to memory – as in the case of Neratova's father – and to literature for appropriate interpretive means. Ginzburg recalled that "during the war years, people used to read *War and Peace* avidly, comparing their own behavior with it (not the other way round – no one doubted the adequacy of [Lev] Tolstoi's responses to life)."[31] The state's decision in the first days of the Nazi invasion to style the Soviet-German war the "Great Fatherland War" (*Velikaia Otechestvennaia voina*) constituted a vulgarized version of the same impulse. Soviet propaganda recognized that the original Fatherland War fought in 1812 against Napoleon offered useful lessons in appropriate and patriotic behavior.[32] For Petrograders and, as we shall see, for

[27] Volkov, *St. Petersburg*, 223.

[28] Ol'ga Berggol'ts, *Govorit Leningrad* in *Stikhi-proza* (Moscow: Gosudarstvennoe izdatel'stvo khudozhestvennoi literatury, 1961), 375–76.

[29] Mikhail Kalinin quoted in O. F. Berggol'ts, V. N. Druzhinin, A. D. Dymshits, A. G. Rozen, and N. S. Tikhonov, eds., *900 dnei* (Leningrad: Lenizdat, 1957), 5. Leonid Brezhnev quoted in N. D. Shumilov, *V dni blokady* (Moscow: Mysl', 1977), 3. Harrison E. Salisbury, *The 900 Days: The Siege of Leningrad* (New York: Harper and Row, 1969), 513–14.

[30] A similar search for precedents characterized the London Blitz. Angus Calder, *The Myth of the Blitz* (London: Jonathan Cape, 1991), 1, 18.

[31] Ginzburg, *Blockade Diary*, 3. See also Ol'ga Berggol'ts, "'Slushai nas, rodnaia strana!'" in Soiuz zhurnalistov SSSR, Leningradskoe otdelenie, *S perom i avtomatom: Pisateli i zhurnalisty Leningrada v gody blokady* (Leningrad: Lenizdat, 1964), 431.

[32] John Barber, "The Image of Stalin in Soviet Propaganda and Public Opinion during World War 2," in John Garrard and Carol Garrard, eds., *World War 2 and the Soviet People* (New York: St. Martin's Press, 1993), 41. David Brandenberger, *National Bolshevism:*

Leningraders, the myth of the city – celebrating the city's civilization and its terrors, elaborating both its destruction and redemption – also provided a vital means of making sense of unprecedented circumstances, of imagining an eternal community.[33]

The Myth of the Center

The Petersburg myth drew on local topography, climate, events, and architecture: the flooding Neva, the white nights, Peter's audacious urban planning, the city's rectilinear prospects. However, the power of the myth also depended on an identification of the city with the nation – as at once its apotheosis and its antithesis. The local landscape not only provided the basis of local solidarity, a sense of ongoing community, but also embodied the contradictions and contests central to Russian identity. The rivalry with Moscow that animated so many Petersburg texts constituted the clearest symptom of the national significance of the Petersburg myth. From the Slavophile point of view, "soulless, bureaucratic, official, unnaturally regular, abstract, bleak, escheated, un-Russian" Petersburg stood against "soulful, domestic-intimate, patriarchal, cozy, 'down-to-earth' [*pochvenno-real'noi*], natural, Russian" Moscow. From the Westernizer's perspective, "Petersburg, as a civilized, cultured, systematically organized, logically rectilinear, harmonious, European city opposed Moscow, as a chaotic, disorderly, contrary-to-logic, semi-Asiatic village."[34] Either way, the city occupied the center of a contested Russian national identity.

Neither changes in regime nor changes in the city's name, or even the return of the national government to Moscow stripped Petersburg, Petrograd, and, after 1924, Leningrad of its multivalent power as a symbol. The return of the national capital to Moscow inflicted a serious loss of status on the city on the Neva. All at once it became obvious how far from the geographic center of the nation the erstwhile capital stood – threatened

Stalinist Mass Culture and the Formation of Russian National Identity, 1931–1956 (Cambridge, MA: Harvard University Press, 2002), 43–62.

[33] Aileen G. Rambow makes a similar point in "The Siege of Leningrad: Wartime Literature and Ideological Change," in Robert W. Thurston and Bernd Bonwetsch, eds., *The People's War: Responses to World War II in the Soviet Union* (Urbana: University of Illinois Press, 2000), 158.

[34] Toporov, "Peterburg," 268. See also Ladis K. D. Kristof, "The Geopolitical Image of the Fatherland: The Case of Russia," *Western Political Quarterly* 20 (December 1967): 943–44; Monas, "St. Petersburg and Moscow," 26–39; Richard Wortman, "Moscow and St. Petersburg: The Problem of Political Center in Tsarist Russia, 1881–1914," in Sean Wilentz, ed., *Rites of Power: Symbolism, Ritual, and Politics since the Middle Ages* (Philadelphia: University of Pennsylvania Press, 1985), 244–74.

by German and then White armies, cut off from food supplies, Petrograd became an increasingly provincial city. As hungry workers returned to the countryside or joined the Red Army, and the middle class and the gentry fled abroad, the city's population plummeted from over two million before the war to 720,000.[35] And yet, the cityscape itself seemed to belie this second-rate standing. The grand imperial boulevards and façades remained. Moreover, the city was the site of a new myth of origins – the so-called cradle of Revolution. The nation's two great founders raised their arms in salute on opposite sides of the Neva – Peter on his rearing stallion in Senate Square, Vladimir Lenin, a mile or so upstream, atop an armored car rendered in stone in front of the Finland Station (see Illustration 2).[36] As the author of a review embracing the notion of a "Leningrad theme" – the Soviet successor to the "Petersburg theme" – pointed out in 1945, while a new era began with the October Revolution, the "symbol of this new epoch was once again the city on the Neva."[37]

Leningraders continued to claim for their city a symbolic power generally reserved for capital cities.[38] As the British journalist Alexander Werth, who grew up in Petersburg, emphasized, Leningraders had a clear "superiority complex."[39] Among the local intelligentsia, the provincial city with the crumbling imperial façade increasingly came to be regarded as an alternate capital, a refuge – both real and symbolic – from the ugliness and brutality of the Soviet state. They privileged the mythical Petersburg that was civilized, cultured, and European.[40]

Treating Leningrad as a mythical center made it possible to endow local events with national – even international – significance and to understand national events in primarily local terms. Only in Petrograd could the third anniversary of the October Revolution be staged where it occurred, with a significantly embellished reenactment of the storming of the Winter Palace.[41] On Palace Square in 1920, the local action defined

---

[35] Ruble, *Leningrad*, 41. Musaev, "Byt gorozhan," 61.

[36] Joseph Brodsky, "A Guide to a Renamed City," in *Less Than One: Selected Essays* (New York: Farrar Straus Giroux, 1986), 69–70.

[37] G. Makogonenko, "Leningradskaia tema," *Znamia*, 1945, no. 1: 207.

[38] Clifford Geertz, "Centers, Kings, and Charisma: Reflections on the Symbolics of Power," in *Rites of Power*, 30. See also Maurice Agulhon, "Paris: La traversée d'est en ouest," in Pierre Nora, ed., *Les lieux de mémoire* (Paris: Gallimard, 1992), vol. 3, *De l'archive à l'emblème*, 869.

[39] Alexander Werth, *Leningrad* (New York: Knopf, 1944), 65.

[40] Clark, *Petersburg*, 7. Brodsky, "A Guide," 93.

[41] James von Geldern, *Bolshevik Festivals, 1917–1920* (Berkeley: University of California Press, 1993), 199–207.

2. Monument to Vladimir Lenin, the city's other namesake, at the Finland Station.
Photo by John K. Conway.

the national holiday, and the nation seemed to be celebrating the city.
For Leningraders – even if they had not participated in the day's fateful
events – what was reenacted was at once of national, local, and personal
significance.[42]

A similarly complicated interaction of the personally, locally, and
nationally significant occurred during World War II. In a poem published
in Berlin in 1923, Anna Akhmatova had addressed herself "to my fellow
citizens" (*sograzhdane*), a term that implied "a group with which she
shares both irrecoverable loss and an unshakable loyalty."[43] When
Akhmatova, whose poetry had not been published in the Soviet Union
since 1922, spoke on Leningrad radio in September 1941, at the very outset of the blockade, she returned to her post–Civil War language of deeply
felt local solidarity. She addressed her listeners as "my dear fellow citizens

---

[42] Nikolai Nikitin, "Nasha slava," *Moskva,* 1957, no. 6: 5–6.
[43] Leiter, *Akhmatova's Petersburg,* 53. Volkov, *St. Petersburg,* 243.

[*sograzhdanki*], mothers, wives, and sisters of Leningrad." For Akhmatova, Leningrad itself was at once real, mythical, and literary: "The enemy threatens the city of Peter, the city of Lenin, the city of Pushkin, of Dostoevskii, and of [the poet Aleksandr] Blok with death and shame." Conflating her personal ties to the city with the community of Leningraders and the larger national struggle, she said, "All my life is connected with Leningrad. In Leningrad I became a poet.... I, like all of you now, live with one unwavering belief – that Leningrad will never be fascist."[44] Representing besieged Leningrad as a large extended female family – mothers, wives, and sisters – Akhmatova suggested that local and intensely personal motivations gave meaning to the struggle against Germany.

Leningraders viewed the city with hometown pride as the symbolic center of the nation. As curator of the State Public Library's Petersburg–Leningrad collection, the librarian Vera Karatygina was steeped in the history and myths of the city. During the blockade, she took charge of the library's Leningrad in the Great Fatherland War project, an effort to acquire and catalog everything printed about the siege – from ration coupons to newspaper articles.[45] In a lecture presented at the library in November 1942, she emphasized the special symbolic role of Petersburg, its connection to Leningrad, and Leningraders' profound attachment to their city. Karatygina began her talk with Lenin's contention that "Petersburg as a separate locality does not exist. Petersburg is the political, geographic, and revolutionary center of Russia. The whole of Russia follows the lead of Petersburg." Tracing the persistence of this view of the city after the Revolution, Karatygina quoted Sergei Kirov, the Leningrad Party leader assassinated in 1934: "For 200 years the capital of the empire, Petersburg was the center of the country's life. Socialist Leningrad in many ways remains the center [*takovym*], especially for us Leningraders." For Karatygina, the symbolic centrality of Leningrad had distinctly local consequences. She echoed a commonly expressed sentiment when she noted that it was the sense of the special character of the city that made it possible for Leningraders to brave cold, hunger, bombs, and artillery attack in order "to have the right after the war to say, 'I was in Leningrad during the blockade, and I did all that was in my power to defend my city.'"[46]

---

44 Quoted in Berggol'ts, "'Slushai nas,'" 432–33. Salisbury, *900 Days,* 285.
45 On the Leningrad in the Great Fatherland War collection, see Chapter 3.
46 "O 'Kollektsii Petersburg-Leningrad': Istoriia goroda po materialam kollektsii. Doklad V. A. Karatyginoi" (November 1942), Arkhiv Rossiiskoi Natsional'noi Biblioteki (hereafter Arkh. RNB) f. 12, T. 297, ll. 1–4.

Here, what mattered was membership in the community of Leningraders who stayed and struggled.

Leningraders, like Londoners during the Blitz, created a "small-scale political 'we'" that was in many ways defined by and identified with well-known urban spaces.[47] Thus a London printer acknowledged, "I ain't a religious bloke.... But I should hate to see dear old St. Paul's hurt or damaged...well, blast it all, it's *London*, ain't it?" At the same time, London, the nation's cultural and political center under attack, rather unproblematically stood in for the nation. The Christopher Wren churches damaged or destroyed by German bombs in London represented not just the city but "British heritage."[48] Leningraders, too, had a habit of imagining familiar buildings as embodiments of Leningrad. Thus, Neratova remembered that in March 1942, just as the city was emerging from the deadliest period of the blockade, "even the palaces" seemed "broken down, somehow exhausted, like the people."[49]

However, while Leningrad under siege, like London during the Blitz, constituted a compelling symbol of "civilization" withstanding "barbarism," it was a more complicated and potentially troublesome national symbol. If in Neratova's reminiscences the palaces seemed to empathize with Leningraders, other buildings constituted enemies in their midst. She recalled that "all Leningraders very much hoped that bombs would fall on the NKVD [political police] building on Liteinii and destroy its archives. But the building, with its grandiose marble entryway, remained standing – enormous, terrible."[50] Here, local defense became something quite distinct from the Soviet cause, and Leningrad functioned as an alternative capital. After all, the NKVD was headquartered in Moscow, the real capital, and Josef Stalin, for one, had deep misgivings about Leningraders' "myth" of the self-sufficiency and unique fate of their city.[51] Nonetheless, during the war the myth proved a useful resource – for the state working to mobilize the population and for Leningraders in search of a way to make sense of their experiences.

[47] Jean R. Freedman, *Whistling in the Dark: Memory and Culture in Wartime London* (Lexington: University of Kentucky Press, 1999), 29.

[48] Quoted in Susan Briggs, *The Homefront: War Years in Britain, 1939–1945* (London: George Weidenfield and Nicolson, 1975), 68, emphasis in original. On "British heritage" see Malcolm Smith, *Britain and 1940: History, Myth, and Popular Memory* (New York: Routledge, 2000), 96.

[49] Neratova, *V dni*, 97.

[50] Ibid., 99.

[51] V. Kutuzov, "Muzei oborny Leningrada," *Dialog*, 1988, no. 24: 24–25.

"Urban Names Are the Language of the City"

The city currently known as St. Petersburg is a city of multiple names. As the poet Joseph Brodsky playfully noted in his "A Guide to a Renamed City," written when the city was still Leningrad:

> So this two-hundred-and-seventy-six-year-old city has two names, maiden and alias, and by and large its inhabitants tend to use neither.... In a normal conversation they would rather call it simply "Peter."... Both "Leningrad" and "Petersburg" are a bit cumbersome phonetically, and anyway, people are inclined to nickname their habitats.... On top of that, since the real name of the emperor in Russian is Pyotr, "Peter" suggests a certain foreignness and sounds congenial.[52]

That the city was for a decade "Petrograd" does not fit into Brodsky's scheme but further complicates the historical picture, as does the fact that the citizens – in a very close vote – rebaptized the city St. Petersburg in 1991, although most of them still call it Peter or Petersburg. In addition, the city boasts an array of epithets, including the already mentioned Venice of the North, northern Palmyra, window on Europe, and the cradle of Revolution, as well as Red Petrograd, the northern capital, the northern Rome, the city of the white nights, the city of three revolutions (1905, and the two in 1917), the city of the great Lenin, the prosaic city on the Neva, and the poetic Petropol'.[53]

The revolutionary propensity for renaming streets and squares added to the toponymic confusion in Petrograd–Leningrad. In the first "wave" of revolutionary name changing that coincided with the first anniversary of October, many of the city's most well-known places lost their imperial names.[54] Nevskii Prospekt became Twenty-fifth of October Prospekt, the date of the Bolshevik Revolution, according to the Julian calendar.[55] (The Bolsheviks overthrew the old calendar in February 1918, and the anniversary was celebrated on 7 November, the Western-Gregorian date.) The Field of Mars (Marsovo pole), a military parade ground under the tsars, became the Square of the Victims of the Revolution (ploshchad' Zhertv Revoliutsii).[56] Here, the Bolsheviks were in a sense completing the work

---

[52] Brodsky, "A Guide," 70–71.

[53] Anatolii Sobchak, *Iz Leningrada*, 30–36.

[54] *Gorodskie imena segodnia i vchera: Peterburgskaia toponimika: Spravochnik-putevoditel'*, 2d ed. (St. Petersburg: Informatsionno-izdatel'skoe agentsvo "LIK," 1997), 15.

[55] Ibid., 84.

[56] Ibid., 73. Iu. I. Smirnov, *Sankt-Peterburg XX vek: Chto? Gde? Kogda?* (St. Petersburg: Izdatel'stvo "Paritet," 2000), 44–46.

of the Provisional Government, which had authorized the burial on the
site of those who died during the February Revolution. In March 1917,
a group of preservationists, led by the architect Ivan Fomin, had successfully argued that the Field of Mars, rather than Palace Square (Dvortsovaia ploshchad') should become the site of the monument to the martyrs
of February.[57] But the square – the heart of imperial Petersburg and the
scene of what the Bolsheviks came to view as the primary action during
the October Revolution – proved too symbolically rich for the Bolsheviks
to ignore.[58] In October 1918, the local authorities renamed it Uritskii
Square (Uritskogo ploshchad'), in honor of Moisei Uritskii, the first head
of the Petrograd Cheka (the precursor of the NKVD), who had been, in
the course of a very tumultuous first year of revolution, assassinated by a
moderate socialist at number 6 Palace Square.[59]

In 1923, a second wave of renamings brought a phalanx of revolutionaries and radicals into Petrograd's streets. Senate Square, the home
of the Bronze Horseman, became Decembrists' Square, in honor of the
officers who in 1825 had led an abortive revolt against Nicholas I on the
site. Voskresenskaia (Resurrection) Embankment became (and remains)
[Maximillen] Robespierre Embankment. Aleksandrovskii Prospekt became Dobroliubov Prospekt, after the nineteenth-century radical Nikolai Dobroliubov. The so-called father of Russian Marxism, Georgii
Plekhanov, also had a street named in his honor, although he was a
Menshevik. New Soviet-style terms also found their way onto the map
of Petrograd: Street of the Red Textile Worker, Strike Street, Uprising
Street.[60]

Street names, as the historian Daniel Milo points out in reference to
the French Revolution, "tell us about the *establishment's* representations
of the national memory and the nation's great men."[61] In the Soviet case,
the waves of name changes in 1918 and 1923, along with the rebaptism
of the city in 1924, were part of an official effort to consecrate Petrograd
as the city of the Revolution. The substitution of, for example, Street
of the Village Poor for Gentry Street, and the appearance of boulevards
named to honor Karl Marx (1925, since 1991 Bol'shoi Sampsonievskii),

[57] Yudina, "Metropolis," 135–38.
[58] On the emerging importance of Palace Square in narratives of the Revolution, see
      Frederick C. Corney, *Telling October: Memory and the Making of the Bolshevik Revo-
      lution* (Ithaca, NY: Cornell University Press, 2004), 75–82, 182–83.
[59] Lev Sidorovskii, "Dvortsovaia ploshchad'," *Dialog*, 1987, no. 14: 28.
[60] *Gorodskie imena*, 15, 42, 106, 43, 96.
[61] Daniel Milo, "Street Names," in Kritzman, *Realms of Memory*, 366, emphasis in original.

Jean-Paul Marat (1918), and Mikhail Bakunin (1918), had much in common with the name changes that swept French cities in the early 1790s.[62] For revolutionaries in Russia as in France, "street names were a means of propaganda, an instrument of revenge, and an arm of punishment."[63]

At the same time, the city's streets, squares, boulevards, and parks remained everyday urban spaces, with personal associations, uses – and names – that the state could never entirely control.[64] In other words, the new official names did not always become part of Leningraders' internal maps – a common outcome wherever authorities change long-standing urban names. An anecdote from the 1920s had an old women asking a *militsioner* how to get to the Passazh department store. He replies, "Take Third of July to Twenty-fifth of October . . ." "Dear, " she interrupts him, "I have to walk for three months?"[65] (Sadovaia Street had been renamed Third of July, the date on which the Bolsheviks' July Days uprising began in 1917.) Only the local police, it seemed, learned the new names and tried to enforce them.

That these new urban names were the "establishment's representation" did not mean that Leningraders had to accept them. Conceiving of the city as an "organic whole" and of urban names as the natural "language of the city," Antsiferov clearly hinted at disagreement, if not contempt, for the practice of imposing artificial names on the "historical-cultural organism" of the city.[66] One expects that Antsiferov never called Nevskii "Twenty-fifth of October Prospekt." Indeed, twenty years after Petrograd had become Leningrad, many "new" names had yet to become a part of everyday speech. The journalist Werth visited the besieged city in September 1943 and reported that "everybody without exception continued to call the principal streets and most of the others by their old names."[67]

On 13 January 1944, the official maps moved closer to those of individuals who had never stopped using the old names. Four months after Werth's visit, while the offensive that broke the siege was in its last stages, the local government reinstated the prerevolutionary names of some of

---

[62] *Gorodskie imena*, 15, 111, 72, 24.

[63] Milo, "Street Names," 372.

[64] Michel de Certeau, *The Practice of Everyday Life*, trans. Steven Rendall (Berkeley: University of California Press, 1984), xix.

[65] N. A. Sindalovskii, *Mifologiia Peterburga: Ocherki* (St. Petersburg: Norit, 2000), 141–42. For an analogous French anecdote, see Milo, "Street Names," 378.

[66] Antsiferov, *Dusha Peterburga*, 41.

[67] Werth, *Leningrad*, 18.

Leningrad's most notable streets and squares. Nevskii Prospekt, the Field of Mars, Palace Square, and Sadovaia all reappeared.[68] The official return of a few imperial place names was recognition that the popular prerevolutionary names existed as part of the rich symbolic texture of the city, which allowed and reflected multiple, sometimes overlapping, understandings of the city as hometown, the incarnation of Russia's imperial glory, the cradle of Revolution, and – the city's wartime epithet – heroic Leningrad.

A 1944 study of the boulevard emphasized that Nevskii – as a place and a name – was central to Leningrad's identity and to Leningraders' experiences of and stories about their city. "Leningrad," wrote the architect Iakov Rubanchik, "is unimaginable without Nevskii Prospekt, without the splendid palaces and churches that line the avenue, without the bridges spanning the canals, without the squares that lie along the city's remarkable main artery."[69] His phrase "unimaginable without Nevskii Prospekt" suggested that names mattered, and that Leningraders mapped their experiences onto a mental landscape that did not necessarily accommodate the "establishment's representations" – certainly not something as "unimaginable" as Twenty-fifth of October Prospekt.

The return to imperial names did not efface the revolutionary associations of these sites so much as play on the multiplicity of meanings embodied in a single space. Rubanchik's architectural history of Nevskii Prospekt described the city as a collage of imperial and revolutionary events:

Herzen Street [as of 1993, Bol'shaia Morskaia], crossing the prospect, enters Palace Square through the triumphal arch. The arch is the centerpiece of the General Staff Building, designed by Karl [Carlo] Ivanovich Rossi and completed in 1829. Such a work of architectural art could only be born in the atmosphere charged with the people's joy that followed the victory in the Fatherland War against the invading Napoleonic horde.... History may know no other examples of a building of such majesty and ceremony. This remarkable arch became triumphal for the Red Guard, which on the night of 26 October 1917 stormed the Winter Palace – the last stronghold of the bourgeois Provisional Government.[70]

---

[68] Other changes included Kazanskaia pl. (previously Plekhanov Square), Izmailovskii pr. (previously pr. Krasnykh Komandirov), and Suvorovskii pr. (formerly Sovetskii pr). Smirnov, *Sankt-Peterburg XX vek, 27. Gorodskie imena*, 17, 49, 120.

[69] Ia. O. Rubanchik, *Nevskii prospekt: Arkhitekturnye ansambli Leningrada* (Leningrad: Iskusstvo, 1944), 5. A review emphasized Rubanchik's insistence on the importance of the "'Nevskii Prospekt' theme" for "Petersburg–Petrograd–Leningrad." V. V. Stepanov, "Ia. O. Rubanchik, 'Nevskii Prospekt,'" *Arkhitektura Leningrada*, 1944, no. 1–2: 29.

[70] Rubanchik, *Nevskii prospekt*, 14–15.

3. The arch of the General Staff Building on Palace Square, monument to victory in the first Fatherland War. *Source:* ITAR-TASS.

Not bothering – not needing – to make explicit the parallels between the victory over the "Napoleonic horde" and the devoutly wished victory over the "Hitlerite horde," Rubanchik painted a remarkable picture of the square as a multifaceted monument to multiple victories. In his vision, the triumphal arch of Rossi's General Staff Building celebrated two "people's victories" – in 1815 and 1917. (See Illustration 3.)

The architect N. Smirnov similarly represented the Field of Mars as a site that commemorated imperial, revolutionary, and World War II victories. Writing in the magazine *Leningrad* in the summer of 1944, Smirnov treated the square's monument to the Revolutions of 1917 as one moment in its long history as a commemorative space.[71] He paid particular attention to the connections between the Field of Mars and the nearby statue of General Aleksandr Suvorov, best known for successfully managing the astonishing retreat of Russian forces through the French Alps in 1799–1800. Emphasizing the continuity between Soviet and imperial military glory, Smirnov ended his description by noting that "today, in 1944, on the memorable day of the Leningrad salute – 27 January – the Field of Mars once again resounded with the thunder of victory salvos."[72] Like

[71] N. Smirnov, "Marsovo Pole," *Leningrad*, 1944, no. 10–11: 27–28.
[72] Ibid., 28.

Palace Square, the Field of Mars, the location of the monument to the
Revolution's martyrs, had strong associations with imperial military victories as well as October, and thus embodied the wartime tendency to link
the Revolution to the glories of the Russian Empire.

In addition to such imperial cum revolutionary associations,
Leningraders had more personal memories associated with the city's
public spaces. Describing, as many memoirs do, a walk through the
snowdrifts and silence of the city at the beginning of December 1941,
Neratova's reminiscences illustrate how public spaces were mapped into
personal memory. Neratova describes a journey marked by the complex
exchange between eternal architecture and immediate concerns, between
the remembered prewar city and its uncanny wartime counterpart that
is central to the role of the city – as everyday place and as symbol – in
memories of the blockade:

> Every time I went across the Field of Mars, when, thanks to the long vista and
> the open sky I felt especially sharply the lightness and beauty of the city in winter,
> there appeared within me, by some mysterious means, the certainty that I was not
> fated to die here, from hunger and bombs. And this was always connected to the
> feeling of the city's beauty – an eternal beauty. To my internal question, "Really?
> I won't die?" there was always the response: "No, I will live – I can't die, while it
> is given to me to feel such beauty!"[73]

For Neratova, the Field of Mars was neither a monument to revolutionary
martyrs nor to imperial glory but a place of reflection and epiphany, where
she situated herself in the larger context of the city's "eternal beauty." Her
story, in which the hungry turn their attention to the magnificence of the
city, has strong affinities with the Petersburg myth of doom and resurrection. Reworking the "establishment's representations" of the city, she
celebrated the grandeur of the imperial architectural legacy, but the city's
monuments – she mentions the Bronze Horseman encased in a protective
wooden shell (Illustration 4), the Mikhailovskii (Engineers') Palace, and
the Peter Paul Fortress – suggested to her not military victories past and
future but personal salvation.

The importance that both survivors and the state accorded the city's
places and names points to the centrality of the personal and the local
in both the state's efforts to mobilize the population and Leningraders'
efforts to make sense of their suffering and to survive. Once the battle
was won, the state became suspicious of local loyalties, while survivors

[73] Neratova, *V dni*, 72–73.

4. The Bronze Horseman, protected from bombs and artillery fire. *Source:* ITAR-TASS.

continued to privilege them. Indeed fifty years after the blockade started, many survivors defended the name Leningrad against efforts to return St. Petersburg to the map. For some, Leningrad retained the establishment's intended meaning – the symbol of Great October. For many, however, the blockade had transformed revolutionary Leningrad into a byword for their city's – and their own – suffering and redemption.

2

The City Scarred

War at Home

> The verses and songs of the war years possessed some kind of magical power; they inspired hope, and strengthened belief in victory and the coming radiant life.
>
> M. G. Zeger, recollections of a wartime radio engineer in 1991[1]

Just before dawn on 22 June 1941, more than three million troops – the Germans and their allies – rolled across the Soviet border from the Baltic to the Black Sea. At noon on that lovely summer Sunday, Leningraders gathered around public loudspeakers to hear Foreign Minister Viacheslav Molotov inform the country that Kiev, Zhitomir, and Sevastopol' had come under surprise attack. While Soviet propaganda had long predicted a war with the capitalist West, many Leningraders, like other Soviet citizens, remembered scarcely believing what they heard – although what they heard was hardly the full story. Molotov explained neither the extent of the debacle nor the reasons that Soviet forces were unprepared.[2] The broadcast itself remained a vivid memory, clearly marking a rupture in the life of the country and of individuals. It was, as the literary critic Lidiia Ginzburg remembered, a "combination of the intensely

[1] M. G. Zeger, "My eti dni uzhe zavoevali," in P. A. Palladin, M. G. Zeger, and A. A. V'iunik, eds., *Leningradskoe radio: Ot blokady do "ottepeli"* (Moscow: Iskusstvo, 1991), 117.

[2] David M. Glantz, *The Siege of Leningrad, 1941–1944: 900 Days of Terror* (Osceola, WI: MBI Publishing, 2001), 21–22. Reinhard Rürup, ed., *Voina Germanii protiv Sovetskogo Soiuza, 1941–1945: Dokumental'naia ekspozitsiia* (Berlin: Argon, 1992), 41–47. G. N. Peskova, "'Nashe delo pravoe': Kak gotovilos' vystuplenie V. M. Molotova po radio 22 iiunia 1941 goda," *Istoricheskii arkhiv*, 1995, no. 2: 32–39. Iu. I. Smirnov, ed., *Sankt-Peterburg XX vek: Chto? Gde? Kogda?* (St. Petersburg: Izdatel'stvo "Paritet," 2000), 204.

personal (the loudspeaker prophesying each one's fate) and the epochally important."[3]

As the war became an everyday reality for Leningraders, the radio and newspapers remained vital components of their experiences. Within twenty-four hours, the news of the invasion prompted some hundred thousand Leningraders not subject to immediate mobilization to volunteer for service in the home guard (*opolchenie*). Josef Stalin's radio address on 3 July, in which he ordered the formation of home guard units, increased both pressure to enlist and enlistments, particularly among Party members. By October, nearly three hundred thousand Leningraders had been called up for active military service, and over two hundred thousand more – about one-quarter of whom were women – had volunteered to serve in the home guard. Often sent to the front hastily trained and poorly armed, the home guard sustained appalling casualties.[4] At the same time, the official media exhorted teenagers, pensioners, and especially women to "substitute" at work for fathers, brothers, husbands, and sons who had left the factory for the front.[5] During the summer, roughly half a million civilians, again primarily young women, were conscripted to dig tank traps and build fortifications along largely undefended approaches southwest of the city. The air war had reached these areas, and by working in the open, the labor conscripts were particularly vulnerable to strafing.[6]

---

[3] Lidiia Ginzburg, *Blockade Diary*, trans. Alan Myers (London: Harvill Press, 1995), 6. Rimma Neratova, *V dni voiny: Semeinaia khronika* (St. Petersburg: Zhurnal "Zvezda," 1996), 6. Ales' Adamovich and Daniil Granin, eds., *Blokadnaia kniga* (Moscow: Sovetskii pisatel', 1982), 210. Dmitrii Likhachev, "Kak my ostalis' zhivy," *Neva*, 1991, no. 1: 6. E. S. Kots, "'Na moiu doliu vypal schastlivyi lotereinyi bilet': Otryvki iz vospominanii E. S. Kots," *Istoricheskii arkhiv*, 1999, no. 3: 75. O. M. Freidenberg, "Osada cheloveka," *Minuvshee*, 1987, no. 3: 9. Hoover Institution Archives, Lydia Osipov, Folder 80033–10.v. Harrison E. Salisbury, *The 900 Days: The Siege of Leningrad* (New York: Harper and Row, 1969), 119–20.

[4] Richard Bidlack, "The Political Mood in Leningrad during the First Year of the Soviet-German War," *Russian Review* 59 (January 2000): 98–100. Andrei R. Dzeniskevich, "The Social and Political Situation in Leningrad in the First Months of the German Invasion: The Social Psychology of the Workers," in Robert W. Thurston and Bernd Bonwetsch, eds., *The People's War: Responses to World War II in the Soviet Union* (Urbana: University of Illinois Press, 2000), 77–82.

[5] My conclusions regarding newspaper coverage are based on the reading of at least one issue per month of both *Leningradskaia pravda* and *Komsomol'skaia pravda* between June 1941 and June 1945. See, for example, *Komsomol'skaia pravda* (hereafter *KP*), 24 June 1941, 26 June 1941, 9 January 1942, 11 September 1942, 20 December 1942.

[6] *KP*, 22 August 1941. Neratova, *V dni*, 18–28. Elena Kochina, *Blockade Diary*, trans. Samuel C. Ramer (Ann Arbor, MI: Ardis, 1990), 34–35. Richard Bidlack, "Foreword: Historical Background to the Siege of Leningrad," in Cynthia Simmons and Nina Perlina,

Still, Leningraders had no indication of the magnitude of the threat to the city until 21 August, when *Leningradskaia pravda*, the radio, and broadsides posted around the city finally informed them of the "immediate threat of attack by German-fascist forces."[7] The first large-scale bombardment of the city occurred on the night of 6 September 1941. The blockade began two days later when German and Finnish troops severed all land routes in and out of Leningrad. Increased Soviet resistance slowed the German advance, but Nazi forces reached the southern slopes of the Pulkovo Heights, a mere twelve kilometers from the city's center, the terminus of Leningrad's southwest tram line. The city endured twelve more night air raids and eleven daytime raids in the next twenty days.[8] On 16 September, *Leningradskaia pravda* and posters throughout the city carried the ominous warning, "The Enemy Is at the Gates!"

Cut off from what they called the mainland (*bol'shaia zemlia*), subject to frequent air raids and artillery attacks, and, by November, living on starvation rations, Leningraders increasingly looked to the newspaper and the radio for a sense of connection to one another and the wider world and for an explanation of their painful and extraordinary everyday lives. On the first day of the war, fifteen-year-old student Iura Riabinkin waited over two hours in an enormous queue for a newspaper that never arrived. Six months later, by which time food had become the starving teenager's main preoccupation, Riabinkin nonetheless also noted in his diary the frustrations of a lack of information: "I didn't read any newspapers yesterday. I know nothing, have no idea about what's happening."[9]

While Leningraders valued the newspaper, it lacked the intimacy and immediacy and thus the emotional resonance of the radio broadcast that seemed to speak to each Leningrader directly.[10] Leningrad radio was broadcast locally via the city's cable radio transmission system, *po gorodskoi transliatsionnoi seti* (GTS). In 1940, there were more than four hundred thousand household radios in the city. Throughout the winter, Ivan Zhilinskii, who, like the much younger Riabinkin, began keeping a diary,

eds., *Writing the Siege of Leningrad: Women's Diaries, Memoirs, and Documentary Prose* (Pittsburgh, PA: University of Pittsburgh Press, 2002), xii–xiii.

[7] Aleksandr Rubashkin, *Golos Leningrada: Leningradskoe radio v dni blokady* (Leningrad: Iskusstvo, 1975), 23.

[8] The beginning of the blockade is sometimes dated to 29 August, when the rail connection with the rest of the country was cut. Glantz, *The Siege*, 21–41, 65. Bidlack, "The Political Mood," 101.

[9] Adamovich and Granin, *Blokadnaia kniga*, 214, 342.

[10] Berggol'ts, *Govorit Leningrad*, in *Stikhi-proza* (Moscow: Gosudarstvennoe izdatel'stvo khudozhestvennoi literatury, 1961), 369. Rubashkin, *Golos Leningrada*, 14.

assiduously noted the temperature, his daily food intake, the number of air raid alerts, and whether the radio was working. On 3 January 1942 he lamented, "The radio hasn't worked since 1 January, as if cut off from the world."[11] Ol'ga Berggol'ts, one of the best-known voices on radio Leningrad during the war, remembered the same moment: "On one of those very cold January nights in forty-two, probably the third day after the radio had ceased working in almost all neighborhoods," people started showing up at the Radio House from all corners of the city to ask, "Why has the radio fallen silent?" An elderly man, who came all the way from Vasil'evskii Island – a distance of several kilometers – implored, "Let the radio speak . . . it's terrible without it! Without it, is like lying in the grave. Exactly like the grave."[12] Leningraders, it seems, needed, perhaps identified with, official accounts of their own experiences. In any event, they craved radio broadcasts.

Emphasizing the local, intimate dimensions of the blockade along with the connections between the deeply personal and the epochal, the myth of heroic Leningrad constructed in the media contained more than a grain of existential truth. Leningraders, of course, could compare official representations to the realities of the blockade that they saw in their "small radius."[13] They likely noted the omission of gruesome details – most obviously the extent of starvation, most sensationally cannibalism, but also other sorts of crimes and less-than-ideal behavior within the hero city. Nonetheless, whatever its distortions or omissions, the myth of the hero city proffered by the official media – and in large part produced by Leningraders – provided a compelling template for understanding and remembering personal experiences. Thus, this chapter aims less to debunk the myth or to demythololgize the siege than to delineate how public narratives and images of the blockade became part of Leningraders' individual experiences.[14] Contemporary news reports, photographs, and posters

---

[11] *Golos Leningrada*, 53. I. I. Zhilinskii, "Blokadnyi dnevnik," *Voprosy istorii*, 1996, no. 5–6: 24; see also 17. Experiments with wired radio had occurred elsewhere in the early twentieth century, but only the Soviet Union developed the system. "Blokadnyi metronom," *Sankt-Peterburgskie vedomosti*, 18 January 1995. Richard Stites, *Russian Popular Culture: Entertainment and Society Since 1900* (Cambridge: Cambridge University Press, 1992), 81–83, 109–10. S. Frederick Starr, "New Communications Technologies and Civil Society," in Loren R. Graham, ed., *Science and the Soviet Social Order* (Cambridge, MA: Harvard University Press, 1990), 29.

[12] Berggol'ts, *Govorit Leningrad*, 367, 374, ellipses in original.

[13] The term "small radius" comes from the diary of Professor Georgii Kniazev. Adamovich and Granin, *Blokadnaia kniga*, 230.

[14] Malcolm Smith, *Britain and 1940: History, Myth, and Popular Memory* (New York: Routledge, 2000), 6.

not only provided coherent descriptions of what survivors and historians alike came to view as discrete "periods" of the siege – the air raids of the autumn of 1941, the starvation of the first winter, the resumption of something like normal life under artillery fire in the spring of 1942, the offensives in January 1943 and January 1944 that first pierced and then broke the blockade.[15] Such images and stories also offered useful and even comforting interpretations of events.

The Leningrad myth constitutes a particularly powerful example of what the historian Jeffrey Brooks has identified as the wartime "counternarrative" of individual and private motives, as opposed to party discipline, that dominated the centrally controlled press's coverage of the first years of the war.[16] In the case of Leningrad, the official media's unprecedented wartime emphasis on home, family, and native place (*rodina*) as key constituents of Soviet patriotism structured a myth of the blockade that honored local sacrifices and the personal stories of ordinary Leningraders, even as it connected such small stories to both the Leningrad epic and the national cause. In besieged Leningrad, it was possible to overhear, as Ginzburg recalled, "a real grandmother talking like a granny in the articles and stories. That's never happened before."[17] Whether because the creators of state propaganda made a conscious effort to supplement party rhetoric with emotional appeals or because the concerns and fears of the government and the people momentarily, and uniquely, overlapped, the gap between official language and the language of grandmothers could be heard to narrow. In Leningrad, this counternarrative proved tenacious, persisting even after the 1943 victory at Stalingrad, when the press resurrected the prewar convention of attributing successes to the party bureaucracy and to Stalin personally. The "almost insurrectionary" counternarrative available in the press, on the radio, and in propaganda posters shaped a potentially subversive

---

[15] On the notion of "periods" of the blockade, see Rubashkin, *Golos Leningrada*, 10.

[16] Jeffrey Brooks, "*Pravda* Goes to War," in Richard Stites, ed., *Culture and Entertainment in Wartime Russia* (Bloomington: Indiana University Press, 1995), 14. T. M. Goriaeva, "Pis'ma s fronta i na front (po materialam Vsesoiuznogo radio, 1941–1945 gg)," *Sovetskie arkhivy*, 1978, no. 1: 32–35. For a fuller discussion, see Lisa A. Kirschenbaum, "'Our City, Our Hearths, Our Families': Local Loyalties and Private Life in Soviet World War II Propaganda," *Slavic Review* 59 (Winter 2000): 825–47.

[17] Ginzburg, *Blockade Diary*, 56. E. S. Seniavskaia, *Frontovoe pokolenie, 1941–1945: Istoriko-psikhologicheskoe issledovanie* (Moscow: Institut rossiiskoi istorii RAN, 1995), 4. Katherine Hodgson, "Kitezh and the Commune: Recurrent Themes in the Work of Ol'ga Berggol'ts," *Slavonic and East European Review* 74 (January 1996): 6.

memory of a self-sufficient local community and of responsible, cultured, and self-activated citizens.[18]

Soldiers on the City Front: Autumn 1941

When the blockade closed around Leningrad in September 1941, and the Luftwaffe began its campaign to bomb the city into submission, about two and a half million civilians of a prewar population of over three million remained trapped in the city. Moreover, because so many adult men had been called up to active service or evacuated with the war industry, the residual population consisted disproportionately of women, children, and the elderly.

Efforts to evacuate children during the summer had been poorly planned and proved disastrous. The local authorities' decision to evacuate children without their parents inspired little enthusiasm among mothers, who hesitated to separate themselves from their little ones. When trainloads of children finally left Leningrad in July, they were unwittingly directed into the path of the advancing Germans. The trains came under heavy fire and had to be returned to the city. In early August, authorities tried again, this time permitting mothers to accompany their children into evacuation. But frightened by the experience of the first round of evacuations in which many children had been injured or killed and by rumors of typhoid fever, many mothers stalled.[19] By the end of the month, there was no way out. In September, about four hundred thousand children – perhaps half of the prewar population under age fourteen – remained in the city.[20]

---

[18] Brooks deems the wartime press's "expression of humanistic values" "almost insurrectionary." "*Pravda* Goes to War," 19.

[19] V. M. Koval'chuk, "Evakuatsiia naseleniia Leningrada letom 1941 goda," *Otechestvennaia istoriia*, 2000, no. 3: 16–18. Dzeniskevich, "The Social and Political Situation," 73–74. Richard Bidlack, "Survival Strategies in Leningrad during the First Year of the Soviet-German War," in Thurston and Bonwetsch, *The People's War,* 88. Dmitrii Pavlov, *Leningrad 1941: The Blockade,* trans. John Clinton Adams (Chicago: University of Chicago Press, 1965), 46. E. S. Kots, "'Na moiu,'" 79. Elena Skrjabina, *Siege and Survival: The Odyssey of a Leningrader,* trans. Norman Luxenburg (Carbondale: Southern Illinois University Press, 1971), 7–18. Elena Kozhina, *Through the Burning Steppe: A Memoir of Wartime Russia, 1942–1943,* trans. Vadim Mahmoudov (New York: Riverhead Books, 2000), 57–63. Neratova, *V dni,* 33–36. Kochina, *Blockade Diary,* 36.

[20] Pavlov, *Leningrad,* 48. Pavlov does not specify the age range included in the category "children"; however, evacuation efforts focused on those under fourteen. The last prewar census (1939) put the total population of the city at just under 3.2 million,

Among adults, remaining in the city could appear both as a reasonable choice and a patriotic duty. Prewar propaganda had encouraged them to believe that a war would be short and that the city was safe from aerial attack. Many preferred staying at home to turning themselves into refugees.[21] For others, remaining in the city became a badge of honor. Rimma Neratova, a second-year medical student when the siege began, remembered her fellow students' contempt for one woman in their class who decided to get married and leave for the rear. In July and August, some local authorities encouraged the view that to stay was a "patriotic action."[22] Finally, for many Leningraders, leaving was simply never an option, as party leaders and factory directors often reserved spaces on evacuation trains and planes for their own families and friends. Even after the blockade closed, it was possible, though dangerous, to fly in and out of the city; however, the authorities apparently never considered a large-scale air evacuation of civilians.[23]

Unsurprisingly, the Soviet press did not emphasize the fact that so many with so little to contribute to the defense of the city remained in Leningrad – under near constant air and artillery attack, and already in September dangerously short of food. Instead, Soviet propaganda stressed that war's imminent threat to home, family, and native place required that every citizen contribute to the war effort, that every home become an "impenetrable fortress."[24] As early as 30 August 1941, one day after the

23.5 percent of whom (728,500) were fourteen or younger. A report to the city party committee reported the evacuation of almost five hundred thousand children, but many of these may have been refugees who had made their way to Leningrad. A. R. Dzeniskevich, ed., *Leningrad v osade: Sbornik dokumentov o geroicheskoi oborone Leningrada v gody Velikoi Otechestvennoi voiny, 1941–44* (St. Petersburg: Liki Rossii, 1995), 301–5. N. Iu. Cherepenina, "Demograficheskaia obstanovka i zdravookhranenie v Leningrade nakanune Velikoi Otechestvennoi voiny," in A. R. Dzeniskevich and John Barber, eds., *Zhizn' i smert' v blokirovannom Leningrade: Istoriko-meditsinskii aspekt* (St. Petersburg: Dmitrii Bulanin, 2001), 18–34. Iu. A. Poliakov, ed., *Vsesoiuznaia perepis' naseleniia 1939 goda: Osnovnye itogi: Rossiia* (St. Petersburg: Russko-Baltiiskii informatsionnyi tsentr "BLITS," 1999), 25, 33.

[21] Skrjabina, *Siege and Survival*, 21–22. Dzeniskevich, "The Social and Political Situation," 77. Pavlov, *Leningrad*, 46–48. Adamovich and Granin, *Blokadnaia kniga*, 223–30.

[22] Neratova, *V dni*, 28. Pavlov, *Leningrad*, 47.

[23] Bidlack, "Survival Strategies," 89. Bidlack, "Foreword," xv.

[24] *KP*, 15 October 1941. Posters with this civil defense theme included "Smelo beri zazhigatel'nuiu bombu i vybrasyvai na mostovuiu," Library of Congress, Prints and Photographs Division, Washington, DC, Lot 4862, BO-454; "Prevratim kolkhozy v nepristupnuiu krepost' dlia vraga"; Records of the Smolensk Oblast of the All-Union Communist Party of the Soviet Union, 1917–41; Microfilm Publication T-87, Roll 52; National Archives at College Park, MD (NACP). *Leningradskaia pravda* (hereafter, *LP*), 27 August 1941.

German advance had cut rail service to the city, Leningrad radio urged civilians to see themselves as soldiers. In an appeal that spoke directly to "you, Leningrader," Berggol'ts tried to rally civilians: "Remember, fellow Leningrader, that you're on the front, that you're a warrior. Leningrader, you're a warrior wherever you are – in the factory, in the office, or in your own apartment – because you're a Leningrader."[25] The Soviet press designated Leningrad a "city front" – a place where the distinctions between front and rear, soldier and civilian, disappeared – and its civilian population "heroic defenders."

Striking a distinctly local and personal note, the Leningrad leadership's call to defend the city drew on and magnified nationalist themes that had become a part of Soviet propaganda in the mid-1930s.[26] The "new nationalism" of the 1930s had merged a positive reevaluation of the heroes of the Russian imperial past with the positive reevaluation of local, intimate, and emotional ties: "Patriotism is love of one's country. What is one's country? My mountains, my trees, my history, the history of my people, my brothers and sisters, my beloved ones."[27] Such statements marked a significant departure from the glorification of proletarian internationalism and of Communists who sacrificed personal ties to the cause that dominated Soviet propaganda throughout the 1920s.[28] As a means of mobilizing support for the state, Soviet propaganda rehabilitated both Russian imperial heroes – the medieval prince Aleksandr Nevskii and the generals of the Napoleonic wars Aleksandr Suvorov and Mikhail Kutuzov – and motherhood and family. Wartime propaganda likewise enlisted the heroes of the imperial state alongside invocations of "my mountains, my brothers and sisters."

[25] Rubashkin, *Golos Leningrada*, 24.

[26] *KP*, 21 August 1941.

[27] Nicholas S. Timasheff, *The Great Retreat: The Growth and Decline of Communism in Russia* (New York: E. P. Dutton, 1946), 180. See also David Brandenberger, *National Bolshevism: Stalinist Mass Culture and the Formation of Modern Russian National Identity, 1931–1956* (Cambridge, MA: Harvard University Press, 2002), 27–112; Terry Martin, "Modernization or Neo-Traditionalism? Ascribed Nationality and Soviet Primordialism," in Sheila Fitzpatrick, ed., *Stalinism: New Directions* (New York: Routledge, 2000), 348–67.

[28] Victoria Bonnell, "The Representation of Women in Early Soviet Political Art," *Russian Review* 50 (1991): 275. Jeffrey Brooks, "Revolutionary Lives: Public Identities in *Pravda* during the 1920s," in Stephen White, ed., *New Directions in Soviet History* (New York: Cambridge University Press, 1992), 34. Elizabeth Waters, "The Female Form in Soviet Political Iconography, 1917–32," in Barbara Evans Clements, Barbara Alpern Engel, and Christine D. Worobec, eds., *Russia's Women: Accommodation, Resistance, Transformation* (Berkeley: University of California Press, 1991), 235–37.

What set wartime propaganda apart, particularly during the first years of the conflict, was the degree to which the new nationalism displaced the cult of Stalin. While the Leningrad leadership's call to be vigilant suggested the Stalinist obsession with ferreting out internal enemies, it did so in the name of local and familial concerns, not in the name of Stalin and the Soviet socialist state. Moreover, the press increasingly emphasized the local and personal – as opposed to imperial or state-centered – dimensions of Soviet patriotism. The maternal figure of the motherland (*rodina-mat'*, literally, the motherland mother) gained new prominence as the media depicted the war in personal, often sentimental, terms as a defense of home, family, and rodina in the narrow sense of hometown, native village, and – recalling prewar conventions – native factory.[29]

Observations made by party activists and the political police (NKVD) in Leningrad suggested the resonance of such rhetoric. Workers at political meetings spoke relatively rarely of the achievements of socialism or even of nationalism. Rather, they emphasized "revenge, blood ties, and the cause of the fathers passed on to the sons," as well as "anxiety over the future of the city." The workers' speeches recorded in surveillance reports echoed to a remarkable degree those quoted in the press.[30]

The autumn bombing raids cemented the city's status in the media as a front, where, under enemy fire, civilians – specifically women and children – became indistinguishable from soldiers. Early in the war, the party and local government organized local air defense forces (*mestnaia protivovozdushnaia oborona* or MPVO) responsible for staffing round-the-clock sentry posts, spotting enemy planes, enforcing blackouts during air raids, extinguishing incendiary bombs in buckets of sand, fighting fires, defusing delayed-action bombs, and extricating survivors from the rubble. By early September, factories, schools, universities, and housing blocks had organized more than thirty-five hundred MPVO groups staffed by two hundred and seventy thousand people, predominately women, usually young, often Komsomol (Young Communist League) members. Children as young as twelve, and perhaps even younger, stood watch on

---

[29] Geoffrey Hosking, "The Second World War and Russian National Consciousness," *Past and Present*, no. 175 (May 2002): 168–73. Robert J. Kaiser, *The Geography of Nationalism in Russia and the USSR* (Princeton, NJ: Princeton University Press, 1994), 139. On the local meanings of *rodnoi*, see Esther Kingston-Mann, "Breaking the Silence: An Introduction," in Esther Kingston-Mann and Timothy Mixter, eds., *Peasant Economy, Cultures, and Politics of European Russia, 1800–1921* (Princeton, NJ: Princeton University Press, 1991), 15–16.

[30] Dzeniskevich, "The Social and Political Situation," 82. See also Kochina, *Blockade Diary*, 35.

rooftops, ready to extinguish incendiary bombs. In London, by contrast, air raid wardens were predominantly middle-aged and elderly men.[31] In Leningrad, the MPVO girl (*devushka*), along with the young, often female, munitions worker, quickly became emblems of the city's will to resist.[32]

In wartime accounts of the blockade, Leningrad women, perhaps even more clearly than women elsewhere in the Soviet Union, emerged as warriors who combined the steadfastness (*stoikost'*) and courage (*muzhestvo* – from *muzh*, man) of (male) soldiers with an indestructible Soviet femininity that was austere, nurturing, and unfailingly chaste.[33] In December 1943, *Komsomol'skaia pravda* ran a story lauding the wartime exploits of Leningrad Komsomols, including Zina Timofeeva, who during the war had become a factory worker. In the course of one apparently typical air raid – the article did not specify the date – she stood watch on the factory roof, reporting her observations by telephone as German bombs exploded almost on top of her. "Was she terrified now, alone on the roof of a building hit by the Germans?" the reporter asked rhetorically:

Probably. But she didn't think about that. She firmly gripped the telephone receiver, and instinctively ducking at the sound of an incoming shell, she looked down the street at a house. An ordinary, large stone house, like hundreds of others in Leningrad. But for her this was not simply a house. People near and dear to her lived there. Does she see them? . . . And she reports her observations to headquarters.[34]

[31] Smith, *Britain and 1940*, 78. David M. Glantz, *The Battle for Leningrad, 1941–1944* (Lawrence: University Press of Kansas, 2002), 128. Pavlov, *Leningrad*, 26–28, 36. On children's participation in the MPVO, see M. V. Chernorutskii, ed., *Alimentarnaia distrofiia v blokirovannom Leningrade* (Leningrad: Medgiz, 1947), 241; Vera Ketlinskaia, "Pokolenie, vyrosshee na voine," in *Rasskazy o Leningradtsakh* (Leningrad: Lenizdat, 1944), 250–61; Skrjabina, *Siege and Survival*, 37; Anna Moizhes, ed., *Deti goroda-geroia* (Leningrad: Lenizdat, 1974), 43, 154, 231; Adamovich and Granin, *Blokadnaia kniga*, 107, 153–54.

[32] *LP*, 16 August 1941, 23 July 1942. *KP*, 22 August 1941, 1 November 1941, 2 October 1941, 1 June 1943, 11 December 1943. A. Fadeev, "Deti geroicheskogo goroda," *KP*, 12 May 1943. Nikolai Tikhonov, *Geroicheskaia zashchita Leningrada* (Moscow: Gosudarstvennoe izdatel'stvo politicheskoi literatury, 1943), 19–20.

[33] Kirschenbaum, "'Our City,'" 840. Boris Skomorovsky and E. G. Morris, *The Siege of Leningrad: The Saga of the Greatest Siege of All Time as Told by the Letters, Documents, and Stories of the Brave People Who Withstood It* (New York: E. P. Dutton, 1944), 83–84. Fadeev, "Deti geroicheskogo goroda." *KP*, 7 March 1942, 1 June 1943. Karen Petrone, "Masculinity and Heroism in Imperial and Soviet Military-Patriotic Cultures," in Barbara Evans Clements, Rebecca Friedman, and Dan Healy, eds., *Russian Masculinities in History and Culture* (New York: Palgrave, 2002), 172–93.

[34] Ol'ga Chechetkina, "Leningradtsy," *KP*, 11 December 1943. German bombardment, which had largely ceased in April 1942, became intense again in the fall of 1943.

Here the domestic, familial motive behind Zina's toughness – "'come what may, I'm staying,' thought Zina" – was explicit. She stood her ground against the bombers, doing her bit to protect not only, and seemingly not primarily, the state, the city, or even her factory, but rather those "near and dear to her."

In keeping with the emphasis on heroic defense, the wartime press emphasized the threat of German shells and bombs – not deaths due to starvation. Even in Leningrad itself, where by the end of 1941 the reality of starvation was plain to see, and where the blockade afforded the local media unprecedented freedom from central control if not the local party's authority, the newspapers and radio rarely mentioned the word *golod* (famine) while it was occurring.[35] Ignoring the physical limits imposed by starvation, *Leningradskaia pravda* chided workers who no longer bothered to rush to bomb shelters during air raids.[36] As the death toll due to starvation mounted in early December, *Smena* emphasized that the Nazis "destroy the peaceful population" by bombing and shelling women, children, and old people.[37]

Once the worst period of starvation was passed, the press spoke more openly about famine, but still pictured Leningraders mainly as fighters and survivors rather than victims. In a radio broadcast of September 1942, Berggol'ts observed, "Just like last year, Leningrad is the front, and just like last year, the Germans have not stopped thinking of taking the city by storm." Among the differences, she noted "the new strength that was born among us during the cruel days of winter."[38] Starvation had made Leningraders not victims but battle-hardened soldiers.

The Responses of "Heroic Defenders"

Of course, such reporting could not wholly determine how Leningraders saw their own local situation. Some Leningraders, like the classicist Ol'ga

---

[35] Rubashkin, *Golos Leningrada*, 33, 60. Berggol'ts, "Iz dnevnikov," *Zvezda*, 1990, no. 5: 190. William Moskoff, *The Bread of Affliction: The Food Supply in the USSR During World War II* (New York: Cambridge University Press, 1990), 205. A review of the local papers – *Leningradskaia pravda*, which continued to publish throughout the winter, and *Smena*, which published until 9 January 1942 and resumed on 5 February 1942 – turned up a few cursory mentions of famine. *LP*, 1 January 1942. On the active role of the local party leaders in shaping media coverage, see Rubashkin, *Golos Leningrada*, 39; Soiuz zhurnalistov SSSR, Leningradskoe otdelenie, *S perom i avtomatom: Pisateli i zhurnalisty Leningrada v gody blokady* (Leningrad: Lenizdat, 1964), 54.

[36] *LP*, 29 November 1941.

[37] *Smena*, 6 December 1941. See also *KP*, 11 December 1943, 1 November 1941; *LP*, 23 July 1942; Nikolai Tikhonov, "O muzhestve i skromnosti," *LP*, 1 January 1942.

[38] Berggol'ts, *Govorit Leningrad*, 399. See also *KP*, 23 June 1942.

Freidenberg (Boris Pasternak's cousin), rejected the myth of heroic defenders on the city front as a bombastic and offensive fiction. She was among the minority who blamed Stalin for the war and called for Leningrad to be declared an open city.[39] In her retrospective diary, begun in March 1942, Freidenberg remembered that in October 1941, "the raids and shelling were merciless and inhuman.... Oh, this was more terrifying than the front. At the front there are not five-story buildings filled with children, women, old people.... Peaceful people, not taking part in war, locked into the ill-fated city despite their wishes, were killed and wounded, like a sin offering. What was the point of this?"[40] Asking "what was the point," Freidenberg declared herself unpersuaded by the media's claims that Leningraders spotting planes and putting out fires had become "defenders," working to save their beloved city if not the nation. Starving civilians, much more than so-called heroic defenders on rooftops, stood not only as a potential reproach to the state that lacked the means to feed them, but also as a potential challenge to the notion of heroic, meaningful, willing sacrifice.[41]

Objections such as Freidenberg's notwithstanding, Leningraders more commonly came to embrace some version of the story of heroic Leningrad.[42] Even for the minority that, like Freidenberg, advocated surrendering the city, defeatist attitudes often did not last very long and left little mark in memory. By the winter of 1941, German tactics "had come to be viewed as monstrously barbaric," and "popular hatred of and contempt for the enemy grew during the winter."[43] At the same time, official accounts provided a pervasive and, if internalized, adaptive framework for interpreting and coping with difficult and unprecedented circumstances. The media both encouraged Leningraders to see themselves as connected to others in "purposeful action" and facilitated such connections.[44]

Moreover, the media's contention that Leningraders were not passive victims but active defenders may well have matched Leningraders' own sense of the momentousness and importance of their experiences. Lidiia Ginzburg, like Freidenberg, refused to see Leningraders as soldiers,

---

[39] Dzeniskevich, "The Social and Political Situation," 77.
[40] Freidenberg, "Osada cheloveka," 13. See also Cynthia Simmons, "Lifting the Siege: Women's Voices on Leningrad (1941–1944)," *Canadian Slavonic Papers* 40 (1998): 60.
[41] Elaine Scarry, *The Body in Pain: The Making and Unmaking of the World* (New York: Oxford University Press, 1985), 112.
[42] Nina Perlina, *Ol'ga Freidenberg's Works and Days* (Bloomington, IN: Slavica, 2002), 189.
[43] Richard Bidlack, "The Political Mood," 108.
[44] Judith Herman, *Trauma and Recovery: The Aftermath of Violence – from Domestic Abuse to Political Terror* (New York: Basic Books, 1997), 58.

maintaining that "it's those in the front line who are at war." All the same, she concluded, in language that suggested official myths, that Leningraders were not "just keeping themselves alive" but instead were "doing what has to be done in this fighting city, to prevent the city from dying."[45] The notion that Leningraders, even as they starved, were somehow fighting on the city front answered the burning and terrible question, "What was the point?" It offered a useful truth, a meaningful struggle.

Even for anti-Stalinist skeptics like Freidenberg, the radio and the newspaper were influential sources of stories and information that profoundly shaped the experience of the blockade. The radio itself became a kind of mythic hero. Freidenberg joyfully recalled that in December, she managed to realize her "dream" of acquiring a radio: "All day long the radio notified us of our victories. People revived. With tears in our eyes we listened to reports and correspondents. Hope rose up."[46] It was this power to revive hope that gave the myth of heroic defenders its purchase among people who, like Freidenberg, may have also felt at times like targets trapped in a box.[47]

"Heroism" and heroic community became central, if ambivalent, motifs of personal stories for many Leningraders.[48] In reminiscences published in 1996, Aleksei Pavlovskii described himself during the war as "an ordinary Leningrad boy of the sort that *Leningradskaia pravda* and *Smena* loved to write about – how we extinguished incendiaries, how cunning and brave we were. All of that is, of course, true." True, that is, within certain limits: "We really wanted to be and sometimes in fact were fearless and cunning. But so many of us died" – all but five of the forty-three students in his class in 1941. Nonetheless, in Pavlovskii's memory, even as the media minimized the extent of the tragedy, the newspapers and especially the radio endowed civilian deaths with meaning. He recalled and mythologized Berggol'ts's radio voice: "The *voice* . . . united people in what Ol'ga Berggol'ts called 'the great blockade brotherhood,' the name

[45] Ginzburg, *Blockade Diary*, 76, 55.
[46] Freidenberg, "Osada cheloveka," 18. See also N. D. Khudiakova, "'I vse zhe verili v pobedu' (Iz blokadnogo dnevnika 1941–1943 gg.)," in *Zabveniiu ne podlezhit*, vyp. 2 (St. Petersburg: Izdatel'stvo "EGO," 2001), 61.
[47] Kochina, *Blockade Diary*, 30, 64–65.
[48] A. N. Boldyrev, *Osadnaia zapis': Blokadnyi dnevnik* (St. Petersburg: Evropeiskii Dom, 1998), 26, 48. Kochina, *Blockade Diary*, 83. "38 dnei iz zhizni umiraiushchikh," *Smena*, 27 January 1994. Roza Livshits, "Pochemu my vystoiali," in L. A. Aizenshtat, ed., *Kniga zhivykh: Vospominaniia evreev-frontovikov, uznikov getto i konstlagerei, boitsov partizanskikh otriadov, zhitelei blokadnogo Leningrada* (St. Petersburg: Acropol, 1995), 75–78.

by which the general courage of Leningrad set right the death of hundreds of thousands of its citizens."[49] Seeing the limits of the myth did not preclude accepting at least some of its consolations.

Indeed, those who produced wartime accounts of the blockade, and who perhaps knew their limits better than anyone, also seem to have taken comfort in the notion that there was something special, even epic, about not only the situation in Leningrad but Leningraders' responses to it. In her diary (published only in 1990), Berggol'ts, briefly evacuated to Moscow in early 1942, struggled to define what it was that made it possible for Leningraders to survive. She concluded that Muscovites "do not speak the truth about Leningrad; they do not speak about famine, and without that, there is no sort of Leningrad 'heroics.' (I put the word heroics' in quotation marks only because I believe that heroism in general does not exist on earth)."[50] Unable to embrace fully the notion of "heroics," she also was unable to do without it entirely.

In 1996, Leonid Rakhmanov recalled a similar personal commitment to the theme of heroic Leningrad. In October 1941, he, together with the writers Vladimir Orlov and Evgenii Ryss, sketched out a plan for documenting "A Day in the Besieged City." They envisioned an extensive project that would result in a book tracing everything from the activities of the armies on the Leningrad front to the extraordinary situations in Leningrad's factories, schools, universities, apartment houses, theaters, nurseries, museums, party and government organizations, churches, and bomb shelters.[51] Rakhmanov's post-Soviet reminiscences corroborate Berggol'ts's immediate postwar description of the "pride and happiness, and... marvelous flow of strength" that she and her colleagues at the Radio Committee felt in January 1942, when they devised a plan for an even more comprehensive account of Leningraders' experiences.[52] That the myth of heroic Leningrad deflected attention from the state's failure to evacuate civilians or to protect them from air raids and starvation did not necessarily diminish its psychological utility. More than an official

---

[49] Aleksei Pavlovskii, "Golos," in Zakhar Dicharov, ed., *Golosa iz blokady: Leningradskie pisateli v osazhdennom gorode (1941–1944)* (St. Petersburg: Nauka, 1996), 240, 242, emphasis in original.

[50] Berggol'ts, "Iz dnevnikov," 190. On her visit to Moscow, see Katharine Hodgson, *Voicing the Soviet Experience: The Poetry of Ol'ga Berggol'ts* (New York: The British Academy in association with Oxford University Press, 2003), 23–25.

[51] Leonid Rakhmanov, "Den' osazhdennogo goroda," in Dicharov, *Golosa,* 150–52.

[52] Berggol'ts, *Govorit Leningrad,* 367. The book was never realized; however, Berggol'ts used the title as the title of her collection of wartime radio broadcasts.

fiction, the story of heroic Leningrad – an embattled, united, and courageous community – provided a shared narrative that helped Leningraders
to make sense of their own experiences and to sustain hope.

Cold, Hunger, Darkness: The Winter of 1941–1942

As the air raids of fall gave way to the starvation of winter, official representations of the blockade increasingly emphasized the notion of the city
front as a place where civilians defended not only their homes and their
families but also the very essence of their own humanity – civilization
itself. By the end of 1941, starvation had replaced bombs and artillery as
the primary cause of death among civilians in Leningrad. While explicit
talk of famine remained impossible, the local media, particularly the radio,
marked the horrors of starvation with prose and poetry that celebrated the
moral strength of Leningraders and the remarkably high cultural level of
citizens under agonizing conditions. Such depictions of the city omitted
the crimes, both petty and murderous, that accompanied mass starvation. Nonetheless, many Leningraders internalized, even if they did not
fully accept, the depiction of the brutal winter as a protracted, painful,
and largely successful struggle to retain human dignity in the face of the
degradations of starvation.

Leningrad as a city of culture standing against Nazi barbarism emerged
as an important theme of Soviet and Allied coverage of the blockade. German bombs took out Leningrad's long-wave radio tower, but shortwave
broadcasts from the city, introduced with the refrain "Leningrad calling,"
almost immediately reconnected Leningrad to the rest of the world.[53]
Before the authorities evacuated them in October, both the composer
Dmitrii Shostakovich and the poet Anna Akhmatova brought the plight
of Leningrad to a national and international radio audience. Both artists
had been severely criticized in the 1930s, but with German bombers in the
skies over Leningrad, both became important, internationally respected
icons of world culture – as opposed to distinctly Soviet culture – under
attack. Shostakovich began his 17 September 1941 national radio address
with the statement, "An hour ago, I completed the second movement of
my new symphonic work," his Seventh Symphony, which became known

---

[53] Rubashkin, *Golos Leningrada*, 26–29, 53. V. N. Tishunin, "Publitsistika blokadnogo
goroda," in I. A. Rosenko and G. L. Sobolev, eds., *Voprosy istorii i istoriografii Velikoi
Otechestvennoi voiny: Mezhvuzovskii sbornik* (Leningrad: Izdatel'stvo Leningradskogo
Universiteta, 1989), 117–18.

as the *Leningrad Symphony*. The composer working on his score even as he took his turn on duty on the roof of the conservatory became a powerful emblem of Leningrad's resistance. On the eve of the U.S. premiere of the symphony in July 1942, a drawing of Shostakovich in his firefighting helmet appeared on the cover of *Time* magazine.[54]

These early broadcasts equated Nazi aggression with bombs and artillery shells, yet almost as soon as the blockade closed, the feeding of more than two million civilians, many of whom in September and October were working eleven-hour shifts in defense plants, constituted a pressing problem. In September, doctors in Leningrad's hospitals saw the first cases of what they called alimentary dystrophy (what doctors in the West often term hunger disease) among one of the city's most vulnerable populations, refugee children from Leningrad's suburbs. However, city officials – overwhelmed by the damage caused by the near-constant bombardment and by Stalin's demands that Leningrad's factories supply artillery and ammunition for the defense of Moscow – did little to prepare for a prolonged siege. Rationing had been introduced in Leningrad, as in the rest of the Soviet Union, in July, but restaurants and so-called commercial stores where people could buy without ration coupons at inflated prices had remained open, depleting the city's reserves.[55]

The media did little to prepare Leningraders for the possibility of starvation. The 8 September 1941 bombardment of the Badaev food warehouses acquired mythical status as the beginning of the famine only in retrospect – and despite the efforts of Soviet officials to downplay the event's importance. According to Ales' Adamovich and Daniil Granin, the burning warehouses figured prominently in half of the oral testimonies they collected in the 1970s, but showed up far less often in the diaries.[56] As survivors worked to construct coherent accounts of the blockade, the warehouse bombing provided a useful and compelling turning point. Such

[54] Berggol'ts, *Govorit Leningrad*, 370. Rubashkin, *Golos Leningrada*, 29–30. Berggol'ts, "'Slushai nas, rodnaia strana!'" in *S perom*, 425–27. Laurel E. Fay, *Shostakovich: A Life* (New York: Oxford University Press, 2000), 125–30. Solomon Volkov argues that Shostakovich had probably completed much of the symphony in his mind before the German invasion, and that it thus must be seen as a condemnation of Stalin's crimes as much as Hitler's. Volkov, *St. Petersburg: A Cultural History*, trans. Antonina W. Bouis (New York: Free Press, 1995), 427–35. *Time*, 20 July 1942. The cover is available at http://www.time.com/time/covers//0,16641,1101420720,00.html (accessed 17 February 2006).

[55] Bidlack, "The Political Mood," 103–4. Chernorutskii, *Alimentarnaia*, 241. Pavlov, *Leningrad*, 48–55.

[56] Adamovich and Granin, *Blokadnaia kniga*, 249.

TABLE 1. *Daily Bread Rations in Grams, July 1941–March 1942*

Date	Workers in "Hot Shops"	Workers	Office Workers	Dependents	Children under 12
18 July 1941	1000	800	600	400	400
2 Sept. 1941	800	600	400	300	300
12 Sept. 1941	700	500	300	250	250
1 Oct. 1941	600	400	200	200	200
13 Nov. 1941	450	300	150	150	150
10 Nov. 1941	375	250	125	125	125
25 Dec. 1941	500	350	200	200	200
24 Jan. 1942	575	400	300	250	250
11 Feb. 1942	700	500	400	300	300
22 Mar. 1942	700	600	500	400	400

Source: Richard Bidlack, *Workers at War: Factory Workers and Labor Policy in the Siege of Leningrad* (Pittsburgh, PA: The Carl Beck Papers, University of Pittsburgh Center for Russian and East European Studies, 1991), 44. Reprinted with permission.

stories were likely already circulating in the late 1950s, when Dmitrii Pavlov, the official sent from Moscow at the outset of the blockade to oversee food supply, worked to quash the rumor of the decisiveness of the destruction of the warehouses – and thus of the poor planning that had left Leningrad's food reserves so vulnerable to attack. He argued, probably somewhat optimistically, that only a small quantity of flour and sugar had been lost, in part because much of the charred sugar was later recovered and processed into candy.[57] Even before the bombing, however, on 2 September, the local authorities had cut the daily bread ration from 800 to 600 grams for factory workers and engineers. Ten days later, recognizing the seriousness of the situation, they cut rations again, as can be seen in Table 1.[58]

The difficulty of bringing food into the city prompted city officials to cut rations three more times before the end of the year (see table). The city's primary supply route was Lake Ladoga, just east of Leningrad. In the fall, a tenuous water link across the lake, subject to air and artillery attack, provided little relief. In January 1942, when the ice on the lake became thick enough to support convoys of five-ton trucks, conditions

[57] N. A. Sindalovskii, *Mifologiia Peterburga: Ocherki* (St. Petersburg: Norit, 2000), 374–75. Elena Skrjabina's diary, which frequently dates events incorrectly and often seems more like a retrospective account than a diary, emphasizes the Badaev fires as a primary cause of the starvation winter. Skrjabina, *Siege and Survival,* 27. Kochina, *Blockade Diary,* 39, 46. Pavlov, *Leningrad,* 56–57. Moskoff, *Bread of Affliction,* 205.
[58] Pavlov, *Leningrad,* 49, 79.

slowly improved. Known officially as the "Road of Life," and somewhat sardonically among Leningraders as the "Road of Death," the ice road across Lake Ladoga remained a difficult and dangerous connection to the mainland. Only in February was the road bringing substantial supplies of food and fuel into the city and evacuating the sick and the young, many of whom died along the arduous route.[59] For thousands who remained behind, increased rations were too little too late. Mortality rates peaked in January and February 1942, and deaths attributed to prolonged semi-starvation continued well into the spring and summer. Doctors considered dystrophy to have disappeared only in late 1943.[60]

Although the ice road provided an increasingly reliable bridge to the mainland, as the winter progressed Leningraders became more and more isolated from one another and from their prewar, pre-famine selves. They became fixated on food – finding it, preparing it, eating it, document-ing it, dreaming of it. Diaries written during the starvation winter speak eloquently and clearly of this narrowed field of concern. As is common among people experiencing famine, which entails not only food short-age but also "the consumption of a strange diet," Leningraders who kept diaries described everything related to food in meticulous detail. I would venture to say that any diary that does not focus almost obsessively on food was probably written or substantially rewritten after the events of the starvation winter. Many Leningraders reported keeping "notes" during the worst part of the blockade, and constructing their "diaries" later.[61]

---

[59] Bidlack, "Foreword," xiv–xv. Pavlov, *Leningrad*, 43–66. On the "Road of Death," see Kochina, *Blockade Diary*, 69, 108; Likhachev, "Kak my," 18; Sindalovskii, *Mifologiia*, 384. Émigré Kyra Petrovskaya Wayne, who worked as a medic along the Road of Life, offers a rather romantic account in *Shurik: A Story of the Siege of Leningrad* (New York: Lyons Press, 2000).

[60] Chernorutskii, *Alimentarnaia*, 196–203. Bidlack, "Foreword," ix. A. R. Dzeniskevich, *Blokada i politika: Oborona Leningrada v politicheskoi kon"iunkture* (St. Petersburg: Nestor, 1998), 45–68. V. M. Koval'chuk, "Tragicheskie tsifry blokady (K voprosu ob ustanovlenii chisla zhertv blokirovannogo Leningrada)," in A. A. Fursenko, ed., *Rossiia v XIX–XX vv: Sbornik statei k 70-letiiu so dnia rozhdeniia Rafaila Sholomovicha Ganelina* (St. Petersburg: Dmitrii Bulanin, 1998), 357–69.

[61] Quotation from J. P. W. Rivers, "The Nutritional Biology of Famine," in G. Harrison, ed., *Famine* (New York: Oxford University Press, 1988), 59. See also Ancel Keys, J. Brožek, A. Henschel, O. Mickelsen, and H. L. Taylor, *The Biology of Human Starvation* (Min-neapolis: University of Minnesota Press, 1950), 832–34; Harold Steere Guetzkow and Paul Hoover Bowman, *Men and Hunger: A Psychological Manual for Relief Workers* (Elgin, IL: Brethren Publishing House, [1946]), 21–23; Chernorutskii, *Alimentarnaia*, 130–31; T. Doxiadès, "Considérations biologiques et cliniques sur la famine en Grèce (1941–1943)," *Revue médicale de la Suisse romande* 70 (1950): 226–27. On retrospec-tive diaries, see Adamovich and Granin, *Blokadnaia kniga*, 256–58; Kochina, *Blockade Diary*, 29.

A fairly typical entry dated 9 December 1941 from the diary of Aleksandr Boldyrev, a specialist in Oriental studies at the Hermitage Museum, illustrates the importance – personal and historical – attached to cataloging everything related to food:

> Yesterday everyone was transfixed by rumors of an increase in the bread ration on the eleventh. This pushed into the background even gossip about world events – the Japanese-American war started.... Already seven days of the first ten-day period have gone by, and no sweets. The sudden cut in rations has made this the worst ten-day period of the siege so far. For two days I had three unused fifty-gram portions of meat, i.e., three cutlets. Not a single soup, not a single kasha. The university canteen didn't have even yeast soup.[62]

Leningraders recorded their precise food intake and described the wet, dense, claylike texture of bread cut with cellulose, flax cake, moldy grain retrieved from a barge sunk in Lake Ladoga, and other flour substitutes. To spill a small amount of cooking oil or to lose a bit of food in the communal kitchen to the quick fingers of the neighbor's child counted as tragedies. Diarists noted their ingeniousness in turning the inedible – wallpaper paste, leather belts, fur coats – into food.[63] They concocted what the scientist Elena Kochina called an original "Leningrad cuisine": "We've learned to make doughnuts out of mustard, soup out of yeast, hamburgers out of horseradish, and gelatin out of joiner's glue."[64]

For the starving, food lost its social functions, its ability to bring people together.[65] On the contrary, the aching need for food often divided families, as hungry husbands and teenage boys in particular – men suffered first from famine – secretly ate rations meant for sick children or devoured the small makeweight pieces on the way home from the bakery.[66] An uncontrollable appetite coexisted in some accounts with debilitating bouts of guilt and self-loathing – after the extra portion had been consumed.[67] A sense of solidarity that extended beyond the family was even more difficult

[62] Boldyrev, *Osadnaia zapis'*, 25. See also Adamovich and Granin, *Blokadnaia kniga*, 116. Only the bread ration was generally available in full and on time. Pavlov, *Leningrad*, 75–81.
[63] Adamovich and Granin, *Blokadnaia kniga*, 36–39. See also Pavlov, *Leningrad*, 60; Skrjabina, *Siege and Survival*, 30–38; Boldyrev, *Osadnaia zapis'*, 25–59; Simmons and Perlina, *Writing the Siege*, 62–63.
[64] Kochina, *Blockade Diary*, 46.
[65] Ginzburg, *Blockade Diary*, 64. Kochina, *Blockade Diary*, 98.
[66] Chernorutskii, *Alimentarnaia*, 194. Josef Brožek, Samuel Wells, and Ancel Keys, "Medical Aspects of Seminstarvation in Leningrad," *American Review of Soviet Medicine* 4 (1946): 73–74. Kochina, *Blockade Diary*, 45–48. Ginzburg, *Blockade Diary*, 48, 60.
[67] Adamovich and Granin, *Blokadnaia kniga*, 358. Ginzburg, *Blockade Diary*, 7–8.

to maintain. Diarists noted the real and imagined efforts of bakery workers to cheat them of part of their ration, and the overall unfairness of
the rationing system, as well as their own attempts to take advantage of
connections, to acquire ration cards illegally, to trade on the black market, and even to steal in order to increase their own allotment. Rumors
of cannibalism circulated widely.[68]

In Leningrad, extreme cold, the breakdown of water and sewage systems, the lack of public transportation, the sparse and erratic generation
of electricity, the closure of public baths and laundries, and the overall
shortage of firewood and fuel added to the agonies of starvation. Starvation lowers body temperature, and people suffering from lack of food
almost always feel cold. In Leningrad, the sensation was intensified by a
bitter-cold winter. Most Leningraders ventured out only to wait in bread
queues and, after bombs and cold destroyed water pipes, to fetch water
from ice holes in the Neva. When the trams ceased to run in mid-December
and snowdrifts blocked the streets, even short journeys became difficult
and dangerous for people severely weakened by starvation.

The home became at once the center of existence and a cold and alien
place. Few Leningraders were able to heat their apartments adequately.
Small, makeshift stoves of the sort Petrograders had used during the Civil
War (called *burzhuiki*) became available in January. They usually did a
poor job of warming even a single room.[69] An apartment's cold, empty
rooms might serve as temporary morgues if relatives lacked the strength
to bring the dead to the cemetery, or even the courtyard. People lit their
dark apartments – most of the windows were boarded or taped up – with
homemade wick lamps (*koptilki,* also a feature of life during the Civil
War). Under these conditions, maintaining even the most rudimentary
levels of personal hygiene and sanitation often proved impossible. By

[68] Ol'ga Freidenberg, "'Chelovecheskaia priroda otmenialas',''" *Chas pik,* 11 February
1991. Freidenberg, "Osada cheloveka," 33–34. *Smena,* 27 January 1994. Adamovich
and Granin, *Blokadnaia kniga,* 69–71. Kochina, *Blockade Diary,* 60, 78. Simmons and
Perlina, *Writing the Siege,* 98. Bidlack, "Survival Strategies," 90–101. Bidlack cites the
figure of approximately 1,500 arrests for cannibalism. Ibid., 99. Dzeniskevich, *Leningrad
v osade,* 421–22. Bidlack, "The Political Mood," 104–12. Nikita Lomagin, *Neizvestnaia
blokada* (St. Petersburg: Izdatel'stvo Dom "Neva," 2002), 275–88. Constantine Krypton,
"The Siege of Leningrad," *Russian Review* 13 (October 1954): 259, 262–64.

[69] The stoves may have been so named because they resembled contemporary caricatures
of the potbellied bourgeois class enemy (*burzhui*), who consumed much and produced
little, or because the formerly comfortable bourgeoisie were reduced to using them. Yuri
Zarakhovich, "Bring Back the Burzhuika!" *Time Europe,* 15 January 2001, http://www.
time.com/time/europe/webonly/europe/2001/01/yuri.html (accessed 17 February 2006).
Adamovich and Granin, *Blokadnaia kniga,* 67, 294–311. Likhachev, "Kak my," 12.

February, as Kochina noted in her diary, "human waste, like petrified rocks, covers all the courtyards."[70] Corpses were stacked in courtyards and basements, and the authorities feared that epidemics would engulf the city as soon as the ice melted.[71]

Later, when Leningraders tried to communicate the experience of starvation to outsiders, they often described its visible disruption of social roles and identities. Hunger effaced the distinctions between men and women, between intellectuals and housewives, as all busied themselves with finding and preparing food.[72] Starvation also created a body devoid of physical markers of age and gender. In the late stages of starvation, the voice became uniformly hoarse, "lost age and sex."[73] At puberty, boys' voices did not break. Women's breasts disappeared. Few women specifically mentioned amenorrhea in their diaries or in later reminiscences, but Leningrad doctors viewed it as one of the earliest and longest-lasting symptoms of alimentary dystrophy.[74]

Some Leningraders described starvation as a more general attack on human identity and dignity. Kochina reflected that "we came to know a hunger that degraded and crushed us, that turned us into animals." She recounted that in April 1942, on the difficult train journey from the Finland Station to Lake Ladoga, Leningraders stuffed themselves on unaccustomed rations. At each stop, "we all crawl out of the train and squat beside the cars, side by side – men, women, and children. The local population crowds around the train, looking at us with horror.... But we are indifferent to all that.... We ate well, and now it's so pleasant to free the stomach in order to stuff it again."[75] Freidenberg's account of the

---

[70] Kochina, *Blockade Diary*, 87. See also Freidenberg, "Osada cheloveka," 18–43; Ginzburg, *Blockade Diary*; Simmons and Perlina, *Writing the Siege*, 47–52, 62–63, 87–91, 156–62; Pavlov, *Leningrad*, 110–35.

[71] Dzeniskevich, *Leningrad v osade*, 289, 307–8. Neratova, *V dni*, 93. Kots, "'Na moiu,'" 84. Wayne, *Shurik*, 146. Bidlack, "Foreword," xxi. M. V. Ezhov, "Leningradskii gorodskoi sovet deputatov trudiashchikhsia v dni blokady (sentiabr' 1941-ianvar' 1944 g.)," *Vestnik Leningradskogo Universiteta: Istoriia, iazyk, literatura*, 1982, vyp. 3, no. 14: 121–22. Iu. I. Khromova, "Deiatel'nost' politorganizatorov sredi naseleniia Leningrada vo vremia Velikoi Otechestvennoi voiny (1941–1942 gg.)," *Vestnik Leningradskogo Universiteta: Istoriia, iazyk, literatura*, 1967, vyp. 3, no. 14: 59–60.

[72] Ginzburg, *Blockade Diary*, 42–43, 71. Adamovich and Granin, *Blokadnaia kniga*, 75–76.

[73] Adamovich and Granin, *Blokadnaia kniga*, 49. See also Julian Fliederbaum, "Clinical Aspects of Hunger Disease in Adults," in Myron Winick, ed., *Hunger Disease: Studies by the Jewish Physicians of the Warsaw Ghetto*, trans. Martha Osnos (New York: John Wiley, 1979), 19.

[74] Brožek et al., "Medical Aspects," 73. Chernorutskii, *Alimentarnaia*, 132, 196–99. Rivers, "Nutritional Biology," 79.

[75] Kochina, *Blockade Diary*, 85, 102. See also Adamovich and Granin, *Blokadnaia kniga*, 336.

blockade contains an even more despairing assessment of the degree to which the experience of starvation stripped Leningraders of their essential humanity. Describing her interaction with a musician visiting the besieged city in 1943, she noted that the pianist Mariia Iudina "was prewar; I was out-and-out a person of the siege. . . . I felt the desecrated soul within me, dying desires, my appreciation of life humiliated and destroyed forever."[76]

In the face of such devastation, Leningraders developed strategies not only for surviving but also for retaining their sense of themselves, their human identity. Honoring, even in a token way, everyday rituals that reinforced social and cultural norms – whether shaving, dividing the bread ration into "meals," reading, or studying – constituted one means of maintaining a connection to one's pre-famine self. Attending cultural events similarly served not only to preserve ties to the community but also to demonstrate continuing adherence to civilized standards. As late as December, it was possible to hear Petr Chaikovskii's "1812 Overture" at the Philharmonic.[77] Some factories set up support services and living quarters for workers. Brigades of young women in the Komsomol, who in January visited the homebound with food and firewood and in February delivered the mail, not only maintained vital services but also found a way to look beyond their own pressing needs.[78] For those who kept journals, often for the first time, writing offered the possibility of establishing a critical distance from, if never really mastering, the insistent thoughts of food that dominated thought, imagination, and action. More ambitious memory projects, such as the planned "A Day in the Besieged City," aimed to record events self-consciously defined as historically significant and offered the possibility of putting present suffering into a broader context.[79]

[76] Freidenberg, "The Race of Life," in Simmons and Perlina, *Writing the Siege,* 74.

[77] Adamovich and Granin, *Blokadnaia kniga,* 146–53. Grigorii Rozin, "Ia posedel v odinnatsat' let," in Aizenshtat, *Kniga zhivykh,* 13–16. Inber, *Leningrad Diary,* trans. Serge M. Wolff and Rachel Grieve (New York: St. Martin's Press, 1971), 31, 34. Dzeniskevich, *Leningrad v osade,* 487–554. V. G. Bortnevskii, "Kinoteatry Leningrada v gody Velikoi Otechestvennoi voiny," in Rosenko and Sobolev, *Voprosy istorii,* 133–42.

[78] The brigades began as a grassroots initiative. Rubashkin, *Golos Leningrada,* 59–60. N. D. Shumilov, *V dni blokady* (Moscow: Izdatel'stvo "Mysl'," 1977), 131–33. Bidlack, "Survival Strategies," 90–95. Alexander Werth, *Leningrad* (New York: Alfred A. Knopf, 1944), 63–69, 74–75. Neratova, *V dni,* 94. V. N. Tishunin, "Publitsistika blokadnogo goroda," 114. N. N. Amosov and L. A. Suetov, "Komsomol – Vernyi pomoshchnik partii v bor'be za spasenie zhizni leningradtsev v gody Velikoi Otechestvennoi voiny," *Vestnik Leningradskogo Universiteta: Istoriia, iazyka, literatura,* 1983, vyp. 3, no. 14: 19–20.

[79] Adamovich and Granin, *Blokadnaia kniga,* 288–91, 332–38. G. L. Sobolev, "Leningrad v Velikoi Otechestvennoi voine (nekotorye itogi i nereshennye voprosy)," *Vestnik Leningradskogo Universiteta: Seriia 2: Istoriia, iazykoznanie, literaturovedenie,* 1989, vyp. 1, no. 2: 4.

As conditions worsened and people became increasingly alienated from one another and their prewar lives, the radio played a vital role in reminding Leningraders that they remained part of a larger human community. Broadcasting fewer and fewer hours in December and January, and often silent in many quarters of the city, the radio assumed an increasingly important role as the symbol of continued social connection. Indicative of the shift was the attitude of listeners and broadcasters alike to the sound of the metronome that sounded continuously on Leningrad radio when there was no other programming. Before the German invasion, radio engineers had proposed the metronome as an air raid warning device. When enemy planes approached, the metronome increased its beat from a calm fifty to fifty-five strikes per minute to a frenetic one hundred fifty to one sixty beats per minute. As air raids diminished in number and finally broke off in early 1942, the metronome continued to fill breaks in radio programming. Now, however, it functioned less as a warning system than as the "heartbeat of the city" that encouraged Leningraders, who were cut off from one another in their freezing, dark apartments, to consider themselves part of a larger organism defiantly resisting evil forces trying to destroy it.[80]

That diarists remarked at least as frequently on whether the radio worked as on the content of the programming suggests the meaning they attached to the mere existence of the radio broadcast. In late March 1942, Zhilinskii's sorrow in the aftermath of his wife's death was deepened by the fact that she died just days before the thaw and the return of the radio – two important improvements that he seemed to believe might have sustained her. The faith in the radio is particularly striking in this case, given that Zhilinskii himself was later arrested for anti-Soviet agitation.[81]

For those who wrote for the radio and the newspaper, poetry took on wide personal and social significance as a means of turning, in Berggol'ts's words, "physical and moral suffering into art." The Radio House itself,

[80] Rubashkin, *Golos Leningrada*, 46. "Blokadnyi metronom." Smirnov, *Sankt-Peterburg XX vek*, 204–5. E. Ignat'eva, "Olimp blokadnykh muz," in Vera Arkharova, ed., *Pamiat': Pis'ma o voine i blokade* (Leningrad: Lenizdat, 1985), 253–54. G. S. Bat', "Pod stuk metronoma," in Mezhdunarodnaia assotsiatsiia blokadnikov goroda-geroia Leningrad, *Deti blokada: Vospominaniia, fragmenty dnevnikov, svidetel'stva ochevidtsov, dokumental'nye materialy* (St. Petersburg: IPk, "Vesti," 2000), 63–64. The collection *Blokadnaia kniga* featured a metronome on the cover.
[81] Zhilinskii, "Blokadnyi dnevnik," *Voprosy istorii*, 1996, no. 8: 14–15. See also K. V. Polzikova-Rubets, *Dnevnik uchitelia blokadnoi shkoly: 1941–1946* (St. Petersburg: Izdatel'stvo "Tema," 2000), 66. P. M. Samarin, "'Kak schastliv budet tot, kto vse eto perezhivet' (Iz blokadnogo dnevnika 1941–1942 gg.)," in *Zabveniiu ne podlezhit*, 69–93. Kochina, *Blockade Diary*, 64. Simmons and Perlina, *Writing the Siege*, 49. Rubashkin, *Golos Leningrada*, 43–46. Inber, *Leningrad Diary*, 37, 41.

where this transformation often occurred, became a crucial, supportive collective. After her husband's death in January 1942, Berggol'ts moved into the barracks set up at the station. Her colleagues Iakov Babushkin and Georgii Makogonenko (later her third husband) tried to buoy her strength by commissioning a long poem to be broadcast on Red Army Day (23 February 1942). The resulting work, "February Diary," began with an image of the persistence and gravity of small human connections in the midst of vast tragedy: The widowed poet and a friend, who had lost the man she loved but could not cry, sat silently together overnight.[82]

Other poets imagined the community of Leningraders in somewhat wider and more ideological terms. In "Kirov Is with Us," written in November 1941 when a newspaper requested an article commemorating the 1934 assassination of the Leningrad party leader Sergei Kirov, Tikhonov described a spectral Kirov dressed in an army greatcoat and forage cap, making the rounds of the besieged city. A sort of Communist guardian angel, Kirov walked under the "iron sky" and observed the bombing raids and the daring response of the young women in the MPVO.[83] His reassuring presence among his fellow Leningraders offered a nominally party-minded embodiment of the hope, perhaps the conviction, that a sense of community mitigated pain and loss. In *Pulkovo Meridian,* read on radio before it was published in late 1942, the poet Vera Inber, who had returned to the city at the beginning of the blockade with her husband, a doctor, portrayed starvation in "almost clinical detail" – "a gray hand almost without a pulse. The onset of death. Breakup of proteins."[84] However, Inber also appealed to the "spirit of Leningrad," a community united in a just cause: Surrounded on three sides, the city's hearbeat did not "oscillate a micron."[85]

---

[82] Berggol'ts, *Govorit Leningrad,* 373. Hodgson, *Voicing,* 24, 75. Berggol'ts, "Fevral'skii dnevnik," in *Sobranie sochinenii v trekh tomakh* (Leningrad: Khudozhesvennaia literatura, 1989), 2: 34.

[83] Nikolai Tikhonov, "Kirov s nami," in *Stikhi i proza* (Moscow: Gosudarstvennoe izdatel'stvo khudozhestvennoi literatury, 1945), 5–6. Tikhonov, "Iz perezhitogo," in A. M. Beilin, ed., *Riadom s geroiami* (Leningrad: Sovetskii pisatel', 1967), 7–10. Katharine Hodgson, *Written with the Bayonet: Soviet Russian Poetry of World War Two* (Liverpool: Liverpool University Press, 1996), 67. On the poem's popularity, see Salisbury, *900 Days,* 425.

[84] The characterization of the poem and the translation are from Hodgson, *Written,* 79. Rubashkin, *Golos Leningrada,* 101. Vera Inber, *Dusha Leningrada (Izbrannoe)* (Leningrad: Lenizdat, 1979), 18. Inber, *Leningrad Diary,* 123.

[85] Inber, *Dusha,* 25. On the importance of this "heroic moment" for the poet herself, see Anna Krylova, "In Their Own Words? Soviet Women Writers and the Search for Self," in Adele Marie Barker and Jehanne M. Gheith, eds., *A History of Women's Writing in Russia* (New York: Cambridge University Press, 2002), 250.

For listeners and readers, such poetry could provide a model of how to turn pain into a narrative of unity, moral purpose, sacrifice, and survival. It is likely that much of the poetry written during the worst of the blockade reached a wider audience only in the spring, when it was rebroadcast and published, particularly in the newspaper.[86] Nonetheless, in later oral histories and reminiscences, Leningraders attested to the ways in which the official representations of the blockade winter that they heard on the radio or read in the newspaper framed and shaped their own experiences. In the late 1970s, Valentina Moskovtseva, who was a child during the war, remembered that Leningrad radio had taught her how to survive. The radio advised: "'Don't eat your whole 125 grams at once, eat it by halves.'... And I did it this way: eat a little piece in the morning, a little piece in the evening. I paid attention to what they said on the radio."[87] Her story suggested that her own personal willpower coupled with the radio's message had saved her.

Survivors remembered Berggol'ts's poetry in particular as a powerful source and confirmation of the spiritual resources that had allowed them to survive. More than thirty years after the war, Galina Ozerova recalled that Berggol'ts's verses were "so simple that they just stuck in your mind, the rhythm just sunk into your head. You'd be walking along, muttering this verse of hers. 'Let it stand this way forever, painted with the dawn...' Once I knew that by heart, it somehow was a big help when I climbed up to the watchtower and was standing there on our library roof under shelling." Maia Babich recalled when "they started reading Ol'ga Berggol'ts's verses on the radio. I clearly remember how splendid that was, how they fit our mood. They really shook us out of that animal brooding about food."[88]

None of which is to suggest that poetry somehow made it possible for Leningraders simply to forget or ignore the degrading, dehumanizing

---

[86] Indeed, it is not even clear that "February Diary" was broadcast in February. In an autobiography written in 1952, Berggol'ts recounted that a last-minute phone call from the censor prevented the poem's broadcast, although it was published in full in May 1942. Other sources describe the poem as an important radio event that went off as planned. Berggol'ts, "Avtobiografiia," in _Sobranie sochineniia,_ 3: 491. G. Makogonenko, "Pis'ma s dorogi," in G. M. Tsurikova and I. Kuz'michev, eds. _Vospominaniia O'lgu Berggol'ts_ (Leningrad: Lenizdat, 1979), 138. Rubashkin, _Golos Leningrada,_ 108–09. Nikolai Tikhonov, "V dni ispytanii," in _S perom,_ 20.

[87] Adamovich and Granin, _Blokadnaia kniga,_ 148.

[88] Ibid., 73. Ozerova is slightly misquoting a line from Berggol'ts's "February Diary." Berggol'ts, "Fevral'skii," 2: 37. See also Polzikova-Rubets, _Dnevnik uchitelia,_ 135. Simmons and Perlina, _Writing the Siege,_ 110.

effects of starvation. Instead, blockade poetry and official accounts more generally offered a way of fitting painful memories into a narrative that defined starvation as a spiritual struggle and that emphasized the ultimate moral strength of Leningraders as individuals and as a community. In a position to see and understand the worst effects of starvation, Leningrad's doctors documented a profound and disturbing "lowering of moral levels" and "lack of shame." The starving, "without constraint, and despite generally accepted rules, choose to urinate in the most incongruous places, and do so openly.... The sick are slovenly and careless in relation to their appearance, often strikingly untidy in relation to food and the demands of personal hygiene." However, alongside this "moral decline," they also documented an unspecified, but apparently not inconsequential, number of cases of starving people who retained "genuinely human traits of steadfast self-sacrifice." The doctors' reports of an ability to "maintain personality," to preserve "human traits" in the face of the "wolfish hunger" that constitutes the primary symptom of hunger disease, are particularly striking given their relative rarity in other clinical studies of starvation.[89] The symptoms that doctors characterized as moral breakdown may have predominated – the study was not explicit one way or the other – but doctors ended their discussion of the psychological effects of starvation with the finding that in at least some cases, humanity triumphed.

Even Leningraders who held official narratives in contempt seemed to accept their basic premise that a person's reaction to starvation was essentially a measure of humanity – and stopped short of claiming that most Leningraders had failed to measure up. Looking back on the blockade in the late 1950s, the cultural historian Dmitrii Likhachev emphasized the distance between published accounts and reality. It is interesting to note that he pointed to Leningrad doctors as among the only people who spoke something approaching the truth of starvation. He dismissed officially sanctioned representations of the siege as "pap," and singled out Inber's *Pulkovo Meridian* for special disdain as "Odessa pap" – she was not a native Leningrader. Nonetheless, the narrative of moral triumph remained a necessary part of his story. For Likhachev, starvation revealed the essence of each individual's character: "Only people dying of hunger live a real life, are able to achieve utter baseness [his account described

---

[89] Chernorutskii, *Alimentarnaia*, 164–65, 130. See also Guetzkow, *Men and Hunger*, 31–32; Fliederbaum, "Clinical Aspects," 36. The fact that doctors in Warsaw, like their colleagues in Leningrad, carried out detailed clinical studies even as they themselves suffered from hunger offers corroboration of the Leningrad findings.

incidences of cannibalism] and the greatest self-sacrifice, without fear of death."[90]

The myth of the starvation winter elaborated in the Soviet media downplayed the "baseness," but it was not thereby a lie. Indeed, it could be embraced even by critics of the Soviet state. Leningraders certainly recognized that more than a few had succumbed, morally and physically. But they, like the doctors, also witnessed acts of selflessness. Moreover, the stories and poetry that depicted Leningraders as retaining their humanity and their moral community despite the horrors of starvation were not merely descriptions of the blockade but crucial elements of the experience itself. The concept of the "spirit of Leningrad" provided a useful basis for coping with, understanding, and remembering traumatic events.

Renewal and Rebirth: Spring and Summer 1942

With the arrival of spring in 1942, images of renewal and rebirth became ubiquitous features of Soviet accounts of the blockade. Much evidence on the streets of Leningrad supported such optimistic reporting. The snow had begun to melt; the sun warmed emaciated bodies; the trees bloomed. The radio returned, and newspapers became more widely and readily available. The city government ordered all Leningraders who were able to stand to take part in a massive effort to clear streets and courtyards of snow, ice, excrement, and corpses. For twelve days in late March and early April, as many as three hundred thousand Leningraders, primarily women, found the strength to break up snow and ice with shovels and picks, to haul away the detritus of winter, and to dump it into the still-frozen canals. The feared epidemics never materialized. The trams began running again on 15 April. Scurvy-ridden Leningraders ate the dandelions that grew in the parks and planted vegetable gardens in every available patch of ground. Rations increased, and queues shortened. Water and sewage systems were slowly repaired. By June, public baths, laundries, hairdressers, and movie theaters, not to mention most workplaces, had reopened. The heroic efforts of workers, predominantly women, in Leningrad's war industry once again became an important theme of media coverage. The renewal that had begun with the early thaw found its apotheosis in the August 1942 performance in blockaded Leningrad of Shostakovich's Seventh Symphony. Preparations for a second blockade

[90] Likhachev, "Kak my," 23.

winter – stockpiling food and fuel, laying electrical cable under Lake Ladoga – began. The city returned to something approaching normal, even as air and artillery attacks increased and the threat of a German summer offensive loomed.[91]

Admitting somewhat more detailed descriptions of the conditions that had prevailed during the winter, the press omitted any mention of how many Leningraders had died and largely ignored the long-term physical and psychological effects of the traumas through which Leningraders had passed. That the losses were staggering was clear to all. However, only after the war did the Soviet government release a figure – more than six hundred thousand deaths due to starvation – widely believed by historians to be too low.[92] The slow physical and psychological recovery of survivors observed by doctors also failed to become part of the media's representation of the blockade. Leningrad doctors connected alimentary dystrophy with a growing number of cases of hypertension, but their findings were not widely publicized.[93] Instead, the press pictured Leningraders as quickly regaining strength following the deprivations of winter. At the end of March 1942, *Leningradskaia pravda* suggested that Leningraders had no legitimate excuse for failing to join their neighbors in cleaning up streets and courtyards. At house number 213 on Pestel' Street, the paper reported, one could find "a large group of kids, and even old men and old women" doing their part.[94]

The spring and summer thus emerged as a happy or at least optimistic ending to the story of the cruel winter. In her radio broadcasts, Berggol'ts emphasized that the blockade had fortified, if not forged, a powerful shared identity. In May 1942, Berggol'ts assured her listeners that "the city revived! Now smiles glimmer on the darkest winter faces." She ended

---

[91] Bidlack, "Survival Strategies," 97–98. Bidlack, "The Political Mood," 111. Glantz, *The Siege,* 112–13. Likhachev, "Kak my," 26–27. Adamovich and Granin, *Blokadnaia kniga,* 184–97. Wayne, *Shurik,* 155–77. Ezhov, "Leningradskii," 121–22. On Leningrad industry, see *LP,* 6 October 1944, 4 April 1945. On the *Leningrad Symphony,* see *KP,* 19 August 1942; *LP,* 11 August 1942; V. Bogdanov-Berezovskii, "Triumf antifashistskoi simfonii," *Zvezda,* 1942, no. 3–4: 201–5.

[92] Dzeniskevich, *Blokada i politika,* 45–68.

[93] *Raboty leningradskikh vrachei za gody otechestvennoi voiny,* vyp. 8 (Leningrad: Medgiz, 1946). The volume had a pressrun of two thousand copies. Pär Sparén, et al., "Long Term Mortality after Severe Starvation during the Siege of Leningrad: Prospective Cohort Study," *BMJ: British Medical Journal* 328 (3 January 2004): 11–14.

[94] *LP,* 31 March 1942. See also *KP,* 12 May 1943; Aleksandr Fadeev, *Leningrad in the Days of the Blockade* (New York: Hutchinson, 1946), 40–45; Skomorovsky and Morris, *The Siege,* 42.

with a poem, proclaiming, "By one unprecedented battle.../We all are marked. We are Leningraders." In her broadcasts, the revival of spring offered a means of demonstrating that starvation, far from destroying the city, had renewed Leningraders' essential humanity, their culture, their community.[95]

The power of images of spring in Leningrad stemmed from their conflation of the incremental improvements that came with warmer weather and the hopes that the damage of winter would be fully and quickly healed. The novelist Vera Ketlinskaia's 1942 "The Story of a Simple Girl" illustrates how spring – a state of mind as much as a time of year – transformed pain into a radiant future. Olia, Ketlinskaia's Leningrad everywoman, joined in the spring cleanup. Her weak hands made it difficult to handle a shovel,

but with every hour in the spring wind, in the cheerful sunshine, her strength grew, and happiness gave birth to song – quiet, but exultant. And the day came when Olia, climbing up the watchtower, saw her city purified, tidied up, beautiful.... The ruined, bombed-out houses and the shell craters visible here and there did not upset her – she believed that the houses would soon be restored, reconstructed, adorned as never before.... Narrowing her eyes, she looked into the sunny spring sky, and felt grown up, strong, worthy of her Leningrad.[96]

Having struggled and survived, like the city, Olia looked forward to a time – not so very distant – when both she and the city would no longer bear the marks of war. The spring promised not just easier living conditions but personal and urban renewal.

Diaries, memoirs, and oral histories suggest that however unrealistic, such sanguine expectations were urgently necessary and deeply felt. For some, the promise of evacuation across Lake Ladoga functioned much like the anticipation of spring – a fantastic land of bread and sunshine just over the horizon whose call fueled efforts to survive. Vera Miliutina, a graphic artist who lived near the Finland Station where journeys across Lake Ladoga originated, remembered thinking when she met those preparing to leave, "These people are going to the Mainland! There they will recover. They will live and have bread to eat.... Grandfather Serezha and I will follow them there to eat fried potatoes."[97] Iura Riabinkin, who did

---

[95] Berggol'ts, *Govorit Leningrad*, 388. See also the broadcasts of 3 June 1942 and 29 December 1942. Ibid., 390–98, 403–10.

[96] *KP*, 23 June 1942.

[97] Vera Vladimirovna Miliutina, "Evacuation and the Scottish Album," in Simmons and Perlina, *Writing the Siege*, 80.

not live to see the spring, wrote in the second-to-last entry of his diary, dated 4 January 1942: "Only the hope of an answer from Pashin at the district committee – 'you're going' – keeps me on my feet. If it weren't for this, I'd die." When orders for evacuation finally came, Iura was too weak to walk. His sister Ira later remembered that their mother left him behind when on 8 January they departed for the station. His mother, like many evacuees, died after she and Ira reached Vologda.[98] Escaping from starvation remained more a wish than a fact, but it was not less real for that.

Evacuation and spring both produced moments of unreasoned joy. Elena Kozhina, who was eight when she left Leningrad, remembered the initial euphoria of evacuation: "All of us, not just children but adults too, lost our heads. . . . The feelings of freedom and safety, which I was experiencing for the first, yes, first time in my life (my prewar childhood now seemed like somebody else's life, not mine), brought uncontrollable exhilaration."[99] In her diary, nineteen-year-old Galina Bobinskaia described summer in Leningrad with similar elation. In an entry dated 27 June 1942 – during Leningrad's white nights, a time that under normal circumstances produced a festival mood – Bobinskaia wrote:

Anyone who didn't spend the winter here, who didn't personally feel and go through all those burdens, can't understand Leningraders' joy as they observe the rebirth of their native [*rodnogo*] city. . . . In the garden by the theater the public is especially well-dressed: women with fashionable hair-dos, elegant shoes, and elegant dresses in all the colors of the rainbow . . . and the girls themselves are healthy, glowing, and merry. . . . The hairdressers are full of women getting manicures and hot waves – they bring their own paraffin![100]

For some, the spring and summer – the end of the miseries of winter – constituted moments of exaltation, a colorful reassertion of conventionally gendered appearances, a carnival of survival.

However, for other Leningraders, the long-anticipated moment of better rations and warmer weather had the opposite effect, deepening depression as the horrors of winter became fully visible in the light of spring,

---

[98] Adamovich and Granin, *Blokadnaia kniga*, 363, 417–25. See also Kochina, *Blockade Diary*, 95–98. Neratova, who never returned to Leningrad, offers a more nostalgic view of evacuation. Neratova, *V dni*, 96–97, 101–8.

[99] Kozhina, *Through the Burning*, 84.

[100] Adamovich and Granin, *Blokadnaia kniga*, 185–86. See also Nadezhda Azhgikhina and Helena Goscilo, "Getting Under Their Skin: The Beauty Salon in Russian Women's Lives," in Helena Goscilo and Beth Holmgren, eds., *Russia – Women – Culture* (Bloomington: Indiana University Press, 1996), 94–121.

intensifying hunger as food became somewhat more available but hardly plentiful. In her diary entry for 7 June 1942, Anna Likhacheva, a doctor, noted, "Spring has awakened frozen human emotions and has cruelly reminded us of our private grief." In the medical literature, doctors emphasized that increased rations often produced not satiation but rather an intensification of hunger.[101] Ginzburg structured much of her retrospective blockade diary around this paradox: Spring brought not renewal but new agonies. For N, the generic intellectual "siege person" at the core of Ginzburg's account, the hunger of winter was "less humiliating and bestial than what happened to him when things were starting to improve. He felt hungry all the time.... He raked three portions of porridge into his plate, to make it look more, then fell into despair because there was actually so little."[102]

Such despair found little reflection in the press. The media reported not the bodily and psychological strains of the tail end of famine but Leningraders' hopes. It insisted on the reality of the clichéd ending: the return of life that follows the winter, the calm after the storm, the light at the end of the tunnel, the suffering that purifies and strengthens. Far from the full story, wartime accounts of the blockade suggest an uneasy coexistence of "levels of truth," "the tensions between the truth as it was experienced by the people in the city, and the truth that was necessary to convince them of the need for continued resistance."[103] The socialist-realist convention of eclipsing the often wretched present with the fairy-tale future fostered representations of blockaded Leningrad that sometimes flew in the face of reality but that also provided powerful means of imagining – and perhaps beginning to accomplish – real recovery. Freidenberg summed up the paradox: "No one believed the radio. It had been long assumed that it spoke for someone, but no one believed it or relied on the truth of what was heard. All the same, one listened and believed."[104]

---

[101] Anna Likhacheva in Simmons and Perlina, *Writing the Siege*, 60. Doctors' studies are cited in Chernorutskii, *Alimentarnaia*, 131. See also Simmons and Perlina, *Writing the Siege*, 83, 198–200; Adamovich and Granin, *Blokadnaia kniga*, 190–93; Polzikova-Rubets, *Dnevnik uchitelia*, 64; Keys, *Biology*, 843–47, 894–95; M. Elia, "Hunger Disease: Review Article," *Clinical Nutrition* 19 (2000): 384–85.

[102] Ginzburg, *Blockade Diary*, 62. See also Neratova, *V dni*, 94–95.

[103] Hodgson identifies these tensions in Berggol'ts's wartime poetry. Hodgson, *Voicing*, 73, 78.

[104] Freidenberg, "Osada cheloveka," 29. On socialist realism, see Katerina Clark, *The Soviet Novel: History as Ritual* (Chicago: University of Chicago Press, 1981), 138.

Local Victories

In 1942, evacuation provided the ending to the personal blockade stories of more than one million Leningraders. At the same time, the lake fleet delivered more than three hundred thousand soldiers, combat replacements for the Leningrad front. With a total population of about 640,000 at the end of 1942, Leningrad came to resemble the urban fortress that the press had declared it in the fall of 1941. When the blockade was finally lifted in January 1944, only about 575,000 people, less than 20 percent of the city's prewar population, remained in Leningrad.[105]

Leningraders who stayed celebrated three victories in the city. The first two were local: 18 January 1943, when Soviet forces cracked the blockade, opening an eight- to ten-kilometer-wide corridor that allowed the resumption of rail service; and 27 January 1944, when the Leningrad-Novgorod Offensive lifted the blockade. The last victory was national and international: 9 May 1945, when Germany surrendered and the red flag was raised over the Reichstag. (Victory in Europe Day was celebrated one day earlier in the West than in the Soviet Union, where the day that the news reached Moscow became a holiday.) As in 1941, most Leningraders learned of these developments from the radio.

No longer as critical as it had been during the first winter of the war, the radio remained in early 1943 the best source of breaking news and a relatively unscripted forum in which Leningraders could communicate with one another. On the night of the partial opening of the blockade, it broadcast until dawn, and Leningraders stayed up to listen. In her diary entry for 18 January 1943, schoolgirl Evgeniia Shavrova recalled, "Nonstop on the radio we heard from workers, soldiers of the Civil Defense (MPVO). Ol'ga Berggol'ts spoke."[106] Recalling the same night, Berggol'ts, too, remembered the pilgrimage of Leningraders to the Radio House. According to Berggol'ts, "What happened that night in the building of the Radio Committee happened spontaneously, without a plan, without preparation – music, verses written on the spot, speeches – everything went in an unbroken, exultant flow." Berggol'ts recalled the story of one old woman who traveled on foot all night from Novaia Derevnia, a district some six or seven kilometers northwest of the city center and the Radio House. When the police stopped her for a pass permitting travel

---

[105] Glantz, *The Siege*, 79, 114. Bidlack, "Foreword," xxii, xxiv. Blair A. Ruble, *Leningrad: Shaping a Soviet City* (Berkeley: University of California Press, 1990), 49.

[106] "Excerpts from Evgeniia Shavrova's 'A Schoolgirl's Diary,'" in Simmons and Perlina, *Writing the Siege*, 43.

after curfew, she replied, "Dear, I'm going to the radio to congratulate Leningraders." The police let her pass. She arrived toward morning, and "congratulated."[107] The ordinary grandmother in the queue became the granny in the media.

Berggol'ts asserted that Leningraders remembered the night of 18–19 January "as the most joyous, as the night when all hearts were boundlessly open to one another." However, this was joy with a strong admixture of sorrow.[108] The media's coverage of victory reflected some of this ambivalence, but also reassured Leningraders that the losses – however seemingly unrelated to the eventual victory – were meaningful. Like the spring and evacuation, the three victories offered the possibility of turning the experience of the blockade into a story of trials and triumph. "The blockade has been broken!" Berggol'ts declared on the night of 18 January 1943. She offered a redemptive ending to the story of starvation:

> We have long awaited this day. We always believed it would come. We were sure of it even during Leningrad's blackest months – January and February of last year. Our relatives and friends who died in those days ... stubbornly whispered as they died, "we will be victorious." They gave their lives for the honor, the life, and the victory of Leningrad. And we ourselves, made stone by sorrow, without even the strength to relieve our hearts with tears, buried them in the frozen ground, in fraternal graves, without any sort of honors.[109]

Whether or not it was true in all particulars – how many really died with the words "we will be victorious" on their lips? – Berggol'ts's story incorporated and evoked details familiar to all who lived through the first winter of the war in Leningrad. She provided an object lesson in how to view the starvation winter through the lens of victory – local victory – a prototype that other Leningraders could appropriate and reshape as they constructed their own blockade stories.

A year later, when the blockade was lifted, Berggol'ts's radio address insisted on the connections between civilian suffering and military victory. The language of the hero city predominated. She granted that "perhaps, only now, when the city has become quiet, will we begin to understand what sort of life we lived for those thirty months." But she also

[107] Berggol'ts, *Govorit Leningrad*, 374–75. See also Rubashkin, *Golos Leningrada*, 135–37.
[108] Berggol'ts, *Govorit Leningrad*, 375, 411–12. See also Simmons and Perlina, *Writing the Siege*, 113.
[109] Berggol'ts, *Govorit Leningrad*, 411.

characterized the entire experience as a "path to the day of 27 January, the unforgettable day of the Leningrad salute."[110]

After the fall of Berlin, when Leningraders celebrated not just local victory but also national triumph, Berggol'ts reiterated with even less qualification the claim that the happy ending redeemed the sorrow and losses of war. Climbing up to an old MPVO post in order to watch the victory fireworks, Berggol'ts and her colleagues retold – and for the first time were able to laugh about – stories from the first months of the war. "We remembered everything," Berggol'ts recounted on the air, "in a new way. . . . And as never before we realized that everything, absolutely everything, that we had done constituted a continuous movement toward victory."[111] Suffering Leningraders, as much as the troops, had made victory possible.

What is particularly striking about these local representations of victory is the degree to which they eschewed the emphasis on the party and Stalin that, beginning in early 1943, had become increasingly prominent features of war reportage in the national newspapers. In central newspapers such as *Komsomol'skaia pravda,* stories about orphans, mothers, reunited families, and the liberation of native villages continued to appear, but often came subordinated to invocations of Generalissimo Stalin's military genius.[112] In the Leningrad press, local stories, while certainly joined by those reinstating Stalin's cult, often had pride of place. Love for the city, the determination and self-motivation of the city's residents, and the heroism of troops from Leningrad continued to figure prominently in local coverage of the last years of the war.[113]

The unremitting emphasis on the local was even clearer on the radio. Although it increasingly rebroadcast programming from Moscow, the local radio continued to produce its own shows, if never again as spontaneously as on the night of 18 January 1943.[114] Berggol'ts, in particular, frequently insisted on the local meanings of the war. She suggested that while the Soviet victory gave meaning to Leningraders' losses, Leningraders'

[110] Ibid., 463, 466, 461.

[111] Ibid., 504–5.

[112] Jeffrey Brooks, *Thank you, Comrade Stalin! Soviet Public Culture from Revolution to Cold War* (Princeton, NJ: Princeton University Press, 2000), 185–88.

[113] See for example, *LP,* 4 June 1943, 2 July 1943, 11 October 1944, 4 April 1945; Aileen Rambow, *Überleben mit Worten: Literatur und Ideologie während der Blockade von Leningrad, 1941–1944* (Berlin: Berlin Verlag, 1995), 214–25.

[114] Rubashkin, *Golos Leningrada,* 138–41, 176–77.

"brotherhood" provided a model for the future of the Soviet Union. She, and the Leningrad press more generally, continued to retell the story of the blockade that local journalists and authors had developed during the first bitter years of the war.[115] Indeed, it was this continued insistence on Leningrad's "unique fate" that helped to precipitate the postwar crackdown on memoirs, museums, and archives devoted to the blockade.

The wartime narratives offered by the local media reflected and shaped individual experiences – and therefore individual memories. In large part, they did so by validating and inspiring the sense that Leningraders were living though and making history. The writers who contributed to the radio and newspapers, like the scores of Leningraders who kept diaries during the blockade, produced images and narratives under the most difficult circumstances because they felt a responsibility to record local, personal events of epochal significance. Wartime narratives of the hero city, the suffering city, the redeemed city structured memories and monuments. Even as the blockade continued, Leningraders telling their own and the city's stories began the work of commemoration.

---

[115] Berggol'ts, *Govorit Leningrad,* 506. On the generally negative reaction of frontline veterans to the reassertion of the Stalin cult, see Seniavskaia, *Frontovoe pokolenie,* 90–91.

3

Life Becomes History

Memories and Monuments in Wartime

> We felt that the fate of the motherland was in our hands, and we conducted
> ourselves in accordance with that idea, feeling ourselves to be *citizens* in the
> full and authentic sense of the word.... For our generation, the war was
> the most essential event of our lives, the most *essential*.
>
> Viacheslav Kondrat'ev[1]

From the moment that the war with Nazi Germany began, the Soviet
media represented it as history in the making – history made by brave,
steadfast, and self-sacrificing Soviet people. Just two days after the German army crossed the border, *Smena,* the newspaper of the Leningrad
Komsomol (Young Communist League), reported that efforts to chroni-
cle the war and to place it in the narrative of Russian and Soviet history
had already begun. The Leningrad movie studio Lenfilm announced plans
to produce short war documentaries and promised that the first five or six
films would be released in ten or twelve days. Meanwhile, workers at the
State Public Library planned an exhibition on the war against Napoleon –
the original Fatherland War – that would also include material on the
German invasion during the Civil War.[2] In December 1942, an exhibit
on "The Komsomol in the Fatherland War" commemorated the ongoing conflict in which "life becomes history." The display of family photographs, diaries, letters, commendations, and blood-soaked Komsomol

---

[1] V. Kondrat'ev, "Ne tol'ko o svoem pokolenii: Zametki pisatelia," *Kommunist,* 1990, no.
7: 113, 123.
[2] *Smena,* 24 June 1941.

cards attested to the epochal importance of the war and to the historic significance of everyday life in wartime.[3]

In Leningrad, the local media encouraged Leningraders to view local episodes as world historical events. Leningraders saw themselves, or an idealized version of themselves, in the press every day. They heard themselves on the radio. Official representations of the blockade ranging from art exhibitions to documentary films, celebrated the everyday heroism of ordinary Leningraders, and invited the city's inhabitants to recognize themselves as actors in the Leningrad "epic." Discussions of how best to commemorate the heroic events of the blockade appeared regularly in the press and on the radio. As early as December 1941, Ol'ga Berggol'ts predicted that the 125-gram daily bread ration of the worst period of the siege would soon become a museum exhibit. Less than three years later, it was.[4] The documentary film *Leningrad v bor'be* (Leningrad in Battle), released in July 1942, incorporated recent and familiar scenes into a comprehensive, ostensibly objective visual history of the blockade. In October 1942, the local branch of the Union of Architects organized a competition for a Monument to the Heroic Defenders of Leningrad.[5] In 1943, the Leningrad Institute of the History of the Communist Party published a history, *Heroic Leningrad,* that emphasized the links between 1917 and the war, and in 1944 a collection of documents – propaganda posters, poetry, official declarations – relating to the blockade.[6] Besieged Leningrad became one of those "events ... that are immediately invested with symbolic significance and are treated,

---

[3] *Komsomol'skaia pravda* (hereafter *KP*), 20 December 1942.

[4] Ol'ga Berggol'ts, *Govorit Leningrad,* in *Stikhi-proza* (Moscow: Gosudarstvennoe izdatel'stvo khudozhestvennoi literatury, 1961), 377. See also *Leningradskaia pravda* (hereafter *LP*), 24 December 1942, 16 April 1943, 4 June 1943; *Na strazhe Rodiny,* 29 December 1943.

[5] E. N. Andogskaia, "V soiuze arkhitektorov (Khronika 1942–1945 gg.)," *Arkhitektura Leningrada,* 1945, no. 1: 28. *LP,* 30 October 1942, 27 November 1942. "Monumenty geroiam Velikoi Otechestvennoi voiny," *Arkhitektura SSSR,* vyp. 5 (1944): 3–11.

[6] Leningrad institut isotrii VKP(b) – filial Instituta Marksa-Engel'sa-Lenina pri TsK VKP(b), *Geroicheskii Leningrad, 1917/42* (Leningrad: OGIZ-Gospolitizdat, 1943); idem, *Leningrad v Velikoi Otechestvennoi voine Sovetskogo Soiuza: Sbornik dokumentov i materialov* (Leningrad: OGIZ-Gospolitizdat, 1944), vol. 1, *22 iiunia 1941 g-22 iiunia 1943 g.* On a similar project proposed by the Academy of Sciences, see Andrei Dzeniskevich, ed., *Leningrad v osade: Sbornik dokumentov o geroicheskoi oborone Leningrada v gody Velikoi Otechestvennoi voiny, 1941–1944* (St. Petersburg: Liki Rossii, 1995), 520–21; E. Bochkareva, "Leningradskoe otdelenie Instituta istorii Akademii nauk SSSR v dni Velikoi Otechestvennoi voiny," *Istoricheskii zhurnal,* 1943, no. 7: 101–2.

even as they are unfolding, as if they were being commemorated in advance."[7]

The largely female and feminized experience of war on the city front – where survival required not just steadfastness under fire but the ability to accomplish routine domestic tasks under extreme conditions – complicated these contemporary commemorations. The bread ration preserved in the museum hinted at ways in which the housewife's traditional work had become heroic. In a 1941 poem, Berggol'ts stretched the concept of heroism in war, imagining the construction of a war memorial that honored not a soldier but a simple housewife in a headscarf, clutching her purse as she went out for bread under artillery fire. She celebrated the Leningrad housewife "as an exemplary heroine, and the equal to any soldier."[8] By contrast, Nikolai Tikhonov's January 1942 proposal for a postwar monument to the "unknown female worker," a female companion for the monument to the "unknown [male] soldier," valued women's wartime contributions to the extent that they mimicked, in a suitably supportive way, the familiar patterns set by male heroism.[9] As Berggol'ts herself recognized later in the war, the state was unlikely to commemorate people who "didn't blow up any tanks."[10]

These complications notwithstanding, many Leningraders shared the sense that they were living through historic events. Some felt the need to publicize their personal tragedies, to endow private loss with public recognition and meaning. Berggol'ts recounted that during one of the bombing raids of September 1941, a mother who lost two children in the attack came directly to the Radio House demanding, "Put me on the radio.... I want to speak."[11] Those who kept diaries recorded the daily details that they imagined would eventually allow historians to reconstruct their experiences. Some, as the archivist and diarist Georgii Kniazev described the situation, recorded only "facts," as he himself did. One colleague kept a count of the air raid alarms since the beginning of the war – 359 as

---

[7] Pierre Nora, "General Introduction: Between Memory and History," in Lawrence D. Kritzman, ed., *Realms of Memory: Rethinking the French Past*, trans. Arthur Goldhammer (New York: Columbia University Press, 1996), 1: 18.

[8] Ol'ga Berggol'ts, "Razgovor s sosedkoi," in *Sobranie sochinenii v trekh tomakh* (Leningrad: Khudozhestvennaia literatura, 1988), 2: 31. The quotation is from Katharine Hodgson, "The Other Veterans: Soviet Women's Poetry of World War 2," in John Garrard and Carol Garrard, eds., *World War 2 and the Soviet People* (New York: St. Martin's Press, 1993), 90.

[9] *LP*, 1 January 1942.

[10] Berggol'ts, "Vtoroi razgovor s sosedkoi," in *Sobranie*, 2: 66.

[11] Berggol'ts, *Govorit Leningrad*, 371.

of May 1942. Others with a different understanding of historians' future needs filled their diaries, as Kniazev disdainfully noted, with all the rumors that they heard.[12]

With the end of the first winter, Leningraders talked obsessively about the trials through which they had just passed, and imagined how they might be commemorated. In May 1942, Kseniia Polzikova-Rubets, a teacher, wrote in her diary that someone had told her of an old man who, before he died, had made himself a medal with the inscription "I lived in Leningrad in 1942." Whether this was true or an urban legend of the blockade, it resonated with Polzikova-Rubets, who mused, "Perhaps after the war such a medal will be given to all Leningraders."[13] As it turned out, civilians who remained and worked in the city received medals "for the defense of Leningrad" in 1943. A report prepared for party secretary Andrei Zhdanov confirmed that Leningraders cherished the awards. One "old worker" vowed that although his clothes were often dirty, the medal never would be: "I'll wear it only on holidays. We Leningraders will forever be respected for this award."[14]

Drawing on a shared sense of the gravity of the war in general and the blockade in particular, and employing the gender-obfuscating language of heroic defenders, official and individual commemorations could converge. In its official commemorations of the siege, notably the exhibition (later the museum) the Heroic Defense of Leningrad, the state employed small, personal blockade stories as a means of establishing the emotional authenticity of the national struggle, bolstering patriotism, and sustaining the "war mood."[15] At the same time, individuals wove state-sponsored images and narratives into their "personal" memory projects as a means of investing their wartime experiences with historic significance. For Leningraders like the librarians at the Saltykov-Shchedrin State Public Library, who organized the Leningrad in the Great Fatherland War document collection, turning life into history constituted an important means of coping with traumatic loss and of maintaining hope for a better future. Commemoration, after all, usually assumes an "after," not only

---

[12] Ales' Adamovich and Daniil Granin, *Blokadnaia kniga* (Moscow: Sovetskii pisatel', 1982), 399–400.

[13] K. V. Polzikova-Rubets, *Oni uchilis' v Leningrade: Dnevnik uchitel'nitsy* (Moscow: Gosudarstvennoe Izdatel'stvo Detskoi Literatury Ministerstva Prosveshcheniia RSFSR, 1948), 93–94.

[14] Dzeniskevich, *Leningrad v osade*, 482–83. See also V. S. Grigor'ev, "'Za oboronu Leningradu': K 50-letiiu uchrezhdeniia medali," *Sankt-Peterburgskaia panorama*, 1992, no. 12: 22–23; *LP*, 4 June 1943, 2 July 1943.

[15] Gaynor Kavanagh, "Museum as Memorial: The Origins of the Imperial War Museum," *Journal of Contemporary History* 23 (1988): 80.

survival but also victory. It also assumes grateful descendants – and perhaps grateful leaders – ready to hear, to understand, and to honor those who made victory possible.

At the Front of History

The uncanny city, at once made strange by war and strangely recognizable, played a crucial role in wartime representations of the siege both as particularly poignant for natives of Leningrad and as particularly "historic." In wartime images of Leningrad, the jarring contrast between the traces of modern war and the beautiful avenues and buildings constructed a cityscape that was at once epic and familiar, a symbol of war's threat to civilization and to home and family. The visual ironies emphasized in wartime photographs, drawings, and literary descriptions of the city front called attention to Leningrad's overlapping identities and histories: the hero city, the cradle of Revolution, the imperial city, the remembered city of childhood. Intertwining places, historic events, and individual memories, the cityscape held together historic and personal events.[16]

The official media emphasized that war transformed the everyday life of the city into the raw material of history. Looking back on the "most difficult period of the blockade" from the vantage of the spring of 1942, the writer Il'ia Gruzdev recalled how, in January 1942, he had taken it upon himself to inspire a roomful of cold, hungry writers, since "not all the comrades were equally steadfast in enduring the difficulties of those days." Certain of the historic importance of life and literary work in the blockaded city, Gruzdev saved the shorthand minutes of his speech. Five months later, he published the text "as a document of those days":

Comrades! Think about what *luck* [or happiness, *schast'e*] it is to live in Leningrad, about the writer's good fortune that in these days puts us not in the backwoods of history, but at the front of history, face to face with awesome events, in a great city, whose bleak days will go down in the history of the millennium. And if we have ears that hear, and eyes that see, think about the fact that to us falls the luck of engraving that which we see and hear. Not a single person in the world can replace us. Every day in Lenin's city is *unique*, not in the banal calendar sense, but in the sense that for seven months, every day has changed the historic aspect of our city.[17]

---

[16] Edward Casey's observation that "a given landscape, whether actually experienced or entirely imagined, holds narrated events together" is relevant here. Casey, *Representing Place: Landscape Painting and Maps* (Minneapolis: University of Minnesota Press, 2002), 274.

[17] Il'ia Gruzdev, "O Leningrade," *Literatura i iskusstvo*, 16 May 1942, emphasis in original.

Ignoring the price that individuals paid to live "at the front of history,"
Gruzdev represented the city as a place where each day and every action
carried profound historical significance.

In the 1960s, Valerian Solovtsev, the head of the film studio that produced *Leningrad in Battle,* recalled a similar sense of living through a
remarkable time in a place with a new "historic aspect." Looking back on
the process of making the documentary, he remembered that "it was precisely in those terrible days that we realized that every meter, every frame
of film shot in the besieged city, every episode of the heroic Leningrad
epic would become a priceless historical treasure. We knew we wouldn't
be able to forgive ourselves if we failed to preserve the great victory of
Leningrad's defenders for future generations."[18] Thus, he concluded, the
filmmakers found the strength to brave the winter streets with a camera on
a sled in tow and to record for posterity the disturbing images of familiar
streets transformed into a wasteland. At the same time, the act of filming
was itself an expression of hope. Film shot during the winter could not
be developed until the photo lab reopened in the spring.

The propaganda posters produced during the blockade and visible
throughout Leningrad carried the same message: Leningraders on the
city front stood at the forefront of history. Typical of the genre was V.
Serov's 1941 "We defend Lenin's city," in which a soldier, a sailor, a male
worker, and a female worker, confronting the viewer with stern and steadfast gazes, stood against the distinctive Leningrad skyline – the Admiralty
spire, St. Isaac's Cathedral, and smokestacks.[19] These Leningrad icons
managed simultaneously to evoke the Revolution; Russian military, cultural, and industrial power; and a very specific locale. Posters that did
not explicitly refer to the defense of the city took on distinctively local
meanings when affixed to Leningrad's bombed-out or boarded-up buildings. In the context of visibly damaged but familiar surroundings, the
two-story-high poster of a mother holding a dead child in her arms under
the caption "Death to the Child Killers!" (Illustration 5), or of a mother

[18] V. M. Solovtsov, "Kinoletopis' groznykh let," in Soiuz zhurnalistov SSSR, Leningradskoe otdelenie, *S perom i avtomatom: Pisateli i zhurnalisty Leningrada v gody blokady*
(Leningrad: Lenizdat, 1964), 361.

[19] P. Gorbunov, "O leningradskom plakate," *Leningrad,* 1944, no. 2: 17. See also "Okna
TASS," *Propaganda i agitatsiia,* 1941, no. 17–18: 65. The discussion of images of the
city during the war draws on my analysis of a large sample of the posters, postcards,
broadsides, and other ephemera that are part of the collection Leningrad v Velikoi Otechestvennoi voine housed at the Fontanka branch of the Russian National Library (hereafter
RNB) in St. Petersburg. See also Red Baltic Fleet (KBF) posters held at the RNB, L3–310
p/7/2.

5. Nevskii Prospekt during the winter of 1941–1942. The poster proclaims "Death to the Child Killers!" *Source:* ITAR-TASS.

and child threatened by a bayonet marked with the swastika, encouraged the sense that history was happening on the streets of Leningrad.[20]

The ubiquitous posters and broadsides in turn became essential elements of the wartime cityscape, at once chronicling and constituting the history of the blockade. In May 1942, the diarist Kniazev, who was the director of the Soviet Academy of Sciences Archives, recorded that a colleague helped him take down a poster about the defense of the city that had hung on the wall "through the whole winter, through rain, snow, blizzard, shelling: 'We will not surrender our native [*rodnogo*] city.'" He observed that "in fifty or a hundred years, this poster will be a rare museum piece. Our descendants will bow their heads before it. This scrap of paper, carefully preserved, will tell more about Leningrad's experience than hundreds of written pages."[21] The notion that the posters plastered around the city ought to be preserved in a museum, where "future people will stand before them reverently as before an eternally living slice of history," also occurred to Berggol'ts. In a June 1942 broadcast, she suggested that her listeners look carefully at the walls of their own apartment buildings, "where last year's leaflets and posters are pasted alongside of today's – scan them, and how much feeling is stirred in you." To reread the signs or, as other survivors emphasized, the wartime newspapers was to relive events. Indeed for Berggol'ts and Kniazev, these written relics of the blockade had the power to conjure the experience even for those who did not live through it. Berggol'ts concluded that "the walls of our houses are like an open stone diary – the whole city's diary, each Leningrader's diary."[22] The official pronouncements and hand-lettered signs that covered the city's walls blurred the boundaries between the experience and its representations, between the everyday lives of individual Leningraders and the larger-than-life stories that would inspire the reverence of their descendants.

Berggol'ts perceptively traced the power of the wartime notices and posters to their obvious incongruity "on the walls of a huge, civilized, beautiful, contemporary city." (See Illustration 6.) Stenciled signs along

---

[20] Gosudarstvennyi muzei istorii Sankt-Peterburga, *Leningrad v blokade: Fotografii B. P. Kudoiarova iz sobraniia muzeia* (St. Petersburg: GMI SPB, 2000), 1. See also the photographs reproduced in David M. Glantz, *The Siege of Leningrad 1941–1944: 900 Days of Terror* (Osceola, WI: MBI Publishing, 2001), 60.

[21] Adamovich and Granin, *Blokadnaia kniga*, 399–400.

[22] Berggol'ts, *Govorit Leningrad*, 390–91. See also L. Nikol'skii, "Slovo o druz'iakh poligrafistakh," in *S perom*, 344; Maksim Gordon and F. Samoilov, "Pero priravniali k shtuku," in ibid., 110; Arkhiv Rossiiskoi Natsional'noi Biblioteki (hereafter Arkh. RNB), f. 12, T. 517, ll. 12–13.

6. Palace Square and the Alexander Column in protective scaffolding. The sign warns pedestrians that in the event of an artillery attack, they stand on the dangerous side of the street. *Source:* ITAR-TASS.

the city's main streets that advised Leningraders on everything from how to fight and prevent fires ("Don't leave children near burning wick lamps!") to the need to tend their vegetable gardens ("You can supply your family with vegetables for the whole year") normalized concerns that should not have existed in a "civilized" city. Other ironies were more painful and glaring. Berggol'ts recalled the notice that hung for a long time on the boarded-up display window of a formerly luxurious shop on Lev Tolstoi Square: "Citizens! I take the deceased to the cemetery by sled, and other everyday transportation."[23] An ordinary advertisement proffered unimaginable services. Such notices encapsulated the strangeness and the significance of the war at home.

Visual depictions of wartime Leningrad similarly relied on the surreal and incongruous juxtapositions of war occurring against the backdrop of "classical porticoes."[24] Throughout the fall and winter of 1941–42,

---

[23] Berggol'ts, *Govorit Leningrad*, 391–92.
[24] "Leningrad zimoi 1941–1942 gg.: Risunki arkhitektorov," *Arkhitektura SSSR*, vyp. 2 (1943): 16. See also "Iz okna ermitazha: Zarisovki akad. arkh. A. S. Nikol'skogo," ibid., 19–20; Iu. M. Piriutko, "V dni geroicheskoi oborony," *Stroitel'stvo i arkhitektura Leningrada*, 1974, no. 1: 19–20.

photographs in the local press focused on Leningrad's still-functioning industry and on the men defending the city at the front.[25] By 1943, however, representations of the first winter of the war that emphasized the macabre beauty of the city front became common in the press and on postcards produced in pressruns of twenty thousand. Rich in visual ironies, many of the wartime images became indelible icons of the siege, endlessly reproduced in histories, museums, and newspapers on important anniversaries. Barrage balloons – airborne barriers against low-level air attacks – floating over the elegant façades along Nevskii Prospekt, searchlights illuminating the skyline of domes and spires, antiaircraft batteries installed on the granite embankments, the Bronze Horseman encased in wood, young women in firefighters' uniforms standing watch on the roof of the Hermitage, the grand square in front of St. Isaac's Cathedral transformed into a massive cabbage patch (Illustration 7), all provided condensed and compelling evidence of Leningrad's unique frontline status and of the resilience of the eternal city on the Neva.[26] The images demonstrated that Leningrad was passing though a remarkable and unforgettable moment in its storied history.

These wartime images played on the multivalent and slippery symbolism of the city's notable sites. Unexpected views of the scarred city underscored the local, personal, and emotional, along with the national and ideological, dimensions of war. A 1943 postcard view of Uritskii Square (Palace Square) the previous winter depicted citizens shoveling snow in the shadow of the Alexander Column. The column itself, a 47.5-meter monument to the Russian victory over Napoleon, appeared wrapped in scaffolding designed to protect it from air and artillery attack. In the context

---

[25] Looking for photographs to illustrate their collection of oral histories and diaries published in the late 1970s, Adamovich and Granin went through thousands of photographs in the TASS archives. They found that "very few pictures showed the true state of things." Initially "outraged," they interviewed reporters who explained that they had "considered it their duty to the war effort to show that despite the blockade, the hunger, the cold, and the shelling, people continued to work." Adamovich and Granin, *A Book of the Blockade*, trans. Hilda Perham (Moscow: Raduga Publishers, 1983), 369–70. This passage does not appear in the 1982 Russian edition.

[26] RNB, "Otkrytki iz kollektsii 'Leningrad v Velikoi Otechestvennoi voiny,'" L3–310 0129/6/13 (Bronze Horseman), L3–310 0129/6/1 (pr. 25 Oktriabria). For similar sketches, see Piriutko, "V dni," 19–20; "Leningrad zimoi 1941–42 gg.," 16–18; "Iz okna ermitazha," 19–20. A review of the local press from 1960 to 1995 reveals that a relatively small number of images were reproduced on important anniversaries related to the blockade. For example, the image of MPVO "girls" on a rooftop, with the dome of St. Isaac's visible in the background, appeared in *LP*, 21 June 1961, 27 January 1967, 7 September 1991, and in *Sankt-Peterburgskie vedomosti*, 8 September 1994. Soviet newspapers frequently reproduced iconic photographs on important anniversaries.

7. Cabbage growing in front of St. Isaac's Cathedral, spring 1942. *Source:* ITAR-TASS.

of wartime propaganda that emphasized the connections between the current Great Fatherland War and the original Fatherland War of 1812, the column evoked continuity with the imperial past at least as much as the square and its current name suggested the events that had ushered in the Soviet era. Likewise, a drawing of the Kazan Cathedral on what was still Plekhanov Square showed soldiers hauling wood in the shadow of the imposing statue of Mikhail Kutuzov. The great general's statue, along with the statues of his peers Mikhail Barclay de Tolley and Aleksandr Suvorov, were among the few left exposed in the besieged city. Like the Bronze Horseman, the statue of Lenin in front of the Finland Station was encased in sandbags and wood. Petr Klodt's statues of men taming wild horses that grace the Anichkov Bridge were buried for the duration. In this context, the exposed generals stood as tangible reminders of imperial victories and points of reference that established the historic lineage of the current war.[27]

---

[27] RNB, "Otkrytki," L3–310 0/29/6/11 (Uritskii square), L3–310 0/29/5/2 (Kazan Cathedral).

The Leningraders who produced media representations of the city emphasized that for natives, who necessarily had their own detailed and personal mental maps of the city, the changes brought by war were particularly moving, disturbing, unnerving, and momentous. In one of his stories from the fall of 1941, Tikhonov described the war as a defense of places deeply embedded in local memories. With sentimental irony he observed, "young Leningraders, who became soldiers, fought in the glades and in the groves where they ran in childhood."[28] In a poem read on the radio in July 1942, Berggol'ts characterized war-torn yet familiar streets as personal roads of memory: "I went to the front through childhood."[29] In blockaded Leningrad, personal histories and the war occupied the same places. The groves of childhood became battlefields; the streets of childhood became the setting for an urban apocalypse of cold, snow, and fire.

Leningrad's many bombed-out buildings stood as dramatic evidence of a historic rupture of everyday life. The house ripped open by a bomb blast impressed neighbors and photographers for the local media alike as a clear demonstration of the war's brutal erasure of the boundaries between public and private spaces and stories.[30] In February 1942, Elena Kochina described in her diary a half-demolished building from which "a round stove hung like a bright blue paradox, timidly recalling the recent comfort and warmth."[31] Arif Saparov, a writer for *Na strazhe Rodiny,* remembered the night the paper's photographer rushed into the editorial offices and insisted that he see the nearby building sheared in half by a bomb, where an upright piano hung precariously on the edge of the abyss. What impressed the writer, however, was less the improbably intact piano

---

[28] Nikolai Tikhonov, "Iz rasskazov voennykh let: Vrag u vorot," in O. F. Berggol'ts, V. N. Druzhinin, A. L. Dymshits, A. G. Rozen, and N. S. Tikhonov, eds., *900 dnei* (Leningrad: Lenizdat, 1957), 83. See also Evgenii Shvarts, "Leningradskie rebiata," in ibid., 129–30; *KP,* 26 September 1941, 21 August 1942, 11 December 1943.

[29] Berggol'ts, *Govorit Leningrad,* 397. See also Vera Ketlinskaia, "Na vyshke," in *Rasskazy o Leningradtsakh* (Leningrad: Lenizdat, 1944), 287–303.

[30] Paula Hamilton, "Memory Remains: Ferry Disaster, Sydney, 1938," *History Workshop Journal,* no. 47 (Spring 1999): 205.

[31] Elena Kochina, *Blockade Diary,* trans. Samuel C. Ramer (Ann Arbor, MI: Ardis, 1990), 93. See also Lidiia Ginzburg, *Blockade Diary,* trans. Alan Myers (London: Harvill Press, 1995), 25; Adamovich and Granin, *Blokadnaia kniga,* 299, 303–05. Rimma Neratova's and architect Igor' Chaiko's unpublished drawings employed similar visual ironies. Rimma Neratova, *V dni voiny: Semeinaia khronika* (St. Petersburg: Zhurnal "Zvezda," 1996), facing 288. A. O. Evlanova, ed., "Arkhitektor I. M. Chaiko i ego blokadnyi dnevnik," in *Trudy gosudarstvennogo muzeia istorii Sankt-Peterburga,* vyp. 5 (2000), 110–24.

than the clothes rod one floor higher that still held a light-colored man's coat and hat: "The coat was barely swinging." The nearby Admiralty spire that seemed "like an opera decoration" made the scene even stranger and more memorable.[32] Such images visually verified that Leningrad was a city in which the quotidian had become historic.

The Simple Human Voice of History

Looking back on the war in the 1950s, Berggol'ts argued that the erasure of the boundary between the personal and the public, the intimate and the national, the everyday and the heroic, constituted a general feature of life during the siege. In her memoirs, she described the "many blockade diaries" she had read:

Singed and icy, the triumphant Leningrad tragedy breathes from the many, many pages of these diaries, where a person writes with total candor about his or her own [*svoikh*], everyday cares, efforts, sorrows, joys. And, as a rule, his or her "own," the "deeply personal," is at the same time more universal, or more general. The people's [*narodnoe*] becomes deeply personal, indeed humane. History suddenly speaks with a living, simple human voice.[33]

Berggol'ts suggested that in besieged Leningrad, the line between personal and national history disappeared because individuals were living an epic.

In blockaded Leningrad, the "simple human voice" that Berggol'ts heard in individual diaries also spoke in spaces that were controlled by the state. Indeed, the conviction that personal, intimate stories held historic significance became a central feature of official efforts to commemorate the siege. In these public contexts, private sorrows and joys made compelling propaganda. Official monuments appropriated and attempted to contain powerful emotions by inscribing personal losses and suffering into a narrative of national unity and eventual triumph.

Familiar images of everyday life in besieged Leningrad provided visual and thus "irrefutable" and "true" raw material for state-sponsored commemorations that found a "way of making a disaster sound glorious without even denying that it is a disaster."[34] The documentary *Leningrad in Battle* contained scenes of air raids and snowbound streets

---

[32] A. Saparov, "'Drozhat doma-gromady,'" in *S perom*, 468.

[33] Berggol'ts, *Dnevnye zvezdy*, in *Stikhi-proza*, 33.

[34] Malcolm Smith, *Britain and 1940: History, Myth, and Popular Memory* (New York: Routledge, 2000), 3, 46.

that Leningraders recognized as reflective of their personal experiences. Contemporary reviewers and the viewers quoted in the press emphasized the absolute accuracy of the documentary. One reviewer, a self-identified Leningrader, stressed that "for us, everything in this film is familiar." Leningraders watched and affirmed: "Yes, it was like that. I know that exactly. I saw that myself." The film, another reviewer opined, "speaks not a part of the truth, but the whole, the full truth."[35] Certainly the film contained remarkable footage of the wartime city. The scenes of the first blockade winter were relatively graphic and unsparing in comparison to the images of the city that had appeared in the Soviet media before the film's release. The film also stood in sharp contrast to the general run of Soviet newsreels, which a 1944 report for the U.S. Office of Strategic Services described as "so similar ... that they are sometimes difficult to distinguish."[36]

Yet even if the film included, as the reviewer in *Zvezda* emphasized, "not a single 'staged' frame," it nonetheless cut its documentary footage into a very clear and unequivocal narrative of struggle and redemption. Containing scenes that replicated the average Leningrader's local and homebound points of view, the film also repositioned viewers as "omniscient spectators" of an epic.[37] Its peaceful prologue showed, as the reviewer in *Komsomol'skaia pravda* noted, the places that every Leningrader instantly recognized as home: the Neva, Nevskii Prospekt, the Peter Paul Fortress, the monument to Vladimir Lenin at the Finland Station, the Bronze Horseman, the smokestacks of Leningrad's factories. News of war – represented by the commonly recalled moment of people gathered around loudspeakers listening to Viacheslav Molotov's announcement – shattered this idyll. (The film omitted the fact that Leningrad had been mobilized for the Winter War against Finland in 1939–40.) From the solemn faces in the crowd – one reviewer saw "anger burning in their eyes" – the film cut to scenes of Leningraders volunteering to join the home guard.[38] Footage of the fierce battles on Leningrad's outskirts gave way to images of housewives and children serving in the local

---

[35] A. Dymshits, "Fil'm, zovushchii k bor'be i pobede (O dokumental'nom kinofil'me 'Leningrad v bor'be')," *Propaganda i agitatsiia*, 1942, no. 14: 15. N. Lesiuchevskii, "Leningrad v bor'be," *Zvezda*, 1942, no. 3–4: 199. See also *KP*, 11 July 1942, and *LP*, 11 July 1942.

[36] In 1944, Soviet studios produced six newsreels per month. "Motion Picture Questionnaire"; Record Group (RG) 226; Entry 16, 68434; National Archives at College Park, MD (NACP).

[37] Hamilton, "Memory Remains," 195.

[38] Dymshits, "Fil'm," 15.

air defense squadrons (MPVO) and of workers at their benches despite air and artillery attack, producing tanks that went directly from the factory floor to the front. The sequence of images suggested that war had taken Leningraders by surprise, and that they had responded with patriotism and courage.

In this filmic context, the starvation winter became an episode in the larger national struggle. Indeed, as a means of emphasizing the press's insistence that "Leningrad is not alone," the film "carried us," as the reviewer in *Literatura i iskusstvo* described it, from the "snowy streets" of Leningrad in November 1941 "to the heart of the motherland, to the mausoleum [Lenin's tomb] on Red Square" for the celebration of the October Revolution. "And the wise words of the *vozhd'* [leader] sound above the country. And Leningrad hears Stalin's voice: 'May the triumphant banner of the great Lenin shield you.'"[39] With this lead-in, the winter scenes – dark houses, stopped trams, a woman pulling a sled with a corpse, a person who has fallen in the snow, dead or dying – could be taken to demonstrate, as one reviewer insisted, not only Leningraders' "torment and suffering" but also the "utmost self-sacrifice, the highest heroism."[40] The apposition of images from the blockaded city with footage of the construction of the ice road and the operations of local partisan units also encouraged viewers to connect personal experiences to the larger battle and to aid from the "mainland." Personal sorrows became part of history; the blockade became at once tragic and glorious. Visual confirmation that the winter struggles were not in vain came in the film's final sequence. Images of spring and renewal – the Neva free of ice, the trams running, the wet asphalt shimmering in the sunlight, children playing – and the decision to omit the words "The End" pointed toward imminent victory. It is interesting to note that these images of local victory did not refer back to the vozhd'. The film provided a panoramic telling of the Leningrad epic that used scenes of personal hardship to visually authenticate and commemorate the myth of the hero city.

In what must have been intended as praise for the film's veracity, a factory worker quoted in *Leningradskaia pravda* noted that after seeing *Leningrad in Battle*, she felt as if she had relived the past year (*god snova perezhila*) because "each frame is a slice of our life." Given that reexperiencing the sensations of air raids and hunger was likely to be

[39] *Literatura i iskusstvo*, 11 July 1942.
[40] Dymshits, "Fil'm," 16.

at least somewhat painful (and thus unlikely to produce enthusiasm for the film), her sense of having "lived through the year anew" can also be taken to mean that the film had permitted remembered images and sensations to become part of a new, "objective," at least somewhat consoling and meaningful story.[41] The film turned lived experience into part of an epic.

In 1943 and 1944, two important exhibitions devoted to the history of the blockade likewise employed personal, small stories and images as a means of documenting and commemorating the defense of Leningrad. In June 1943, the Political Administration of the Leningrad Front sponsored the "first exhibition of front artists." Works depicting battle scenes and portraits of heroes, especially fliers, dominated the exhibition. Yet the artistic "documents of the defense of Leningrad, which the future historian of our great times will consult often," also included representations of the everyday life of the besieged city.[42] As in the film, depictions of the wartime city familiar to Leningraders lent authority to the larger story that they had not witnessed.

In the summer of 1943, the Leningrad military authorities undertook the organization of an ambitious exhibition devoted to the Heroic Defense of Leningrad. Military exhibitions had been a feature of life in the city almost since the beginning of the war and had proved quite popular. The first, which opened in August 1941, displayed German tanks, planes, and artillery captured on the approaches to Leningrad. The second, The Great Fatherland War of the Soviet People against Fascism, which also opened in 1941, ran to the end of 1943. It told the story of the defeat of the Livonian and Teutonic knights – presented as the precursors of the fascists – of the "treacherous" attack on the Soviet Union, and of partisan activities and German atrocities in the occupied territories. Cases displayed the personal effects of German officers and soldiers. Visitors could also see a captured Tiger tank and other German arms and artillery. The Heroic Defense of

[41] *LP*, 11 July 1942. See also Lesiuchevskii, "Leningrad," 199–200. In 1944, U.S. observers noted that Soviet movie audiences expressed "indifference to war films but pleasure with even bad foreign films." "Motion Picture Questionnaire"; RG 226; Entry 16, 68434; NACP.

[42] V. Saianov, "Na vystavke khudozhnikov-frontovikov," *LP*, 1 June 1943. See also Politicheskoe upravlenie leningradskogo fronta, *Pervaia vystavka khudozhnikov-frontovikov: Katalog* (Leningrad: Voennoe izdatel'stvo Narodnogo Komissariata Oborony, 1943), 7–8, and reproductions following 47; Ven. Vishnevskii, "'Boevoi karandash': Na vystavke leningradskikh khudozhnikov," *Trud*, 13 October 1943; Bor. Brodianskii, "Khudozhniki nashego fronta," *Na strazhe Rodiny*, 29 December 1943.

Leningrad exhibition that the local military soviet authorized in August 1943 focused more explicitly on the heroes of the Leningrad front – in battle and in the city. It opened in April 1944, four months after the siege had been lifted.[43]

Like London's Imperial War Museum, which was likewise organized while Britain was still at war in 1916, the Leningrad exhibition can be understood as "an ethnographic collection whose ethnographic subject was the nation-in-arms," and, in the case of Leningrad, also the city-in-arms. Both museums "solicited souvenirs, ephemera, films, and photographs so that the war could be represented simultaneously as a national and a personal achievement."[44] The personal effects collected in Leningrad were particularly charged with emotion because in addition to celebrating the soldiers at the front, they documented the lives of women and children who had become "defenders" within the city. It was here that Berggol'ts's prediction that "we will see our daily bread ration, this poor little piece of black bread, behind the glass in some kind of museum" was realized.[45]

Alongside Soviet military hardware and captured German tanks and artillery, the museum displayed not only the starvation ration of the winter of 1941–42 but also diaries, letters, and personal possessions that suggested the local and familial dimensions of the city's experience. The poet Vera Inber, who lived through the siege, recalled the bread, installed in a diorama behind the iced-over window of a bakery, as one of the most effective parts of the siege museum. She also reacted strongly to finding on display the unexploded bomb that had played an important part in her own personal blockade story.[46] The bread hardly constituted the centerpiece of the enormous 20,000 square meter (over 215,000 square feet) exhibition space organized by the military authorities to celebrate Soviet might. The three rooms devoted to "Leningrad in the period of the blockade famine" included a display of German artillery shells of

---

[43] V. P. Kivisepp and N. P. Dobrotvorskii, "Muzei muzhestva, skorbi i slavy," *Leningradskaia panorama*, 1991, no. 8: 24. N. P. Dobrotvorskii and Iu. K. Khriashchev, "Relikvii oborony i blokady Leningrada," *Muzei Rossii*, vyp. 2 (1993): 7–8. *LP*, 7 January 1942, 30 April 1944, 22 August 1944. Adamovich and Granin, *Blokadnaia kniga*, 245.

[44] Sue Malvern, "War, Memory and Museums: Art and Artefact in the Imperial War Museum," *History Workshop Journal*, no. 49 (Spring 2000): 187.

[45] Berggol'ts, *Govorit Leningrad*, 377.

[46] Vera Inber, *Leningrad Diary*, trans. Serge M. Wolff and Rachel Grieve (New York: St. Martin's Press, 1971), 207.

8. Leningrad During the Great Fatherland War exhibition. Opened in 1964 and currently part of the State Museum of the History of St. Petersburg, it recreates the look of the blockaded city. The case displays drawings of Leningraders during the starvation winter. Photo by author.

different calibers, photographs of the "best people" of the MPVO, a model of an American Douglas transport plane, and artifacts relating to the Road of Life in addition to the bread. The exhibit's centerpiece, the halls devoted to "the great victory at Leningrad," featured an impressive array of Soviet and captured German artillery pieces, tanks, and planes – the attraction, as one survivor recalled, that brought flocks of teenage boys to the museum. Still, the inclusion of the modest bread ration, and the powerful response of visitors to it, underscores the process of commemorating the national emergency in terms accessible and memorable to average citizens. More than forty years later, those who had visited the exhibit vividly recalled the bread as well as a tram destroyed by German artillery and strewn with the tattered clothes of the dead.[47]

The siege museum established on the basis of the wartime exhibition (and shut down in 1953), the new exhibit on Leningrad during the Great Fatherland War that opened in 1964 (in the Rumiantsev Palace; see Illustration 8), and the reconstituted Heroic Defense of Leningrad museum, established on the original site in 1989 (see Illustration 9), all adopted the practice of juxtaposing the artifacts of battle and of everyday life as a means of writing the tragic tale of the city into the grand narrative of Soviet military victory. The American journalist Harrison Salisbury recognized this dynamic in his complaint that by situating the mock-up of the bakery among exhibits devoted to the heroic dimensions of the battle for Leningrad, the wartime exhibit "had not captured the simplicity and triviality of real life," but instead had "romanticized" civilian suffering. Nonetheless, the exhibit proved enormously popular, attracting more than four hundred and fifty thousand visitors before the end of 1945.[48]

History Becomes Life

Although official commemorations of the siege "romanticized" their everyday experiences, Leningraders nonetheless recognized themselves

---

[47] S. Kara and A. Mikhailov, "Zhivaia istoriia," *Na strazhe Rodiny,* 30 April 1944. L. Rakov, "Vystavka 'Geroicheskaia oborona Leningrada,'" *Leningrad,* 1944, no. 8: 14–15. *LP,* 30 April 1945. *Vystavka "Geroicheskaia oborona Leningrada": Ocherk-putevoditel'* (Leningrad: Iskusstvo, 1945), 65–66. V. Kutuzov, "Muzei oborony Leningrada," *Dialog,* 1988, no. 24: 21–27. Adamovich and Granin, *Blokadnaia kniga,* 16. When the campaign to revive the museum began in the late 1980s, articles and letters to the editor in various local publications contained recollections of the original exhibit and the museum. "Vosstanovim muzei oborony Leningrada!" *Dialog,* 1988, no. 35: 22–23. *LP,* 27 August 1988, 13 December 1988. *Vechernii Leningrad,* 25 April 1989.

[48] Salisbury, *The 900 Days: The Siege of Leningrad* (New York: Harper and Row, 1969), 571. Attendance figures may be found in Kutuzov, "Muzei," 23. The museum organized in November 1945 on the basis of the exhibition was almost 40,000 square meters. Kivisepp and Dobrotvorskii, "Muzei muzhestva," 24. *Muzei oborony Leningrada: Putevoditel'* (Leningrad: Iskusstvo, 1948), 44. On the exhibit in the Rumiantsev Palace, see http://www.spbmuseum.ru/rus/index.php?site=rum4 (accessed 17 February 2006). The original museum reopened in 1989, in a corner, roughly 1,000 square meters, of its former 40,000 square meter site. V. Petrov, "Muzeiu oborony Leningrada – byt'!" *LP,* 13 December 1988. "Ob organizatsii Muzeia oborny Leningrada: Reshenie ispolnitel'nogo komiteta Leningradskogo gorodskogo Soveta narodnykh deputatov ot 24 aprelia 1989 goda No. 318," *Biulleten' Ispolnitel'nogo Komiteta Leningradskogo gorodskogo Soveta narodnykh deputatov,* 1989, no. 14: 6–7. Gosudarstvennyi memorial'nyi muzei oborony i blokady Leningrada, *Muzei oborony i blokady Leningrada* (St. Petersburg: "AGAT," 1998). *Nevskoe vremia,* 30 April 1991.

9. The Museum of the Defense and Blockade of Leningrad. Opened in 1989 on the site of the wartime Heroic Defense of Leningrad exhibit, the museum displays a school desk and a list of schools that remained open during the starvation winter. Photo by author.

and their personal stories in the state's productions. The essays in a famine scrapbook compiled by children at a local school offer a clear illustration of how Leningraders' contemporary commemorations interleaved personal experiences and the slogans and stories of the official media. In one young girl's essay, the simple and moving image of "sitting in the shelter, round improvised stoves, with our coats and fur caps and gloves on" existed alongside the widely circulated story of the Nazis' thwarted plans for a victory celebration in Leningrad: "The German General von Leeb was already licking his chops at the thought of the gala dinner he was going to order at the Astoria," one of Leningrad's finest hotels. Another pupil explicitly linked the children's war work to the larger story of the defense of Leningrad: "In August [1941] we worked for twenty-five days digging trenches. We were machine-gunned and some of us were killed, but we carried on, though we weren't used to this work. And the Germans were stopped by the trenches we had dug."[49] Thus, stories read in the press or heard on radio framed, validated, and finished individual memories.

The memory project undertaken by a small group of librarians at the State Public Library provides an unusually well-documented example of how Leningraders integrated the state's rhetoric, images, and narratives into individual stories that emphasized collective work, shared experience, and meaningful sacrifice.[50] Initiated neither by the party nor the state, the work of the "brigade" grew out of the assumption that wartime publications constituted a central feature of the experience, and hence the memory, of the blockade. For the librarians, who interacted with state propaganda more intensely than did most Leningraders, the work of collecting and cataloging everything published about the siege, from ration coupons to concert tickets to newspaper clippings, could not be separated from the work of preserving individual memories.

Employees of the Public Library began collecting the published artifacts of the siege almost immediately after the Germans blockaded the city in the fall of 1941. Even as air raids and artillery attacks disrupted the operations of the library's branches – closing reading rooms, forcing the evacuation of rare volumes, and damaging buildings – two librarians who found themselves without work to do, M. A. Briskman, the head of the acquisitions department, and Iu. A. Mezhenko, the head of the bibliographic department, had the idea of collecting everything published in the besieged city.[51] Initially, the only criteria for inclusion in the proposed

[49] Alexander Werth, *Leningrad* (New York: Alfred A. Knopf, 1944), 84–85.

[50] V. A. Karatygina, "Rabota gosudarstvennoi Publichnoi Biblioteki nad Kollektsiei i Bibliografiei 'Leningrad v Velikoi Otechestvennoi voine,'" Arkh. RNB, f. 12, T. 517. V. A. Karatygina, "'Leningrad v Velikoi Otechestvennoi voine' (Kollektsia Publichnoi biblioteki)," *Trudy Gosudarstvennoi-Publichnoi Biblioteki imeni M. E. Saltykova-Shchedrina*, 1964, no. 12: 253–62. *Leningrad v Velikoi Otechestvennoi voine: Katalog izdanii, khraniashchikhsia v fondakh Gosudarstvennoi Publichnoi biblioteki*, vyp. 1, *Knigi i broshiury* (Leningrad: Gosudarstvennaia Publichnaia biblioteka, 1971); vyp. 2, *Listovki, plakaty, otkrytki, al'bomy* (Leningrad: Gosudarstvennaia Publichnaia biblioteka, 1972).

[51] L. Frankfurt, "Na bibliotechnoi vakhte," in A. F. Volkova et al., eds., *Zhenshchiny goroda Lenina: Rasskazy i ocherki o zhenshchinakh Leningrada v dni blokady* (Leningrad: Lenizdat, 1944), 104–11. Cynthia Simmons and Nina Perlina, eds., *Writing the Siege of Leningrad: Women's Diaries, Memoirs, and Documentary Prose* (Pittsburgh, PA: University of Pittsburgh Press, 2002), 163–69. M. Bronshtein, "Biblioteki goroda

collection was place of publication: blockaded Leningrad. The idea was to preserve the publications that constituted, and therefore would help to reconjure, the material and intellectual milieu of the city. Vera Karatygina, who took over the collection in the fall of 1942, remembered that it initially included the edition of Henri Beyle Stendhal's *The Red and the Black*, which was a ubiquitous fixture in the windows of Leningrad bookshops, *War and Peace*, and a primer of fairy tales for children, along with "war orders-of-the-day, appeals, instructions for citizen conduct during air raids" – all works considered "extremely characteristic of blockaded Leningrad."[52] As originally conceived, the collection enshrined the published materials that Leningraders saw and held in their hands in those difficult days.

The following year, when the collection became the responsibility of Karatygina, whose prewar work had included the management of the library's St. Petersburg–Leningrad collection, the emphasis shifted toward an effort to compile an exhaustive catalog of published materials pertaining to the siege, regardless of their place of publication. In her wartime presentations, Karatygina emphasized the distinctiveness of her "thematic" approach, but it too allowed the collection of materials of a "general" nature. *The Red and the Black* had to go. Still, Karatygina deemed most interesting those objects in the collection that captured the look and feel of the city at a particular moment. She emphasized the importance of leaflets, posters, slogans, and ephemera (*melkii material*) – labels, tickets, ration coupons – in the reconstruction of the experience of the siege in memory and in history.[53] In a paper presented in 1945, she argued that "for those who lived through the blockade in Leningrad, who along with everyone defended our city, each document, each scrap of paper will be a memory, will make it possible to realize the whole past."[54] Without sharing her tendency to reify memory, it is possible to see in her argument a

Lenina v dni voiny," *Bibliotekar'*, 1946, no. 2–3: 24–39. Werth, *Leningrad*, 138–44. On the origins of the collection, see Karatygina, "'Leningrad v Velikoi Otechestvennoi voine,'" *Trudy*, 253; Karatygina, "Rabota," Arkh. RNB, f. 12, T. 517, ll. 5–6. A fuller description may be found in the album, Karatygina, *Brigada Kollektsii "Leningrad v Velikoi Otechestvennoi voine" Gosudarstvennoi publichnoi biblioteki k 20-letiiu sniatiia blokady Leningrada, 1944 27 I 1964* (Leningrad, 1964), a volume included in the siege collection.

[52] Karatygina, "Rabota," Arkh. RNB, f. 12, T. 517, l. 6.
[53] Ibid., l. 7. Karatygina, "O 'Kollektsii Peterburg-Leningrad': Istoriia goroda po materialam kollektsii: Doklad V. A. Karatyginoi" (November 1942), Arkh. RNB, f. 12, T. 297, l. 22.
[54] Karatygina, "Rabota," Arkh. RNB, f. 12, T. 517, l. 7.

recognition of the importance of public materials in the process of making individual memories.

Under Karatygina's leadership, the siege collection's "brigade" became one of the library's most active and visible groups. When Karatygina became director of the collection in the fall of 1942, she had only one associate, Elena Kots, the head of the Dom Plekhanova. By 1945, the collection employed seventeen women and two men. Karatygina remembered that "it was absolutely natural that all of GPB's [the State Public Library's] best workers, left without work in connection with the evacuation of materials [*fondov*] or the temporary interruption of their job, drifted to us."[55] This "small collective," undertaking what Karatygina characterized as the task, "unprecedented for GPB," of cataloging a wide variety of materials, quickly came to occupy an "absolutely exceptional position" in the library.[56] The project attracted a fair amount of media attention, which the librarians themselves cataloged in their file on the Leningrad press. When the journalist Alexander Werth visited the library in September 1943, the collection, in contrast to the rest of the library, was "buzzing with activity." He found fifteen "old ladies – most of whom looked like rather decrepit old gentlewomen who had seen better times – ... up to their ears in cuttings and posters and bills and ... so absorbed in their work that they scarcely seemed aware of our existence – any more than the shelling that was continuing outside."[57]

For its members, the brigade was an "oasis" that provided refuge and support. The librarians created a physical space that emphasized both the warmth of home and the historic importance of their work. They

---

55 The Dom Plekhanova was the library's branch (*filial*). V. Karatygina herself was the head of Branch II, the Biblioteka mestnogo khoziahstva i kraevedeniia (Regional Studies). Karatygina, *Brigada*, 14. E. S. Kots, "'Na moiu doliu vypal schastlivyi lotereinyi bilet,'" *Istoricheskii arkhiv*, 1999, no. 3: 79–89. *LP*, 4 November 1942. *Trud*, 27 October 1942.

56 Karatygina, *Brigada*, 14. *Izvestiia*, 2 July 1943. *LP*, 3 September 1943. *Trud*, 24 September 1943.

57 His tour guide, the library's director, took strong exception to Werth's characterization of "qualified librarians" as "old ladies." Werth, *Leningrad*, 143, 144. By 1943, the librarians may have looked much older than they were. Karatygina was 47; Kots, the oldest member of the brigade, was 63. A half dozen others were in their fifties. Three women listed themselves as having at least one parent from the nobility (Filatova, Semenova, Zinov'eva). Three were Jewish (Kots, Rubina, Leibzon). Arkh. RNB, Karatygina lichnoe delo, f. 10/1 (1949); Filatova lichnoe delo, f.10/1(1947); Shmidt lichnoe delo, f.10/1 (1953); Rubina lichnoe delo, f. 10/1 (1956); Kots lichnoe delo, f. 10/1 (1959); Semenova lichnoe delo, f. 10/1 (1946); Ozerova lichnoe delo, f. 10/1 (1944); Kosichkina-Bogoslovskaia lichnoe delo, f. 10/1 (1946); Dinze lichnoe delo, f. 10/1 (1946); Zinov'eva lichnoe delo, f. 10/1 (1948).

furnished their large room in the library's main building with furniture brought from the temporarily closed Branch II – portraits, rugs, a mirror, showcases, vases – and a rug from Branch V. Karatygina remembered that "our room looked beautiful, elegant, even imposing, and it happily stood out from the rest of the building."[58] They kept objects from the collection "artistically" on display, and hung propaganda posters on the walls.

In an account of the brigade put together in 1964, Karatygina noted that "our work supported many of us, and helped many of us to bear all the severity of the blockade and the sorrow of loss."[59] Many involved in working on the collection had lost a husband, child, or parent during the siege.[60] Yet only the most extreme circumstances kept the librarians away from their work. In a description of Karatygina's wartime work included in her personnel file, the library's director claimed that "during the time of the Great Fatherland War, work was not interrupted for a single day. When the room in the branch was without light – she brought work home; when she was sick, she worked lying in bed."[61] In March 1942, a month in which thousands died of starvation, one of the members of the brigade, Mariia Zinov'eva, asked for two weeks off because severe malnutrition made it impossible to walk to the library from her home on the Petrograd side, a district roughly three or four kilometers from the library. Recurrent poor health occasionally forced fifty-five-year-old Zinov'eva to work shorter hours or take brief sick leaves, but she always returned to full-time work. The librarians missed few days of work.[62]

For the librarians, collecting and cataloging became a means of coping with catastrophe. As Karatygina noted: "It was easier to live, having before you a clear aim, devoting all your strength to work, and living with a harmonious, united collective."[63] An architect who spent the famine winter of 1941–42 preparing blueprints of the city's historical buildings echoed her sentiments. He told Werth that the blueprint project

---

[58] Karatygina, *Brigada*, 15.

[59] Ibid., 21.

[60] Karatygina's mother died in November 1941. Kots's mother died in the summer of 1942. The collection's artist, Z. N. Kosichkina-Bogoslovskaia, lost her only daughter and later her husband. Arkh. RNB, Karatygina lichnoe delo, f. 10/1 (1949), l. 13; Kots lichnoe delo, Arkh. RNB, f. 10/1 (1959), l. 8. Kots, "'Na moiu,'" 82. Karatygina, *Brigada*, 21.

[61] Arkh. RNB, Karatygina lichnoe delo, f. 10/1 (1949), l. 11. See also Arkh. RNB, Kosichkina-Bogoslovskaia lichnoe delo, f. 10/1 (1946), l. 78.

[62] Arkh. RNB, Zinov'eva lichnoe delo, f. 10/1 (1948), ll. 29–36. Valentina Filatova requested ten days leave when her husband died in April 1942. Arkh. RNB, Filatova lichnoe delo, f. 10/1 (1947), l. 13. See also Arkh. RNB, Dinze lichnoe delo, f. 10/1 (1946), l. 8.

[63] Karatygina, *Brigada*, 21.

had been "a double blessing." With the city under air attack, the task itself "had now become really vital." The sense of the overriding importance of the work "was the best medicine that could be given us during the famine.... The moral effect is great when a hungry man knows he's got a useful job of work to do."[64] Work helped individuals to cope with the continuing trauma of air raids and artillery attacks by restoring a sense of internal control, and by connecting individuals to both co-workers and a larger purpose.[65]

In her wartime presentations on the collection, Karatygina merged personal memory and public commemoration. In a talk at a library conference in the fall of 1942, she cataloged the slogans of the posters that had covered the walls of the city: "All for the defense of Lenin's city against the fascist barbarians"; "Youths of Leningrad! Volunteer to go to the front!"; "Stand up for the defense of your freedom, your honor, your motherland!" She concluded that "everyone of us has seen these posters and slogans, and in each of us they rouse the same feelings." This shared response effectively turned each poster into an "exact representation of how Leningrad lived in those heroic months."[66] Ignoring the large number of military publications in the collection, she used the posters and slogans that constituted a visible presence in the city as a means of framing the story of average Leningraders.

Karatygina maintained that propaganda had to be preserved because it resonated so strongly for survivors. She noted, "I don't know how it is with others, but for me, seeing the matchbook covers of that time, there rises up before my eyes the long, dark, sleepless nights of the winter of 1941–42, without light and heat, interrupted by air raid sirens and the explosions of bombs."[67] The matchbook covers that Karatygina claimed so forcefully had brought back the experience of the blockade (although she neglected to mention starvation) featured the simplest sorts of propaganda. They carried patriotic slogans demanding "All strength to the front" or more locally oriented messages proclaiming "Glory to heroic Leningrad" and

---

[64] Werth, *Leningrad*, 44.

[65] The work of the librarians and the architects has much in common with the strategies of Vietnam veterans who effectively coped with trauma. They "consciously focused on preserving their calm, their judgment, and their connection with others, their moral values, and their sense of meaning, even in the most chaotic battlefield conditions." Judith Herman, *Trauma and Recovery: The Aftermath of Violence – from Domestic Abuse to Political Terror* (New York: Basic Books, 1997), 59.

[66] None of the posters she listed included references to Stalin or the party. Arkh. RNB, f. 12, T. 297, ll. 22–23. See also Arkh. RNB, f. 12, T. 517, ll. 9–16.

[67] Arkh. RNB, f. 12, T. 517, ll. 12–13.

drawings of the city's most beloved landmarks.[68] Even the state's seemingly most banal propaganda touched living memory for survivors.

For Karatygina, officially sponsored representations of the siege in photographs and poetry also expressed the personal experiences of Leningraders. She argued that the frequently reproduced photographs from the winter of 1941–42 that showed corpses being transported on children's sleds, lines for water, or the "characteristic faces of the malnourished [*distrofikov*]" spoke "better than any words of the unprecedented sufferings of Leningraders."[69] At the same time, she was willing to grant that "the terrible blockade winter was excellently represented by Vera Inber in *Pulkovo Meridian,* by Ol'ga Berggol'ts and by other Leningrad writers and poets, who lived through those black days together with all Leningraders."[70] Karatygina recognized her personal story in the public, state-sponsored pictures and words that everyone in the city saw and knew – from straightforward propaganda to literary representations.

When it came time for the librarians to commemorate their own efforts to commemorate the siege, the album they produced, *Leningrad v blokade* (Blockaded Leningrad), constructed a memory of the siege out of news photos and the words of Leningrad's siege poets, primarily Berggol'ts and Inber.[71] Mentioning neither Lenin nor Josef Stalin or the party, the album focused on the destruction of the city and the shared suffering of Leningraders. With its emphasis on the siege as a clear break in the lives of those who lived through it, and its preference for images over sustained narrative, the album gave concrete form to the difficulties of speaking about traumatic events and seamlessly integrating them into life stories. At the same time, the album's use of poetry suggests an effort to establish the sense of collective solidarity and purpose that can provide "the strongest protection against terror and despair, and the strongest antidote to traumatic experience."[72] The librarian's siege album began with Berggol'ts's affirmation from the poem broadcast in May 1942 that the blockade had forged an indissoluble community: "We are Leningraders."

[68] *Etiketi kollektsiia Leningrad v Velikoi Otechestvennoi voine, 1941–44 gg,* handmade album, RNB, II L-3-304/5/1–57.

[69] Arkh. RNB, f. 12, T. 517, l. 11.

[70] Arkh. RNB, f. 12, T. 517, l. 13. On the emotional, personal tone of Soviet World War II poetry, see Katharine Hodgson, *Written with the Bayonet: Soviet Russian Poetry of World War II* (Liverpool: Liverpool University Press, 1996), 44–50.

[71] *Leningrad v blokade, 1941–44* [handmade album] (Leningrad, 1946), RNB, L3 3646. On the importance of the albums that are part of the collection, see Arkh. RNB, f. 12, T. 517, l. 22. Arkh. RNB, Kosichkina-Bogoslovskaia lichnoe delo, f. 10/1 (1946), l. 78. Karatygina, *Brigada,* 13.

[72] Herman, *Trauma and Recovery,* 38, 214.

Suggesting that the siege divided the lives of all who lived through it into "before" and "after," Berggol'ts gave voice to a common refrain among survivors. Emphasizing the shared identity of all who lived through the siege – "We are Leningraders" – and representing the blockade as a collective struggle – a "battle" – she also echoed the heroic rhetoric of the official myth. The librarians who structured their own memories around the poet's words apparently agreed that because all Leningraders suffered a "unique fate," the poet could speak for all of them. They too became Leningraders marked by battle. Berggol'ts's verses set an appropriate tone for an album that commemorated not only the siege but also the efforts of a small group of library workers to survive by making the public and mythic narratives of the siege a part of their everyday lives.

Life after History

Long before the Great Fatherland War, Soviet citizens had been encouraged to understand themselves as participating in a grand, glorious, and historic march to the radiant future. The events of the Great October Revolution had happened too quickly to be commemorated as they unfolded, but the Revolution soon became the subject of what the historian Frederick Corney has called a "veritable memory project" – a far-reaching effort to collect oral and written reminiscences – that aimed to "make October part of the personal and collective experience of large parts of the population."[73] The Civil War and the Great Break (*velikii perelom*) of collectivization and industrialization likewise became subjects of contemporary commemorations – document collections, interviews, written reminiscences, novels, museums – that enshrined their historic status.[74] While what came to be known in the West as the Great Purges could hardly

---

[73] Frederick Corney, "Rethinking a Great Event: The October Revolution as Memory Project," *Social Science History* 22 (Winter 1998): 407, 401. See also Lisa A. Kirschenbaum, "Scripting Revolution: Regicide in Russia," *Left History* 7, no. 2 (2000): 28–52; Daria Khubova, Andrei Ivankiev, and Tonia Sharova, "After Glasnost: Oral History in the Soviet Union," in Luisa Passerini, ed., *Memory and Totalitarianism* (New York: Oxford University Press, 1992), 91–92.

[74] Katerina Clark, *The Soviet Novel: History as Ritual* (Chicago: University of Chicago Press, 1985), 82. Josette Bouvard, "Histoire d'un livre: *L'histoire du metro de Moscou*," *Cahiers de l'Institut d'Histoire du Temps Présent* 35 (1996): 161–78. Cynthia Ruder, *Making History for Stalin: The Story of the Belomor Canal* (Gainesville: University of Florida Press, 1998). M. Gor'kii, L. Averbakh, et al., eds., *Belomorsko-Baltiiskii kanal imeni Stalina: Istoriia stroitel'stvo* (Moscow: OGIZ, 1934). Stephen Kotkin, *Magnetic Mountain: Stalinism as Civilization* (Berkeley: University of California Press, 1995), 371–73.

become the subject of public monuments in the Soviet Union, the accompanying show trials took on the status of epic historic events.[75] Already in 1927, amid growing fears of anti-Soviet conspiracies, the Soviet press had begun preparing its readers for an imminent war with the enemies of socialism. After 1936, the year that the media declared the achievement of socialism in the Soviet Union, a victory heralded by the Stalin Constitution, warnings of war became ubiquitous – a question not of "if" but of "when." The press promised that the generation too young to have fought in the Civil War would have its own historic moment. The German invasion came as the long-anticipated but ironically unexpected fulfillment of these predictions of an inevitable clash of systems.[76] The historian Amir Weiner goes so far as to argue that "for all [Soviet citizens] the war signaled the climax in the unfolding socialist revolution," the apotheosis of Soviet history, the "Armageddon of the Revolution."[77] With the Great Victory of May 1945, the Soviet Union's "Heroic Age" came to an end.[78]

On the morning after the war, the nature of the everyday life that would follow the storm remained unclear. As Berggol'ts observed on 15 July 1945, the "sixty-eighth day of peace," the end of the war brought hope as well as fears. Indeed, by adopting the wartime convention of counting the days, she suggested that peace, too, was a noteworthy event. "We also know," she told her listeners two weeks after Petr Klodt's statues of young men taming horses reappeared in their familiar places on the Anichkov Bridge, "that nothing will return to us exactly as it was before the war: neither children, nor feelings, nor even immobile monuments. We are living as it were at daybreak, in the early morning of peace.... but one wants to believe that the midday of peace will be even brighter, even more generous, even freer, even more excellent than we imagine now, in the first days after victory." In the meantime, her neighbor, who had fearlessly

---

[75] Jeffrey Brooks, *Thank You, Comrade Stalin! Soviet Public Culture from Revolution to Cold War* (Princeton, NJ: Princeton University Press, 2000): 126–49.

[76] Anna Krylova, "Soviet Modernity in Life and Fiction: The Generation of the 'New Soviet Person' in the 1930s" (Ph.D. diss., Johns Hopkins University, 2001), 209, 211, and more generally 206–29. *KP*, 14 February 1938. See also Brooks, *Thank You*, 150–58.

[77] Amir Weiner, *Making Sense of War: The Second World War and the Fate of the Bolshevik Revolution* (Princeton, NJ: Princeton University Press, 2001), 7. For his discussion of the "Armageddon of Revolution," see ibid., 21–39.

[78] Clark uses the term "Heroic Age" to describe "the 1917 Revolution, the Civil War, and certain moments in Stalin's life that became a kind of canonized Great Time that conferred an exalted status on all who played a major part in them." She notes parenthetically that "World War II has since been added to the list." Clark, *The Soviet Novel*, 40.

withstood air raids and shelling, found herself trembling in terror when someone dropped a saucepan in the kitchen or a child playing at war banged a garbage can against the roof.[79]

The central media pictured the return of peace, somewhat less ambivalently, as a return of gender and generational hierarchies – and as a reassertion of the power of Stalin and the party to shape public policy and private lives. The approach of peace substantially reduced the state's tolerance for the emphasis on the personal and emotional dimensions of the war that it had done so much to promote in the first years of the fighting. However, rather than rejecting personal, even sentimental, war stories as petit bourgeois nonsense, the official media worked to adapt the wartime rhetoric of motherhood and family, love and sacrifice, loss and revenge, to a program of reinvigorated party control of daily life. The press represented state policies that aimed to raise birthrates, encourage adoption, and strengthen parental authority in the family as rooted in the desire both to reestablish family bonds in the wake of war and to serve the nation. It thus glorified family life while attempting to infuse state efforts to manage private relationships with the warm glow of motherhood.[80]

Such efforts to convert private values into public values constituted a key element in what the literary historian Vera Dunham has identified as the postwar "embourgeoisement of the entire system." Dunham argues that the state authorized private aspirations, material contentment, and the small pleasures of domestic life – all of which Soviet ideology had long held in contempt – as a means of containing and redirecting the wartime emphasis on personal, local, and familial concerns. She reads the postwar fiction that equated peace with feminized domestic bliss – pink divans and scalloped bedspreads – as evidence that the regime had exchanged its historic revolutionary mission for what she terms "monumental and ponderous *meshchantsvo* [philistinism]."[81] History ended in a well-appointed living room.

In the popular fiction that constitutes the basis of Dunham's study, the most notable arguments against the new legitimacy of middle-class

[79] Berggol'ts, *Govorit Leningrad*, 517–18, 515.

[80] I discuss this process in Lisa A. Kirschenbaum, "'Our City, Our Hearths, Our Families': Local Loyalties and Private Life in Soviet World War II Propaganda," *Slavic Review* 59 (Winter 2000): 845. Anna Krylova, "'Healers of Wounded Souls': The Crisis of Private Life in Soviet Literature, 1944–1948," *Journal of Modern History* 73 (June 2001): 307–31.

[81] Vera Dunham, *In Stalin's Time: Middleclass Values in Soviet Fiction* (New York: Cambridge University Press, 1976), 18, 79, 22.

meshchantsvo often came from veterans and blockade survivors.[82] Dunham explains such reservations as a reflection of the ambiguities inherent in the task of reconfiguring the rhetoric of proletarian heroics without jettisoning it entirely.[83] She makes little of the fact that the fictional doubters appeared in the form of those who had fought, suffered, and triumphed on the front or the city front. Taking these wartime identities and experiences seriously, however, reveals not just the residual power of the earlier ideology of private life subordinated to public deeds and the great cause, but also the continued power of the wartime counternarrative of individual agency and spontaneous community. Particularly among those who viewed themselves as having fought for a better world, the conflict raised expectations of somehow reaching the promised land of a harmonious and conflict-free society. The world of well-kept homes, well-fed children, and happy wives depicted in postwar fiction was one such orderly, managed, and modern (if not specifically socialist) utopia.

A darker side of the dream of homogenizing, purifying, and "sculpting" the body politic emerges in Weiner's study of the Ukrainian region of Vinnytsia. Focusing on an area marked by tremendous state violence – both Nazi and Soviet – and on the experiences of adult, male soldiers, Weiner emphasizes the "postwar drive for purity along ethnic lines" that originated in the wartime deportations of entire ethnic groups and "the extermination of separatist nationalist movements." Although he notes that the war "forced and inspired individuals to reassert themselves, take up new roles, and make new claims," Weiner views the war's primary outcome as the "ethnicization" and "radicalization of Soviet state violence" that "brought to fruition the desires for a comprehensive plan to transform and manage society."[84]

In addition, as a focus on Leningrad makes clear, the experience and memory of war also fueled dreams of an "unruly" modernity of personal freedom and freely chosen community.[85] The experience of war and its representation in Soviet propaganda raised fragile hopes across Soviet society of a freer postwar life, hopes at odds with the continuation of the

[82] Among the examples Dunham cites are Iurii Trifonov, *Studenty, Novyi mir,* 1950, no. 10–11; Aleksandr Chakovskii, "Mirnye dni: povest'," *Zvezda,* 1947, no. 9: 3–58; Vladimir Lifshits, "Petrogradskaia storona," *Novyi mir,* 1946, no. 10–11.

[83] Dunham, *In Stalin's Time,* 18, 7.

[84] Weiner, *Making Sense,* 7–8, 27.

[85] Alan O'Shea, "English Subjects of Modernity," in Mica Nava and Alan O'Shea, eds., *Modern Times: Reflections on a Century of Modernity* (New York: Routledge, 1996), 20.

Stalinist system. Peasants anticipated the end of the hated collective farms. Prisoners in the gulag expected a large-scale amnesty. Intellectuals looked forward to a continuation, if not broadening, of the wartime relaxation of censorship, and imagined that a repeat of the terror of the late 1930s was now unlikely, if not yet impossible.[86] Perhaps nowhere were expectations more palpable than in Leningrad. The blockaded city resounded with the music of Dmitrii Shostakovich and the poetry of Anna Akhmatova – two Leningraders whom the prewar Soviet state had roundly condemned. In 1943, Werth "noticed in Leningrad a slight aloofness towards Moscow, a feeling that, although this was part of the whole show, it was also in a sense a separate show, one in which Leningrad had largely survived thanks to its own stupendous efforts and those of its local chiefs," Andrei Zhdanov and Petr Popkov. The myth of heroic Leningrad, forged by party propagandists and the emotionally resonant poetry of Berggol'ts, Inber, and others, opened the possibility of a resurgence of the city's cultural, if not political, preeminence.[87] The blockade reinforced Leningrad's status as a symbolic alternative to Moscow, a potential source of alternative visions of the future and alternative identities.

Because wartime commemorations of the blockade had encouraged Leningraders to understand the besieged city as a community purified and unified by suffering and collective struggle, Leningraders' visions of the postwar world could take particularly liberationist forms. The "blockade brotherhood" celebrated in the media seemed to presage the spontaneous emergence of a true, natural, harmonious community – the sort of radiant future that, as much as state-directed modernization, had constituted a strand of Russian revolutionary thinking, albeit one largely swamped by prewar Stalinism.[88] The unprecedented wartime emphasis on private life

[86] Ludmilla Alexeyeva and Paul Goldberg, *The Thaw Generation: Coming of Age in the Post-Stalin Era* (Boston: Little, Brown, 1990), 19. Golfo Alexopoulos, "Amnesty 1945: The Revolving Door of Stalin's Gulag," *Slavic Review* 64 (Summer 2005): 274. Elena Zubkova, *Russia After the War: Hopes, Illusions, and Disappointments, 1945–1947,* trans. Hugh Ragsdale (Armonk, NY: M. E. Sharpe, 1998), 18, 59–67, 88–98. Werner G. Hahn, *Postwar Soviet Politics: The Fall of Zhdanov and the Defeat of Moderation, 1946–53* (Ithaca, NY: Cornell University Press, 1982), 9–10. Il'ia Erenburg, *Post-War Years, 1945–1954,* trans. Tatiana Shebunina (Cleveland: World Publishing, 1967), 13.

[87] Werth, *Leningrad,* 64–65. Blair A. Ruble, "The Leningrad Affair and the Provincialization of Leningrad," *Russian Review* 42 (1983): 301–2. C. N. Boterbloem, "The Death of Andrei Zhdanov," *Slavonic and East European Review* 80 (April 2002): 279.

[88] S. Alexiyevich, *War's Unwomanly Face* (Moscow: Progress, 1988), 123. Moshe Lewin, "Leninism and Bolshevism: The Test of History and Power," in *The Making of the Soviet System: Essays in the Social History of Interwar Russia* (New York: Pantheon Books, 1985), 194. Gail Warshofsky Lapidus, "Sexual Equality in Soviet Policy: A

and on active, self-assertive citizenship produced nostalgic recollections of the purity and honesty of wartime life. Pavel Gubchevsky, a researcher at the Hermitage, remembered the blockade as a moment of freedom and clear, meaningful purpose: "I felt as though something within me had been lifted, set free. . . . I knew what I had to do, what I was obliged to do, but for me that 'obliged' was freedom."[89] That so many veterans and blokadniki remembered the war years as "the best years of our lives" underscores the degree to which the freedom and sense of community associated with the war provided an (unrealized) model for the Soviet future and an implicit critique of both the postwar embourgeoisement of the system and the violence of postwar purification drives.[90] Particularly in Leningrad, those who lived through the war viewed themselves and their community as already purified and transformed.

In a remarkable story written in the liminal period between war and peace – April to July 1945 – Vera Ketlinskaia imagined peacetime not in terms of the return to family that dominated the central press, but instead as a moment of ultimate and even terrible individual freedom. Set on the eve of the arrival of the engineer Pavel Viktorovich's wife and children from evacuation, the story focused on a moment of decision: Would Pavel remain with his wartime mistress Nastia or return to his wife of twelve years and their children? Looking back on the wartime relationship that he was preparing to abandon, Pavel recalled its beginnings in the "gray dawn" that followed the destruction of his building in an air raid. His colleague Nastia unexpectedly arrived on the scene, a natural, no-nonsense savior. "A comical figure in a beret, boots, and a quilted jacket held together by a thin belt with an elegant buckle," Nastia kept repeating "Thank god," and insisted that Pavel move into the communal apartment in which she now lived alone. During the worst period of the blockade, Nastia sacrificed her own bread in order to keep Pavel

Developmental Perspective," in Dorothy Atkinson, Alexander Dallin, and Gail Warshofsky Lapidus, eds., *Women in Russia* (Stanford, CA: Stanford University Press, 1977), 117–18. Barbara Evans Clements, "The Utopianism of the Zhenotdel," *Slavic Review* 51 (Summer 1992): 485–96. Jane Burbank, "Lenin and the Law in Revolutionary Russia," *Slavic Review* 54 (Spring 1995): 41.

89 Adamovich and Granin, *Blokadnaia kniga*, 61.

90 V. Kardin, "Luchshie gody nashei zhizni," *Ogonek*, no. 19 (5–12 May 1990): 17–19. E. S. Seniavskaia, *Frontovoe pokolenie, 1941–1945: Istoriko-psikhologicheskoe issledovanie* (Moscow: Institut rossiiskoi istorii RAN, 1995), 3–5, 79–93. Kondrat'ev, "Ne tol'ko," and Kondrat'ev, "Paradoks frontovoi nostal'gii," *Literaturnaia gazeta*, 9 May 1990. Geoffrey Hosking, "The Second World War and Russian National Consciousness," *Past and Present*, no. 175 (May 2002): 173–75.

alive. They confessed their fears to each other and knew that they were in love. Nonetheless, when word reached him of his family's return, Pavel arranged to repair the apartment, and the two lovers parted.[91]

In contrast to Nastia, Ketlinskaia depicted Pavel's wife Zoia as an exceedingly feminine and, it soon appeared to Pavel, a scheming, artificial, and shallow woman. Meeting Zoia and his children at the train station, Pavel "was horrified at the quantity of things" she had brought with her. Nevertheless, he allowed himself to be charmed and gladdened by the return of "familiar domestic tyranny": "So ends the blockade life." But doubts returned as Zoia coyly hinted that she knew what he was up to while she was away. Her "flirtatiousness, credulous tone, and caresses," Pavel decided, were nothing but a premeditated and manipulative strategy to win him back. When she phoned him at work, her "insincerely affectionate voice irritated him. And at home, he's annoyed by her artificially cheerful face with watchful, alert eyes." The critical moment came during an elegant and ostentatious homecoming party arranged by Zoia. When the conversation turned to the blockade, Pavel waxed nostalgic, proclaiming that "for many of us, all the deprivations and calamities notwithstanding, these were the loftiest, the most beautiful days of our lives." To the suggestion that these were not, however, the "most sinless" days, Pavel replied, "When the chances of life and death are even, or possibly the chances of death are higher, then words like 'mischief' and 'sin' are simply out of place."[92] He ended up leaving for Nastia's apartment, arriving just before dawn to embrace an uncertain future.

Once the postwar cultural crackdown began in 1946 – with an attack on the journals *Leningrad* and *Zvezda* – "it was generally considered not good literary decorum to allow positive heroes to actually indulge in adultery."[93] Yet here, Ketlinskaia unabashedly made adultery the foundation of a freer, if not necessarily easier, neater, or more harmonious, future. Pavel's choice recalls the early Soviet fiction of one of the most forceful Bolshevik advocates of women's emancipation, Aleksandra Kollontai, with its free unions based on love and mutual respect. The winged Eros has alighted among practical engineers.[94] Zoia, her petit bourgeois

---

[91] Vera Ketlinskaia, "Nastia," in *Den' prozhityi dvazhdy* (1945; reprint, Leningrad: Sovetskii pisatel', 1964), 367–99, quotation 369.

[92] Ibid., 385–86, 389, 395.

[93] Clark, *The Soviet Novel*, 208.

[94] Richard Stites, *The Women's Liberation Movement in Russia: Feminism, Nihilism, and Bolshevism, 1860–1930* (Princeton, NJ: Princeton University Press, 1978), 356–58. Aleksandra Kollontai, *Love of Worker Bees*, trans. Cathy Porter (London: Virago, 1977).

obsession with having enough forks for all her guests notwithstanding, may not, as Dunham argues, come off too badly.[95] But the real way forward emerged as the uncharted, "true," "natural" path chosen by the lovers. If the state – and indeed many people tired by the chaos of war – welcomed peace as a moment of reasserted order embodied in the reestablishment of traditional family ties and gender roles, Ketlinskaia expressed the hope that peace would bring not constraining relationships but the risk and unpredictability of individual emancipation – the freedom of citizens, not cogs in the machine. The story's ending was firmly grounded in the shared memory of the blockade. Nastia and Pavel undertook a literal continuation of the "lofty" life of the besieged city that had been mythologized in contemporary narratives and inscribed in memories and monuments.

[95] Dunham, *In Stalin's Time*, 57.

PART II

RECONSTRUCTING AND REMEMBERING THE CITY

4

The City Healed

Historical Reconstruction and Victory Parks

> Today, thirty-three years later, however repainted and stuccoed, the ceilings
> and façades of this unconquered city still seem to preserve the stain-like
> imprints of its inhabitants' last gasps and last gazes. Or perhaps it's just bad
> paint and bad stucco.
>
> Joseph Brodsky, 1979[1]

"On 8 July 1945," wrote architect A. K. Barutchev in 1946, "Leningrad
met its defenders." In the southern reaches of the city, not far from the
former front line, three wood and gypsum triumphal arches provided
grandiose – if ephemeral – backdrops for the crowds greeting the troops
returning victorious from the West. The arch on Stachek Street near the
Kirov Factory was topped with an artillery piece and adorned with silhouettes of Vladimir Lenin and Josef Stalin (Illustration 10). The Kirov
men treated the returning soldiers to shots of vodka; the women gave
them wildflowers. On Obukhovskoi Oborony, an architrave set on two
massive pylons declared "Glory to the Red Army." Under the arch on
Mezhdunarodnii (now Moskovskii) Prospekt that proclaimed "Glory to
the Hero Victors," Ekaterina Leonidova, a "hero mother" with at least
seven children, offered the commanding general a loaf of bread, the traditional symbol of hospitality.[2]

---

[1] Joseph Brodsky, "A Guide to a Renamed City," in *Less Than One: Selected Essays* (New
York: Farrar Straus Giroux, 1986), 91.

[2] A. K. Barutchev, "Arki pobedy," *Arkhitektura i stroitel'stvo Leningrada: Sbornik* (June
1946), 1, 4. Il'ia Erenburg, *Post-War Years, 1945–1954*, trans. Tatiana Shebunina (Cleveland: World Publishing, 1967), 13. A. G. Raskin, *Triumfal'nye arki Leningrada* (Leningrad:
Lenizdat, 1977), 220. Ol'ga Berggol'ts, *Govorit Leningrad*, in *Stikhi-proza* (Moscow:
Gosudarstvennoe izdatel'stvo khudozhestvennoi literatury, 1961), 515–17.

10. Temporary victory arch constructed near the Kirov Factory, 1945. *Source:* ITAR-TASS.

The three triumphal arches had been hastily constructed. Planned by groups of Leningrad architects in just twenty-four hours, they were built in a week. Nonetheless, Barutchev emphasized that they drew upon a glorious precedent. He noted that in 1814, following the defeat of Napoleon and the occupation of Paris, the soldiers of the first Fatherland War had entered the capital through the newly constructed Narva Triumphal Gate. Like its Soviet counterparts, the Narva Gate, designed by the architect Giacomo Quarenghi, had begun as a temporary wooden structure. Only in 1829 did another famous Petersburg architect, Vasilii Stasov, design the stone replacement that still stands on Stachek Square. Barutchev promised that a similar future awaited the arches celebrating victory in the Great Fatherland War. "The wooden arches," he concluded, "will be replaced by stone."[3]

As it turned out, the wood and plaster arches quickly disappeared, and a competition that opened on Victory Day (9 May) 1946 and aimed to replace them with a permanent structure produced no concrete results.[4]

[3] Barutchev, "Arki," 4.
[4] Raskin, *Triumfal'nye*, 221–22.

Building victory monuments did not become part of the immediate post-war effort to repair and revitalize the city. Until the mid-1950s, planners largely followed the prescription for the city articulated by the architect Valentin Kamenskii in 1945: "Quickly heal the wounds inflicted by the German-fascist barbarians." For Kamenskii, who became the city's chief architect in 1951, "healing" meant not only rehabilitating damaged buildings but also "creating a more monumental, a more powerful architectural form that is a fitting reflection of heroic events unprecedented in human history."[5] A survivor of the blockade, Kamenskii proposed restoring and beautifying the city as the most appropriate form of commemoration. The program of healing paradoxically removed all traces of war from the cityscape in the name of memorializing "heroic events."

Kamenskii imagined a cityscape that both remembered and forgot the war. Historians, by contrast, have generally focused on the element of forgetting – particularly in the realms of history and literature – entailed in postwar "healing." They have held Stalin accountable for enforcing amnesia. By 1945, the Soviet press was full of praise for the generalissimo's military genius, but Stalin had reason to be concerned about the memory of the war. Certainly he had no interest in remembering the early "catastrophic losses caused in large part by his failure to heed repeated warnings of the German attack."[6] Moreover, the early catastrophes had afforded Soviet citizens unprecedented autonomy and freedom of expression, and raised expectations of a postwar liberalization of the system. Rather than meet such expectations, Stalin exhorted "his country to curtail talk about the war, to move past the ordeal and on to the tasks of economic reconstruction and the waging of the Cold War against capitalist nations."[7] The decision to curb plans for building a massive museum and memorial on Moscow's Poklonnaia gora, the demotion of Victory

---

[5] V. A. Kamenskii, "Pervoocherednye zadachi arkhitektorov Leningrada," *Arkhitektura Leningrada*, 1945, no. 1: 2, 1. O. A. Chkanova, "Valentin Kamenskii," in V. G. Isachenko, ed., *Zodchie Sankt-Peterburga XX vek* (St. Petersburg: Lenizdat, 2000), 420. Anatolii Mikhailovich Kuchumov, *Pavlovsk Palace and Park*, trans. V. Travlinsky and J. Hine (Leningrad: Aurora Art Publishers, 1975), 2. Geoffrey Barraclough, "Late Socialist Housing: Prefabricated Housing in Leningrad from Khrushchev to Gorbachev" (Ph.D. diss., University of California, Santa Barbara, 1990), 4–5.

[6] Lazar Lazarev, "Russian Literature on the War and Historical Truth," in John Garrard and Carol Garrard, eds., *World War 2 and the Soviet People: Selected Papers from the Fourth World Congress for Soviet and East European Studies* (New York: St. Martin's Press, 1993), 30–31.

[7] Nina Tumarkin, *The Living and the Dead: The Rise and Fall of the Cult of World War II in Russia* (New York: Basic Books, 1994), 103.

Day 1947 from official state holiday to ordinary workday, and the refusal to publish memoirs and histories of the war advanced the state's program of selective remembering.[8]

In the case of Leningrad, the state ultimately aimed not merely to manage memory but to obliterate it. If any one place embodied Stalin's fears about the memory of the war, it was the city on the Neva. Projects like the popular Museum of the Heroic Defense of Leningrad emphasized the local dimensions of the Leningrad epic and stoked local pride in the city's unique fate at the expense of the cult of Stalin's wisdom and talent. In 1949, the so-called Leningrad Affair, a purge of the party hierarchy that began with the current and former bosses of the Leningrad party organization, effectively silenced such memories. Asserting its power to shape the public memory of the war, the state shut down the museum and practically excluded the Leningrad blockade from Soviet histories of the war.[9] At the same time, it lavishly commemorated other episodes. Books on the Leningrad blockade ceased to appear in the same year that a massive complex honoring the Soviet soldiers who, as the memorial declared, "saved European civilization from German fascism" opened in East Berlin's Treptower Park.[10]

Without minimizing the role of state-enforced silence, this chapter recovers the impulses to forget as well as remember that came from both below and above, as survivors struggled to heal themselves and their city, to at once return to life and to commemorate death.[11] If veterans and blokadniki resented the ban on histories and memoirs of the blockade that made it impossible for them to tell their stories, they often embraced efforts to remove all traces of the war from the city's streets. No Leningrader, I would venture to say, favored the neglect of war graves that persisted into the early 1950s. But it is also the case that despite differing motives, the state's and survivors' interests in reordering the urban landscape – an activity that required both forgetting and selective remembering – could converge.

Particularly on the terrain of the city, remembering and forgetting tended to interact in sometimes paradoxical and unexpected ways.

---

[8] Nurit Schleifman, "Moscow's Victory Park: A Monumental Change," *History and Memory* 13 (2001): 10. The Victory Park opened in 1995.

[9] A. R. Dzeniskevich, *Blokada i politika: Oborona Leningrada v politicheskoi kon"iunkture* (St. Petersburg: Nestor, 1998), 10–11.

[10] Sergiusz Michalski, *Public Monuments: Art in Political Bondage, 1870–1997* (London: Reaktion Books, 1998), 125–31.

[11] Catherine Merridale, "Death and Memory in Modern Russia," *History Workshop Journal*, no. 42 (Autumn 1996): 2.

The restoration of historical façades covered up the wounds of war – and thereby served the state's amnesiac agenda – but it also allowed Leningraders to preserve the familiar places in which they had led their prewar lives and survived the blockade. As the poet Joseph Brodsky suggests in the epigraph, paint and stucco could not entirely efface the past that stained Leningrad's walls and ceilings. A review of a few other cities' efforts to rebuild illuminates the difficulty of resolving tensions – on the levels of policy, politics, and emotion – between the desire to forget and the impossibility of forgetting, between the revival of urban life and the commemoration of loss. Leningraders' immediate postwar efforts to reconstruct historic buildings and to disguise war damage with "Victory Parks" reveal the complexity, if not impossibility, of fixing or effacing memories and meanings in the urban landscape.

Tensions Between Rebuilding and Remembering

Every building destroyed during World War II raised questions about the past and the future. From Hiroshima to London, citizens and city planners had to decide whether and how to reconstruct, remodel, or completely remake buildings and whole cityscapes. They faced the challenge of bringing cities back to life while honoring the dead. Whether cities stood on the winning or losing side of World War II did not necessarily determine the appearance of reconstructed environments. On one hand, both winners and losers often embraced modern urban forms. On the other hand, two cities destroyed by the Nazis, Rotterdam and Warsaw, effectively marked the extremes of postwar planning, with Rotterdam constructing itself as a modern city and Warsaw reconstructing the ruins of one of its historical centers.[12]

However, whether a reconstructed city stood on the winning or losing side has been crucial in structuring critical evaluations of similar urban plans. Differentiating, for example, the Poles' laudable desire to recuperate the past from the Germans' attempts to deny theirs, critics have understood the restoration of historic city centers in overarching political terms. Thus, the Berlin filmmaker Hubertus Siegert distinguishes the

---

[12] Carola Hein, "Hiroshima: The Atomic Bomb and Kenzo Tange's Hiroshima Peace Center," in Joan Ockman, ed., *Out of Ground Zero: Case Studies in Urban Reinvention* (Munich: Prestel, 2002), 82. Robert E. Alvis, "The Berliner Dom, the Kaiser Wilheim Gedächtiniskirche, and the Ideological Manipulation of Space in Postwar Berlin," *East European Quarterly* 31 (1997): 359.

Poles' rebuilding of Warsaw's castle, which he regards as "really a continuity of invention because they had lost everything," from the proposed reconstruction of the royal palace in post-reunification Berlin, which he dismisses as "just stupid traditionalism."[13] The historian Gavriel Rosenfeld goes further, denouncing the architect Erwin Schleich's equation of historical reconstruction in Munich and Warsaw as demonstrating "the tendencies to relativize the causes of these cities' destruction, to deny German guilt."[14] While highlighting key motives on both sides, such approaches largely ignore the complex relationship between the urban environment and the people who live in it. The cityscape is reduced to a fixed abstraction disconnected from the inhabitants' understandings and uses of urban places.[15]

By contrast, the interest here is not in assessing the global meanings or legitimacy of one reconstruction strategy or another, but in examining the wide potential for unintended outcomes that accompanied efforts to fix either acts of remembering or forgetting in the repaired cityscape. I am interested in local, situated interactions with the urban environment. Regardless of the strategy chosen by planners – exact historical reproduction or radical modernization – the (re)built environment never entirely dominated the multiple meanings, memories, and habits that inhabitants brought to urban spaces.[16] In the city, meanings and memories are public but also intensely personal, and thus inherently kaleidoscopic.

If the architects and urban planners who built modern cities in the wake of war intended them as a means of "remembering to move on," for city dwellers the modern city could, ironically, evoke the past more forcefully than the future.[17] In Rotterdam, where a May 1940 Nazi bombing raid destroyed sixty-five hundred acres and eleven thousand buildings in the city center, reconstruction meant modernization. Planners jumped at the

---

[13] Hubertus Siegert and Ralph Stern, "Berlin: Film and the Representation of Urban Reconstruction since the Fall of the Wall," in Ockman, *Out of Ground Zero*, 131. Brian Ladd, *The Ghosts of Berlin: Confronting German History in the Urban Landscape* (Chicago: University of Chicago Press, 1997), 47–70.

[14] Gavriel D. Rosenfeld, *Munich and Memory: Architecture, Monuments, and the Legacy of the Third Reich* (Berkeley: University of California Press, 2000), 178.

[15] On the concept of "place" as "lived and living space," see Kenneth Hewitt, "Place Annihilation: Area Bombing and the Fate of Urban Places," *Annals of the Association of American Geographers* 73 (June 1983): 258.

[16] Michel de Certeau, *The Practice of Everyday Life*, trans. Steven Rendall (Berkeley: University of California Press, 1984), 29, 18. Sarah Bennett Farmer, "Oradour-sur-Glane: Memory in a Preserved Landscape," *French Historical Studies* 19 (Spring 1995): 37.

[17] Deyan Sudjic, "Remembering to Move On," *Architecture* 92 (May 2003): 144.

chance to replace what they viewed as a medieval, backward, poorly built city with a showplace of modern planning and modern architecture. By the 1950s, "Rotterdam was lauded as a courageous and progressive example of postwar reconstruction."[18]

Erasing traces of the prewar city along with evidence of wartime destruction, the modernization of Rotterdam can be understood as an act of forgetting, a leap into the future. Yet the city's destruction remained a present reality in its ostensibly forgetful modern counterpart. In 1951, the city commissioned a commemoration of its wartime experience in the form of Russian-born sculptor Ossip Zadkine's *The Destroyed City,* an anguished, twice-life-size figure that, like the city, had a gaping hole at its center. By the time it was unveiled in 1953, Zadkine's monument to the horror of war stood in sharp contrast to the reborn city around it. Some observers predicted that the statue would become "Rotterdam's only sign pointing clearly back to the ravages of May, 1940."[19]

However, by the late 1960s, the new city itself worked to remind citizens of all that had been lost. Increasingly criticized by its inhabitants as empty, uninviting, and lacking character and intimacy, modern Rotterdam fueled what the planning historian Han Meyer has called "waves of misplaced nostalgia" for the idealized prewar city center. Such sentiments are hardly unique to Rotterdam. In London and other cities, where modern buildings similarly mark wartime destruction, there has been a similar nostalgic backlash against postwar construction.[20] Despite the presumptive meaning of the modern cityscape, it became for many in Rotterdam less an image of renewal than an afterimage of the vanished past. By the 1990s, city planners were looking for ways to restore aspects of the prewar city, a project which, if successful, would further complicate the memory and forgetting of the damage done both during and after the war.

---

[18] Han Meyer, "Rotterdam: The Promise of a New, Modern Society in a New, Modern City: 1940 to the Present," in Ockman, *Out of Ground Zero,* 85–94, quotation 95. E. R. M. Taverne, "The Lijnbaan (Rotterdam): A Prototype of a Postwar Urban Shopping Center," in Jeffry M. Diefendorf, ed., *Rebuilding Europe's Bombed Cities* (New York: St. Martin's Press, 1990), 145–55.

[19] Joan Pachner, "Zadkine and Gabo in Rotterdam," *Art Journal* 53, no. 4 (Winter 1994): 79–80, quotation 80.

[20] Meyer, "Rotterdam," 95. Hewitt, "Place Annihilation," 278. L. Dudley Stamp, "Replanning London," *Geographical Review* 35 (October 1945): 665. Alan Powers, "Plymouth: Reconstruction after World War II," in Ockman, *Out of Ground Zero,* 98–115. Paul Jürgen, "Reconstruction of the City Center of Dresden: Planning and Rebuilding during the 1950s," in Diefendorf, *Rebuilding Europe's Bombed Cities,* 170–89.

If in Rotterdam the modern city had the ironic effect of calling attention to destruction, in Warsaw the painstaking reconstruction of the historic city center, intended by the state as an emblem of the legitimacy of the communist present, became, perhaps no less ironically, a nostalgic reminder of the possibility of a noncommunist future. Rather than abandoning the devastated city center or building a modern city on the old site, planners in Warsaw decided to recreate the royal palace and the Old Town virtually from scratch. Initial efforts to clear rubble and to rebuild relied on the spontaneous and voluntary labor of locals. Thus, many observers have interpreted the decision to reconstruct the seventeenth-century city as a defiant reclamation project aimed at "wresting national identity back from the ruins."[21] In the late 1940s, the communist state centralized and regularized the reconstruction project, which became, as the design historian David Crowley argues, "central to the Party's claim on political legitimacy."[22]

Nonetheless, the state was unable to dictate the meanings of the reconstructed cityscape.[23] Moreover, as Stanisław Jankowski, a participant in the 1944 Warsaw uprising who worked in the Town Planning Office from 1946 to 1976, has emphasized, the rebuilt Old Town did not exactly reproduce the prewar cityscape. Architects and planners unearthed "previously unknown fragments of medieval architecture and frescoes" and restored "long-obliterated arrangements of houses and streets." The new Old Town thus at once reaffirmed city dwellers' sense of place and remade it, offering the possibility of a more authentic Warsaw.[24] While Varsovians viewed the Soviet "gift" of a Stalinist skyscraper, the Palace of Culture and Science, as an unwelcome "imposition on the urban and architectural traditions of the city," the multiple pasts and futures associated with the reconstructed Old Town made it a popular site of anticommunist rallies in the 1980s – despite the fact that the Communists had sponsored the reconstruction.[25]

---

[21] Rudolph Chelminski, "Warsaw, the City That Would Not Die," *Smithsonian* 28, no. 8 (November 1997): 108–16 (online version, no pagination). Ladd, *Ghosts*, 67. José M. Faraldo, "Medieval Socialist Artefacts: Architecture and Discourses of National Identity in Provincial Poland, 1945–1960," *Nationalities Papers* 29 (2001): 610–11.

[22] David Crowley, "People's Warsaw/Popular Warsaw," *Journal of Design History* 10 (1997): 205.

[23] Ibid., 217, 219.

[24] Stanisław Jankowski, "Warsaw: Destruction, Secret Town Planning, 1939–44, and Postwar Reconstruction," in Diefendorf, *Rebuilding Europe's Bombed Cities*, 88.

[25] Crowley, "People's Warsaw," 213. David Crowley, *Warsaw* (London: Reaktion Books, 2003), 68–83.

For people who have seen their city destroyed, the reconstructed city is a palimpsest. The city of memory remains visible, however faintly, beneath the modern architecture or the historic replicas. As a result, much as architects, planners, and especially "totalitarian systems" might have wished to maintain "absolute control over the production of meaning" in the built environment, the urban landscape layered in memories often worked against them.[26] Widened streets and modern buildings did not entirely efface public and private memory mapped onto the prewar cityscape. For those who survived the war, the reconstructed city remained a city built not only on ruins but on the remains of the prewar past, even as it became a living site of new memories and meanings. Because city dwellers have prewar, wartime, and postwar memories of any given urban place, any analysis of the meanings of postwar reconstruction must attend to residents' interactions with the once-destroyed – now restored or modernized – city.

Wartime Damage in Leningrad: Icons and the Everyday City

Leningrad suffered far less damage to its physical plant than, for example, Stalingrad, Warsaw, Berlin, and Hiroshima. When the British journalist and Petersburg native Alexander Werth visited the city in late 1943, he informed his hosts that the city seemed to him quite well preserved. The author Vsevolod Vishnevskii, who participated in the defense of Leningrad in 1941 and 1942, sought to disabuse Werth of this notion: "That's a first impression. If you look closely, you will see hidden destruction that does not immediately catch the eye." Having just returned from the Volga, Werth remained unconvinced, noting, "All the same, it's not Stalingrad."[27]

Leningrad was not leveled. Nonetheless, citizens experienced it as profoundly wounded. Some of the city's best-known landmarks – the Hermitage, the Tauride Palace, Gostinyi Dvor, the eighteenth-century

---

[26] John Grech, "Empty Space and the City: The Reoccupation of Berlin," *Radical History Review*, no. 83 (Spring 2002): 132.

[27] Conversation quoted in "Kak mog vystoiat' Leningrad," *Podvig Leningrada: Dokumental'no-khudozhestvennyi sbornik* (Moscow: Voennoe izdatel'stvo Ministerstva oborony Soiuza SSR, 1960), 529. Werth's own account of the meeting does not mention this exchange. However, he does suggest that damage was minimal in comparison even to London. Alexander Werth, *Leningrad* (New York: Alfred A. Knopf, 1944), 119–34, 27 for the London comparison. See also Constantine Krypton, "The Siege of Leningrad," *Russian Review* 13 (October 1954): 255–56.

shopping arcade on Nevskii Prospekt – sustained extensive damage.[28] Moreover, because iconic buildings and bridges were often part of their neighborhoods, Leningraders were likely to be more sensitive to traces of war than an American visitor, who dismissed "small gashes in the plaster of many buildings from fragments of bursting shells and bombs."[29] Such "small" damage was widespread. In May 1944, *Pravda* reported that of two hundred and forty buildings deemed to have particular historic-artistic value, not a single one had escaped some level of injury.[30]

Leningraders, however, measured destruction not only in terms of damage to the city's icons but also in terms of the disorder, damage, and emptiness of their everyday places. "Hidden" destruction operated at the level of the neighborhood, the street, the workplace, the apartment. German bombs and artillery destroyed 16 percent of Leningrad's housing stock, along with much of the city's infrastructure of streets, sewer lines, and water lines. Nearly half of the city's school buildings and 78 percent of its hospitals were knocked out of commission.[31]

Even this damage to the everyday fabric of the city was not the full story in Leningrad. The relatively intact cityscape barely hinted at the vast human losses. The most assiduously covered-up – if not the most hidden – aspect of Leningrad's destruction was the number of people who starved to death in the city. Postwar estimates submitted to the authorities at Nuremberg pretended to statistical exactness, setting the number of dead at 632,253. Given the problems and omissions of the available records, an exact accounting remains impossible, but the Leningrad Funeral Trust's competing figure of 1.2 million appears more likely.[32]

---

[28] A. V. Karasev, "Vozrozhdenie goroda-geroia (Iz istorii vosstanovleniia Leningrada)," *Istoriia SSSR*, 1961, no. 3: 116–17.

[29] "Report of Observations in Leningrad, September 1944"; Record Group (RG) 226; Entry 16, 109691; National Archives at College Park, MD (NACP).

[30] O. N. Arsiutkina, "Leningradskaia partiinaia organizatsiia v bor'be za vosstanovlenie zhilogo fonda (1944–1945 gg)," *Vestnik Leningradskaia Universiteta: Seriia istorii, iazyka i literatury*, 1964, vyp. 19, no. 20: 17.

[31] Edward Bubis and Blair A. Ruble, "The Impact of World War II on Leningrad," in Susan J. Linz, ed., *The Impact of World War II on the Soviet Union* (Totowa, NJ: Rowman and Allanheld, 1985), 189. S. P. Kniazev puts the percentage of lost housing stock at 28 percent. Kniazev, "Kommunisty Leningrada v bor'be za vosstanovlenie goroda," *Voprosy istorii KPSS*, 1961, no. 1: 64. Arsiutkina, "Leningradskaia partiinaia," 17.

[32] Dzeniskevich, *Blokada i politika*, 45–68. The Nuremberg figure appears on p. 59. Kniazev, "Kommunisty," 65. V. M. Koval'chuk, "Tragicheskie tsifry blokady (K voprosu ob ustanovlenii chisla zhertv blokirovannogo Leningrada)," in A. A. Fursenko, ed., *Rossiia v XIX–XX vv: Sbornik statei k 70-letiiu so dnia rozhdeniia Rafaila Sholomovicha Ganelina* (St. Petersburg: Dmitrii Bulanin, 1998), 357–69. Boris Gusev, "'Pokhoronnoe delo,'" in

Leningraders' own estimates ran much higher. Rumors circulating in the winter of 1941–42 put the number of dead as high as 3.5 million – an estimate larger than the city's prewar population. Such guesses had a certain local plausibility. As the classicist Ol'ga Freidenberg noted in reminiscences written in the spring of 1942, "Whole families, whole apartments with collectives of families disappeared. Houses, streets, blocks disappeared."[33]

Outside of the city, the devastation of the iconic palaces in Pavlovsk, Peterhof, Pushkin, and Gatchina was dramatic, thorough, and as seemed to many observers, irreparable. Before abandoning the former imperial palaces in Leningrad's suburbs, the occupying Nazis looted, burned, and booby-trapped the buildings and laid mines in the gardens. Visiting Pushkin (Tsarskoe Selo) shortly after the blockade had been broken, the architect Evgenii Levinson found buildings ravaged by bombs and fire.[34] At Peterhof, the damage to the palace was so extensive that an American observer deemed it "hopeless."[35] Stalin's right-hand man, the foreign minister Viacheslav Molotov, reached the same conclusion about the palace at Pavlovsk and advocated razing the building.[36]

Emblems of the power of the imperial state and its Soviet successor, the palaces also held more personal meanings for many Leningraders. Lamenting the destruction at Pavlovsk, Levinson related that "the park was close to me, as much as I'd spent a series of years there in my youth, walking its length and breadth."[37] The museum workers at Pavlovsk took the destruction of "their palaces" personally and immediately took up the cause of restoration – both as a matter of local and national pride and as a personal mission.[38]

Zakhar Dicharov, ed., *Golosa iz blokady: Leningradskie pisateli v osazhdennom gorode (1941–1944)* (St. Petersburg: Nauka, 1996), 302–8. Harrison E. Salisbury, *The 900 Days: The Siege of Leningrad* (New York: Harper and Row, 1969), 514–17. Relevant documents may be found in A. R. Dzeniskevich, *Leningrad v osade: Sbornik dokumentov o geroicheskoi oborone Leningrada v gody Velikoi Otechestvennoi voiny, 1941–1944* (St. Petersburg: Liki Rossii, 1995), 279–80, 313–43.

[33] Ol'ga M. Freidenberg, "Osada cheloveka," *Minuvshee*, 1987, no. 3: 21. Freidenberg reported the 3.5 million rumor. Salisbury reported rumors of 2 million deaths circulating in 1944. Salisbury, *900 Days*, 516.

[34] E. E. Levinson, *O druz'iakh, o zhizni i nemnogo o sebe* (St. Petersburg: Stroiizdat SPb, 1998), 88.

[35] "Report on Observations in Leningrad"; RG 226; Entry 16, 109691; NACP.

[36] Suzanne Massie, *Pavlovsk: The Life of a Russian Palace* (Boston: Little, Brown, 1990), 278.

[37] Levinson, *O druz'iakh*, 87.

[38] Massie, *Pavlovsk*, 277.

Leningrad's grand vistas and architectural masterpieces were integral to Leningraders' everyday sense of place. The former imperial palaces that graced its suburbs were at once icons of Russian glory and beloved parks that Leningraders enjoyed visiting on summer weekends. Damaged buildings carried both personal and public meanings. In Leningrad, the symbolic and the everyday overlapped and coexisted, more or less peacefully, often in a single building. Whatever architects and planners intended, the repair and reconstruction of Leningrad's icons inevitably interacted with the revitalization of its everyday places.

The Meanings of Historical Reconstruction

During the war, the first impulse among Leningrad planners and architects was the preservation and, if necessary, reconstruction of historic buildings.[39] After the war, architects undertook both historic reconstruction and new construction based on what they tactfully called the "Leningrad tradition" in architecture. The repair and reproduction of historic buildings, as well as the creation of new buildings that paraphrased their historic neighbors offered a means of restoring visible order in the city. If we approach the urban environment as not only a physical space but also a place constituted by imagination and memory, the insistence on preserving and perpetuating the Leningrad tradition can be understood as recovering what was lost (or an idealized version of what was lost), covering the memory of destruction with simulated continuity, preserving the landscapes of memory, and asserting a distinctively Leningrad (or Petersburg) identity.

Not surprisingly, the most important and prestigious location for preservation and reconstruction work was Nevskii Prospekt, the central artery, if not the heart, of the historic city. Here, any effort to modernize damaged or destroyed façades risked the opposition of the local architectural elite. A German bomb had largely demolished the façade of Number 30 at the intersection of Nevskii and the Griboedov Canal – the historic Small Hall of the Philharmonic. With little of the original to work with,

---

[39] Werth, *Leningrad*, 43–44. E. N. Andogskaia, "V soiuze arkhitektorov (khronika 1942–1945 gg.)," *Arkhitektura Leningrada*, 1945, no. 1: 28. O. N. Shilina, "Vrachevateli krasoty," in V. A. Kutuzov and E. G. Levina, eds., *Vozrozhdenie: Vospominaniia, ocherki i dokumenty o vosstanovlenii Leningrada* (Leningrad: Lenizdat, 1977), 222–23. Karasev, "Vozrozhdenie," 117–18. Massie, *Pavlovsk*, 291. A. I. Zelenova, "Pavlovskii dvortsovo-parkovyi ansambl'," in Kutuzov and Levina, *Vozrozhdenie*, 250.

Kamenskii's initial plan for the site created an "independent and wholly contemporary composition." While praising Kamenskii's work, critics suggested that the building's new and bolder façade threatened to overpower its neighbors on the prospect, especially the nearby Kazan Cathedral. Thus, "under pressure from the architectural community and the chief architect of the city," Nikolai Baranov, Kamenskii produced a "second version that reproduced, almost exactly" the 1829 façade designed by Paul Jacot.[40] This second plan provided the basis for the building's reconstruction.

The repaired Nevskii Prospekt featured buildings with "authentic" neoclassical façades. Perhaps learning from Kamenskii's experience, the architect in charge of restoring Gostinyi Dvor, Oleg Lialin, undertook extensive archival and archeological work with the intention of "recreating the original look" of the exterior, while modifying some of the interior spaces.[41] As the chief architect Baranov emphasized, the aim was not to "mechanically reproduce that which had been destroyed during the war."[42] Instead, the war damage became an opportunity to recreate the austere neoclassical grandeur that architects imagined had existed in the time of Catherine II and Alexander I. Architects ignored buildings' early-eighteenth-century baroque incarnations and eliminated the "tinsel" that dated to the late nineteenth century.[43] Thus, many of the historical reproductions resembled not their prewar counterparts but their late-eighteenth-century ancestors.

Architects embarked on a similar program of historical reproduction and purification in relation to the ruined palaces. Drawing on archival records, paintings, engravings, and their own prewar studies, restorers aimed to resurrect the palaces as their original designers had intended them, before successive monarchs remodeled them. In 1943, local architects organized a school to train a hundred and fifty children returning from evacuation in the skills necessary for reconstructing the palaces,

---

[40] Ia. O. Rubanchik, "My otstoiali tebia, Leningrad, my tebia i vosstanovim!" *Arkhitektura Leningrada*, 1945, no. 1: 16, 18. See also M. S. Burenina, *Progulki po Nevskomu propektu* (St. Petersburg: Litera, 2002), 116–24; R. A. Somina, *Nevskii prospekt: Istoricheskii ocherk* (Leningrad: Lenizdat, 1959), 232.

[41] Rubanchik, "My ostoiali," 19. See also Isachenko, *Zodchie*, 672; Karasev, "Vozrozhdenie," 125.

[42] N. V. Baranov, "O plane vosstanovleniia Leningrada," *Arkhitektura Leningrada*, 1945, no. 1: 3.

[43] Rubanchik, "My otstoiali," 18–19. See also Burenina, *Progulki*, 145–47; Karasev, "Vozrozhdenie," 124.

ranging from marble cutting to cabinet making.[44] Utilizing modern techniques to restore the structures – recreating pillars out of poured concrete, for example – architects insisted that the palaces appear "original."[45]

In other cases, architects substituted historical simulacra for historical reproductions. The one important building on the central historic stretch of Nevskii Prospekt that was wholly redesigned after the war – Number 68, adjacent to the Anichkov Bridge, where Nevskii crosses the Fontanka River – mimics the neoclassical façades that surround it. The effectiveness of the simulation was the subject of some rather caustic commentary immediately after the war. The original building had been almost totally destroyed and was slated to be converted from residential to administrative use. The architects Igor' Fomin and Boris Zhuravlev proposed a brand new neoclassical building, the most striking feature of which was a central portico framed by columns extending from the third to the fifth floors. Before the building was constructed, the architect Iakov Rubanchik attacked its "lack of architectural logic and architectural truth." Rubanchik found the purely decorative portico and the building's height – a true "Petersburg empire" building should have no more than three stories – especially "vexing."[46] Rubanchik's criticism of the portico was grounded in the socialist-realist principle that architectural "elements must be used in their proper tectonic or structural functions. Arches must span, columns must bear loads."[47] By contrast, Baranov supported Fomin's building as "answering the historically formed character of the architecture of worthiest buildings" on the prospekt.[48] Despite the criticism, Fomin and Zhuravlev's project was built in 1947 as the Kuibyshev District soviet (Illustration 11). Currently, the building houses the Central District Tax Office. It has become, according to a post-Soviet architectural

---

[44] I. A. Vaks and N. M. Ol', "Budushchie restavratory," in Kutuzov and Levina, *Vozrozhdenie*, 228–31.

[45] Massie, *Pavlovsk*, 312–16. Kuchumov, *Pavlovsk*, 9–10. "Orden na znameni goroda Petrodvortsa," *Stroitel'stvo i arkhitektura Leningrada*, 1974, no. 1: 8–9. Vivian Craddock Williams, "Beautiful Ghosts from the Past: The Paradox of Leningrad's Revival," *Smithsonian* 3, no. 2 (May 1972): 69–70. M. Kirby Talley, Jr., "The Beautiful and the Damned: Preserving Peter the Great's Dream on the Neva," in Frank Althaus and Mark Sutcliffe, eds., *Petersburg Perspectives* (London: Fontanka, 2003), 171–84. Boris Metlitskii, "Iantarnaia komnata: Segodnia i zavtra," *Sankt-Peterburgskie vedomosti*, 26 March 1994. Elizabeth Kolbert, "Forever Amber: A Room Built for a King and Treasured by an Empress Haunts Two Countries," *New Yorker*, 14 April 2003, 36–45.

[46] Rubanchik, "My otstoiali," 20–21.

[47] Catherine Cooke, "Beauty as a Route to 'the Radiant Future': Responses of Soviet Architecture," *Journal of Design History* 10 (1997): 151.

[48] Baranov, "O plane," 5–6.

11. No. 68 Nevskii Prospekt, a new neoclassical building constructed after the war. One of the horses on the Anichkov Bridge is visible in the foreground. *Source:* ITAR-TASS.

critic, "a familiar and integral part of Nevskii Prospekt." To the average visitor, it is scarcely recognizable as a twentieth-century building.[49]

Away from the historic center, architects planned many new buildings and ensembles along the lines of Fomin and Zhuravlev's neo-neoclassicism. The expanded Lenin Square in front of the Finland Station provided a suitably grandiose setting for the monument commemorating Vladimir Lenin's return in April 1917. Local architects emphasized its debt to the "Leningrad" tradition of monumental public spaces.[50] Similarly, architects described the gigantic square that Fomin imagined uniting Rastrelli Square and Dictatorship Square in front of Smol'nyi – the Bolshevik headquarters in October 1917 – as an homage to the quintessentially "Leningrad" architecture of the imperial Smol'nyi ensemble, rather

[49] A. G. Vaitens, "Igor' Fomin," in Isachenko, *Zodchie,* 305. *St. Petersburg: Eyewitness Travel Guides* (New York: DK Publishing, 1998), 49. Burenina, *Progulki,* 219–22.

[50] Baranov, "O plane," 7. V. G. Isachenko, "Arkhitektura," in Iu. I. Smirnov, ed., *Sankt-Peterburg XX vek: Chto? Gde? Kogda?* (St. Petersburg: Izdatel'stvo "Paritet," 2000), 64–65. O. A. Chekanova, "Nikolai Baranov," in Isachenko, *Zodchie,* 345–47. I. A. Nosikov, "S imenem Lenina," *Stroitel'stvo i arkhitektura Leningrada,* 1974, no. 1: 2–3.

than to the revolutionary events that transpired there. (The square was never built.)[51] Both projects had much in common with Ivan Fomin's (Igor's father) turn-of-the-century "New Petersburg," a largely unbuilt project that transplanted the grandeur, pomp, and unity of Petersburg neoclassicism to Golodai (now Decembrist) Island.[52] Leningrad architects promoted the architectural legacy of imperial Petersburg as the local lodestar.

The local devotion to neoclassicism meshed well with the aesthetic preferences of the Stalinist state. Stalinist architecture often relied on the legitimizing power of classical forms. The austere, monumental, well-ordered city lent substance to the "fantasy of modernization as an end to dissonance and conflict" that Marshall Berman has identified as a key element in the thought of nineteenth-century Russian revolutionaries and that remained vital to the Stalinist project. The Stalinist state found in the Petersburg–Leningrad cityscape a powerful emblem of the rational, centralized state – of what Berman labels "modernization as routine," as opposed to "modernization as adventure."[53] The values of centralization and rationalization can be seen at work in the prewar plan for Moscow that demolished seventeenth-century churches, widened streets and squares, and featured buildings in the neoclassical style – that, in short, made the Bolshevik capital more like imperial Petersburg.[54] Likewise, Stalinallee, East Berlin's grand Stalinist boulevard, drew on the Berlin neoclassicism of Karl Friedrich Schinkel, which in turn had strong affinities with the "Leningrad" neoclassicism that East German architects encountered when they visited the Soviet Union. A showpiece at the farthest reaches of Soviet power, the rebuilt East Berlin streetscape embodied and sought to legitimize communist order.[55]

[51] Baranov, "O plane," 4–5. Vaitens, "Igor' Fomin," 303–5.

[52] Blair A. Ruble, *Leningrad: Shaping a Soviet City* (Berkeley: University of California Press, 1990), 40–41, 44–45. Isachenko, *Zodchie*, 697. Katerina Clark, *Petersburg, Crucible of Cultural Revolution* (Cambridge, MA: Harvard University Press, 1995), 63.

[53] Marshall Berman, *All That Is Solid Melts into Air: The Experience of Modernity* (New York: Penguin Books, 1988), 243–45. Clark, *Petersburg,* 71.

[54] Antonina Manina, "Der Generalplan zur Stadterneuerug Moskaus 1935," in Peter Noever, ed., *Tyrannei des Schönen: Architektur der Stalin-Zeit* (Munich: Prestel, 1994), 165–69. Stephen V. Bittner, "Green Cities and Orderly Streets," *Journal of Urban History* 25 (1998): 22–56. Andrew Elam Day, "Building Socialism: The Politics of the Soviet Cityscape in the Stalin Era" (Ph.D. diss., Columbia University, 1998), 92–109. Ruble, *Leningrad,* 42–45.

[55] Ladd, *Ghosts,* 181–89. Greg Alan Castillo, "Exporting the Model City and its Citizens: Berlin's Stalinallee" (Paper delivered at the Thirty-fourth National Convention of the American Association for the Advancement of Slavic Studies, Pittsburgh, PA, 23 November 2002).

In the wake of their dangerous and tragic wartime adventures, many Leningrad architects and planners shared the state's preference for a controlled, visibly harmonious urban environment that signaled the return of peace and that materialized the spirit of the unconquered city. For G. P. Chulkevich, who spent the blockade working to save people and buildings as a brigade leader in the local air defense forces (MPVO), the static orderliness of Lenin Square was a "symbol of the postwar rebirth of Leningrad."[56] The monumental cityscape could also be understood as a sort of victory monument. Echoing Kamenskii's call for a grand postwar architectural aesthetic, Baranov deemed it "obvious" that just as the Fatherland War of 1812 had "found its reflection in the Russian classical style," so too should the recent war "be strongly reflected in postwar construction in Leningrad."[57] Baranov scrupulously emphasized the national dimensions of his program, noting that the great foreign architects who defined the tradition in which Leningrad architects worked – Bartolomeo Rastrelli, Quarenghi, Carlo Rossi – were deeply influenced by the Russian environment and "created genuinely Russian things."[58]

While Leningrad architects recognized the importance of the state's national agenda, their emphasis on neoclassicism included a large measure of local self-assertion. After all, neoclassicism was not Stalinism's sole architectural mode, as the so-called seven sisters, the neo-Gothic skyscrapers constructed in postwar Moscow, and their cousin in reconstructed Warsaw attest.[59] Leningrad architects insisted, as the chief architect Baranov put it, that "obviously" every city has a "right to its own, distinctive individuality." He emphasized the importance in Leningrad of a uniform five- or six-story roofline, large-scale buildings, green space, and monumental sculpture.[60] Levinson located the "architectural tradition of Leningrad . . . in the nobility of form; in the large scale; in the modulation among neighboring structures."[61] Both emphasized the need to honor local traditions and forms.

[56] G. P. Chulkevich, "Put' k ploshchadi Lenina," in Kutuzov and Levina, *Vozrozhdenie,* 213.

[57] Baranov, "O plane," 6.

[58] Ibid.

[59] Werth, *Leningrad,* 43. Andrej Ikonnikov, "Gli 'edifici alti' di Mosca," in Alessandro De Magistris, ed., *URSS anni '30-'50: Paesaggi dell'utopia staliniana* (Milan: Edizioni Gabriele Mazzotta, 1997), 260. Michalski, *Public Monuments,* 129–31. Cooke, "Beauty," 143. Greg Castillo, "Classicism for the Masses," *Design Book Review,* no. 35/36 (Winter 1995): 78–88.

[60] Baranov, "O plane," 6–7. "Report on an Interview with Mr. N. V. Baranov"; RG 226; Entry 16, 109571; NACP.

[61] E. A. Levinson, "Eshche o novatorstve i traditsii," *Arkhitektura Leningrada,* 1945, no. 1: 22–23.

By highlighting the specifically local dimensions of their architectural practice, Leningrad architects proclaimed both their identity as Leningraders and the uniqueness, if not superiority, of Leningrad, the heir of imperial Petersburg. Already a provincial city in relation to Moscow, postwar Leningrad became increasingly marginalized, in large part because so many native Leningraders had either died in the blockade or failed to return to the city.[62] Nonetheless, Leningrad's cityscape continued to embody Leningraders' cultural if not political pretensions. While, as Baranov noted, the "Russian" architecture of Leningrad reflected national glory, he along with Kamenskii and Levinson also viewed the grandeur of the Leningrad cityscape as a reflection of the city's illustrious past and its "brilliant" chapter in the Great Fatherland War. Thus, the desire among architects who lived through the blockade to build distinctively Leningrad-style buildings and streets can be understood in very local terms as an effort to honor, protect, and purify the "beloved city" in which they had suffered and survived.[63]

Domestic Places in the Rebuilt City

The affinity of both architects and the Stalinist state for grand and imposing public spaces had important, if largely unintended, repercussions for the city's more personal spaces. The emphasis on restoring Leningrad's status "as one of the world's most beautiful and well-built cities" meant that high-profile administrative and public buildings – along with industry – had the first claims on the labor and resources necessary for repairs.[64] Moreover, as Baranov informed American General Phillip Fleming, the Federal Works administrator, who interviewed the chief architect in order to collect information on postwar reconstruction in the Soviet Union, planners committed to building a grand city agreed that "small houses and dwellings of a temporary nature are . . . out of place in Leningrad."[65]

[62] Bubis and Blair, "The Impact," 202–3.
[63] Karl D. Qualls observes a similar negotiation between the local and the national in Sevastopol'. Qualls, "Accommodation and Agitation in Sevastopol: Redefining Socialist Space in the Postwar 'City of Glory,'" in David Crowley and Susan E. Reid, eds., *Socialist Spaces: Sites of Everyday Life in the Eastern Bloc* (Oxford: Berg, 2002), 40.
[64] Arsiutkina, "Leningradskaia partiinaia," 18–19. Intelligence Division, Office of Chief of Naval Operations, Navy Department, "Intelligence Report" (18 November 1944); RG 226; Entry 16, 102427; NACP. V. M. Reshkin, "Tsifry, kotorye ia budu pomnit' vsegda," in Kutuzov and Levina, *Vozrozhdenie,* 32–34. N. L. Staskevich, "V kazhduiu kvartiru – gaz," in ibid., 195–97. Kniazev, "Kommunisty," 65–66.
[65] "Report on an Interview with Mr. N. V. Baranov"; RG 226; Entry 16, 109571; NACP.

The preference for the low-rise, high-quality apartment buildings that architects deemed appropriate for a monumental city substantially slowed efforts to provide adequate housing. Returning Leningraders crammed into garrets, basements, barracks, and converted railway cars. In 1951, approximately three families shared the average Leningrad apartment.[66]

Behind the glorious façades, Leningrad remained the communal-apartment capital of the nation. The postwar *kommunalka* immortalized by Brodsky in his essay "In a Room and a Half" illustrates some of the central paradoxes of Leningraders' personal spaces. The apartment itself was located in a once-elegant turn-of-the-century Moorish-style apartment house that, while not embodying Leningrad neoclassicism, was architecturally striking and had caused quite a sensation when it was completed in 1903. After the Revolution, the apartment had been partitioned, and four unrelated families shared the single toilet, bathroom, and kitchen. Brodsky and his parents' personal space was the "room and a half" of the essay's title. By Soviet standards, this was a relatively spacious forty square meters.[67] Housing norms put the minimum square meterage per person at nine (approximately 97 square feet), but this standard was rarely met, least of all in Leningrad. The family's good luck meant that by filling the two nearly ceiling-high Moorish arches that separated his "half" from his parents' room with bookshelves and suitcases, the young Brodsky created ten square meters of almost private space.[68] Yet even the most cramped Leningrad apartment might have, as did Brodsky's, fourteen-foot (approximately 4.7 meter) ceilings – the now cracked and stained token of a bygone era. The room and a half's balcony offered a view of what Brodsky described as a "typically Petersburgian, impeccable perspective" – as if the Leningrad communal apartment,

---

[66] Barraclough, "Late Socialist," 3–4. Ruble, *Leningrad*, 64. Karasev, "Vozrozhdenie," 123.

[67] Brodsky, "In a Room and a Half," in *Less Than One*, 451–54. Zinaida Gippius and her husband had been the prerevolutionary residents.

[68] As late as 1998, 40 percent of Petersburg households had less than nine square meters of living space per person. James H. Bater and John R. Staples, "Planning for Change in Central St. Petersburg," *Post-Soviet Geography and Economics* 41 (2000): 87. On the establishment of "sanitary norms" of meterage per person, see Leslie Dayna Kauffman, "Building Castles in the Sky: The Domestication of Daily Life in Urban Russia" (Ph.D. diss., Columbia University, 2000), 34–38; Steven E. Harris, "Moving to the Separate Apartment: Building, Distributing, Furnishing, and Living in Urban Housing in Soviet Russia, 1950s–1960s" (Ph.D. diss., University of Chicago, 2003), 34–37; Katerina Gerasimova, "Public Privacy in the Soviet Communal Apartment," in Crowley and Reid, *Socialist Spaces*, 207–30.

with all its foul smells and noises, opened onto an entirely different and enchanted city.[69]

The careful preservation of Leningrad's exteriors, its façades and streetscapes, facilitated an unplanned preservation of its domestic interiors. Communal apartments became museums, almost archeological sites, where the history of the displaced bourgeois owners remained visible beneath the Soviet-era partition walls, and the traces of the blockade could be seen beneath the postwar paint.[70] When Ales' Adamovich and Daniil Granin began collecting oral histories of blokadniki in the late 1970s, they visited numerous apartments that bore the physical marks of war. "The people we visited," Adamovich and Granin wrote, "are like soldiers who now live a life of peace but are still surrounded by the same things, the same walls, as if still in the same dug-out, the same trench." Aleksandra Den pointed out a damaged patch of parquet floor, "where, towards the end, my husband chopped up the furniture. Until he died on this sofa. Here." Lidiia Usova directed Adamovich and Granin's attention to a yellow stain that marked the spot where the *burzhuika*, the small makeshift stove, had stood. Thirty years after the end of the war, Galina Bobinskaia "sees her flat as a kind of museum of what her family went through during the blockade. She showed us fragments of glass still sparkling in the damaged glossy surface of the grand piano."[71] Into the 1990s, many blokadniki still lived in the apartments in which they had survived the war.[72]

Unlike Berlin, Hiroshima, and Coventry, postwar Leningrad retained no ruins as monuments to the destructiveness of war.[73] Planners explicitly rejected the modernism that dominated postwar Rotterdam.[74] Instead,

---

[69] Brodsky, "In a Room," 465. Yury Arabov, "The Petersburger's Psychology: A Moscow View," in Althaus and Sutcliffe, *Petersburg Perspectives*, 43.

[70] Svetlana Boym, *Common Places: Mythologies of Everyday Life in Russia* (Cambridge, MA: Harvard University Press), 142. Ilya Utekhin, "Filling Dwelling Place with History: Communal Apartments in St. Petersburg," in John J. Czaplicka and Blair A. Ruble, eds., *Composing Urban History and the Constitution of Civic Identity* (Baltimore: Johns Hopkins University Press; Washington, DC: Woodrow Wilson Center Press, 2003), 96–99.

[71] I have used the translation in Ales' Adamovich and Daniil Granin, eds., *A Book of the Blockade*, trans. Hilda Perham (Moscow: Raduga Publishers, 1983), 7, 9, 81. Adamovich and Granin, *Blokadnaia kniga* (Moscow: Sovetskii pisatel', 1982), 3, 4, 68.

[72] *Chas pik*, 25 March 1991. Utekhin, "Filling," 107.

[73] Alvis, "The Berliner Dom." Hein, "Hiroshima." Stefan Goebel, "Commemorative Cosmopolis: Coventry after 1945" (Paper delivered at the conference "Metropolitan Catastrophes," Centre for Metropolitan History, London, 13 July 2004).

[74] Levinson, "Eshche o novatorstve," 22.

Leningrad architects chose a strategy of renewal closer to that undertaken in Warsaw – historical reconstruction and purification. The acceptability of Petersburg neoclassicism as a symbol of communist order made the retaining of Leningrad's historic character relatively unproblematic. It was spared the Stalinist skyscraper so loathed in Warsaw. At the same time, Leningrad's restored façades not only eliminated war damage and created an idealized version of the prewar cityscape but also asserted local identity. The Soviet second city remained visually and symbolically a capital city. The restoration of Leningrad's public face also had the unintended result of preserving its wartime domestic spaces. Largely covered up in the city's streets, the memory of the war remained visible in the plaster of its communal apartments.

Victory Without Monuments

During the war, architects had assumed that victory would bring monuments. As early as 1942, Leningrad architects began to sketch victory monuments and memorials to the civilian victims of the blockade. Planning for monuments and memorial cemeteries continued into the postwar period, and architects expressed their commitment to constructing them as soon as possible.[75] In 1947, the architects T. I. Skripnik and S. V. Petrov presented to the city government their plans for a Victory monument that they had first conceived in 1942. It featured a tank on the march, a flag emblazoned with Lenin's likeness, and a statue of Stalin.[76]

All these plans notwithstanding, postwar Leningrad raised no memorials to the "destroyed city." The failure to build monuments can be explained as a result of the need to allocate scarce reconstruction funds to restoring essential services. At the same time, the state's preference – shared by many survivors – for moving forward and healing the city's wounds thwarted plans to build the memory of the war into the cityscape. Until 1949, only a few of the blue and white warning signs that marked the dangerous side of the street in the event of an artillery attack – most had been painted over as soon as the blockade was broken – stood as

[75] V. Tvel'kmeier, "Pamiatniki geroicheskoi oborny Leningrada," *Leningrad*, 1946, no. 1–2: 51–52. V. F. Tvel'kmeier, "Synov svoikh rodina ne zabudet, vragov ne prostit," *Arkhitektura i stroitel'stvo Leningrada*, June 1946, 17–21. M. E. Rusakov, "Proekty pamiatnikov na Serafimovskom kladbishche," *Arkhitektura i stroitel'stvo Leningrada*, November 1946, 40–41.

[76] "Ekskiznni proekt narodnogo pamiatnika 'Pobeda' v Leningrade," Tsentral'nyi Gosudarstvennyi Arkhiv Sankt-Peterburga (hereafter TsGA SPb), f. 7384, op. 29, d. 260, l. 2.

12. Warning sign on Nevskii Prospekt, 1944. *Source:* ITAR-TASS.

reminders of the war (Illustration 12).[77] However, not a single obelisk, funeral mound (*kurgan*), or tank proposed by architects was constructed within the city limits until after Stalin's death in 1953.

Instead of war monuments, the local government built two enormous victory parks that remembered not so much the war as the return of tranquility and order. Whereas in Berlin's Treptower Park, as in the Tiergarten and on Vienna's Schwarzenbergplatz, the Soviet state constructed imposing war memorials complete with tanks and bronze soldiers, in Leningrad the local authorities created quiet green spaces. One park stood close to the former front line in the south; the other was on Krestovskii Island, where the Neva meets the Gulf of Finland. The southern Moskovskii Victory Park, named after the district in which it is located, explicitly covered up wartime damage. The Primorskii (Seafront) Park reflected chief architect Baranov's dream of making Leningrad a "true maritime city" with a "face to the sea."[78] Erasing wartime damage and anchoring new development in outlying districts, both parks looked more to building the future than to memorializing the past.

The victory parks constituted part of a larger effort to restore the order, beauty, and pleasures of Leningrad's green spaces. The government

[77] Salisbury, *900 Days*, 580. *Nevskii prospekt v dni voiny i mira: Reportazh fotokorrespondenta Davida Trakhtenberga* (Leningrad: Izdatel'stvo "Avrora," 1970).
[78] Ruble, *Leningrad*, 51.

13. Arts Square and the monument to Aleksandr Pushkin. This sculpture by Mikhail Anikushin was erected in 1957. Photo by John K. Conway.

estimated that during the blockade, bombs, artillery, fires, and – it seems reasonable to add – Leningraders' desperate need for fuel destroyed some hundred thousand trees and eighty thousand shrubs along with two hundred hectares of lawn.[79] Emphasizing that "the blockade and the war have ended," Petr Popkov, the first secretary of the city and regional party committees, made the restoring of parks and gardens a local priority. The city undertook numerous restoration projects in the historic center, including the gardens around Engineer's Castle, Arts Square (ploshchad Iskusstv) (Illustration 13), and the Tauride Gardens.[80]

City officials understood the effort to put parks and gardens "in order" as a way of marking the return of peace and of restoring life to normal. At a meeting of the city soviet's executive committee in 1946, Popkov advocated the dismantling of a wartime aerodrome that had been constructed on the site of a park, "where, before the war," as he fondly recalled, "workers often went with their teapots and samovars and spent the whole day." In the city center, restoring parks and gardens complemented the project of historic reconstruction. The first secretary

[79] V. D. Kirkhoglani, "Geroicheskii peizazh," in Kutuzov and Levina, *Vozrozhdenie*, 260.
[80] "Stenograficheskii otchet: soveshchanie u Predsedatelia Ispolkoma Lengorsoveta t. Popkova" (February 1946), TsGA SPb, f. 7384, op. 29, d. 37, ll. 70–72.

underlined the "need to put the Field of Mars – the most beautiful spot in our city – in order." The job required filling in trenches and replanting grass. Popkov proposed directing funds to the restoration of the Tauride Gardens, which had suffered extensive artillery damage, and stressed the need to "put in order" the gardens around the monument to Peter I, "because this is the very center of the city, an obligatory destination for foreign tourists."[81]

The construction of the victory parks, which served the needs of locals more than tourists, attracted extensive public involvement. On 7 October 1945, some twenty-five thousand Leningraders took part in a massive tree-planting effort that initiated the two victory parks.[82] Just how voluntarily Leningraders undertook this unpaid labor is difficult to gauge. The city government published brochures and posters promoting the significance of the planting campaign, and charged the newspapers *Leningradskaia pravda* and *Smena* with additional publicity.[83] The blandishments of party activists, who worked to enforce norms of unpaid labor, helped to bring out thousands of Leningraders on a blustery fall day.[84] Anna Akhmatova's 1950 poem "Primorskii Victory Park"– a poem often excluded from the Akhmatova canon because she wrote it as an attempt to appease Stalin and obtain the release of her arrested son – emphasizes the large numbers of Leningraders who participated. However, its explicitly laudatory intentions notwithstanding, the poem suggests a lack of spontaneous feeling – if not a dose of regimentation – in the proceedings:

> But early one morning the Leningraders turned out
> At the seashore in countless crowds.
> And each one planted a tree
> On that strip of land, swampy and empty,
> In memory of the great Day of Victory.[85]

---

[81] Ibid., ll. 72–73.

[82] "Parki Pobedy v Leningrade," *Krasnaia zvezda*, 23 October 1945. Karasev, "Vozrozh-denie," 122.

[83] "O stroitel'stve 'parkov pobedy' i provedenii massovykh drevonasazhdenii v gorode Leningrade," TsGA SPb, f. 7384, op. 29, d. 37, ll. 2–4.

[84] Kniazev, "Kommunisty," 72–74.

[85] Excerpt from "Seaside Victory Park," from The *Complete Poems of Anna Akhmatova*, translated by Judith Hemschemeyer, edited and introduced by Roberta Reeder. Copyright © 1989 by Judith Hemschemeyer (Somerville, MA: Zephyr Press, 1990), 2: 841. Reprinted by permission of Zephyr Press. On the controversy over the poem, see Eric Lozowy, "La Recueil Slava miru et l'oeuvre poétique d'Axmatova," *Canadian Slavonic Papers* 34 (December 1992): 419–27; Brodsky, "The Keening Muse," in *Less than One*, 48.

Reporting his observations at Moskovskii Park to the city soviet, Professor Tkachenko of the Forestry Academy (Lesotekhnicheskaia akademiia) noted, by contrast, that the Leningraders who showed up with shovels on 7 October worked "with great enthusiasm" and "much lack of coordination," as volunteers planted, for example, elms where the plans called for ash trees.[86] Unruly Leningraders perhaps found their own meanings and pleasures in a ritual structured by the state.[87] Twenty years later, when the city finally committed itself to building a war monument, many blokadniki suggested parks, where the misery of war could be forgotten, as the most appropriate memorials.[88]

At the Moskovskii Victory Park, Leningraders planting trees "in memory of the great Day of Victory" covered up the traces of war. Leningrad's southern industrial districts, just a few kilometers from the front, were among the most badly damaged in the city. Planners thus envisioned the Moskovskii Victory Park as, first and foremost, a means of reclaiming a scarred landscape. Before Leningraders came to plant trees, city workers dismantled concrete and wooden pillboxes and filled trenches. They removed a brick factory, which had been used as a crematorium during the starvation winter, and converted the site into the source of a system of lakes. Bomb craters became ponds (Illustration 14). A newly created pastoral landscape obliterated war damage.[89]

Likewise, the design of the Primorskii Victory Park scarcely alluded to the war. Its focal point, the 75,000-seat Kirov Stadium at the western end of the island, had been under construction since 1933. A formal central alley lined with oaks, ashes, and some cedars led to the stadium. Designers conceived of the rest of the park as a restful landscape of meandering paths among trees and ponds. In the first stage of construction, Leningraders planted some forty-five thousand trees on the island.[90]

---

[86] "Stenograficheskii otchet," TsGA SPb, f. 7384, op. 29, d. 37, l. 69. See also Kirkhoglani, "Geroicheskii peizazh," 261.

[87] Crowley makes a similar point in relation to Varsovians' celebration of the reconstruction of new quarters of the city. Crowley, "People's Warsaw," 206.

[88] "Pis'ma," Tsentral'nyi Gosudarstvennyi Arkhiv Literatury i Iskusstva Sankt-Peterburga (hereafter TsGALI SPb), f. 341, op. 6, d.1, ll. 123–24; "Pis'ma," TsGALI SPb, f. 341, op. 6, d. 7, ll. 20, 112.

[89] E. I. Katonin, "Parki Pobedy," *Arkhitektura i stroitel'stvo Leningrada*, June 1946, 11–12. V. D. Kirkhoglani, "Parki slavy narodnoi," *Stroitel'stvo i arkhitektura Leningrada*, 1977, no. 8: 12–13. Smirnov, *Sankt-Peterburg XX vek*, 221.

[90] Katonin, "Parki," 10–11. Smirnov, *Sankt-Peterburg XX vek*, 218–19. A. V. Povelikhina, "Aleksandr Nikol'skii," in Isachenko, *Zodchie*, 55–58. A. S. Nikol'skii and K. I. Kashin, "Stadion imeni S. M. Kirova," *Arkhitektura i stroitel'stvo Leningrada*, 1950, no. 2: 5–16.

14. At the Moskovskii Victory Park, shell craters became ponds. Photo by author.

    As constructed between 1945 and 1948, the victory parks were emblems of the city's rebirth. Celebrations of the return of peace, the parks were designed to forget the blockade. A single reinforced concrete pillbox can still be found in the Primorskii Park; however, the planners made no effort to call visitors' attention to this relic of the war, and contemporary descriptions of the park completely ignored it. A Victory Square stood midway between the park's entrance and the stadium, but it initially contained no monuments or memorials.[91] At the Moskovskii Park, a broad Victory Alley, nearly 35 meters wide and 860 meters long, bisected the park. Initial plans called for "sculptures" of an unspecified sort along its length. However, it contained no monuments to the war until the late 1970s, when the city added statues of two national heroes – murdered partisan Zoia Kosmodem'ianskaia and Aleksandr Matrosov, a soldier who saved his comrades by throwing himself in front of a German machine-gun emplacement – as well as busts of locals who had twice been honored as heroes of the Soviet Union or heroes of socialist labor (Illustration 15). The latter group included Leonid Brezhnev's

---

[91] Smirnov, *Sankt-Peterburg XX vek*, 219. Katonin, "Parki," 9–11.

15. Monuments erected in the Moskovskii Victory Park in the 1970s. Photo by author.

prime minister, Aleksei Kosygin.[92] Such monuments did little to recall Leningraders' wartime experiences.

For blokadniki, however, the ponds, paths, and trees never entirely displaced the memory of trenches, pillboxes, and bomb craters. In 1990, the freer atmosphere of perestroika allowed survivors who remembered the park as it had been during the war to lobby for a memorial to mark the location of the brick factory, where thousands of Leningraders had been cremated. At the time, a tennis court stood on the site of the proposed memorial.[93] On 25 January 1995, the fifty-first anniversary of the end of the blockade, eleven survivors from among the women who had worked at the brick factory during the war dedicated a small monument on the former factory grounds (Illustration 16). Imagining a building that no longer existed, Anna Kadykova told a reporter, "Right here stood two tunnel ovens, each 100 meters long. They were fired round the clock. And we worked in three shifts."[94]

[92] Smirnov, *Sankt-Peterburg XX vek*, 221. Katonin, "Parki," 11–12. On Kosmo-dem'ianskaia and Matrosov, see Richard Stites, *Russian Popular Culture: Entertainment and Society since 1900* (Cambridge: Cambridge University Press, 1992), 99.

[93] S. Vital'ev, "Vremia vozrashchat' dolgi," *Vechernii Leningrad*, 29 January 1990.

[94] *Sankt-Peterburgskie vedomosti*, 26 January 1995. See also *Chas pik*, 25 January 1995; *Nevskoe vremia*, 26 January 1995.

16. Monument on site of crematorium, Moskovskii Victory Park. Photo by author.

The Leningrad Affair: Enforced Forgetting

The project of healing the wounds of war – restoring damaged buildings, parks, and gardens – drew support from the local party hierarchy, from the architectural establishment, and probably from a fair number of blokadniki who turned out to plant trees in 1945. The state's interest in eliminating the traces of the recent war and restoring the economy converged with survivors' desire to rebuild their homes and lives and, as local architects emphasized, to memorialize the city's wartime epic in monumental architecture. However, as the state's program of moving past the blockade went beyond efforts to heal the city, it relied on increasingly coercive measures. The state's enforcement of forgetting initially manifested itself in the reprimand of Leningrad authors who remembered the war and portrayed their city in allegedly anti-Soviet ways. It culminated in a thoroughgoing purge of the city's party and soviet leadership that effectively shut down all local efforts to tell and memorialize the story of the blockade.

By April 1945, the wartime celebration of Leningrad's unique fate and the commitment to constructing monuments that would "give to future generations the unique details of the life of besieged Leningrad" produced official efforts to rein in the practice of emphasizing the city's unique spirit and wartime experiences.[95] At a meeting of the Leningrad section of the Soviet Writers' Union, the critic P. Gromov, whose remarks the journal *Leningrad* cited extensively, attacked Vera Inber's "repulsive" and "clinical" descriptions of the city's starvation winter as "tortuous to read." Moreover, her all-too-personal account lacked "the air of the epoch" and the "feeling of history."[96] At the same meeting, the Leningrad poet Aleksander Prokof'ev defined the "Leningrad theme" in literature in explicitly Soviet and national terms – rejecting any connection to the "Petersburg theme" – as "strongly reflecting the splendid qualities of the Soviet person: selfless love and devotion to the mighty Bolshevik Party, to the people's leader Comrade Stalin; selfless love and devotion to the Motherland."[97] Wartime propaganda had emphasized the local and private loyalties that made sacrifice meaningful and urgent. By 1945, efforts to universalize the Leningrad epic by reconnecting it to Soviet patriotism marked the limits of official tolerance of local pride and identity.

After the war, as the historian Sheila Fitzpatrick has noted, "the regime wanted to tighten controls on the society, not loosen them."[98] Stalin was particularly keen to tighten control of Leningrad. He had harbored a special hatred, perhaps fear, of the city since 1925, when the Leningrad party organization, led by the locally powerful Grigorii Zinoviev, "openly opposed" the party's Central Committee in Moscow.[99] In the early 1930s,

---

[95] G. Makogonenko, "Leningradskaia tema," *Znamia*, 1945, no. 1: 209–10.

[96] "Diskussiia o Leningradskoi teme," *Leningrad*, 1945, no. 7–8: 27.

[97] Ibid., 26.

[98] Sheila Fitzpatrick, "Postwar Soviet Society: The 'Return to Normalcy,' 1945–1953," in Linz, *The Impact*, 130.

[99] Clayton Black, "Party Crisis and the Factory Shop Floor: Krasnyi Putilovets and the Leningrad Opposition, 1925–1926," *Europe-Asia Studies* 46 (1994): 121–22. Leonard Schapiro, *The Communist Party of the Soviet Union* (1960; reprint, New York: Vintage Books, 1971), 294–302. T. H. Rigby, "Stalinism and the Mono-Organizational Society," in Robert C. Tucker, ed., *Stalinism: Essays in Historical Interpretation* (New York: W. W. Norton, 1977), 68. C. N. Boterbloem, "The Death of Andrei Zhdanov," *Slavonic and East European Review* 80 (2002): 280.

another popular Leningrad party boss, Sergei Kirov, emerged as a potential rival. Stalin exploited Kirov's 1934 murder to generate the climate of fear that fed the terror of the late 1930s and that produced particularly devastating effects on the Leningrad party and intelligentsia.[100] Leningrad's wartime sense of autonomy – Werth observed that portraits of local hero Andrei Zhdanov were almost as plentiful as those of Stalin in the blockaded city – could only have troubled the leader. In 1946, when Zhdanov left his post in Leningrad to join the secretariat of the party's Central Committee in Moscow, the cultural crackdown that he orchestrated, the so-called *Zhdanovshchina,* took uppity Leningrad as one of its first targets.

The party's reassertion of cultural control began with the Central Committee's August 1946 condemnation of the journals *Leningrad* and *Zvezda.* The episode is best known as an attack on the high-profile targets of Akhmatova and the satirist Mikhail Zoshchenko, who were expelled from the Writers' Union in September 1946.[101] The brief against the journals also included a broader critique of fictional accounts of the war, the blockade, and the Petersburg–Leningrad theme. The critic N. Maslin took Akhmatova to task for failing to write poetry that reflected "the theme of the great struggle of the Soviet people with the enemy." Zoshchenko's story "A Monkey's Adventure" (Prikliucheniia obez"iany), about a monkey who escapes from the zoo during an air raid and learns the pleasures of eating kasha with a spoon, the critic dismissed as "absurd" and an "empty farce."[102] He also denounced Gennadii Gor's story "Dom na Mokhovoi" (House on Mokhovaia) for depicting not a "typical" Leningrad woman, who would presumably demonstrate courage and steadfastness, but instead an introspective, ambivalent – that is "passive" and "indifferent" – woman coping with the war's disruption of her marriage.[103] The state effectively proscribed stories that depicted the war as

---

[100] The evidence remains inconclusive, but some historians accuse Stalin of planning the murder. Robert Conquest, *Stalin and the Kirov Murder* (New York: Oxford University Press, 1989). Amy Knight, *Who Killed Kirov? The Kremlin's Greatest Mystery* (New York: Hill and Wang, 1999). Matt Lenoe, "Did Stalin Kill Kirov and Does It Matter?" *Journal of Modern History* 74 (June 2002): 352–80. Melanie Ilic, "The Great Terror in Leningrad: A Quantitative Analysis," *Europe-Asia Studies* 52 (December 2000): 1515–34.

[101] Roberta Reeder, "Mirrors and Masks: The Life and Poetic Works of Anna Akhmatova," in Reeder, *Complete Poems,* 124–25. Brandenberger, *National Bolshevism,* 186.

[102] N. Maslin, "O literaturnom zhurnale 'Zvezda,'" *Kul'tura i zhizn',* 10 August 1946.

[103] Quotations from ibid. Gennadii Gor, *Dom na Mokhovoi* (Leningrad: Lenizdat, 1945). In 1952, Georgii Malenkov defined the typical as "that which most pervasively expresses

local, personal, painful, or absurd – in short, as anything other than a "great struggle."

The anti-Western and xenophobic program of cultural repression soon spread beyond the sphere of literature. It became increasingly "anti-cosmopolitan," which in practice usually meant anti-Semitic, following the mysterious 1948 murder of Solomon Mikhoels, the Jewish actor who had been an official of the Jewish Anti-Fascist Committee during the war.[104] In Leningrad, the broadened cultural crackdown merged in 1949 with a political purge of the city's leaders and an attack on the memory of the blockade. Zhdanov's untimely demise in August 1948 provided an opportunity for his rivals in the Central Committee, Georgii Malenkov and Lavrentii Beria, to move against Zhdanov's protégés in Leningrad and throughout the country, notably Central Committee member A. A. Kuznetsov, who was, like Zhdanov, a former first secretary of the Leningrad party organization.[105]

Apparently fueled by struggles for power, as well as by disagreements over economic policy and ideology, what came to be known as the Leningrad Affair also had an important local component. The charge that the Leningraders advocated the establishment of a Russian Communist Party with its headquarters in Leningrad seems to have particularly provoked Stalin, who was sensitive to the threat to the Soviet Union that might emanate from a Russian party ensconced in the rival capital. On one level, what Stalin feared, as David Brandenberger emphasizes, was that rising Russian nationalism would undermine the Soviet state – a fear that produced a repudiation of the wartime emphasis on Russian heroes and the glorification of Russian history.[106] The Leningrad Affair also operated

the essence of a given social force." Quoted in Boris Groys, *The Total Art of Stalinism: Avant-Garde, Aesthetic Dictatorship, and Beyond,* trans. Charles Rougle (Princeton, NJ: Princeton University Press, 1992), 50.

[104] Peter Kneen, "Physics, Genetics, and the Zhdanovschina," *Europe-Asia Studies* 50 (November 1998): 1183–202. Werner G. Hahn, *Postwar Soviet Politics: The Fall of Zhdanov and the Defeat of Moderation, 1946–1953* (Ithaca, NY: Cornell University Press, 1982), 12, 115–22. Nikita Khrushchev, *Khrushchev Remembers,* trans. Strobe Talbott (Boston: Little, Brown, 1970), 258–62, 269–71.

[105] Boterbloem, "The Death," 285–87. Hahn, *Postwar,* 122. Jonathan Harris, "The Origins of the Conflict Between Malenkov and Zhdanov, 1939–1941," *Slavic Review* 35 (1976): 287–303. Ruble, *Leningrad,* 59–60. Richard Bidlack, "Ideological or Political Origins of the Leningrad Affair? A Response to David Brandenberger," *Russian Review* 64 (January 2005): 90–95. Benjamin Tromly, "The Leningrad Affair and Soviet Patronage Politics, 1949–1950," *Europe-Asia Studies* 56 (July 2004): 707–29.

[106] David Brandenberger, "Stalin, the Leningrad Affair, and the Limits of Postwar Russocentrism," *Russian Review* 63 (April 2004): 241–55. Dzeniskevich, *Blokada i politika,* 12.

against more local identities, putting an end to the wartime tolerance of local loyalties in general and of Leningraders' insistence on the uniqueness of their experiences in particular.

The attack on the Leningrad leadership began in February 1949, when the Politburo brought unpublicized charges against Popkov, as well as the party's second secretary Iakov Kapustin, Kuznetsov, and Mikhail Rodionov, the chair of the Council of Ministers of the Russian Federation. In late March 1949, a mass purge of Leningrad party and soviet workers began; by 1952, two thousand people had lost their jobs. As the purge widened, Popkov, Kuznetsov, and the others were tried in September 1950 on charges of "turning the Leningrad organization into a support base for carrying on a struggle with the party and its Central Committee."[107] Six of the nine defendants were sentenced to death and immediately shot. Additional trials and executions followed.[108]

The widening purge targeted not only party and state functionaries who had links to Zhdanov but also those who had played roles in the defense of blockaded Leningrad. The coincidence of the arrests with the appearance of work crews who painted out the remaining blue and white warning signs on Nevskii Prospekt made the linkage between the alleged political threat and the memory of the blockade unmistakable.[109] When Malenkov visited the city in February 1949 in order to oversee his political handiwork, he "immediately demanded the guidebook" for the Museum of the Defense of Leningrad. Not surprisingly, he found it to be dangerously antiparty. One former museum worker remembered Malenkov waving the guidebook and shouting, "It has created a myth of Leningrad's special 'blockade' fate! It has minimized the role of the great Stalin."[110] In the wake of Malenkov's visit, a commission organized by the Central

[107] Quoted in Elena Zubkova, *Russia After the War: Hopes, Illusions, and Disappointments, 1945–1957*, trans. Hugh Ragsdale (Armonk, NY: M. E. Sharpe, 1998), 133.
[108] Those executed in October 1950 were Kuznetsov, Popkov, Kapustin, Rodionov, Chair of Gosplan (the State Planning Agency) N. A. Voznesenskii, and Chair of the Leningrad Soviet Petr Georgievich Lazutin. V. Kutuzov, "Istoriia bez belykh piaten: 'Leningradskoe delo,'" *Dialog*, 1987, no. 18: 17, 20–21. Kutuzov, "Istoriia bez belykh piaten: 'Leningradskoe delo' (okonchanie)," *Dialog*, 1987, no. 19: 15–19. V. A. Kutuzov, "Tak nazyvaemoe 'Leningradskoe delo,'" *Voprosy istorii KPSS*, 1989, no. 3: 53–67.
[109] Salisbury, *900 Days*, 580.
[110] V. Kutuzov, "Muzei oborony Leningrada," *Dialog*, 1988, no. 24: 24. See also Gosudarstvennyi memorial'nyi muzei oborony i blokady Leningrada, *Muzei oborony i blokady Leningrada* (St. Petersburg: AGAT, 1998), unpaginated [8]. The guidebook did focus on local events and people. *Muzei oborony Leningrada* (Leningrad: Iskusstvo, 1948).

Committee in Moscow descended on the museum, and likewise judged it to be not only "distorted" but also "antiparty." The commission saw the museum's collection of artillery shells, mines, and other explosive devices – some of which had been brought to the museum directly from the front during the war and in fact remained operable – as the armory of the antiparty group led by Popkov, Kuznetsov, and Kapustin, whose portraits still hung in the galleries.[111]

The former directors of the museum, along with the museum itself, became victims of the Leningrad Affair. S. I. Abbakumov, who had headed the wartime precursor of the museum, and Lev Rakov, the museum's first director, were both arrested. In August 1949, Rakov was the head of the Public Library, a further taint, inasmuch as the party commission viewed the library as a nest of "enemy elements."[112] He was sentenced to twenty-five years. The museum was "temporarily" closed to visitors as its exhibits were reworked to better reflect Stalin's greatness. However, the new exhibits – including one devoted to Stalin's role in the 1919 Civil War defense of Petrograd – failed to pass muster. The USSR Council of Ministers transferred the museum's building to the Navy. In 1953, the museum was officially liquidated, and its collection – more than thirty-two thousand items including 123 dioramas and models, 131 maps, 6 airplanes, and a Panzer – scattered or destroyed.[113]

In postwar Leningrad, the Museum of the Defense of Leningrad had been the most prominent and, from the point of view of the party elite in Moscow, the most dangerous repository of the memory of the siege. It functioned at once as a museum, preserving a purportedly comprehensive and accurate account of the blockade, and as a memorial, "provoking empathy and insight through emotional identification."[114] Like

---

[111] Kutuzov, "Muzei," 25. *Muzei oborony* (1998), [8].

[112] Kutuzov, "Muzei," 25.

[113] *Muzei oborony* (1998), [10–12]. N. P. Dobrotvorskii and Iu. K. Khriashchev, "Relikvii oborony i blokady Leningrad," *Muzei Rossii,* vyp. 2 (1993): 10–11. V. P. Kivisepp and N. P. Dobrotvorskii, "Muzei muzhestva, skorbi i slavy," *Leningradskaia panorama,* 1991, no. 8: 24. Iu. B. Demidenko, *Muzei Sankt-Peterburga: Spravochnik* (St. Petersburg: Izdatel'stvo Bank Petrovskii, 1994), 122. Historians at the Leningrad branch of the Institute of History of the USSR Academy of Sciences were charged with, among other things, exaggerating the role of Petersburg–Leningrad in the nation's history. V. M. Paneiakh, "Uprazdnenie Leningadskogo otdeleniia Instituta istorii AN SSSR v 1953 godu," *Voprosy istorii,* 1993, no. 10: 21.

[114] Naomi Stead, "Memory and Museology," *Architecture Australia* 91 (January/February 2002), online version, no pagination. See also Sue Malvern, "War, Memory, and Museums: Art and Artefact in the Imperial War Museum," *History Workshop Journal,* no. 49 (Spring 2000): 179.

the warning signs that Leningraders passed everyday – and which were also eliminated – the museum turned artifacts into sites of memory and mourning.[115] Before its closure, the museum had been the second most popular museum in the city, behind only the Hermitage. By 1949, more that a million visitors had seen the exhibit – a number roughly equivalent to the city's postwar population.[116] Its closure underscores the degree to which the Leningrad Affair aimed not only to discipline local leaders but also to erase the memory and the myth of the blockade.

A small story from the Public Library provides a glimpse of how the general postwar tightening of the system and the local attack on memory insinuated itself into the lives and memories of Leningraders who survived the blockade. In September 1949, with the library's director under arrest, all employees were required to fill out a new questionnaire (*lichnyi listok*) for their files, even if they had filled one out just a few months before. In general, employees answered the familiar questions far more thoroughly than usual. Where previously a simple "da" or "net" would have been sufficient, they now answered in full sentences, leaving no blank empty. The questionnaire of Vera Karatygina, the leader of the library's Leningrad in the Great Fatherland War project, hints at unexpressed fears. Whereas on earlier questionnaires she had listed herself as "divorced," on a form dated 31 January 1949, she described herself as married to Mir Abramovich Tseitlin. On a more fully filled-out form, completed nine months later, the husband with the apparently Jewish name disappeared, and Karatygina once again described herself as "divorced in 1930." On earlier questionnaires and in autobiographies, she detailed her wartime work collecting and cataloging materials about the blockade; now she avoided any mention of the Leningrad in the Great Fatherland War project. She described her postwar work as consisting only of the organization of a catalog for party researchers and of the preparation of the "Petersburg–Leningrad" collection for the city's 250th anniversary in 1953. No member of the wartime brigade recorded current work on the collection in their personnel files.[117]

By 1950, the cityscape was visibly healed. Façades had been repaired, streets repaved, gardens replanted. Additional repairs and improvements of Nevskii Prospekt and new construction projects, notably Lenin Square,

---

[115] Jay Winter, *Sites of Memory, Sites of Mourning: The Great War in European Cultural History* (New York: Cambridge University Press, 1995).

[116] Dobrotvorskii and Khriashchev, "Relikvii," 10. Kutuzov, "Muzei," 23.

[117] Arkhiv Rossiiskoi Natsional'noi Biblioteki (hereafter Arkh. RNB), Karatygina lichnoe delo, f. 10/1 (1949), l. 40; Karatygina lichnoe delo, f. 10/1 (1966), l. 70b.

pointed to the realization of architects' dreams of making Leningrad more beautiful and monumental than it had been before the war. If these efforts won the support of locals who survived the blockade, the party's more aggressive efforts to extirpate the memory of the siege – purging wartime officials, shutting down the popular museum – likely did not. The state's power to control urban space effectively wiped out both the scars of war and local commemorations of it.

The Limits of Forgetting: The City Preserved in Memory

In the wake of the Leningrad Affair, the restoration of historic parks and buildings continued. By 1950, few signs of the blockade remained in the city. War cemeteries constituted an important, but geographically marginal, exception to the postwar reimposition of order.[118] However, while the party could close museums and eschew victory monuments and memorial cemeteries, it could never entirely control the city of memory. At home, Leningraders preserved domestic siege museums. And even on the repaired city streets, beneath the order, the wartime city could be felt, if not seen.

The reborn city continued not only to preserve the memory of the blockade but also to offer survivors a narrative framework – a map – for memory. Because the war in Leningrad occurred in familiar spaces that Leningraders knew before the war and continued to use after, the physical environment of the city became central to the sometimes unbidden recall of blockade memories and to the telling of blockade stories. Before the official crackdown, as the novelist and author Il'ia Erenburg, who visited Leningrad in 1946, noted, "Those who had lived through the blockade described its horrors for hours on end."[119] If they talked less freely four years later, they still might "hear" the stories they had told – and that they had read in the wartime press, heard on the radio, or seen in the museum – in the streets, squares, and courtyards that provided the settings for their memories.

The ability to see the wartime past beneath the postwar present sometimes proved essential for the task of healing the city, if not the self. In the winter of 1947, the crew called out to repair an underground power cable

---

[118] "Spravka o Piskarevskoem kladbishche v g. Leningrade" (9 October 1953), TsGA SPb, f. 7384, op. 37, d. 1197, l. 24. "Sekretariu Leningradskogo oblastnogo Komiteta KPSS" (20 November 1953), TsGA SPb, f. 7384, op. 37, d. 1197, l. 21.

[119] Erenburg, *Post-War Years*, 11.

near Suvorovskii Prospekt concluded that the problem stemmed from wartime damage in the area. As Granin, a member of the repair crew, later described the situation, "The rubble had been cleared away, any holes filled in, house façades repaired, and yet the shooting, shelling, and bombing still seemed to go on underground, and cables would suddenly be ripped apart in the depths of long-filled in, asphalted-over craters." Electric repairs required a detailed knowledge of the wartime history of the city – when and how a shell exploded, how and whether the cable had been previously repaired. But no one had a memory of this particular stretch of Ligovskaia Street.[120]

As his co-workers brooded over the location of the rupture, the "cold and gloom and the creaking snow stirred something" in Granin's memory. Slowly he pieced together the history of a day on leave from the front spent in blockaded Leningrad six years earlier:

By the Obvodnyi Canal I heard a slightly hoarse female voice, issuing forth from a black loudspeaker, a very special voice not to have been forgotten from that day on. That was Ol'ga Berggol'ts reading her poetry.... Later I found myself on Sadovaia Street, at the flat of Galia, an old school friend. Her rooms were full of snow. From there I had gone to Boria Abramov. The neighbors told me he had died. So then I had taken the food to Vadim's mother.... That was how I found myself near Suvorovskii Prospekt. That was how it had been, it was not in the least difficult to reconstruct that day from my memory: it had been the first time I had got leave to come to the city. The blockade had made Leningrad unrecognizable, so everything struck me and was firmly implanted on my memory.

Remembering the air raid and the Father Frost doll carried by the woman who took cover under the archway with him, Granin solved the puzzle of the power outage. He told the foreman, "A bomb fell here. It was toward the end of December."[121]

What is particularly striking about Granin's recollection is the degree to which his memory returned spontaneously, prompted only by the cold and the gloom and the crunching snow. His mental map of the wartime city remained linked to the city as it appeared after the war. Long-exploded bombs remained powerful beneath newly repaved streets and in the memories of Leningraders. Granin's story also underscores the intricate links between the public and the private city. His city of memory was a web of radio broadcasts, chance encounters, and apartments of dead friends.

---

[120] I have used the translation in Adamovich and Granin, *A Book of the Blockade*, 397. Adamovich and Granin, *Blokadnaia kniga*, 346–47.

[121] Second ellipses in original. I have used the translation in Adamovich and Granin, *Book of the Blockade*, 398–99. Adamovich and Granin, *Blokadnaia kniga*, 348.

The fact that war invaded familiar places in Leningrad helps to account for Leningraders' ability to "see" the prewar and wartime city as they walked postwar streets. For many, like Granin, the hometown made unfamiliar by war left an indelible impression. In her reminiscences, Avgusta Saraeva-Bondar', a teenager when the war began, described how, more than fifty years later, she still saw the traces of war in the people and places of her native city. Amid the festivity of the bazaar held before New Year's, she discerned fellow survivors of the blockade. Likewise, she saw the city's wounds beneath the holiday decorations. For Saraeva-Bondar', the "place near the Rossi Pavilion where the garden railing begins" remained the site of a "huge crater full of metal pipes that had been blown to bits," the spot where a massive bomb exploded just steps from the shelter where she and her mother had taken cover.[122] The elegant Rossi Pavilion – an architectural icon along Nevskii Prospekt – contained at once the living city and the powerful memory of its destruction.

Walking around the city with childhood companions in 1991, Grigorii Brailovskii similarly connected famous sites to his personal history and "saw" the city as it had been in 1941, on the eve of the war. He and three surviving friends visited sites connected to their memories of the war and of their comrades. They began at the enlistment office that constituted the start of their "long army road," the nineteenth-century Iusupov Palace, better known as the place the notorious Grigorii Rasputin was murdered in 1916. When the boyhood friends reached the courtyard where they had grown up, time and place lost their solidity, as the past completely overwhelmed the present: "The surrounding world disappears, an astonishing merging of time occurs, and everything looks to us at it did so many years ago."[123] In order to remember the friends who did not return from war, the three veterans visited the local landmarks that marked their prewar lives. When they reached their old home, the real city gave way entirely to the city of memory.

In Leningrad, the "restored" city was not always a forgetful city. The survivors' ability, or perhaps propensity, to see the city simultaneously as it is and as it was constitutes a vital point of reference in the examination of how Leningraders rebuilt their city after the war. After 1949, Leningraders lacked a public repository of artifacts and stories about the blockade. They lacked places to mourn the dead. But because memories were so closely

---

[122] I have used the translation in Simmons and Perlina, *Writing the Siege*, 142–43. See also R. Zubova, "'Pomnitsia eshche sil'nei,'" *Vechernii Leningrad*, 8 September 1987.

[123] Grigorii Brailovskii, "Minuty molchaniia," *Nevskoe vremia*, 22 June 1991.

associated with spaces that they continued to interact with and "see" – even if they had changed substantially – the erasure of memory was never complete.

The stories just recounted, dating to the early 1980s and early 1990s, suggest the importance of the city of memory in preserving stories, of the city itself as a kind of enormous and unmarked museum of the blockade. Even in the early 1990s, signs designating the sites of war damage remained relatively rare. However, if one knew where and how to look, the Rossi Pavilion, the Iusupov Palace, an unassuming intersection near Suvorovskii Prospekt all became artifacts with stories to tell. The stories remained compelling because they were linked to well-known places, to family and friends. When in the wake of Stalin's death it became possible once again to tell stories about and commemorate the blockade, these local and emotional connections remained important despite a dense overlay of stilted paeans to the party.

5

The Return of Stories from the City Front

The voice of memory sounds like a pledge and a promise.

– Andrei Siniavskii[1]

Kitsch is the aesthetic ideal of all politicians and all political parties and movements. . . . kitsch is a folding screen set up to curtain off death.

– Milan Kundera[2]

On 5 March 1953, Soviet radio broadcast a report that struck the novelist and journalist Il'ia Erenburg as inconceivable. More than ten years later he recalled, "We had long lost sight of the fact that Stalin was mortal. He had become an all-powerful and remote deity. And now the deity had died of a cerebral hemorrhage." The next day incredulity gave way to uncertainty, if not dread: "What would happen now?"[3] A month later, a previously unimaginable story was published in *Pravda;* "it was broadcast, it was said openly for all the world to hear."[4] Erenburg emphasized that an unprecedented revelation produced an incredible twist in the Doctors' Plot: The mostly Jewish doctors were released, and the investigator arrested. In the same month, April 1953, Erenburg began the novel whose title – *The*

---

[1] Andrei Siniavskii, "The Poetry and Prose of Olga Berggol'ts," in *For Freedom of Imagination,* trans. Laszlo Tikos and Murray Peppard (New York: Holt, Rinehart and Winston, 1971), 48.

[2] Milan Kundera, *The Unbearable Lightness of Being,* trans. Michael Henry Heim (New York: Harper and Row, 1984), 251, 253.

[3] Il'ia Erenburg, *Post-War Years, 1945–1954,* trans. Tatiana Shebunina (Cleveland: World Publishing, 1967), 301. Erenburg's fears for the future appear to have been shared by much of the population. See Elena Zubkova, *Russia After the War: Hopes, Illusions, and Disappointments, 1945–1957,* trans. Hugh Ragsdale (Armonk, NY: M. E. Sharpe, 1998), 151–54.

[4] Erenburg, *Post-War Years,* 320.

Thaw – became shorthand for the decade of political and cultural liberalization that followed Stalin's death. The state's new story encouraged
Erenburg to write a new story of his own, one that broached taboo subjects – notably Soviet anti-Semitism and the insincerity of Soviet art – and
thereby "caused a tremendous stir."[5]

For Erenburg, stories – the state's and his own – played a central role
in defining the thaw. Without minimizing the enormity of the political
and economic problems that Stalin bequeathed to his successors – the
Cold War, an agricultural crisis, shortages of consumer goods, overflow-
ing prison camps – historians have often followed Erenburg's lead and
adopted his terminology.[6] Critical junctures in the political cum cultural
struggle to come to terms with, if not overcome, Stalin's legacy included
Erenburg's *The Thaw*, the revelations of Nikita Khrushchev's secret speech
at the Twentieth Party Congress in 1956 and of his public speech at
the Twenty-second Congress in 1961, and the publication in 1962 of
Aleksandr Solzhenitsyn's novella of life in the camps, *One Day in the
Life of Ivan Denisovich*.

Khrushchev's decision – upheld by his successors – to lift Stalin's ban on
war stories that focused on something other than Stalin's military genius
constituted an essential and durable, if less-sensational, part of the de-
Stalinization process. In the years between Khrushchev's ouster in 1964
and the implementation of Mikhail Gorbachev's policy of glasnost, revelations of Stalin's crimes ceased. Nonetheless, the slow, fitful, and ultimately
incomplete recovery and revision of narratives of the war years continued. Throughout the 1970s, a swelling stream of stories about ordinary
Soviet citizens during the Great Fatherland War appeared in print. Indeed,
it was late in Leonid Brezhnev's tenure that the most remarkable and
unvarnished Soviet collection of stories of the blockade, Ales' Adamovich
and Daniil Granin's *A Book of the Blockade* (Blokadnaia kniga), was
published and promptly sold out.[7]

---

[5] George Gibian, "New Aspects of Soviet Russian Literature," in Stephen Cohen, Alexander Rabinowitch, and Robert Sharlet, eds., *The Soviet Union Since Stalin* (Bloomington:
Indiana University Press, 1980), 255. See also Katerina Clark, *The Soviet Novel: History
as Ritual* (Chicago: University of Chicago Press, 1985), 214.

[6] Nancy Condee, "Cultural Codes of the Thaw," in William Taubman, Sergei Khrushchev,
and Abbott Gleason, eds., *Nikita Khrushchev* (New Haven, CT: Yale University Press,
2000), 160, 161. On the problems faced by Stalin's successors, see William Taubman,
Khrushchev: The Man and his Era (New York: W. W. Norton, 2003), 241–44.

[7] Ales' Adamovich and Daniil Granin, *Blokadnaia kniga* (1979; revised, Moscow: Sovetskii
pisatel', 1982). It was published in English as Ales' Adamovich and Daniil Granin,
A Book of the Blockade, trans. Hilda Perham (Moscow: Raduga Publishers, 1983). On

Focusing increasingly on personal and detailed depictions of individual suffering and heroism, Soviet accounts of the war attempted to revive the regime's wartime legitimacy by exposing (or reexposing) Soviet citizens to the conditions in which it had emerged and to the language in which it had been framed.[8] Few of the reminiscences, interviews, and diaries of the blockade that were published during the Brezhnev years aimed at synthesis or analysis. As the state saw it, memoirs were not supposed to break new historical ground.[9] Instead, the flood of stories that accompanied the burgeoning cult of the war aimed to recreate the moment when, to return to Lidiia Ginzburg's image, it was possible to overhear "a real grandmother talking like a granny in the articles and stories."[10] As the historian Geoffrey Hosking argues, "even at the height of the war" the regime itself had done much to squander this "newfound national cohesion." Among the state's "serious mistakes" he counts the abandonment of prisoners of war, the mistrust and often imprisonment of citizens returning from German prisons or occupied territory, the wholesale deportations of minority ethnic groups from the Soviet borderlands, and Stalin's postwar prohibition of wartime memoirs.[11] The stories of the war cult sought to repair this last error by encouraging veterans and blokadniki to tell moving, personal, and tragic tales, and by positioning such war stories in an overarching narrative of the unity of the party and the people.

It is thus tempting – but, I would argue, ultimately inadvisable – to read the numerous stories from the city front that appeared in the 1960s and 1970s as a species of what the Czech dissident author Kundera called "totalitarian kitsch." Certainly the war stories of those years were rife with sentimental clichés and prepackaged emotions. With their formulaic

the difficulty of finding a copy in Leningrad, see Cynthia Simmons and Nina Perlina, eds., *Writing the Siege of Leningrad: Women's Diaries, Memoirs, and Documentary Prose* (Pittsburgh, PA: University of Pittsburgh Press, 2002), 174. Aleksandr Rubashkin, "O podvige i tragedii Leningrada (Razmyshleniia o 'blokadnoi' literature)," in Zakhar Dicharov, ed., *Golosa iz blokady: Leningradskie pisateli v osazhdennom gorode (1941–1944)* (St. Petersburg: Nauka, 1996), 424–28.

[8] Boris Gasparov, "On 'Notes from the Leningrad Blockade,'" *Canadian-American Slavic Studies* 28 (Summer–Fall 1994): 217. Jeffrey Brooks, *Thank You, Comrade Stalin! Soviet Public Culture from Revolution to Cold War* (Princeton, NJ: Princeton University Press, 2000), 243.

[9] A. R. Dzeniskevich, *Blokada i politika: Oborona Leningrada v politicheskoi kon"iunkture* (St. Petersburg: Nestor, 1998), 18. Catherine Merridale, *Night of Stone: Death and Memory in Twentieth-Century Russia* (New York: Viking, 2000), 273.

[10] Lidiia Ginzburg, *Blockade Diary*, trans. Alan Myers (London: Harvill Press, 1995), 56.

[11] Geoffrey Hosking, "The Second World War and Russian National Consciousness," *Past and Present*, no. 175 (May 2002): 179, 180–86.

paeans to the organizational role of the party and redemptive victory, the cult's stories seemed to banish doubt and irony. In the war cult, as in Kundera's totalitarian kitsch, "everything must be taken quite seriously."[12] Nonetheless, the war cult stories were as much a cultural product of the thaw as of the years of stagnation that followed. They often managed to communicate a sense, however attenuated, of unredemptive loss and of the irony of victory that is completely alien to Kundera's supreme example of communist kitsch, the May Day parade. As the literary historian Denis Kozlov has noted, "officially sanctioned" interest in the history of the war "offered a legitimate, fertile ground for postwar social contemplation and collective doubt."[13] A careful reading of state-sanctioned stories from the city front reveals that the deployment of the language – ubiquitous during the first years of the war – of the personal and the local worked not only to sentimentalize the memory of the siege but also potentially to subvert narratives that emphasized the role of the party over the experiences of individuals. Published reminiscences of the war can be read not only as hopelessly compromised totalitarian kitsch but as a "pledge and a promise," an incomplete return of the wartime "counternarrative" of self-directed Soviet citizens.[14]

The Thaw and the Memory of the War

The thaw was uneven and sporadic, but it nonetheless exposed vast stretches of the memoryscape that had long been covered in secrecy or silence.[15] Three periods of thaw – one precipitated by Stalin's death, the second by Khrushchev's secret speech, and the third by his public denunciation of Stalin in 1961 – were cut short by cold snaps marked by

---

[12] Kundera, *Unbearable Lightness,* 251–52. See also Merridale, *Night of Stone,* 251.

[13] Denis Kozlov, "The Historical Turn in Late Soviet Culture: Retrospectivism, Factography, Doubt, 1953–91," *Kritika: Explorations in Russian and Eurasian History* 2 (Summer 2001): 585. See also Susan Reid, "The 'Art of Memory': Retrospective Soviet Painting under Brezhnev," in Matthew Cullerne Bown and Brandon Taylor, eds., *Art of the Soviets: Painting, Sculpture and Architecture in a One-Party State, 1917–1992* (Manchester: Manchester University Press, 1993), 161–87; Denise Youngblood, "A War Remembered: Soviet Films of the Great Patriotic War," *American Historical Review* 106 (June 2001): 850–54.

[14] On the "counternarrative" see Chapter 3. I have borrowed the phrase from Jeffrey Brooks, "*Pravda* Goes to War," in Richard Stites, ed., *Culture and Entertainment in Wartime Russia* (Bloomington: Indiana University Press, 1995), 14.

[15] Lisa Yoneyama, "Taming the Memoryscape: Hiroshima's Urban Renewal," in Jonathan Boyarin, ed., *Remapping Memory: The Politics of TimeSpace* (Minneapolis: University of Minnesota Press, 1994), 99–134.

the still-jittery post-Stalinist leadership's crackdown on the journal *Novyi mir* in 1954, the Soviet invasion of Hungary in 1956, and Khrushchev's forced retirement in 1964.[16] Nonetheless, much that had been hidden was revealed, and the process of bringing the problems, even crimes, of the Stalinist past to light became a defining activity of the thaw. Among the works that charted new territory were Evgenii Evtushenko's 1961 poem "Babi Yar," which condemned the Soviet regime's failure to commemorate the Jewish victims of the Nazi massacre, and Solzhenitsyn's stunning *One Day in the Life of Ivan Denisovich*. Among the works that marked the shifting, erratic borders of disclosure stood Boris Pasternak's *Doctor Zhivago*, rejected by the censor and published abroad in 1957, and Vasilii Grossman's epic World War II novel *Life and Fate*. In 1961, Mikhail Suslov, one of the old Stalinists in the party leadership, told Grossman that the novel, which centered on the battle of Stalingrad and drew extended parallels between Stalinism and Nazism, covered ground so forbidden that it could not be published for two hundred years. It was published in the Soviet Union in 1988.[17]

The recovery project that defined the thaw also included the excavation of state-produced myths that had been obscured by the cult of personality. This process, too, entailed risk. The return of Lenin's cult and the nascent cult of the war can be understood as efforts on the part of the leadership to balance what they (correctly) viewed as potentially dangerous disclosures of Stalin's crimes with legitimizing and optimistic tales of Lenin's revolutionary rectitude and of the heroism of the Soviet people during the Great Fatherland War. The celebration of past victories was supposed to limit the damage caused by revelations of terror and to signal a return to the true and idealistic path.[18] Yet war narratives also provided, however unintentionally, the raw materials for imagining a transformation of the post-Stalin state more profound than the leadership was prepared – or able – to grant.

---

16 In some cultural fields, notably theater and architecture, the thaw lasted beyond Khrushchev's ouster. Condee, "Cultural Codes," 162. Stephen V. Bittner, "Remembering the Avant-Garde: Moscow Architects and the 'Rehabilitation' of Constructivism, 1961–1964," *Kritika: Explorations in Russian and Eurasian History* 2 (Summer 2001): 575.

17 Condee, "Cultural Codes," 160–61. Nina Tumarkin, *The Living and the Dead: The Rise and Fall of the Cult of World War II in Russia* (New York: Basic Books, 1994), 113–17, 119–24. "Babi Yar" appeared in *Literaturnaia gazeta*, 19 September 1961. Taubman, *Khrushchev*, 525–28. Robert Chandler, "Translator's Introduction," in Vasilii Grossman, *Life and Fate* (London: Harvill Press, 1985), 9.

18 Hosking, "Russian National Consciousness," 187.

Almost immediately after Stalin's death, the war emerged in literary discussions as a compelling model of a freer future. In mid-April 1953, just over a month after Stalin's funeral, *Literaturnaia gazeta* published Ol'ga Berggol'ts's passionate appeal for a poetry of individuality, sincerity, intimacy, and love. Like other cultural productions of the early post-Stalin period – notably Erenburg's "On the Work of the Writer," Vladimir Pomerantsev's article "On Sincerity in Literature," and Vera Inber's attack on the "same old steam shovel, same old dam" school of poetry – Berggol'ts's essay raised crucial questions of self-expression and truthfulness in literature.[19] What is particularly striking about her article, and a second one in 1954 that responded to her critics, is Berggol'ts's use of wartime literature as evidence that emotionally honest Soviet art was both possible and necessary.

Berggol'ts built her argument on the (arguably flawed) premise that truth and self-expression, far from undermining the Soviet system, constituted essential elements of that system. She began her discussion of lyric poetry with the assertion that "one of the fundamental and powerful characteristics of lyric poetry is that its hero is the poet himself, an individual [*lichnost'*] speaking of himself and from himself, from his own 'I.' At the same time, the hero of the lyric work is the reader, who pronounces this 'I' as his own, personal, individual [*sobstvennoe, svoe, lichnoe*] 'I.'" To illustrate her point, Berggol'ts asked, "When soldiers in wartime sing, 'I want you to hear how my living voice yearns,' have they really cited [Aleksei] Surkov? No... with the words of the poet they expressed their own, deeply individual condition, which is at the same time typical of the great majority of people." Her article called for verses that, like the best poetry of the war years, "more fully and sincerely [*iskrenne*] express the reader's intimate and multifaceted feelings, thoughts, and aspirations."[20]

---

[19] George Gibian, *Interval of Freedom: Soviet Literature during the Thaw, 1954–1957* (Minneapolis: University of Minnesota Press, 1960), 6–7. V. Pomerantsev, "Ob iskrennosti v literature," *Novyi mir*, 1953, no. 12: 218–45. Erenburg, "O rabote pisatelia," *Sobranie sochinenii v deviati tomakh* (Moscow: Izdatel'stvo "khudozhesvennaia literatura," 1965), 6: 555–87. Originally published in *Znamia*, 1953, no. 10. Vera Inber, "Pomagat' poetam (Za masterstvo literaturnoi kritiki: Vsesoiuznoe soveshchanie molodykh kritikov)," *Literaturnaia gazeta*, 3 October 1953. Zubkova, *Russia After the War*, 156–58. Condee, "Cultural Codes," 160.

[20] Ol'ga Berggol'ts, "Razgovor o lirike," in *Sobranie sochinenii v trekh tomakh* (Leningrad: Khudozhestvennaia literatura, 1989), 2: 367, 369, 377. Surkov's poem "Zemlianka" was a popular wartime song, with music by K. Listov. See also Richard Stites, *Russian Popular Culture: Entertainment and Society since 1990* (Cambridge: Cambridge University Press, 1992), 99–100.

With its insistence on the urgency and virtue of the individual, personal voice, Berggol'ts's article brought down the wrath of poets and critics committed to the orthodoxies of socialist realism.[21] In answering her critics, Berggol'ts proposed a return to wartime norms of life and literature. She reiterated her claim that rather than simply reflecting reality, the "Soviet poet" was "obliged to express the historical moment of Soviet society through himself, as his own personal, individual experience and feeling."[22] The war, she argued, had in fact produced the sort of poetry she advocated. "Where," she asked rhetorically, "do our critics get their incomprehensible mistrust of the personality [*lichnosti*] of the Soviet poet and person? On what basis do they suppose that as soon as he opens his heart there will be an outpouring of neurasthenia, weakness, crackups – a feast of personal inadequacies and mistakes? Don't the best examples of Soviet poetry, particularly the poetry from the period of the Great Fatherland War, speak against this?"[23] She noted that while her critics praised some of her poetry, particularly her blockade poetry, they utterly misunderstood it, failing to "'notice' that all of my lyric poetry . . . and especially the Leningrad, the blockade, lyric poetry – relies on the principle of maximum self-exposure and self-expression even more than faithfulness to the facts of daily life during the blockade."[24] Without mentioning the dead leader's name, Berggol'ts suggested that the war revealed the sincere and deeply felt idealism that Stalin had distrusted – even distorted – but not destroyed.

When two years later Khrushchev decided to name names and expose some of Stalin's crimes, he deployed a similar strategy, contrasting the sincerity and heroism of the Soviet people during the war with the capricious brutality of their leader.[25] In the speech, Khrushchev recovered two distinct but interrelated sets of stories: revelations of Stalin's growing contempt for "Leninist" norms of "socialist legality" and reminders that the people and the party shared credit for the Soviet victory in the Great Fatherland War. Uncovering both the secrets of Stalin's crimes and the wartime narrative that had been silenced by Stalin, Khrushchev attempted to distance himself from his erstwhile boss and to unearth a usable past.

---

[21] B. Solov'ev, "Poeziia i pravda," *Zvezda*, 1954, no. 3: 154–64. I. Grinberg, "Oruzhie liriki," *Znamia*, 1954, no. 8: 171, 179–80. N. Gribachev and S. Smirnov, "'Violonchelist' poluchil kanifol' . . . ," *Literaturnaia gazeta*, 21 October 1954.
[22] Ol'ga Berggol'ts, "Protiv likvidatsii liriki," in *Sobranie*, 2: 386.
[23] Ibid., 2: 387.
[24] Ibid.
[25] Taubman, *Khrushchev*, 283–84.

Khrushchev himself recognized the dangers of the first set of stories. He noted in his speech that "the question arises: Why is it that we see the truth of this [Leningrad] affair only now, and why did we not do something earlier?" Khrushchev's answer was that "the majority of the Political Bureau members" simply did not know and therefore could not intervene.[26] Rank-and-file party members who learned about the speech via special lectures found such explanations unconvincing. Audiences posed pointed questions: "What has our state been over the course of almost thirty years: a democratic republic or a totalitarian state? ... Doesn't single-party status and the almost complete overlap of government and Party organs facilitate the personality cult?"[27]

Khrushchev took the risk of incriminating both himself and the system because he viewed selective revelations of Stalin's crimes as a means of purifying the political landscape, of quieting the ghosts of the terror.[28] He imagined the process that Erenburg had dubbed a "thaw" as a "downpour" that "washed away all the extraneous matter. . . . People felt freshened up, and found that it had become easier to breathe, fight, and create."[29] After the rains, the "extraneous matter" would presumably be forgotten, or at least fall out of public conversation.

The desire to replace secrets with silence was particularly clear in the case of the most dramatic "discoveries" of the Khrushchev years, wrongfully executed old Bolsheviks and the gulag archipelago. Khrushchev blamed Stalin's deficiencies for the terror. Offering no overall statistics or overarching systemic analysis, Khrushchev's 1956 speech consisted of a series of vignettes that graphically illustrated Stalin's willingness to torture the innocent and condemn them to death. As prisoners returned, the state permitted a circumscribed public discussion of the Soviet Union's most hidden places. No shared framework existed for these stories, and the state had little interest in supplying one.[30] Promises of a monument

[26] "Khrushchev's Secret Speech," in Strobe Talbott, ed. and trans., *Khrushchev Remembers* (Boston: Little, Brown, 1970), 598.

[27] Cited in Iurii Aksiutin, "Popular Responses to Khrushchev," in Taubman, Khrushchev, and Gleason, *Nikita Khrushchev*, 186, ellipses in original.

[28] In his memoirs, Khrushchev stated, "In order to prevent the ghosts of those years from coming back from their graves to haunt us, we have no choice but to rehabilitate *all* of Stalin's victims." Khrushchev, *Khrushchev Remembers*, 7, emphasis in original.

[29] Cited in Nancy Condee, "Cultural Codes of the Thaw," 174.

[30] Catherine Merridale, "War, Death, and Remembrance in Soviet Russia," in Jay Winter and Emmanuel Sivan, eds., *War and Remembrance in the Twentieth Century* (Cambridge: Cambridge University Press, 1999), 75. Nanci Adler, "Life in the 'Big Zone': The Fate

to Stalin's victims came to nothing. The leadership permitted the limited publication of stories of the terror and the camps not as a means of commemorating the victims but as a means of giving the past a proper burial.[31]

"Washing away" the excrescences of the Stalin cult allowed Khrushchev to recover the pure memory of Lenin's leadership. In his secret speech of 1956 and in his public speech to the Twenty-second Party Congress in 1961, Khrushchev pledged a return to Leninist ideals. Grounding his argument in the "classics of Marxism-Leninism," Khrushchev spent far less time explicating theory than telling stories that showed Stalin to be a poor imitation of Lenin. Whereas Lenin "called for the most meticulous observance of all norms of Party life," Stalin was rude and in general "acted not through persuasion, explanation, and patient cooperation with people" – a presumptively Leninist approach – "but by ... demanding absolute submission."[32] The denunciation of Stalin had some clear limits. Khrushchev drew a bright line in 1934, before which time stood the "necessary" defeat of the "right deviation" and what he continued to regard as the achievements of collectivization and industrialization.[33] Still, the rehabilitation of the Lenin cult – and Stalin's 1961 eviction from the mausoleum – promised a return to a system of legality that had allegedly operated before the long Stalinist winter.

In the case of the Great Fatherland War, Khrushchev at once attacked Stalin's war record and magnified the myth of the war, recovering the wartime narrative of a people's war that had been concealed beneath the Stalinist cult of personality. In his secret speech, Khrushchev both debunked and mocked the notion of Stalin's "military genius" that since 1943 had shaped histories, films, and journalistic accounts of the war. Khrushchev emphasized the devastating effects of the prewar purge of the Red Army, Stalin's repeated failures to heed credible warnings of the German attack, and the deadly results of the generalissimo's amateurish approach to military strategy. "Yes, comrades," Khrushchev told his stunned audience, "he used to take the globe and trace the frontline on

---

of Returnees in the Aftermath of Stalinist Repression," *Europe-Asia Studies* 51 (January 1999): 5–19.

[31] Khrushchev called for a monument to Stalin's victims in his speech at the Twenty-second Party Congress. Zubkova, *Russia After the War*, 169. Taubman, *Khrushchev*, 275–78, 514–15, 525–28.

[32] "Khrushchev's Secret Speech," 559–60, 570, 562, 564.

[33] Ibid., 565. Erenburg, *Post-War Years*, 321.

it."[34] Having dethroned Stalin, Khrushchev was able to recuperate the stories of individual initiative and bravery – as opposed to Stalin's or even the party's genius – that had dominated Soviet propaganda in the first years of the war.[35]

The tension between Khrushchev's effort to put the party first and his populism constituted a central feature of the emerging war cult.[36] Promising a return of the wartime sense of shared purpose, the recovered narrative served to legitimize the new leadership. Among many who lived through the war, the recovered narrative also kindled hopes of a return of the freedom and sense of real citizenship that they associated with the war's first years. Writing at the end of the thaw, Solomon Ezerskii, who had worked for *Leningradskaia pravda* during the war, recalled that at the bleakest moment of the blockade, in November 1941, "I wrote, without following the canons or models. I wrote what I thought.... I understood that in such circumstances, the most important thing is to speak the truth."[37] The hopes born of such memories found some concrete realization in the state's tolerance of somewhat greater freedom of expression and in Khrushchev's idealistic – if ultimately quixotic – efforts to fulfill the promises of the Revolution. Schemes such as the so-called Virgin Lands program that opened new agricultural lands in central Asia generated real enthusiasm, if generally meager results.[38] In the long run, however, the attempt to conjure wartime feelings that "were in practice unrecoverable" worked against the credibility and legitimacy of Stalin's heirs.[39] Like Khrushchev's overly optimistic 1961 prediction that "a Communist society will be just about built by 1980," the recovery of the memory of the people's war raised expectations that the Soviet system could not meet.[40]

---

[34] "Khrushchev's Secret Speech," 593. Khrushchev singled out Mikhail Chiureli's 1949 film *The Fall of Berlin* (Padenie Berlina), which Youngblood describes as "a panegyric, not a war movie." Youngblood, "A War Remembered," 844.

[35] "Khrushchev's Secret Speech," 595.

[36] Tumarkin argues that despite its "populist statement" the speech made it clear that "the Party comes first." Tumarkin, *The Living and the Dead*, 109.

[37] S. Ezerskii, "Cherez dvadtsat' let," in Soiuz zhurnalistov SSSR, Leningradskoe otdelenie, *S perom i avtomatom: Pisateli i zhurnalisty Leningrada v gody blokady* (Leningrad: Lenizdat, 1964), 526. Hosking, "Russian National Consciousness," 178.

[38] Stites, *Russian Popular Culture*, 144–45. Taubman, *Khrushchev*, 262–63. James R. Millar, "Post-Stalin Agriculture and Its Future," in Cohen et al., eds., *The Soviet Union since Stalin*, 135–54. Michaela Pohl, "The Virgin Lands Between Memory and Forgetting" (Ph.D. diss., Indiana University, 1999).

[39] Brooks, *Thank You*, 240.

[40] Taubman, *Khrushchev*, 507–13.

The Rehabilitation of Leningrad

On 30 April 1954, the Supreme Court of the Soviet Union rehabilitated all those who had been "repressed" as a result of the Leningrad Affair.[41] However, the virtual ban on stories about the blockade persisted.[42] In the wake of Khrushchev's secret speech, an article on the Leningrad party organization's wartime work appeared in the professional journal *Voprosy istorii.* The following year, the local party's celebration of the city's 250th anniversary largely ignored the blockade. Still, the fact that the party bothered to mark the anniversary at all – the actual anniversary had passed in 1953 without pomp or pageantry – signaled at least a tentative rehabilitation of the city's history. The belated commemoration opened the way to reminiscences that elaborated the "Leningrad theme" and also to the republication of wartime poetry and prose. While the 1957 anniversary produced histories that emphasized the central role of the party, it also permitted a public resurgence not only of individual memories of the blockade but also of the local identities that had been so important during the blockade itself.

Published just months after Khrushchev's secret speech, historian F. I. Sirota's account of the "military-organizational work" of Leningrad Communists elaborated the speech's distinction between Stalin's costly mistakes and the selfless and efficient work of the party. Sirota inverted the cult of Stalin's military genius, blaming Stalin alone for the late, poorly planned, and insufficient deployment of troops, tanks, armored vehicles, and artillery along the Leningrad front.[43] In sharp contrast to his assessment of Stalin, Sirota concluded that "the soul of the heroic defense of Leningrad was the party organization." Asserting that local party and Soviet leaders "inspired Leningraders," Sirota praised the organizational work of a number of the most prominent victims of the Leningrad Affair. He emphasized that many of the hastily trained home guards

---

[41] V. A. Kutuzov, "Tak nazyvaemoe 'Leningradskoe delo,'" *Voprosy istorii KPSS,* 1989, no. 3: 64.

[42] Dzeniskevich, *Blokada i politika,* 12–14.

[43] F. I. Sirota, "Voenno-organizatorskaia rabota leningradskoi organizatsii VKP(b) v pervyi period Velikoi Otechestvennoi voiny," *Voprosy istorii,* 1956, no. 10: 10, 16–17. On Stalin's role in the early defeats see David M. Glantz, *The Siege of Leningrad 1941–1944: 900 Days of Terror* (Osceola, WI: MBI Publishing, 2001), 18–30; Mark von Hagen, "Soviet Soldiers and Officers on the Eve of the German Invasion: Toward a Description of Social Psychology and Political Attitudes," in Robert W. Thurston and Bernd Bonwetsch, eds., *The People's War: Responses to World War II in the Soviet Union* (Urbana: University of Illinois Press, 2000), 191.

(*opolchentsy*) who gave their lives to stop the German advance were Communists. In blockaded Leningrad, the party, according to Sirota, effectively orchestrated everything from the training of firefighters to the construction of the Road of Life across Lake Ladoga. Describing party achievements in great detail, he glossed over the conditions faced by civilians. While he omitted any reference to the overall number of people who died in the city, Sirota did mention that "17,000 Communists died as a result of air raids, shelling, and starvation." Thus, the party seemed to have provided both the active heroes and the innocent victims on the city front.[44]

In the interstices of this overwhelmingly party-minded account of the blockade, traces of the wartime emphasis on personal motivations and local identities remained visible. The article's quotation from a letter written by old hands at the Kirov Factory to their young comrades departing for the front – a typical production of the wartime propaganda machine – recovered a moment in which neither Stalin nor the party constituted central concerns. "Be steadfast and brave in battle," advised the older workers. "Add to the glorious traditions of Peter's workers, be worthy sons of the great city of Lenin!" In the context of Sirota's article, the letter, which appeared in the newspaper of the Leningrad home guard, stands out as the sole attempt to hear the voices, however filtered, of the Leningraders supposedly inspired by the party. Yet the wartime letter appealed not to the example of the party but to emotional ties to local places and traditions. Moreover, with its use of the city's familiar nickname, "Peter," and its tone of fatherly advice, the letter created an aura of sincerity unmatched by Sirota's claim that "the Party organization was the organizer and inspirer of the defense of Leningrad."[45] Here, two official narratives appeared to work against each other.

While historians attempted to fit a retrieved wartime narrative that emphasized local, personal motives into a story of the party's leading role, survivors – who published their own reminiscences of the city, as well as collections of wartime poetry, fiction, diaries, posters, and engravings – worked to recover the memory of the individual struggles of the war years. In juxtaposing the construction of history and the recovery of memory in this way, I am not suggesting that the memories were necessarily more authentic than histories. After all, the personal – often first-person – accounts of the blockade published during the thaw were also

---

[44] Sirota, "Voenno-organizatorskaia," 18, 20, 24–28, 29, 31.
[45] Ibid., 31.

state sanctioned. They too had to clear the censor. Indeed, because so many of the first-person accounts published during the thaw had been written during the war, they often minimized or ignored the evidence of catastrophic Soviet defeats later uncovered by the historians and duly blamed on Stalin.

However, the juxtaposition of history and memory does illuminate the competing impulses that structured the development of the war cult. On the one hand, the war cult, as it emerged during the thaw, aimed to enshrine an official history of the war that recast Stalin's victories as the party's.[46] On the other hand, it sought to reignite the spirit of the war years. Here, ideological correctness was sometimes sacrificed to the cause of recovering the wartime feelings of shared purpose, local loyalty, and love for the *rodina* – native place – in its broadest and narrowest senses. Works such as the issue of the journal *Moskva* devoted to Leningrad's anniversary; *900 Days* (1957), a collection of wartime writing and visual material edited by Berggol'ts, among others; and the republication of her own collection of wartime radio broadcasts, *Govorit Leningrad* (Leningrad Calling, 1946, reprinted 1961), demonstrated a clear interest in subjective, personal, individual blockade stories on the part of survivors and, more surprisingly, the state.[47] Even as it endorsed party-centric histories of the blockade, the state supported the telling of small, personal stories in which the party played a subordinate, if not minimal, role.

In the case of Leningrad, recapturing the spirit of the war years required the rehabilitation of the spirit of the city – not only of "the great city of Lenin" but of the more intimate city nicknamed Peter. That the reemergence of blockade stories came in conjunction with the celebration of the city's 250th anniversary was completely appropriate. Not only was the blockade a significant moment in the city's history but also, as the Leningrad authors who contributed reminiscences to the June 1957 issue of the journal *Moskva* made clear, the resilience of the city during the blockade was often understood as inseparable from its history, from its

---

[46] For a list of the "very few" books on the blockaded city – as opposed to the battle for Leningrad – published between 1959 and 1965, see Dzeniskevich, *Blokada i politika*, 15. Other works include B. G. Malkin, "Agitatsionno-propagandistskaia rabota leningradskoi organizatsii KPSS v period oborony goroda (dekabr' 1941-mart 1942 gg.)," *Vestnik Leningradskogo Universiteta: Seriia istorii, iazyka i literatury*, 1964, vyp. 1, no. 2: 8–28; V. V. Stremilov, "Leningradskaia partiinaia organizatsii v period blokady goroda (1941–1943)," *Voprosy istorii KPSS*, 1959, no. 5: 101–21; B. V. Bychevskii, *Gorod-front* (Moscow: Voennoe izdatel'stvo, 1963).

[47] Ol'ga Berggol'ts, *Govorit Leningrad*, in *Stikhi-proza* (Moscow-Leningrad: Gosudarstvennoe izdatel'stvo khudozhestvennoi literatury, 1961).

literary doubles, and from the powerful effects of its places and mystique on its inhabitants. In other words, the contributors presented their memories of the city, and of the blockade in particular, as manifestations of the Petersburg–Leningrad theme, which along with the memory of the blockade had come under attack after the war.

Leonid Rakhmanov explicitly adopted the framework of the Petersburg theme, taking as his point of departure Nikolai Antsiferov's *Soul of Petersburg* (1922), a veritable encyclopedia of literary representations of St. Petersburg.[48] After briefly summarizing nineteenth-century authors' hostility to cold, unrelenting, phantasmagoric Petersburg, Rakhmanov moved from art to life. He proposed that the inhabitants' newfound love for their city stemmed from the fact that the "the world's first socialist revolution was carried out and triumphed in it" – an assertion somewhat tempered by his conclusion that the blockade, beside which "all of the calamities foretold by prophets and poets" paled, further strengthened Leningraders' love for their city.[49]

Rakhmanov set his own blockade memory in the context of the whole of the city's architectural and literary legacy. Remembering a moment that brought him to tears, he emphasized the connections between his emotional responses and the staginess of the city's spaces, their ability to blur the line between life and art, that constituted central elements of the Petersburg theme:

> I remember how, in the worst days of the Leningrad blockade, in January 1942, in the hall of the Academic [or Glinka] Capella near the Pevcheskii Bridge (one of the most beautiful places in Leningrad – behind Palace Square, cattycorner from the Winter Palace) there was a "Literary-artistic matinée."...Outside it was freezing and sunny. In the hall it was also freezing, but the beautiful velvet of the chairs and draperies seemed to partially soften the cold. Both the audience and the participants were dressed in fur coats, in overcoats, in quilted jackets – they guarded every drop of warmth – and I unwittingly recalled how many years earlier, on this same stage, Maiakovskii, when he got hot, spontaneously took off his jacket and hung it on the back of a chair.[50]

Here, literary history, architectural history, and personal memory merged. Both inside and out, the concert hall emerged as a distinctly Petersburg place. The memory of the poet Vladimir Maiakovskii's gesture stood at once a counterpoint to the cold of the blockade and an affirmation that

---

[48] Nikolai Antsiferov, *Dusha Peterburga* (1922; reprint, Paris: YMCA Press, 1978).
[49] Leonid Rakhmanov, "Dusha goroda," *Moskva*, 1957, no. 6: 26.
[50] Ibid., 27.

blockade artists – the author among them – bravely carried on the city's literary traditions.

The portion of the morning's program that moved Rakhmanov was a presentation by Lev Il'in, the chief architect of the city. The professor, visibly weakened by malnutrition, described his walk across the city to the concert. He named streets and buildings that he admired and repeated slogans that appeared in the newspapers: "The enemy will not pass, our city is immortal." Rakhmanov found it "hard to hold back the tears." These were "tears not of pain, not of pity, but of rapture." He realized that "if there were people who, in these terrible conditions of the blockade – of cold and hunger – could still feel the beauty of Leningrad so strongly, then the city and its inhabitants really are immortal."[51] The memory thus linked the blockade to the city's spirit, a force which, Rakhmanov was sure, would turn postwar immigrants into "immortal" Leningraders.

Likewise focusing on the connections between the history of the city and the lives of its inhabitants, Vera Ketlinskaia suggested that such connections were both highly idiosyncratic and deeply personal. Entitling her reminiscences "My Leningrad," she began with the question of whether it was possible to claim the city as one's own. She decided it was appropriate to attach the first-person possessive pronoun to Leningrad because "love is always individual. Even when 200 million love, each of the 200 million loves in his own way. And sees in his own way."[52] For her, the city was an early morning tram ride in spring; a snowy evening on which she joined tens of thousands who marched on Palace Square to protest some now-forgotten capitalist ultimatum; the white nights, when "everyone walks and walks along the embankments."[53] Ketlinskaia represented the remembered Leningrad of her youth as a city defined by individual moments in public spaces.

Such small stories of the big city ended abruptly when Ketlinskaia's narrative reached the blockade. She did not see – or did not want to see – the blockade in her own way. Abandoning "my Leningrad" for what might be called "our Leningrad," Ketlinskaia intoned, "The true Leningrader is the true Soviet person." Rather than a personal memory from the blockade,

---

[51] Ibid. Il'in was sixty-two, and was by this time dangerously malnourished. He died in December 1942 in an artillery attack. E. P. Busyreva and O. A. Chkanova, "Lev Il'in," in V. G. Isachenko, ed., *Zodchie Sankt-Peterburga XX vek* (St. Petersburg: Lenizdat, 2000), 215–17. See also Ol'ga Forsh, "Vchera i segodnia," *Moskva*, 1957, no. 6: 17, and L. Panteleev, "V dni osady (Iz zapisnoi knizhki)," ibid., 21.

[52] Vera Ketlinskaia, "Moi Leningrad," *Moskva*, 1957, no. 6: 8.

[53] Ibid., 11, 12.

Ketlinskaia, who spent the entire war in Leningrad, offered a ritualized litany of horrors and a parade of slogans: "Starvation, frost, bombs, mortar fire, no water, no light, no fuel – all the same, we did not surrender, we stood our ground, we emerged victorious!" In her account, "collective victories" cut personal stories short.[54] Nonetheless, the article's explicit rejection of any distinction between the true Leningrader and the true Soviet person coexisted with richly detailed reminiscences of Ketlinskaia's youth, which pictured the true Leningrader as connected to a beloved local landscape defined by both personal and world-historical events.

Emphasizing the uniqueness of Leningrad's wartime experiences, a uniqueness connected to Petersburg–Leningrad's status as at once symbol and city, the reminiscences collected in *Moskva* echoed a central theme of wartime writing on Leningrad. Moreover, as in wartime writing, the focus on the spirit of the city tended to relegate the party to the margins. Even the October Revolution became a decidedly local and personal event. Nikolai Nikitin's eyewitness account of Lenin's arrival at the Finland Station in 1917 mixed nostalgia for his own revolutionary youth with a detailed travelogue of Lenin's route through the city.[55]

A nearly six hundred–page compilation of mainly wartime works about the blockade published in early 1957 emphasized another central theme of wartime writing: the ordinary people – workers, soldiers, housewives, writers, teenagers – who achieved victory. Here, too, the party played little role in the story of the blockade. For their part, the editors of *900 Days* made clear that the "Leningrad epic" was "one of the most vivid, heroic, and tragic pages of the peoples' struggle [*bor'by narodov*] against fascism." In one of the few contributions told from the point of view of a party activist, Elizaveta Sharypina emphasized less the organizational prowess of the party than the importance of the surrogate maternal care spontaneously provided by female cadres during the blockade. She herself took in a Ukrainian boy abandoned by his relatives.[56] Her maternal instincts seemed to matter more than her party card.

The editors of *900 Days* collected works demonstrating the paradox that during the war, ordinary citizens concerned about love, family,

[54] Ibid., 13.

[55] Nikolai Nikitin, "Nasha slava," *Moskva*, 1957, no. 6: 5–6.

[56] O. F. Berggol'ts, V. N. Druzhinin, A. L. Dymshits, A. G. Rosen, and N. S. Tikhonov, eds., *900 dnei* (Leningrad: Lenizdat, 1957), 3. Elizaveta Sharypina, "Za zhizn' i pobedu: Iz zapisok politorganizatora," in ibid., 155–68. "Pis'mo M. G. Andreeva," in ibid., 218. See also Elizaveta Sharypina, *V dni blokady: Zapiski politorganizatora* (Leningrad: Detgiz, 1960).

hometown, and hearth – the domestic, personal world seemingly outside of history – made history. Nearly all the contributions to the collection emphasized the importance of familial or quasi-familial ties. The first section, "Leningrad Accepts Battle," included Ketlinskaia's story "With All Her Heart," in which a grandmother reconciled herself to her teenage grandson's enlistment when "she recognized her own son [who had died in the war against Finland] in this boy," his son. Here, the war became more family drama than national emergency. Numerous authors emphasized that particularly during the most difficult days of the blockade, Leningraders became, in the words of schoolgirl Z. Vorozheikina, a "single family."[57] As in the wartime "counternarrative," the motives and the concerns of the Leningraders represented in *900 Days* were overwhelmingly local and familial.

The editors themselves suggested why the state tolerated the collection's decidedly nonparty perspective, so at odds with the histories being produced at the same time. Predicting that the collection would allow readers "to imagine the character of those events," the editors presented it as an important "contribution to the communist upbringing of a new generation of Soviet people."[58] Personal, accessible stories, the editors assumed, would transmit the feeling of the war years to those who did not live through them. Showing young people all that their elders had suffered and accomplished promised a means of inculcating Soviet patriotism.

However, the stories included in the collection also suggested the possibility of uncoupling respect for the heroic defenders from devotion to the system that they ostensibly had defended. In what could be read as a criticism of contemporary histories of the blockade, the editors proposed that their work would prove a useful source for "the creation of a future monumental History of the Great Fatherland War."[59] The monument they imagined was to the people, not the party. Moreover, the collection conveyed nostalgia for a time when people acted on their own initiative and "the rules aren't always taken into consideration."[60]

The editors concluded their collection with a wartime essay by Erenburg that expressed thinly veiled hopes for a postwar liberalization of the system. Invoking the Decembrists – the young officers who returned

---

[57] Vera Ketlinskaia, "Vsem serdtsem," in Berggol'ts et al., *900 dnei.*, 48–52. Z. Vorozheikina, "Stranitsa iz dnevnika," in ibid., 258. See also ibid., 11, 90, 126, 145–53, 175–80.

[58] Ibid., 3, 4. See also Ezerskii, "Cherez," 521–23.

[59] Berggol'ts et al., *900 dnei*, 4.

[60] K. Zolotovskii, "Kogda vspykhnul svet...: Zapiski vodolaza," in ibid., 198–99.

from Paris with dreams of liberty after defeating Napoleon in the first Fatherland War – Erenburg suggested that victory in the Great Fatherland War would fulfill their dreams. He structured his essay "The Eternal City" around an exploration of the parallels between Europe's two "beautiful cities" – Paris and Leningrad – and concluded: "We have become the heart of Europe, the bearers of its traditions, the successors of its daring, its builders and poets. And the wind from the sea, full of salt and courage, reminds us of the great voyage, of the great responsibility of every Soviet citizen."[61]

Significantly, Erenburg, who was not a Leningrader, chose Leningrad as the site for these musings. He described himself standing on the Strelka at night, gazing out over the sea through Russia's historic "window on Europe," contemplating "the fate of our Motherland." It was expectations of the sort Erenburg outlined in his essay – specifically the hint that returning soldiers might become neo-Decembrists and the insistence on Leningrad's special, European-oriented role – that had fed Stalin's postwar crackdown on both imagined enemies and the memory of the blockade.[62] The essay underscored the disjunction between the war years, when Soviet citizens demonstrated their "great responsibility" – their ability to act without the guidance of a superior authority – and the postwar distrust, to paraphrase Berggol'ts, of the Soviet poet and person.

Ironic Complications: The Normalcy of War

Paul Fussell, a scholar of the First World War and a veteran of the Second, has noted that "everyone who remembers a war first-hand knows that its image remains in the memory with special vividness. The very enormity of the proceedings, their absurd remove from the usages of the normal world, will guarantee that a structure of irony sufficient for ready narrative recall will attach to them." The war in Leningrad had plenty of the irony, both "gentle" and "extravagant," that Fussell regards as essential to the process of turning wartime experiences into indelible memories or – what amounts to essentially the same thing – memorable narratives. The contrast that World War I soldiers encountered marching from front-line

---

[61] Il'ia Erenburg, "Vechnyi gorod," in ibid., 592.
[62] On concerns about neo-Decembrists, see Zubkova, *Russia After the War*, 24; E. S. Seniavskaia, *Frontovoe pokolenie, 1941–1945: Istoriko-psikhologicheskoe issledovanie* (Moscow: Institut rossiiskoi istorii RAN, 1995), 91–92.

trenches to "reserve-billets in some pretty village" was mirrored, in particularly compressed and startling form, in Leningrad.[63] Ordinary urban trams full of soldiers and civilians ran as far south as the Kirov Factory's gates, where conductors announced: "End of the line. Next – the front!"[64]

In the Soviet case, however, the abnormality of the world that immediately preceded and followed the war created ironic complications of memory unknown in the West. Compared to the often brutal and unpredictable world of everyday Stalinism, wartime seemed normal, or at least not unduly absurd. Erenburg remembered that during an early postwar visit to Leningrad, Berggol'ts had asked him, "Tell me, do you think the year thirty-seven can repeat itself, or is that out of the question now?" He had replied, "No, I don't think it can." Berggol'ts laughed, "You don't sound quite sure."[65] By the late 1940s, it was clear that peace threatened a return to the absurd world of the late 1930s.

The post-Stalinist state prevented the publication of war stories that too explicitly celebrated the war's ability to disrupt "normal usages." Both Grossman's *Life and Fate* and Pasternak's *Doctor Zhivago* clearly registered the blessed normalcy of the hazards of war, and both were banned.[66] Berggol'ts's published reminiscences, by contrast, employed subtler and more personal contrasts between normal times and wartime to produce the implication that the war years offered an ironic vision of a saner world.

In his laudatory 1960 review of portions of her *Dnevnye zvezdy* (Daytime Stars), Siniavskii, later one of the most prominent victims of the post-Khrushchev refreeze, noted that Berggol'ts's reminiscences were characterized not by "the intonation of passive submission to the rush of memories, as for example, 'I cannot forget,' but rather the powerful and proud 'I do not wish, I shall not permit forgetting!'"[67] What Berggol'ts's memoir did not permit the reader to forget was the unfulfilled promises of the Revolution and the war. *Dnevnye zvezdy* scarcely mentioned the purges, but their memory provided an essential point of reference for Berggol'ts's stories of her childhood and of the blockade. Linking personal and national

---

[63] Paul Fussell, *The Great War and Modern Memory* (New York: Oxford University Press, 1975), 326–27. *900 dnei* includes wartime engravings that underscore what Fussell calls the "ridiculous proximity" of the war to the normal life of the city.

[64] Tikhonov, "Iz rasskazov," 83.

[65] Erenburg, *Post-War Years*, 13. See also Bernd Bonwetsch, "War as 'Breathing Space': Soviet Intellectuals and the 'Great Patriotic War,'" in Thurston and Bonwetsch, *People's War*, 137–53.

[66] Grossman, *Life and Fate*, 240, 256, 289.

[67] I have used the translation from Siniavskii, "The Poetry and Prose," 48. A. Siniavskii, "Poeziia i proza Olga Berggol'ts," *Novyi mir*, 1960, no. 5: 225–36.

struggles, Berggol'ts alluded to but did not plumb the depths of the worst of times: "at the end of the thirties, the deaths of my daughters one after the other, then immediately the severe trials of 1937–1939, which left an indelible mark on my consciousness."[68] She declined to explore this "indelible mark," but it nonetheless cast a shadow. The dark memory separated her happy childhood memories of Uglich – where she and her mother and sister had been evacuated during the Civil War – from her tragic, but also hopeful, even nostalgic, memories of blockaded Leningrad.

Instead of addressing directly the irony that the war brought relief from the personal and political tragedies of the 1930s, Berggol'ts structured her published reminiscences around a series of journeys in time and space that highlighted the connections among her youthful revolutionary dreams, the struggles and triumphs of the war years, and the post-Stalinist thaw. Shortly after Stalin's death, she returned to the city of her childhood, where she had often returned in dreams, and where she hoped to recover more innocent times, personally and politically. In her account of the visit, Berggol'ts explicitly equated memories of the early years of the Revolution and the blockade. When she met a child survivor of the siege, who had been evacuated across Lake Ladoga in February 1942 and who asked about Leningrad with tears in her eyes, she realized that the young woman's "blockade childhood was for her exactly what my Uglich childhood was for me" – a moment of sorrow but also of hope and high ideals.[69]

Berggol'ts's recollections of the siege focused on two trips to her father's house – one in the first month of the blockade and one in February 1942, at what was for her the most difficult and deadly moment of the nearly three-year ordeal. In both cases, she structured the memory of the war around signs from the prewar world that unexpectedly penetrated the world of the blockade. On the first of her trips, Berggol'ts passed a warehouse bearing a worn slogan from the early years of the Revolution that conjured up the first flush of youthful revolutionary excitement. She responded with "happy sobs." Breaking off her narration at this point, she addressed her reader directly: "On that day, I remembered none of my countless sorrows. Not for a moment did the apparitions, which before the war were

[68] Ol'ga Berggol'ts, *Dnevnye zvezdy,* in *Stikhi-proza,* 81. On her experiences during the purges, see Berggol'ts, "Avtobiografiia," in *Sobranie sochinenii v trekh tomakh* (Leningrad: Khudozhestvennaia literatura, 1988), 3: 487–88; A. Pavlovskii, "Ol'ga Berggol'ts," in *Sobranie sochinenii,* 1: 14; M. F. Berggol'ts, "Ob etikh tetradiakh," *Zvezda,* 1990, no. 5: 180.

[69] Berggol'ts, *Dnevnye zvezdy,* 41, 174.

invincible, take possession of my soul – not my daughters' deaths, nor the unjust accusation of 1937.... No, I walked along a summit, and I was possessed only by ... happiness and the ecstasy of life."[70] The distance between the war and the promises of revolution – the abyss of the 1930s – momentarily collapsed. The war opened the prospect of a return of youthful optimism, perhaps even innocence.

Four months later, the recently widowed Berggol'ts encountered a different token from the prewar world that produced, instead of transcendent ecstasy, an ironic reinforcement of the distance between revolutionary dreams and Soviet reality. In February 1942, the trams were no longer running, and pedestrians weakened by starvation moved slowly along Nevskii Prospekt, negotiating snowdrifts as they struggled from lamppost to lamppost. On almost every lamppost, Berggol'ts remembered, there was a poster with the words "Anton Ivanovich Is Angry," an advertisement for a movie musical that had been scheduled to play in the first days of the war. Thus, anyone who walked along Nevskii continually encountered the poster, "which, because of the way the war, the assault, the blockade, and the city's disaster had unfolded, had turned into a kind of warning, a reminder, a loud reproach." Ashamed before Anton Ivanovich's anger, Berggol'ts wanted to say on her own behalf and "on behalf of all the people of the earth: 'Anton Ivanovich, dear, dear, Anton Ivanovich, do not be angry at us! We are not to blame. We are still good people. We'll come to our senses somehow. We'll fix this ugliness. We will live humanely.'"[71] If Berggol'ts imagined that Anton Ivanovich was angry at the horrors of the blockade that surrounded him – the bodies of Leningraders killed by starvation or artillery attacks – her entreaty could also be taken more broadly. Her "we will live more humanely" sounded like a "pledge and a promise" to fix the ugliness not only of the war but of the prewar years.

Ordinary Heroes

Eschewing the cliché of the "heroic defense of the city front," Berggol'ts's remarkable memoir managed to represent the war as an ironic return to the ideals of the Revolution. For other survivors, however, the rehabilitated wartime narrative of the blockade provided a prefabricated script that allowed – perhaps encouraged – them to tell their stories as tales of heroic struggle. Like the wartime narratives they took as their model,

---

[70] Ibid., 114.
[71] Ibid., 126.

the stories from the city front that appeared in the 1960s and 1970s cast ordinary Leningraders as heroes, and minimized doubt, death, horror, and filth.[72]

Yet for all their formulaic triumphalism and unearned catharsis, these stories also insisted on the centrality of individual actions, personal losses, and private motivations in the story of the blockade. While the insider memoirs produced by party and government officials ended with images of rebuilt Leningrad and statistics demonstrating booming industry, the small stories of the blockade sought a different sort of closure – not national or local victories but lives resumed, suffering made meaningful. The questions of whether and how, with the advent of glasnost in the late 1980s, the memories that remained hidden, secret, and private in the years of the war cult finally surfaced are taken up in Chapter 7. Here the emphasis is on the degree to which the stories published before it was possible to tell all – and which are so easily dismissed as (self-) deceptive kitsch – expressed something of the trauma and the hopes, the "counternarrative," of the war years. In order to understand why the stories of the war cult outlasted the state that sponsored them, it is necessary to take the sugarcoated stories of ordinary heroes seriously, to explore their ability to endow pain and loss with personal and historical significance.

When librarian Mariia Zinov'eva died in 1960 at the age of seventy-three, Vera Karatygina wrote a memorial note for public display in the library. It was larded with the buzz words of the wartime press and the emerging cult of the war:

At the beginning of the war…Mariia Konstantinovna came to our brigade "Leningrad in the Great Fatherland War," and worked in it through the entire course of the blockade. In those difficult years we learned all about her – courage,

---

[72] In addition to those already mentioned, collections of memoirs and diaries from this period include the following: *Belye nochi* (Leningrad: Lenizdat, 1971). Mikhail Dudin, *Radi tvoei zhizni* (Leningrad: Lenizdat, 1962, 1965). F. F. Grachev, *Zapiski voennogo vracha* (Leningrad: Lenizdat, 1970). P. I. Kapitsa, *V more pogasli ogni* (Leningrad: Lenizdat, 1972). P. Luknitskii, *Leningrad deistvuet* (Leningrad: Lenizdat, 1961). *Na "doroge zhizn"* (Leningrad: Lenizdat, 1970). *Plamia nad Nevoi* (Leningrad: Lenizdat, 1964). *Po signalu vozdushnoi trevogi* (Leningrad: Lenizdat, 1974). A. M. Samsonov, ed., *Oborona Leningrada, 1941–1944: Vospominaniia i dnevniki uchastniki* (Leningrad: Nauka, 1968). *V gody Velikoi Otechestvennoi voiny* (Leningrad: Lenizdat, 1959). *V osazhdennom Leningrade* (Leningrad: Lenizdat, 1969, 1974). V. E. Vasilenko and S. V. Krasnikov, eds., *V ognennom kol'tse: Vospominaniia uchastnikov oborony goroda Lenina i razgroma nemetsko-fashistskikh zakhavatchikov pod Leningradom* (Moscow: Gosudarstvennoe izdatel'stvo politicheskoi literatury, 1963).

steadfastness, self-possession, an always even temper, prepared to morally support and come to the aid of comrades – such are the fundamental characteristics that described Mariia Konstantinovna in those days.[73]

At first blush, this memorial note stands as a clear example of the pervasiveness of state-sanctioned language. A librarian, who spent the war collecting and cataloging, became a steadfast, courageous hero. The phrase "those difficult years" effectively obscured the real, everyday horrors of the blockade.

Nonetheless, Karatygina managed to convey the intensity and persistence of her memory of their shared experience. "With the end of the war," she concluded, "Mariia Konstantinovna returned to her section, and we rarely met, but in memory she remains just as she was in those awful years of the blockade." That Karatygina continued to imagine her colleague as she had been during the war was, perhaps, primarily a straightforward consequence of the rarity of their meetings. However, the continuing power of the wartime image also suggests both the indelible quality of wartime memory and the conviction that what was learned about a person under the conditions of the blockade was what was real and essential about them. In her memorial note, Karatygina used the inflated rhetoric of the war cult to honor a woman and an unpretentious devotion to work and comrades that the language of "heroic defense" seemed designed to efface. She turned the Leningrad epic into a small, local, even lyrical sketch.

The memoirs of officials, by contrast, emphasized the epic scale of the heroic defense of the city and the party's role in organizing and inspiring it. Nikolai Shumilov, who was "no ordinary Leningrader" but the city party committee's secretary for propaganda and the editor-in-chief of *Leningradskaia pravda* during the war, expunged from his reminiscences nearly all trace of his individual memories of the blockade.[74] Averring that "human memory is not a very reliable historical source," Shumilov supplemented his recollections with archival and published sources, and told a story that went well beyond his propaganda bailiwick. Rarely recording his reactions to events, he did note that the January 1945 ceremony

[73] Arkhiv Rossiiskoi Natsional'noi Biblioteki (hereafter Arkh. RNB), Zinov'eva lichnoe delo, f. 10/1 (1957), l. 28.

[74] Nikolai Tikhonov, "O knige *V dni blokady*," in Nikolai Shumilov, *V dni blokady* (Moscow: Izdatel'stvo "Mysl'," 1977), 6. The reminiscences of Shumilov's editorial colleagues at *Leningradskaia pravda* and of the editor of *Smena* struck a similar tone. *S perom*, 24–74, 75–98. Maksim Gordon, *Nevskii, 2: Zapiski redaktora frontovoi gazety* (Leningrad: Lenizdat, 1976).

at which the Presidium of the Supreme Soviet of the USSR awarded
Leningrad the Order of Lenin was for him unforgettable.[75]

Shumilov told the story of the starvation winter from a bureaucrat's-
eye view, so high above the cold and hunger that each individual death
melted into the glorious tableau of heroic struggle and ultimate victory.
"The city's party organizations did everything possible," he concluded,
perhaps betraying the guilt of one who suffered less than most, "to relieve
Leningraders' suffering." Despite these efforts, Leningraders – including,
he emphasized, many Communists – died. Shumilov insisted that all "died
like heroes."[76] He reserved his harshest criticism for "bourgeois falsifiers
of history, who try to demonstrate that the heroic inhabitants of the blockaded city were doomed victims, at the mercy of the authorities. This is
an unscrupulous attempt to disparage Leningraders' victory, to belittle
their steadfastness and heroism."[77] At the same time, official histories
and officials like Shumilov reiterated that the Leningrad story was one
small part of the larger epic of the Great Fatherland War. Leningraders
had not "stood alone," and "the victory at Leningrad is the whole country's victory."[78] At the end, the story ceased to be strictly local.

Stories like Karatygina's, told from Leningrad's neighborhoods,
schools, workplaces, and apartments, also deployed the language of
"steadfastness and heroism," and affirmed that Leningraders were heroes,
not victims. However, by substituting the close-up for the panoramic
view of the battle, they also called attention to individual troubles and
triumphs. The shift in perspective is particularly jolting in stories told

---

[75] Shumilov, *V dni,* 10, 294–95.

[76] Ibid., 119–22, 128.

[77] Ibid., 135. See also the memoirs of Dmitrii Pavlov, the State Defense Committee's supply
representative in Leningrad: D. V. Pavlov, *Leningrad v blokade (1941 god)* (Moscow:
Sovetskaia Rossiia, 1958); Dmitrii V. Pavlov, *Leningrad 1941: The Blockade,* trans. John
Clinton Adams (Chicago: University of Chicago Press, 1965). Shumilov's narrative has
much in common with the histories that he cites. A. V. Karasev, *Leningradtsy v gody
blokady, 1941–1943* (Moscow: Izdatel'stvo Akademii nauk, 1959). S. P. Kniazev, ed.,
*Na zashchite Nevskoi tverdyni: Leningradskaia partiinaia organizatsii v gody Velikoi
Otechestvennoi voiny* (Leningrad: Lenizdat, 1965).

[78] Shumilov, *V dni,* 281. This is a constant refrain in accounts of the blockade from
the 1960s through 1980s. Sometimes the emphasis fell on the central role of the
Communist Party, sometimes on the aid and support offered by ordinary Soviet citizens, sometimes on both. N. D. Khudiakova, *Vsia strana s Leningradom, 1941–1943
gg.* (Leningrad: Lenizdat, 1960). V. E. Zubakov, *Geroicheskii Leningrad* (Moscow:
Ordena Trudogo Krasnogo Znameni voennoe izdatel'stvo Ministerstva Oborony SSSR,
1972), 182. Gennadii Fedorovich Petrov, *Piskarevskoe kladbishche* (Leningrad: Lenizdat,
1971), 11.

by and about women and children – the most ordinary as well as the majority of Leningraders –whom the towering bureaucrat saw primarily as touching and effective symbols of Soviet patriotism and strength.[79] In collections such as *Deti goroda-geroia* (Children of the Hero City, 1974), the broader view appeared in brief excerpts from the local press that framed interviews, diaries, stories, and reminiscences in which ordinary Leningraders operated on their own initiative, and in which, even for heroes, the city's Order of Lenin did not necessarily heal all wounds.[80]

Decades after the end of the war, people who had been children during the blockade recounted their wartime exploits with gusto, but they also suggested that the blockade remained a painful, indelible memory. In his contribution to *Children of the Hero City*, a collection directed at children born after the war, A. Krestinskii, noted that "many of today's kids imagine us, back then, this way: The fascists are pouring incendiary bombs down on the city, and we're extinguishing these bombs. The fascists pour spies into the city, and we catch these spies." Krestinskii clearly saw the romance of such stories, and he affirmed that "all of that happened – the bombs and the spies." However, unlike other contributors, Krestinskii extinguished no bombs. His purpose in writing was to show "today's kids how we really were: ragged, hungry, bereft of loved ones, and at the same time not depressed, resourceful, desperate boys of the besieged city." Alongside this promised gritty realism, Krestinskii continued to deploy the high diction of heroic struggle, declaring that cold and hunger "tested our character and will, our honor and friendship, our human virtue."[81]

Many child survivors told similarly ambivalent stories and projected similarly ambivalent self-images. For A. Lugovtsova, the heroic story offered an ironic contrast to the "real" war. She took as her point of departure not the image that "today's kids" might have of their heroic predecessors, but her own childhood ideas about war that came out of romantic narratives of the Civil War. In the idyllic prewar spring of 1941, a traveling photographer interrupted the children playing "Chapaevtsy" – imagining themselves members of Vasilii Chapaev's legendary Civil War guerrilla force – to ask if he could take their picture. He told them, Lugovtsova

[79] Shumilov, *V dni*, 129–31, 221–27.

[80] Anna Lazarevna Moizhes, ed., *Deti goroda-geroia* (Leningrad: Lenizdat, 1974). See also E. Maksimova, ed., *Deti voennoi pory* (Moscow: Politizdat, 1984).

[81] A. Krestinskii, "Gorod nevdaleke," in *Deti goroda-geroia*, 246. On the "high diction" of honor and sacrifice, which Fussell maintains was a casualty of World War I, see Fussell, *Great War*, 21–23.

remembered, that it would be a memory they could hold for their whole lives. Uninterested in the memento, but fascinated by the camera, the eighteen children who happened to be in the courtyard agreed. Thirty years later, the moment was ripe with irony. The children who had been playing war were soon caught up in a real one that "turned out to be completely unlike what had been described to us, what we had imagined in our naive games," and the picture turned out to be a far more treasured memorial than the photographer could have imagined.[82]

In Lugovtsova's account, the first adventurous, exciting months of the war – in which it seemed truly an epic struggle between great powers – gave way to a deep and quiet sadness. Almost immediately after the German invasion, a woman, perhaps from the house committee, Lugovtsova wasn't sure, came and "ignited us with her energy," telling the residents, "Each Leningrad house must become an impenetrable fortress." Initially banned from standing watch on the rooftop to extinguish incendiaries during air raids, the children eventually took over the job. Lugovtsova recounted that the first time an incendiary bomb came down on their watch, her partner Vil'ka lost his head. Instead of putting out the flaming bomb in the bucket of sand, he sent it into the courtyard, where it landed on a shed, which promptly caught fire. The fire was easily put out, and "no one cursed Vil'ka. They told us: No problem, you'll learn."[83] Such adventures, darkly humorous and mock heroic in hindsight, ended abruptly as Lugovtsova's story turned to winter.

Lugovtsova's narrative screened from view much of the death that surrounded her and focused on the essential objects and routines of her family circle. Fully congruent with the state's efforts to downplay the extent of the tragedy in blockaded Leningrad, Lugovtsova's story also reflected the "narrowed attentional focus" common in stressful circumstances.[84] She made no mention of the dead visible along Leningrad's streets nor of the children's sleds used for transporting corpses to the cemetery that some

---

[82] A. Lugovtsova, "Istoriia odnoi fotografii," in *Deti goroda-geroia*, 231. Dmitrii Furmanov's 1923 novel *Chapaev* spawned films, songs, and an opera, as well as children's games. Stites, *Russian Popular Culture*, 45. A shorter version of Lugovtsova's reminiscences was published as "Rebiata s nashego dvora," in *Deti voennoi pory*, 196–203.

[83] Lugovtsova, "Istoriia," 232.

[84] David Spiegel, "Hypnosis and Suggestion," in Daniel L. Schacter, ed., *Memory Distortion: How Minds, Brains, and Societies Reconstruct the Past* (Cambridge, MA: Harvard University Press, 1995), 131. Christina A. Byrne, Ira E. Hyman, Jr., and Kaia L. Scott, "Comparisons of Memories for Traumatic Events and Other Experiences," *Applied Cognitive Psychology* 15 (December 2001): S130.

Leningraders employed as a synecdoche for mass death.[85] Rather, she provided a small and intimate picture of the blockade, one that scarcely left her own apartment. She and her sister went to the bakery when it opened at six in the morning, and when they returned home, divided their rations into three equal parts. Most of the time, Lugovtsova, her mother, and sister lay together in the same bed – too cold and tired to move.

Lugovtsova described her emotional reactions in terms that suggested both the numbness associated with traumatic events and the ways in which narratives of the Leningraders' shared heroic struggle helped her to overcome numbness and find meaning in her experiences.[86] On 7 February 1942, her sister Valia died; her mother died a few hours later. "I remember, I didn't even cry," she wrote. "All the feeling had died within me." Nonetheless, when the radio began to broadcast at six in the morning, "I realized that I had to go to the bakery."[87]

The radio served to reconnect Lugovtsova to the community, and that social connection, she maintained, saved her. By finding the strength to go to the bakery the morning after her mother's death, she demonstrated precisely the sort of stoic heroism that constituted a central theme of the wartime press. That she ran into a friend who, immediately understanding what had happened, invited Lugovtsova to live with her family, constituted both a confirmation of the virtue central to the heroic epic and the sort of good luck often cited by people who have not only survived, but effectively coped with all sorts of traumatic experiences.[88] Lugovtsova lived with her friend for two months, during which time both Tamara's mother and grandmother died, and the two school friends found themselves alone in the large apartment. The two survived, Lugovtsova

---

[85] See, for example, Ia. Kamenetskii, "Dnevnik Mishi Tikhomerova," in *Deti voennoi pory*, 82–84. Shumilov, *V dni*, 128. Pavlov, *Leningrad 1941*, 123. Harrison E. Salisbury, *The 900 Days: The Siege of Leningrad* (New York: Harper and Row, 1969), 435–46.

[86] Judith Herman, *Trauma and Recovery: The Aftermath of Violence – from Domestic Abuse to Political Terror* (New York: Basic Books, 1992), 43–45. Avril Thorne and Kate C. McLean, "Telling Traumatic Events in Adolescence: A Study of Master Narrative Positioning," in Robyn Fivush and Catherine A. Haden, eds., *Autobiographical Memory and the Construction of a Narrative of Self: Developmental and Cultural Perspectives* (Mahwah, NJ: Lawrence Erlbaum, 2003), 183. The psychiatrist Derek Summerfield emphasizes that "Children, too, are not just 'innocent' and passive victims, but also active citizens whose values and causes are connected to collective meanings and memories." Derek Summerfield, "The Social Experience of War and Some Issues for the Humanitarian Field," in Patrick J. Bracken and Celia Petty, eds., *Rethinking the Trauma of War* (London: Free Association Books, 1998), 23.

[87] Lugovtsova, "Istoriia," 233.

[88] Herman, *Trauma*, 60.

suggested, because they had each other, and also, perhaps – although she mentioned nothing of the sort – by making use of the ration cards of the dead.[89]

Taking her story only as far as the spring of 1942, Lugovtsova conveyed both the joy and the pain of survival. As in many accounts of the blockade, the conventional figure of spring as a moment of rebirth became breathtakingly literal: "Outside, steam rose from the pools glittering brilliantly in the sun, and drying up on the asphalt; from a branch, who knows where, a sparrow chirped. We had to unbutton our coats – it was that warm. Tamara turned toward me: 'Well, now we're going to live!'"[90] By ending her narrative here, Lugovtsova embraced the possibility of rebirth but foreswore the clichéd closure of the victory salute. Instead, she implicitly took up the question of what happened when feeling returned. She concluded the narrative by returning to the photograph of her childhood friends – of her childhood. What, she asked, would have become of them if they had lived? Here she came close to suggesting if not the meaninglessness of these losses then the disproportion between what was lost and what was won: "These kids from our courtyard would have done a lot for people had their lives not been cut off by the war."[91] Pouring over the old photograph and wondering what might have been, Lugovtsova imagined a happy ending for the child whose fate she did not know.

Such narratives of everyday life in blockaded Leningrad illustrate how the small stories authorized and encouraged by the cult of the war could at once validate, complicate, and destabilize the overarching narrative of the "heroic defense of Leningrad." It is certainly possible to dismiss stories like Lugovtsova's as a "folding screen set up to curtain off death." The scale of death in blockaded Leningrad remained invisible in these reminiscences. Survivors offered little description of the physical and emotional effects of starvation. Even people who had been children during the war, and who arguably could have – and perhaps should have – contributed little to the defense of the city, never suggested that they were "doomed victims." In various ways, survivors who published memoirs seemed to accept their suffering as their contribution to the war effort. Hearing similar stories in the 1990s, the historian Catherine Merridale concluded that "kitsch war poetry and film created a consensual world, a fantasy of survival

---

[89] If a death remained unregistered, ration cards remained valid until the end of the month when they had to be renewed in person. Richard Bidlack, "Survival Strategies in Leningrad during the First Year of the Soviet-German War," in Thurston and Bonwetsch, *People's War,* 92.

[90] Lugovtsova, "Istoriia," 234.

[91] Ibid., 235.

and endurance. It was a collective escape, a voluntary anesthetic, and the people who remember it believe that it worked."[92]

However, a close reading of stories from the city front suggests that such stories may be understood not only or primarily as a "collective escape" but also as part of an ongoing effort to cope with unimaginable experiences. Thirty years after the war, survivors' stories echoed "kitsch war poetry and film" because the notion of "heroic defense" made their suffering meaningful, and because believing that their suffering was meaningful had helped – and continued to help – them to survive. The conventions of the story of heroic Leningrad at once celebrated individual agency – the strength of will that got Lugovtsova to the bakery in the aftermath of her mother's death – and membership in the larger collective struggle – the radio that reminded Leningraders of their shared and higher purpose. At the same time, individual survivors hinted that they knew and felt the limits of the heroic story. Concluding his account of the wartime fates of his neighborhood friends, G. Goppe remembered, "At the beginning of the war, we said: 'We are almost a platoon.' Now I must sorrowfully say: This platoon, like any real shock troops, came out of battle with enormous losses."[93] The story of heroic Leningrad offered a way to find some significance in these deaths, not so much anesthetizing pain as allowing survivors to make narrative sense of persistent sorrow.

Stagnation and the Memory of Real Horrors

By the mid-1970s, a decade after Khrushchev's ouster, the optimism of the early post-Stalin years had given way to pessimism and cynicism. Gorbachev later dubbed these years the period of stagnation (*zastoi*). It was quite clear that communism would not be achieved, as Khrushchev had promised, within a decade. Instead, shortages of butter, meat, and sometimes even cabbage, as well as shoddy or, more often, nonexistent consumer goods – along with long lines and a thriving second economy – remained facts of Soviet life. Defense spending soared, and economic growth ground to a halt.[94] Soviet citizens, particularly young people,

---

[92] Merridale, *Night of Stone*, 251.

[93] G. Goppe, "Marshruty odnogo puteshestviia," in *Deti goroda-geroia*, 88.

[94] John Bushnell, "The 'New Soviet Man' Turns Pessimist," in Cohen et al., *The Soviet Union since Stalin*, 179–99. James R. Millar, "The Little Deal: Brezhnev's Contribution to Acquisitive Socialism," *Slavic Review* 44 (Winter 1985): 694–706. Stephen Kotkin, *Armageddon Averted: The Soviet Collapse, 1970–2000* (New York: Oxford University Press, 2001), 25–28. Elizabeth Pond, *From the Yaroslavsky Station: Russia Perceived*, 3d ed. (New York: Universe Books, 1988), 95–107.

increasingly regarded the "master signifiers" – Lenin, party, and Revolution – that permeated official pronouncements as mind-numbingly predictable, immutable, perhaps, but also irrelevant.[95]

Under these circumstances, stories of the Great Fatherland War acquired new importance as a means of, if not inspiring Soviet citizens, at least reminding them of both the sanctity and the great costs of victory. The cult of the war, as the historian Nina Tumarkin has argued, "tried to shame young people into feeling respect for their elders or as a minimum goal, into behaving obediently in their presence."[96] Because stories of the Great Fatherland War celebrated Soviet citizens but paid relatively little obeisance to the "master signifiers," the leadership hoped that they would resonate with both the members of the war generation and their children. In 1974, when authorities drew up the indictment against Solzhenitsyn, whose crime was publishing *The Gulag Archipelago* in France and the United States earlier that year, what chiefly outraged the men in the Politburo was the book's attack on Lenin, the party, and the Revolution. However, Brezhnev insisted that "it is important to show to the people . . . [Solzhenitsyn's] profanation of the memory of the victims of the Great Fatherland War."[97] The party counted on the memory of the holy war to appeal to a populace increasingly resistant to propaganda appeals.

Thus, while the Brezhnev regime tightened its control over cultural and political dissent – exiling the poet Joseph Brodsky in 1964 and arresting Siniavskii and the writer Iulii Daniel in 1965, not to mention invading Czechoslovakia in 1968 – it paradoxically allowed greater honesty and leeway in war stories. Appropriately heroic, if not kitschy, films such as Iurii Ozerov's five-part epic *Liberation* (Osvobozhdenie, 1972) dominated the screen, but the Brezhnev years also saw the production of Larisa Shepit'ko's brutal *The Ascent* (Voskhozhdenie, 1976) and Elem Klimov's even bleaker *Come and See* (Idi i smotri, 1985), from a screenplay by the Belorussian author and veteran Ales' Adamovich. The historian Denise Youngblood credits these films with "returning to the Soviet people an authentic memory of the conflict," free of "the cant and bombast of official history." She attributes their production to the fact that

---

[95] Alexei Yurchak, "The Cynical Reason of Late Socialism: Language, Ideology, and Culture of the Last Soviet Generation" (Ph.D. diss., Duke University, 1997).

[96] Tumarkin, *The Living and the Dead*, 133. Lisa A. Kirschenbaum, "Innocent Victims and Heroic Defenders: Children and the Siege of Leningrad," in James Marten, ed., *Children and War: A Historical Anthology* (New York: New York University Press, 2002), 283–88.

[97] Yurchak, "The Cynical Reason," 172–73.

"working with images rather than words, these directors were able to subvert censorship."[98] Certainly, state officials may have gotten much more than they bargained for when they approved the scenarios for these films – a film may well be made in the editing. At the same time, published memoirs and oral histories also increasingly told uncompromising war stories remarkably free of cant and bombast.

In the case of the siege of Leningrad, the publication of *A Book of the Blockade* (Blokadnaia kniga) in 1979 marked a turn in public discussion.[99] Explicitly committed to ensuring that the younger generation would remember and value the sacrifices of the aging war generation, Adamovich and the Leningrad novelist Daniil Granin, the editors of this collection of oral histories and diaries, provided often disturbing details of life during the blockade that had generally been omitted or downplayed in Soviet accounts. They rejected sanitized representations of the siege, because while it might have once made sense for "those hurt by the war to spare the hearts of their fellow countrymen," forty-years later "it is absolutely vital that the postwar generations should know as much as possible, in all its details, about what happened before their time, that they should get the feel of it all."[100] The effort to impress upon the postwar generation the momentousness and also the tragedy of the war produced stories that to an unprecedented extent confronted its horrors.

Increasing honesty regarding the blockade did not undermine the fundamentally uplifting quality of the story. Virtuous and heroic Leningraders still triumphed in the face of hunger, cold, and death. However, the focus on individual struggles became even more pronounced, and the triumph became more mixed. *A Book of the Blockade* illustrates the degree to which the effect of realism became central to the pedagogical mission of the war cult. It, together with Lidiia Ginzburg's *Blockade Diary*, a memoir published in the Soviet Union in 1984, also illustrates survivors' complicated appropriation of the myth of heroic Leningrad and the concomitant difficulty of categorizing memories as authentic or inauthentic.[101] Their stories simultaneously embraced and questioned redemptive, happy endings.

Hoping to make an impact on the younger generation, Adamovich and Granin worked to include accounts of the blockade from the point of view

---

[98] Youngblood, "A War Remembered," 855.
[99] Cynthia Simmons, "Lifting the Siege: Women's Voices on Leningrad (1941–1944)," *Canadian Slavonic Papers* 40 (1998): 48–49.
[100] Adamovich and Granin, *Blokadnaia kniga*, 22.
[101] Lidiia Ginzburg, "Zapiski blokadnogo cheloveka," *Neva*, 1984, no. 1: 84–108.

of children and teenagers.[102] Indeed, one of the central accounts included in the 1982 edition of *Blokadnaia kniga* was the diary of Iura Riabinkin, who turned sixteen shortly after the blockade closed. The power of his diary stemmed in part from his moving, personal descriptions of taboo subjects: the inadequacy of efforts to evacuate children, the effects of starvation, the strain and breakdown of family relations. Riabinkin recorded his involvement in all sorts of war work, from helping to build bomb shelters to putting out incendiary bombs at school. He thus fit the stereotype of the young heroic defender. At the same time, he emerged as a very real boy, whose motives and reactions were not self-consciously "heroic," but included the desire to be with friends, to keep busy, and to participate in the great adventure of war.

As food rations diminished in the winter of 1941, Riabinkin chronicled a painful struggle between, in the editors' phrase, "conscience and hunger." In December 1941, the starving Iura recorded his "degradation...dishonor and shame": "Like a bastard I sneak their last morsels" from his mother and thirteen-year-old sister Ira. In early January, Riabinkin described the advanced stages of starvation – "I'm bloated...I can't force myself to move about, can't make myself get up from a chair and walk a step or two" – and expressed his soon-realized fears that his sister and mother would leave him behind when they were evacuated.[103] Never intended for publication, the diary revealed not only the objective horrors of the blockade but also the psychological state, oscillating between suicidal and defiant, of the starving.[104]

Few of the interviews and diaries in *Blokadnaia kniga* matched the honesty and self-exposure of Riabinkin's diary. Still, of the more than one hundred interviewees, many told bleak and painful stories that underscored the shame of having managed to set aside "civilized" standards and live through the catastrophe of the starvation winter.[105] Challenging the simplified story of the spring of 1942 as a moment of rejoicing and rebirth, the interviews collected in *Blokadnaia kniga* told of the horrors – emphasized by Ginzburg – of confronting a body whose strangeness had been at least partly concealed under layers of clothes and blankets.[106] Undressing for the first time in months, survivors registered starvation's

---

[102] Adamovich and Granin, *Blokadnaia kniga*, 419.

[103] Ibid., 353, 358, 362.

[104] Rubashkin, "O podvige i tragedii," 429–30.

[105] Such "shame" or "survivor guilt" is a widely observed consequence of traumatic events, a response to "helplessness, the violation of bodily integrity, and the indignity suffered in the eyes of another person." Herman, *Trauma and Recovery*, 53.

[106] Ginzburg, *Blockade Diary*, 11.

destruction of the physical markers of gender and generation.[107] Maiia Ianova remembered that when the baths reopened, people queued up for eight hours or so for the opportunity to take a hot bath. When two weeks later she finally succeeded in getting in, the experience "was so horrible, when they were all naked and kept falling – they didn't have the strength to carry the wash basins. My god! What a nightmare you could see there."[108]

Of course, not everyone remembered such grim scenes. The editors made explicit efforts to include both memories of despair and of recovery.[109] Indeed, survivors themselves often hesitated to emphasize despair. Ianova, for example, distanced herself from the "nightmare" – "*they* fell down." Stories that emphasized the return of clearly gendered and desirable female bodies – the evacuee transformed "from an old woman into a pleasing woman" – also worked to balance reminiscences that focused on the shame of starvation.[110] The return of femininity and youth and of male desire marked the full recovery from starvation.

Ginzburg, whose remarkable *Blockade Diary* unflinchingly explored both the physical and psychological effects of starvation, provided no such unalloyed happy endings. Nonetheless, she too granted – or hoped – that the pain of survival could be overcome or at least offset with the recognition that starving civilians participated in a meaningful struggle. On the one hand, Ginzburg presented a powerful account of the shame of the survivor who, as the starvation winter receded, felt his physical degradation as well as "the inadequacy of the sacrifice...(I survived – that means I didn't sacrifice enough), and along with the inadequacy, remorse." On the other hand, she adopted a point of view very close to the epic narrative of heroism and meaningful sacrifice. She argued that in trying to save themselves and their loved ones from hunger, Leningraders performed work "essential to the war effort, because a living city barred the path of an enemy who wanted to kill it."[111] The narrator's "detached and analytic point of view" – a stance epitomized in Ginzburg's representation of the starving body as genderless – recognized the shame of surviving starvation, but also provided enough distance from this shame to allow the siege to be constructed as a meaningful experience.[112]

First-hand accounts of the blockade published from the late 1970s and early 1980s contained stark depictions of starvation – family members

[107] Adamovich and Granin, *Blokadnaia kniga*, 312, 49, 369, 390.
[108] Ibid., 68–69.
[109] Ibid., 193.
[110] Ibid., 338. See also Galina Bobinskaia's diary, cited in Chapter 2. Ibid., 186.
[111] Ginzburg, *Blockade Diary*, 62, 8, 3.
[112] Gasparov, "On 'Notes,'" 217.

taking bread from one another, mothers abandoning their children, the war on the body. However, many survivors also continued to tell stories that affirmed the resilience and sanctity of the human body and that represented Leningraders not as victims of starvation but as soldiers under enemy fire. The 1979 edition of *Blokadnaia kniga,* which did not include Iura Riabinkin's diary, ended with the lengthy interview of Mariia Ivanovna, who, as a civil defense worker, saved an injured woman and her newborn baby from the rubble, even as German shells continued to fall.[113] That the editors chose to emphasize the story does not negate the fact that survivors – seeking to make sense of their experience or to evade the memory of horror, despair, and shame – told them. The injured mother, with beautiful fair hair that reached her knees, who gave birth in the midst of an air raid, constituted a less painful memory, for both the state and survivors, than the "nightmare" scene at the bathhouse. The state did not need to impose silence in the face of the degradation and destruction of the human body – especially one's own body. Survivors often did that on their own.[114]

Stories from the city front both documented and mythologized the siege. They expressed at once despair and transcendence. Whether or not such emotionally powerful but ambivalent stories had the desired effect on Soviet youth is a question that lies beyond the scope of this study. Anecdotal evidence suggests that many young people found the incessant retellings of wartime heroism and suffering tiresome. They responded with boredom and sometimes derision.[115] Nonetheless, the war has remained in post-Soviet public opinion the single greatest achievement in Russian history.[116] But whether or not the combination of heroic myth and dark reality worked, survivors and war veterans – from those at the pinnacle of

---

[113] Adamovich and Granin, *Blokadnaia kniga,* 193–97.

[114] On "the impossibility of telling" as a central experience of Holocaust survivors, see Shoshana Felman and Dori Laub, *Testimony: Crises of Witnessing in Literature, Psychoanalysis, and History* (New York: Routledge, 1992), 79–80, 190–91.

[115] Tumarkin, *The Living and the Dead,* 24–25. Jennifer Dickinson, "Building the Blockade: New Truths in Survival Narratives from Leningrad," *Anthropology of East Europe Review* 13, no. 2 (1995): 20. Anna Krylova, "Dancing on the Graves of the Dead: Building a World War II Memorial in Post-Soviet Russia," in Daniel J. Walkowitz and Lisa Maya Knauer, eds., *Memory and the Impact of Political Transformation in Public Space* (Durham, NC: Duke University Press, 2004), 91–93. More respectful responses can be found in *Velikaia Otechestvennaia voina glazami dvukh pokolenii: Vospominaiia i ocherki* (Omsk: Izdatel'stvo OmGTU, 2000).

[116] "Sports Are Our All," *Current Digest of the Post-Soviet Press* 55, no. 17–18 (2003): 13. On the familial transmission of blockade memories, see Éléonora Martino-Fristot, "La mémoire du blocus de Léningrad, 1945–1999" (Ph.D. diss., Ecole des hautes etudes en sciences sociales, 2002).

power like Brezhnev, to cultural mediators like Adamovich and Granin, to ordinary Leningraders – increasingly framed stories ostensibly meant for the postwar generation in this way. Internalizing officially sanctioned myths, they found a powerful framework for narrating their own personal stories. Such stories also suited the needs of a state that traced current economic problems to the destructiveness of the war and that insisted on the glorious victory as a key demonstration of its popular support. Yet paradoxically, such stories also largely wrote the state and the party out of the story of the blockade. With their emphasis on individual struggles and triumphs, the stories from the city front at once perpetuated the myth of redemptive victory and called attention to the unfulfilled promises of the "people's war."

6

Heroes and Victims

Local Monuments of the Soviet War Cult

The exhibits inside the Heroic Defenders of Leningrad Memorial are documentary and symbolic at the same time.... The subdued nature of the exposition underscores the memorial's multiple intent as a place haunted with memories for those who lived through the siege, a museum of the city's history, and a venue for gala events.

Museum guide, 2001[1]

During and immediately after the war, a relatively small number of monuments marking the graves of fallen soldiers or commemorating victory appeared in the Soviet Union. After 1947, when Victory Day became an ordinary work day, the state substantially curtailed the ritual spaces and times allotted for reflecting on both the heroes and the victims of the war. The cult of the war that emerged after Josef Stalin's death changed all this. Local governments, with approval and funding from the state, undertook the construction of hundreds of war cemeteries and monuments. In 1965, Victory Day once again became a public holiday. By the early 1970s, monuments to the Great Fatherland War became ubiquitous features of the Soviet landscape.[2]

---

[1] Elena Lezik, *Monument geroicheskim zashchitnikam Leningrada* (St. Petersburg: Litsei, 2001). The guidebook was published in Russian, English, and German; I have used the English in the original.

[2] Nina Tumarkin, *The Living and the Dead: The Rise and Fall of the Cult of World War II in Russia* (New York: Basic Books, 1994), 95–105. V. G. Khol'tsova, *Memorial'nye ansambli i pamiatniki na territorii SSSR, posviashchennye Velikoi Otechestvennoi voine 1941–1945 gg: Bibliograficheskii ukazatel'* (Leningrad: Institut zhivopisi, skul'ptury i akhitektury, 1976). A. I. Gegello, "Pamiatniki na mestakh boev pod Leningradom," *Arkhitektura i stroitel'stvo Leningrada*, June 1946, 5–8.

Soviet monuments to the war ranged from understated markers to monumental statues situated in enormous memorial "complexes." In general, they embraced traditional and idealized images of war. Unabashedly representational and resolutely optimistic regarding the justice of the cause, the heroism of the fighters, and the purity of the victory, Soviet memorials attempted to balance and integrate two essential tasks – mourning the country's staggering losses and celebrating the victory that, according to the myth of the people's war, crowned and redeemed the sorrows. The painful realities of war for both soldiers and civilians often found expression in allegorical images of mothers holding dead children in their arms. By contrast, the blurring of gender and generational roles that had been a necessary response to total war remained largely invisible, as monuments usually marked battlefronts, not home fronts.[3] Replete with obelisks, colonnades, T-34 tanks, stoic Motherland figures, and steadfast, broad-shouldered soldiers, Soviet monuments stood in stark contrast to many World War II memorials in the West, where abstraction became the "privileged," if still "vehemently contested," mode of public sculpture. When the human figure appeared in Western World War II memorials, it was often "anguished, distorted, pared down, or metamorphosed."[4] Such memorials expressed anger or despair, and marked the difficulty of resuscitating sentimental, romantic, heroic language and forms after Auschwitz and Hiroshima. The unbroken bodies that stood at the heart of so many Soviet memorials suggested everything that abstract Western World War II memorials rejected – faith in human progress, "clichés about duty, masculinity, honor."[5]

The scores of monuments constructed in and around Leningrad between 1957 and 1985 constitute a particularly interesting and complicated subset of Soviet war monuments. While most Soviet monuments relied on anodyne allegories of civilian suffering and civilians' contributions to the war effort, the unprecedented degree to which the battlefront in Leningrad had bled into the home front encouraged memorial planners – many of whom had lived through the blockade – to consider ways

[3] Viktor Golikov, ed., *Podvig naroda: Pamiatniki Velikoi Otechestvennoi voiny, 1941–1945* (Moscow: Izdatel'stvo politicheskoi literatury, 1980). I. Betkher-Ostrenko, "Pamiati geroev," *Dekorativnoe iskusstvo SSSR,* 1966, no. 7: 19–20.

[4] Mona Hadler, "Sculpture in Postwar Europe and America, 1944–59," *Art Journal* 53, no. 4 (Winter 1994): 17, 18. See also Sergiusz Michalski, *Public Monuments: Art in Political Bondage, 1870–1997* (London: Reaktion Books, 1998), 125–31, 154–63.

[5] Jay Winter, *Sites of Memory, Sites of Mourning: The Great War in European Cultural History* (New York: Cambridge University Press, 1995), 115.

17. Recreated warning sign and commemorative plaque on Nevskii Prospekt. Photo by author.

of documenting and commemorating Leningraders' unique experiences alongside the shared Soviet victory. As the sculptor Mikhail Anikushin emphasized, a Leningrad memorial had to show "our contemporaries and our descendants how everything really happened."[6] Yet, as Anikushin's himself implicitly admitted, the heroic, romantic visual idiom of the war cult did not easily lend itself to the task of rendering "what really happened" in Leningrad, particularly during the first winter of the blockade.

The desire to document the realities of the besieged city is visible in one of the earliest and most modest memorials of the emerging war cult – a replica of the white and blue signs that had warned pedestrians on Leningrad's main streets, "Citizens: In case of shelling this side of the street is most dangerous" (Illustration 17). Appearing at Number 14 Nevskii Prospekt in 1957 as part of the belated celebration of Leningrad's 250th anniversary, the sign reproduced the original warnings that had been painted over at the time of the Leningrad Affair. A plaque explaining the sign's significance and a small open-work metal shelf on which Petersburgers still leave flowers indicated the memorial purposes of this recreated trace of the blockade.[7]

---

[6] Mikhail Anikushin, "Bol' i muzhestvo," *Avrora*, 1975, no. 5: 19.
[7] *Putevoditel' po Leningradu* (Leningrad: Lenizdat, 1957), 131. Golikov, *Podvig naroda,* 110.

Leningrad's massive memorial complexes similarly included real or simulated documents, relics, and even wartime environments. Designers conceived of the Greenbelt of Glory, which is actually a series of more than sixty monuments constructed in the 1960s and 1970s, as a 1-to-1 scale model of the blockade. Its monuments follow – though, because of postwar suburban sprawl, not always with geographic precision – the ring of the blockade and the route of the Road of Life to the shores of Lake Ladoga.[8]

Paradoxically, the documents and images that communicated "how everything really happened" worked both to reinforce and complicate the myth of the hero city. The warning sign on Nevskii and the plaques that marked shell damage on landmarks, such as the Anichkov Bridge, St. Isaac's Cathedral, and the Church of the Savior on the Blood (Illustration 18), memorialized air raids and artillery attacks, not civilian deaths due to starvation. However, set as they were amid the everyday urban spaces in which Leningraders survived the blockade, such commemorations interacted with Leningraders' individual memories of the war in the city.

The layers of memory evoked by the cityscape worked against official efforts to produce urban memorials with singular and static meanings. Indeed, the difficulty of taming and homogenizing the meanings of urban space may explain why the most ambitious monuments to the blockade stand on the outskirts of the city, on terrain more clearly and narrowly associated with the defense of Leningrad. Yet these monuments also incorporated a variety of meanings and memories.

Western critics, who have few kind words for Soviet architecture in general and Soviet war memorials in particular, often praise the earliest of these Leningrad monuments, Piskarevskoe Memorial Cemetery, as an exceptional and exceptionally effective Soviet memorial.[9] For those who had been unable to bury their loved ones or to visit any sort of grave,

---

[8] "Nikto ne zabyt, i nichto ne zabyto!" *Stroitel'stvo i arkhitektura Leningrada*, 1974, no. 1: 11–13. T. M. Semenova, "'Kamennaia letopis" Velikoi Otechestvennoi voiny," *Trudy gosudarstvennogo muzeia istorii Sankt-Peterburga*, vyp. 5 (2000): 334–41. Golikov, *Podvig naroda*, 113–20. V. Ganshin and O. Serdobol'skii, *Kol'tso pamiati, kol'tso slavy* (Leningrad: Lenizdat, 1988). Iu. A. Luk'ianov, *Rubezhi stoikosti i muzhestva*, 2d ed. (Leningrad: Lenizdat, 1985). B. V. Nekrasov, *Granitnaia letopis': Pamiatniki boevoi slavy v Leningrade* (Leningrad: Lenizdat, 1971). O. I. Bakharev, *Zelenyi poias slavy* (Leningrad: Lenizdat, 1978). E. Rapoport, "'Zelenyi poias slavy' pod Leningradom," *Dekorativnoe iskusstvo SSSR*, 1969, no. 4: 10–11.

[9] W. Bruce Lincoln, *Sunlight at Midnight: St. Petersburg and the Rise of Modern Russia* (New York: Basic Books, 2002), 318. Michael Ignatieff, "Soviet War Memorials," *History Workshop*, no. 17 (1984): 159–60. Tumarkin, *The Living and the Dead*, 31–32.

18. Small commemorative plaque on the Church of the Savior on the Blood marking still-visible artillery damage. Photo by Steven Maddox.

the cemetery, dedicated on Victory Day (9 May) 1960, offered a place to mourn the dead. Its vast horizontal expanse made palpable the enormity of Leningrad's loss. At the same time, the purposes of the state were very much in evidence. An enormous tomb of the unknowns, presided over by a towering figure of the Mother-Motherland (*Mat'-Rodina*) and framed by a museum and the poetry of Ol'ga Berggol'ts, Piskarevskoe Cemetery constructed an account of the siege that remembered personal tragedies even as it fit them into the grand narrative of collective heroism and sacrifice.

Dedicated on Victory Day 1975, the Monument to the Heroic Defenders of Leningrad that greets visitors as they drive into the city from Pulkovo Airport is on the surface a more typical product of the war cult. From the car window, the visitor sees a rather bombastic monument to Victory featuring a red granite obelisk soaring over the strapping, larger-than-life figures of a soldier and a worker. However, behind this façade lies a more complicated monument that both recognizes and attempts to contain memories of the war's devastating impact on the city and its inhabitants. The sometimes public planning process that produced the monument revealed the interactions and interdependence of commitments to honoring the city's suffering and its strength – often given female form – and Soviet victory – personified by courageous, powerful, and protective male soldiers. The finished monument obscured the ugliest realities of war for both civilians and soldiers. At the same time, it evoked local memory. Creating distinct spaces dedicated to military victory and civilian suffering, the monument managed to document as well as to mythologize, to structure emotionally powerful combinations of the allegorical and the realistic, the local and the national, the battlefront and the home front.

Clearly, the Soviet state shaped commemoration and constrained artistic production. Nonetheless, the protracted design processes that stood behind the Leningrad memorials that constitute the focus of this chapter – Piskarevskoe Cemetery and the Monument to the Heroic Defenders – along with the public statements of designers and critics, opened arenas in which personal memories and official narratives and images interpenetrated one another.[10] The explanations and reactions of art critics and artists can be read as both prescriptive – models for how the ideal viewer should see a memorial – and descriptive – personal responses framed in the available and acceptable language of the war cult. The present chapter approaches monuments to the blockade as serious, if fettered, efforts on the part of artists, architects, and poets, many of whom were veterans of the Leningrad front or survivors of the blockade, to give meaningful form to their own memories and to speak on behalf of their fellow survivors.[11]

The Unnamed Dead: Piskarevskoe Memorial Cemetery

Piskarevskoe Cemetery was one of the first memorial complexes constructed during the thaw that followed Stalin's death in 1953. As the largest, but by no means the only, site of mass graves in Leningrad, Piskarevskoe carried undoubted personal and political significance. That the planning and construction of the cemetery occurred with little public scrutiny or intervention suggests the primacy of state interests. Yet the designers, poets, and sculptors who shaped and realized the memorial

---

[10] Peter Jelavich, "National Socialism, Art, and Power in the 1930s," *Past and Present*, no. 164 (August 1999): 248–49.

[11] James E. Young, *The Texture of Memory: Holocaust Memorials and Meaning* (New Haven, CT: Yale University Press, 1993), 155–56.

were predominantly native Leningraders who understood that the cemetery could offer both a place to grieve and a promise of consolation and closure. They turned the cemetery's fraternal graves into a monument to collective struggle and to unspeakable and unforgettable loss.

Mass Death and Fraternal Graves

In the first winter of the siege, few Leningraders were laid to rest in individual, marked graves. As the director of the city's food distribution services, Dmitrii Pavlov, remembered in the 1960s, "There was not enough strength to dig the deeply frozen earth. Civil defense crews would blast the ground to make mass graves, into which they would lay tens and sometimes hundreds of bodies without even knowing the names of those they buried."[12] As the historian Nina Tumarkin has bitterly remarked, "Most of the hundreds of thousands of siege victims had gone from communal apartments to mass graves."[13]

The near impossibility of honoring the dead deepened the tragedy for many families. In his diary, Ivan Zhilinskii recounted his wife's determination to spend the most precious commodity in a city emerging from months of starvation – the still-inadequate bread ration – in order to provide her brother and mother with individual graves amid the reality of mass death. In early March 1942, the cost of each grave was two kilos of bread and 500 rubles. Zhilinskii tried to persuade Olia to bury her relatives in a "general (fraternal) grave," at a total cost of only 40 rubles. The living, he reasoned, needed the bread more than the dead. She would not be persuaded. Olia herself died two weeks later and was buried in a common grave despite her husband's efforts to fulfill her wish to be cremated.[14]

Many survivors have attested to the importance that Leningraders attached to marking an individual grave. In March 1942, Sof'ia Buriakova failed in her efforts to bury her father in a separate grave. Fifty years later, the pain of her failure had not faded: "All my life I have suffered pangs of remorse that I was unable to fulfill this single request that my father made of me." Still, she managed to persuade the cemetery workers to place the body at the edge of a communal grave, and to remember

[12] Dmitrii V. Pavlov, *Leningrad 1941: The Blockade,* trans. John Clinton Adams (Chicago: University of Chicago Press, 1965), 123. See also I. I. Zhilinskii, "Blokadnyi dnevnik (osen' 1941–vesna 1942 g)," *Voprosy istorii,* 1996, no. 7: 9.
[13] Tumarkin, *The Living and the Dead,* 119.
[14] I. I. Zhilinskii, "Blokadnyi dnevnik," *Voprosy isotrii,* 1996, no. 8: 11, 14–15.

the location by orienting herself to the church. "In the postwar years," she noted in her memoirs, "whenever I had the strength, on Papa's birthday and V-Day, I would go to the communal grave and leave flowers."[15] Many Leningraders lacked even that small solace.

Designing the Memorial Cemetery: From Marking Absence to Offering Consolation

Perhaps half a million Leningraders – civilians and soldiers – lie in Piskarevskoe Cemetery's communal graves. A military cemetery before the war, Piskarevskoe became in January 1942 the primary site for the burial of civilians who died of starvation and of soldiers who died in the city's hospitals.[16] Almost immediately, architects recognized the importance of the cemetery as a potential commemorative site. However, turning the place into a memorial cemetery was a difficult operation, in practical as well as conceptual terms. Trenches blasted out of the frozen earth had to be reshaped into graves; the cemetery had to be marked as hallowed ground.

The wartime and immediate postwar plans for a memorial at Piskarevskoe Cemetery took the anonymity of death in besieged Leningrad as a given. Architects never considered including the names of the dead on the memorial, let alone creating and marking individual grave sites, as many victims tried in vain to do during the war. Instead, the architects relied on the sheer expanse of the planned cemetery to communicate the overwhelming, but unspecified, suffering and loss of unnamed citizens.

Evgenii Levinson, one of the primary architects on the project, looked back on the origins of the Piskarevskoe memorial in 1970 and remembered that the bleak appearance of the cemetery grounds in the aftermath of the war shaped his conception of the future memorial. Before the group of visiting architects "opened a sad picture. Fraternal graves were spread haphazardly throughout the territory.... The extraordinary breadth, the

[15] Sof'ia Nikolaevna Buriakova, "A Half-Century Ago," in Cynthia Simmons and Nina Perlina, eds., *Writing the Siege of Leningrad: Women's Diaries, Memoirs, and Documentary Prose* (Pittsburgh, PA: University of Pittsburgh Press, 2002), 101; see also 35, 122, 130, and Catherine Merridale, *Night of Stone: Death and Memory in Twentieth-Century Russia* (New York: Viking, 2000), 235–40.

[16] *Nekropol': Kladbishcha Sankt-Peterburga: Spravochnik*, vyp. 1 (St. Petersburg: Izdatel'stvo zhurnala "Avrora," 1992), 60. Upravlenie predpriiatiiami kommunal'nogo obsluzhivaniia (UPKO) to the executive committee (Ispolkom) of the Leningrad city soviet (29 October 1953), Tsentral'nyi Gosudarstvennyi Arkhiv Sankt-Peterburga (hereafter TsGA SPb), f. 7384, op. 37, d. 1197, l. 22.

extraordinary expanse . . . constituted the chief complexity, if you will. But it was precisely that expanse that defined the solution of the project." The view of the cemetery site that Levinson dated to 1948 became a central feature of the eventual memorial: "The level of the burials was lower than that of the adjoining road, and standing on the road it was possible to survey the whole territory, beyond the limits of which were fields, so unusual for the Leningrad city landscape."[17] A sensation of infinite emptiness defined the memorial.

The first designs for the memorial at Piskarevskoe Cemetery drew on the classical forms that Soviet architects often favored for war memorials, whether dedicated to the Great Fatherland War, the short but bloody war against Finland in 1939–40, or the Civil War.[18] The original plans called for the construction of a "tall obelisk made of clear glass, situated as if squeezed between two stelae, and behind it, a small courtyard, so that visitors would be able to escape for a time the great expanses of the necropolis."[19] The architects imagined an ineffably empty landscape and a small refuge. The transparent obelisk standing at the end of the long alley flanked by mass graves constituted a paradoxical focal point – rendered in glass, the traditional monument marking both victory and death would appear insubstantial, almost invisible.

Though in many ways a fitting monument to absence, the clear obelisk was eventually rejected. In their published writings, the architects offered a number of reasons for their decision. In an article written two years after the cemetery opened, in 1962, Levinson and his collaborator Aleksandr Vasil'ev explained that they abandoned the idea of a glass or granite obelisk "because this traditional architectural form turned out to be less expressive than the statue of the Mother-Motherland."[20] In his later

---

[17] E. Levinson, "Piskarevskii memorial'nyi ansambl'," *Sovetskaia arkhitektura*, 1970, no. 19: 148.

[18] T. G. Malinina, *Tema pamiati v arkhitekture voennykh let: Po materialam konkursov i vystavok, 1942–1945 gg.* (Moscow: Izdatel'stvo NII teorii i istorii izobrazitel'nykh iskusstv AkhSSSR, 1991), 82. "Monumenty geroiam Velikoi Otechestvennoi voiny," *Arkhitektura SSSR*, vyp. 5 (1944): 3–11. Gegello, "Pamiatniki na mestakh," 5–8. V. Tvel'kmeier, "Pamiatniki geroicheskoi oborony Leningrada," *Leningrad*, 1946, no. 1–2: 51–2. Ia. O. Rubanchik, "Diplomnye proekty 'Panorama oborny Petrograda,'" *Arkhitektura Leningrada*, 1940, no. 3: 42–45. I. G. Iavein, "Diplomnye raboty studentov LIIS'a," *Arkhitektura Leningrada*, 1940, no. 3: 46–48. "Proekty monumentov na mestakh boev s belofinnami," *Iskusstvo i zhizn'*, 1940, no. 8: 4–5.

[19] Levinson, "Piskarevskii memorial'nyi ansambl'," 150.

[20] E. A. Levinson and A. V. Vasil'ev, in *Pamiatnik geroicheskim zashchitnikam Leningrada: Piskarevskoe memorual'noe kladbishche-muzei* (Leningrad: Khudozhnik RSFSR, 1962), 26. Gennadii Fedorovich Petrov, *Piskarevskoe kladbishche* (Leningrad: Lenizdat, 1971),

reminiscences, Levinson emphasized that what persuaded the architects to revise their plan was the "fear that the obelisk would 'disappear' in the expansiveness," along with the technical difficulties of producing a transparent monolith.[21] The two concerns were clearly related. The architects, who must have understood when they proposed it that a transparent obelisk would "disappear," gradually, according to Levinson, changed their minds and decided that they needed to do more than mark a void without suggesting its meaning or offering comfort. The "expressive" and very visible Mother-Motherland, in contrast to the clear obelisk, unmistakably embodied both personal sorrows and the national cause. Standing six-and-a-half meters tall, she became the memorial's only vertical element and its symbolic core.

The Cult of the War and the Construction of Piskarevskoe Memorial Cemetery

The construction of the cemetery began only after Stalin's death. Planning had begun earlier, in 1949, when the city's public works administration directed engineers at Lenproekt (a division of the city soviet) to prepare blueprints for the improvement of the cemetery and for the construction of a memorial marking the mass graves. The engineers apparently completed a portion of the plan by 1952, and in December of that year, the council of ministers of the Russian Republic (RSFSR) approved six million rubles for the project.[22]

Why work did not begin immediately is not altogether clear. Simple administrative inefficiency is certainly a possibility. However, circumstantial evidence suggests that political fears played a role as well. The purge of party officials who had led Leningrad during the war, the closure of the Museum of the Heroic Defense of Leningrad, and the removal of the memorial warning signs on Nevskii Prospekt created an inauspicious climate for local officials or survivors interested in constructing memorial cemeteries. Moreover, the rehabilitation of the memory of the war and of

---

16. In 1946, architects N. V. Baranov and G. I. Ivanov proposed a Mother-Motherland statue as the centerpiece of the memorial at Serafimovskoe Cemetery. M. E. Rysakov, "Proekty pamiatnikov na Serafimovskom kladbishche," *Arkhitektura i stroitel'stvo Leningrada,* November 1946, 40.

21 Levinson, "Piskarevskii memorial'nyi ansambl'," 150–51. The architect's widow emphasizes "expressiveness." E. E. Levinson, *O druz'iakh, o zhizni, i nemnogo o sebe* (St. Petersburg: Stroiizdat, 1998), 130. V. G. Isachenko, "Vasil'evy," in V. G. Isachenko, ed., *Zodchie Sankt-Peterburga XX vek* (St. Petersburg: Lenizdat, 2000), 504–5.

22 TsGA SPb, f. 7384, op. 37, d. 1197, l. 22.

Leningrad that followed Stalin's death coincided with an energetic party-sponsored campaign to clean up and repair local cemeteries, both historic and active.[23] The increased attention to blockade cemeteries was thus part of a more general effort in the wake of Stalin's death to restore neglected sites of memory.

In September 1953, the Science and Culture Department of the regional Communist Party organization (Otdel nauki i kul'tury obkoma KPSS) turned its attention to the wretched conditions at Piskarevskoe Cemetery. An investigation had revealed that the "territory of the cemetery is swampy and that plans to drain and improve it have not been implemented." Unfit for visitors in purely practical terms, the cemetery also fell short of accomplishing its symbolic work of honoring the sacrifices of the dead. The report noted that "wooden monuments erected on fraternal [*bratskikh*] graves of fighters who fell during the G[reat] F[atherland] W[ar] are partially rotted, and the nameplates with the names of fighters have been dislodged from many monuments."[24] It is interesting that the memo said nothing about improving or marking the mass graves of civilians on the site. The concern at Piskarevskoe, as at other cemeteries, seems to have been motivated initially by military authorities who pushed local party and government organizations to provide fallen soldiers with a proper resting place.[25]

Almost seven years elapsed before the city completed work on the cemetery. In the fall of 1953, engineers were still working on blueprints for the first stage of technical improvements – the rebuilding of two hundred and fifty mass graves, the installation of water pipes, and the construction of a metal fence around the cemetery. The city government estimated that this phase of the project would take at least a year and cost 667,000 rubles.[26] Finishing the cemetery in time for its scheduled opening in May 1960 ultimately required diverting material and money from one of Leningrad's biggest postwar construction projects: the metro.[27]

---

[23] Ispolkom correspondence (23 September 1953, 16 December 1953), TsGA SPb, f. 7384, op. 37, d. 1197, ll. 13, 26–29.

[24] "Spravka o Piskarevskoem kladbishche v g. Leningrade" (9 October 1953), TsGA SPb, f. 7384, op. 37, d. 1197, l. 24.

[25] Leningradskii gorodskoi voennyi komissariat to Ispolkom (30 June 1956), TsGA SPb, f. 7384, op. 37, d. 1254, ll. 7–12.

[26] Ispolkom to Leningrad oblast party committee (20 November 1953), TsGA SPb, f. 7384, op. 37, d. 1197, l. 21.

[27] Ispolkom to Glavnyi upravlenie tonnelei i metropoletenov (4 October 1956), TsGA SPb, f. 7384, op. 37, d. 1254, l. 13. "V Otdel stroitel'noi industrii Gosplana SSSR" (29 October 1959), TsGA SPb, f. 7384, op. 37, d. 1394, l. 158. On the subway, see Blair A. Ruble,

The city soviet and party organizations solicited no public input into the planning or construction of Piskarevskoe Cemetery. However, the military authorities in Leningrad supported families outraged by the Funeral Trust's decision to disinter soldiers buried in individual graves and rebury them in a mass grave. Families "complained about the improper reburials in a common [*obshchuiu*] grave to the USSR Council of Ministers, the Central Committee of the Communist Party, and the Ministry of Defense." The order was rescinded. Still, the military authorities chided the local government that conditions remained disgraceful: "Individual graves and mass graves are overgrown with grass; grave markers are dilapidated, and many of them have collapsed."[28]

As work to improve the site began, the architects turned to the problem of coordinating the words and sculpture that would constitute the symbolic center of the cemetery. Levinson remembered that "there was no doubt" about choosing the sculptor Vera Isaeva to model the Mother-Motherland statue. Like Berggol'ts, Isaeva was a native Leningrader who had survived the blockade. She collaborated with Robert Taurit, a sculptor with whom she had worked before the war.[29] After much emotional debate, the two sculptors and the architects settled on a female figure holding a garland of oak leaves (Illustration 19). Levinson emphasized the intensity with which Isaeva, in particular, approached the sculpture. "Criticism," he recalled, "often brought her to tears."[30]

Likewise, Levinson had no doubts about who should provide the poetic centerpiece of the memorial. "From the very beginning," he remembered, "I knew which poet would be able to find the right words for the occasion. That was Ol'ga Berggol'ts."[31] In order to persuade the poet to participate, Levinson took her to visit the site. Berggol'ts, like Levinson some ten years before, was moved by the expanse of the still largely unimproved cemetery. In an autobiographical sketch written in 1972, she remembered:

It was a foul, fall Leningrad day, when we made our way to the outskirts of Leningrad. We walked through still absolutely unshaped mounds, not graves, but already behind them there was a huge granite wall, and there stood a woman

Leningrad: Shaping a Soviet City (Berkeley: University of California Press, 1990), 78, 83–84.

[28] TsGA SPb, f. 7384, op. 37, d. 1254, l. 11.

[29] Petrov, *Piskarevskoe kladbishche*, 17–19. Vera Ketlinskaia, "Skul'ptor Isaeva" in A. F. Volkova et al., eds., *Zhenshchiny goroda Lenina: Rasskazy i ocherki o zhenshchinakh Leningrada v dni blokady* (Leningrad: Lenizdat, 1944), 101–11.

[30] Levinson, "Piskarevskii memorial'nyi ansambl'," 152.

[31] Ibid., 148.

19. The Mother-Motherland statue at Piskarevskoe Cemetery. Photo by John K. Conway.

with an oak wreath in her hands. An inexpressible feeling of grief, sorrow, of total alienation overtook me at that moment, when I walked along that planked footway, through that awful earth, among those huge hills of graves, toward that blind and silent wall. No, I didn't think that I personally had to give a voice to that wall. But all the same, someone had to give it words and a voice. And besides, it was such a foul Leningrad fall, and it seemed to me that already not much time remained.[32]

Unlike Isaeva, who struggled with the motherland statue, Berggol'ts recalled that while she was looking at these "awful and heroic graves," the words for the wall suddenly came to her. The reality was probably somewhat less spontaneous, as she had to meet strict requirements regarding the number of characters per line and the number of lines. Still, the

---

[32] Berggol'ts, "Popytka avtobiorgrafii," in *Sobranie sochinenii v trekh tomakh* (Leningrad: Khudozhestvennaia literatura, 1988), 1: 44.

deep connection with the site that both she and Levinson felt suggests that the construction of the Piskarevskoe memorial, a state project of massive dimensions, also held emotional significance for the people who helped produce it.

As the guidebook to the cemetery emphasized, Piskarevskoe was a monument built by and for Leningraders. Isaeva returned to her native Leningrad from the relative safety of Moscow at the outset of the siege, and worked in the city to produce what was known as monumental propaganda, sculptures designed to honor heroes and inspire patriotism.[33] Her collaborator Taurit had fought on the Leningrad front. Berggol'ts, the voice of Radio Leningrad during the war, was widely regarded as "the poet who was able to give voice most convincingly to the trials of life under siege in Leningrad."[34] Mikhail Dudin, a poet who wrote the verses at the entrance to the cemetery, had been a newspaper correspondent on the Leningrad front. The architect Vasil'ev had produced propaganda posters for distribution in the besieged city. In the early days of the war, Levinson had supervised the construction of the defense perimeter around the city, and then returned to the city to oversee efforts to camouflage important monuments and buildings. The memorial at Piskarevskoe was created largely by people whose hearts, as the guidebook noted with regard to Levinson, were in Leningrad.[35]

By promoting the memorial as the work of survivors, the state, it could be argued, was merely attempting to pass off an official cultural production as the work of the "people," and to cover up the fact that in the postwar Soviet Union, the sorts of public contests over war memorials that characterized, for example, the building of memorials in post–World War I France, were impossible.[36] Decisions about the cemetery's ultimate

---

[33] G. Shkoda, "Iskrennost', chelovechnost', patriotizm," *Khudozhnik,* 1963, no. 11: 24–28. E. Turova and L. Kuznets, "V surovye dni blokady: Monumental'naia propaganda v Leningrade v gody Velikoi Otechestvennoi voiny," *Iskusstvo,* 1966, no. 2: 44–48.

[34] Katharine Hodgson, "Under an Unwomanly Star: War in the Writing of Ol'ga Berggol'ts," in Rosalind Marsh, ed., *Women and Russian Culture: Projections and Self-Perceptions* (New York: Berghahn Books, 1998), 157.

[35] Petrov, *Piskarevskoe kladbishche,* 17–19. Isachenko, "Vasil'evy," 501. Levinson was later evacuated from Leningrad. I. I. Lisaevich, "Evgenii Levinson," in Isachenko, *Zodchie Sankt-Peterburga,* 285.

[36] Daniel J. Sherman, *The Construction of Memory in Interwar France* (Chicago: University of Chicago Press, 1999), 215–60. Rubie Watson, "Memory, History, and Opposition under State Socialism: An Introduction," in Rubie Watson, ed., *Memory, History, and Opposition under State Socialism* (Santa Fe, NM: School of American Research Press, 1994), 1–5.

shape, indeed its very existence, rested squarely with city government and party officials. Nonetheless, the poets, sculptors, and architects did bring something of their own to the project. As Berggol'ts's sense that "already not much time remained" suggests, Piskarevskoe was for them a necessary, if belated, part of the process of coping with sorrow and loss. Even as they created an official monument that marginalized individual sacrifices, the monuments' designers managed to express painful and persistent personal memories. Recognizing the mass graves of the unnamed dead as "heroic," as Berggol'ts did when she visited the unfinished cemetery, did not rule out feelings of grief, sorrow, and "total alienation." Personal memory existed not only in the "interstices of public commemoration" – it helped to shape public commemoration.[37]

The Meanings of Piskarevskoe Cemetery

The ceremonies that marked the opening of the cemetery in 1960 linked the memorial's personal significance for Leningraders to the larger meanings of the war. A decade later, F. F. Grachev, who worked as a doctor in the besieged city, remembered that survivors turned the opening of the cemetery into an occasion for exchanging personal memories. The contemporary press coverage – a full page of stories and photographs in *Leningradskaia pravda* on the day after the dedication – emphasized the presence of survivors, who reportedly found in the new memorial both a place to mourn and remember and a monument to the meaningfulness of their sacrifices. A female deputy from the local soviet spoke on behalf of "all the women of Leningrad, who have not forgotten the bleak [*surovye*] years of the war." N. I. Pershin, a current deputy to the Supreme Soviet, who had apparently worked at the Elektrosil Plant during the blockade, spoke with "sincere pain" (*dushevnoi bol'iu*) as he remembered the many workers from the plant buried in the cemetery's fraternal graves. His speech also exemplified the ways in which the emerging cult of the war could serve as a tool of Cold War propaganda. Pershin ended his remarks by connecting the sacrifices memorialized at Piskarevskoe to a recent speech by Nikita Khrushchev that filled him "with pride for the Communist Party, which undertakes wise foreign policy, and defends peace."[38] The account of his pain may ring truer than the paean to Khrushchev's wisdom,

---

[37] Vera Schwarcz, "Strangers No More: Personal Memory in the Interstices of Public Commemorations," in Watson, *Memory, History, and Opposition*, 45–64.

[38] F. F. Grachev, *Zapiski voennogo vracha* (Leningrad: Lenizdat, 1970), 137–39. *Leningradskaia pravda* (hereafter *LP*), 10 May 1960. On the connections between Cold War

20. The eternal flame at the Monument to Revolutionary Fighters on the Field of Mars. Photo by John K. Conway.

but there is little reason to doubt that a survivor might take pride, and perhaps comfort, in the fact that his government seemed to be working for peace.

The newspaper's photograph of P. A. Zaichenko lighting the eternal flame provided the clearest image of a ceremony that both remembered the dead and celebrated the Soviet state. Zaichenko, who, probably not coincidentally, was both a "participant in the defense of Leningrad" and a turner at the Kirov Factory, connected the war to the Revolution. The memorial to the martyrs of 1917 on the Field of Mars had been renovated in 1957, at which time an eternal flame had been added (Illustration 20). A torch from this flame, carried through the entire city, ignited the "sacred

propaganda and the war cult, see Amir Weiner, "In the Long Shadow of War: The Second World War and the Soviet and Post-Soviet World," *Diplomatic History* 25 (Summer 2001): 447–48.

fire" at Piskarevskoe Cemetery.[39] The newspaper account clearly spelled out the significance of the journey from the Field of Mars: "The victory of the heroes of the Revolution served as an inspiring example for thousands of Leningraders during the years of the Great Fatherland War. That is why yesterday a part of the eternal flame from the Field of Mars was brought to the memorial cemetery."[40] The newspaper failed to note what lighting the flame meant to Zaichenko himself, who likely remembered his war even as he participated in a ritual designed to recast the war as a monument to the Revolution.

At Piskarevskoe, mythmaking and forgetting existed alongside images, words, and symbols that elicited and validated individual memory. At the entrance to the cemetery, two exhibits housed in classical propylaea told the story of the hero city, but also provided spaces for quiet introspection and remembering. For the survivor, images such as the photograph of books for sale on Nevskii Prospekt could stir up troubling memories of the desperation and death that brought so many rare editions to the city's bookstalls, along with more comforting reminiscences of the resilience of cultured habits in blockaded Leningrad.[41] Hushed, intimate, and dimly lit, the two pavilions functioned at once as museums that enshrined official narratives and as secular chapels where Leningraders who recognized the photographic icons of the blockade might recall their own stories.

From the terrace behind the propylaea, the site of the eternal flame, there opened a substantially more orderly version of the view that had so impressed the architect in 1948 – an expanse of graves below and, beyond the limits of the cemetery, trees and fields (Illustration 21). A stone staircase led down to a vast open space, 75 meters wide and 300 meters long, of well-groomed grassy mounds – the fraternal graves of the unnamed dead. The overall plan was rigidly symmetrical. This calming, tranquil landscape concealed the grim eyesore produced by hurried, haphazard burials and years of neglect. But if Piskarevskoe failed to mark the horrors of the blockade, it effectively communicated its dimensions. The rows of graves stretched to the horizon.[42]

---

[39] *Nekropol'*, 25. Iu. I. Smirnov, ed., *Sankt-Peterburg XX vek: Chto? Gde? Kogda?* (St. Petersburg: Izdatel'stvo "Paritet," 2000), 46. Nina Tumarkin provides an insightful analysis of the role of "sacred fire" in Soviet memorials. She incorrectly dates the eternal flame on the Field of Mars to 1920. Tumarkin, *The Living and the Dead*, 126–29.

[40] Z. Ustinova, "Vy zhivy v nashikh serdtsakh," *LP*, 10 May 1960. See also *Putevoditel' po Leningradu* (Leningrad: Lenizdat, 1963), 32.

[41] Petrov, *Piskarevskoe kladbishche*, 32–36. Alexander Werth, *Leningrad* (New York: Alfred A. Knopf, 1944), 176–77.

[42] Ignatieff, "Soviet War Memorials," 159. Merridale, *Night of Stone*, 235.

21. The view from the eternal flame at Piskarevskoe Memorial Cemetery. The Mother-Motherland statue is visible in the background. Photo by John K. Conway.

That the graves themselves were marked – with a year and a star, for soldiers, or a hammer and sickle, for civilians (Illustration 22) – constituted the cemetery's most pious fiction. Given the long delay between the original burials and the improvement of the graves, as well as the massive numbers buried at Piskarevskoe, it seems at best unlikely that the markers corresponded to the contents of the graves. Their inclusion points to the complicated interaction of memory and myth at the core of the cemetery. Simultaneously distinguishing and equating deaths at the battlefront and on the home front, the subtle markers on the otherwise identical graves perpetuated the reassuring story that all who died were "heroic defenders." On a more personal level, the tablets responded to the individual mourner's need to find, or at least to imagine that he or she had found, the "right" grave. Visitors still place flowers on the granite slabs with the appropriate symbol and year of death.

22. Civilian graves at Piskarevskoe Cemetery, marked with a hammer and sickle and a year. Photo by John K. Conway.

The cemetery's sculpture, and particularly the mourning motherland figure, similarly evoked both the heroic collective and individual losses. The Mat'-Rodina that presided over the mass graves was at once mother and motherland. A contemporary Soviet art historian noted that "the difficult war years have left their mark on the Mother's face. . . . It seems, she even now sees the torments of the inhabitants of the besieged city." Yet the overall impression – one completely in accord with the myth of the hero city – was one of "strength, courage, steadfastness, and belief in the justness of her cause." She was, in short, the embodiment of the "characteristics of our people that brought us to victory." At the same time, she was a familiar and ordinary woman, who, as the critic noted, was endowed with the features of a typical Russian woman. Her body was of "heavy proportions" with powerful hands and broad hips.[43] An allegory of the

---

[43] V. M. Rogachevskii, "Mat'-Rodina, 1951–1960," in *Iz bronzy i mramora: Kniga dlia chteniia po istorii russkoi i sovetskoi skul'ptury* (Leningrad: Khudozhnik SSSR, 1965), 454.

Motherland, she also recalled actual mothers. If she obscured women's active roles in the blockaded city, as well as the physical realities of starvation, she nonetheless provided a recognizable, if rather turgid, reflection of the sorrows and strengths of the city's real women.[44]

Berggol'ts's poetry, which together with the Mother-Motherland, stood at the center of the memorial, can, like the statue, be understood as both a mythic whitewash and a call to remember. The verses echoed her most declamatory works of the war years.[45] An epitaph for the unnamed dead, the poem began:

> Here lie Leningraders
> Here lie the men, women, and children of the city.
> And alongside of them, Red Army soldiers.
> With all their life
> They defended you, Leningrad,
> The cradle of revolution.
> We are not able to enumerate here their noble names,
> So many are beneath the eternal protection of granite.
> But know, as you consider this stone,
> No one is forgotten, and nothing is forgotten.

In a few brief lines, Berggol'ts managed to stir a sense of hometown patriotism – "Here lie Leningraders" – and to connect local sacrifices to the national cause. They defended the city, the poem suggested, as native sons and daughters and as the heirs of the Revolution that was also born there. Berggol'ts's phrase "no one is forgotten, and nothing is forgotten" became during the 1960s and 1970s the watchword of the war cult, and as such, suggested that a grateful, victorious nation remembered. The phrase can thus be read, as Nina Tumarkin has noted, as a galling bit of hypocrisy, since the war cult effaced, ignored, and distorted so much of the Soviet war experience.[46]

However, even as they voiced the verities of the war cult, the verses called attention to the fact that the official monument did not tell the whole story.[47] In the context of the cemetery, the phrase "no one is forgotten"

---

[44] Irina Ignat'evna Lisaevich and I. Betkher-Ostrenko, *Skul'ptura Leningrada,* 2d ed. (Leningrad: Iskusstvo, 1965), 190.

[45] Katharine Hodgson, *Voicing the Soviet Experience: The Poetry of Ol'ga Berggol'ts* (New York: The British Academy in association with Oxford University Press, 2003), 72–78.

[46] Tumarkin, *The Living and the Dead,* 134–35. Ignatieff, "Soviet War Memorials," 160. Weiner, "In the Long Shadow," 455–56.

[47] Hodgson, *Voicing,* 134 ff. Aileen Rambow, "The Siege of Leningrad: Wartime Literature and Ideological Change," in Robert W. Thurston and Bernd Bonwetsch, eds., *The People's War: Responses to World War II in the Soviet Union* (Urbana: University of Illinois Press, 2000), 161.

evoked personal and individual operations of memory, as well as the consoling power of the myth. Providing what any survivor would recognize as
an attenuated description of the city's sufferings, the poem pledged that the
horrors would not be forgotten – "neither the hungry, cruel, dark/ winter
of forty-one-forty-two,/ nor the savagery of the shelling,/ nor the terror
of the bombs in forty-three." Names could be – would be – remembered
even if they were not inscribed in stone. Leaving much unsaid, but not, it
asserted, unremembered, the poem assured survivors that their suffering
and losses were meaningful. Berggol'ts's verses, indeed the memorial as a
whole, prompted survivors themselves to fill in the unspoken details – the
bodily sensations of hunger, darkness, and cold, the names of the dead.

The most substantial exception to the general rule of the anonymity and
abstractness of death at Piskarevskoe was the display in one of the pavilions of the diary and photograph of Tania Savicheva. During the blockade,
eleven-year-old Tania had kept a log of the dates and time of the deaths
of the members of her family. This "diary" had become an exhibit at the
siege museum opened during the war. Its famous last lines, "Everyone has
died. Only Tania remains," allegedly brought Winston Churchill's wife
Clementine to tears when she visited the museum in 1944.[48] The journal,
along with a prewar photograph of its author, appeared at Piskarevskoe
without caption or comment. Tania herself died of the effects of starvation, not in Leningrad but after being evacuated from the city in the spring
of 1942.[49] (Thus, the only prominent "named" victim of the blockade at
Piskarevskoe was not buried there.) In military cemeteries where remains
are assiduously identified and named, the "unknown" stands in for "every
soldier." By contrast, at Piskarevskoe, the "known" represented "every
Leningrader" in a sea of unmarked mass graves.

Recently, the situation has changed, as local factories, cultural insti-
tutions, and survivors' organizations have placed, along the edges of
the central memorial, rows of easels holding memorial tablets with the
names of civilians who died during the blockade (Illustration 23).[50] This
post-Soviet addition suggests both the emotional resonance of names and

[48] Ales' Adamovich and Daniil Granin, *Blokadnaia kniga* (Moscow: Sovetskii pisatel',
1982), 8. In her telegrams from Leningrad, Churchill did not mention the museum. Mary
Soames, ed., *Winston and Clementine: The Personal Letters of the Churchills* (Boston:
Houghton Mifflin, 1998), 525.

[49] D. Khrenkov, "Po znakomomu adresu," *Literaturnaia gazeta*, 25 January 1964.

[50] "A Gravestone Has Been Set Up on the Memorial Piskarevskoe Cemetery," Petersburg
CITY: Official Internet-portal of St. Petersburg, 7 September 2001, http://petersburgcity.
com/news/city/2001/09/07/memorial (accessed 17 February 2006).

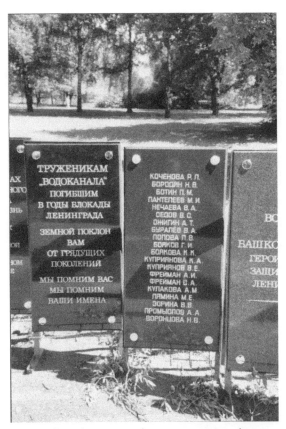

23. Easels with names and commemorative plaques around the periphery of the Piskarevskoe memorial. Photo by author.

dissatisfaction with a design that included so few, and none at its core. That survivors brought movable tablets with names to the memorial also suggests that mourners had long carried mental lists of names to the cemetery with them.[51] The act of adding to the memorial thus indicates less a rejection of Soviet iconography than a concrete recognition of the multiplicity of meanings implicit in the memorial landscape created by the Soviet state. The personal memories evoked by the memorial have gained visibility and some measure of permanence.

[51] On the importance of recovering names, see Young, *Texture,* 189–96; Sherman, *The Construction of Memory,* 68; Thomas Laqueur, "Memory and Naming in the Great War," in John R. Gillis, ed., *Commemorations: The Politics of National Identity* (Princeton, NJ: Princeton University Press, 1994), 161.

Placing a garland on the graves of the unnamed dead, the Mother-Motherland insisted on the meaningfulness and equality of the sacrifices made by the city's "heroic defenders." Nonetheless, the meaning of the sacrifice remained somewhat open. The rodina, after all, might be understood in local terms – as the city or the neighborhood – as well as in broader national terms. Using a maternal figure to represent an ambiguously defined "native place" underscored the importance of the local and the domestic in the process of attributing significance to the losses marked at the cemetery. The story of the siege constructed at the cemetery denied or at least downplayed individual loss. At the same time, the Mother-Motherland emphasized the degree to which the war could, and perhaps should, be understood in personal terms – a mother mourning her children whose names will never be forgotten. Now, some of those names have become part of the memorial.

The Monument to the Heroic Defenders of Leningrad

On 9 May 1975, fifteen years after the opening of Piskarevskoe Cemetery, the Monument to the Heroic Defenders of Leningrad was dedicated on Victory Square. Citizens' contributions funded the project, and in the mid-1960s, the Leningrad city government had actively solicited residents' opinions regarding the memorial's location and its form. The flood of letters from Leningraders, along with the debates occasioned by competitions to choose a design, illuminate the ways in which the veterans and blockade survivors who designed the monument struggled to memorialize the tragic, urban, and domestic experiences of the blockade within the limits imposed by the triumphal visual idiom of the war cult. A celebration of victory that forgot a great deal, the monument was – and remains – a place to mourn and remember.

Finding a Location: City or Front?
The initial planning for what would become the Monument to the Heroic Defenders of Leningrad dates to the war itself, when the local branch of the Union of Architects organized competitions for a "Victory" monument. The first important postwar competition took place in 1958, five years after Stalin's death.[52] Thus, like Piskarevskoe Cemetery, the Victory monument grew out of the recovery of the memory of the war associated

---

[52] E. V. Lezik, "Monument geroicheskim zashchitnikam Leningrada (istoriia sozdaniia)," *Trudy gosudarstvennogo muzeia istorii Sankt-Peterburga*, vyp. 5 (2000): 270–73.

with the thaw and was part of the resurgence of local history that accompanied the belated celebration of Leningrad's 250th anniversary.

Promoting the memorial as a people's rather than a state project, the local press in 1963 asked Leningraders to make contributions to its construction and to suggest possible locations. In advance of the open competition to decide a site for the monument, hundreds of Leningraders sent letters, postcards, even rather expertly drafted sketches to the local newspaper.[53] By the time the public judging in the first round of competition occurred, Khrushchev had been forced out of office. Nonetheless, the letters and the debate generated by the competition reflected more the spirit of the thaw than the refreeze presided over by Leonid Brezhnev.

The debate on where to locate the memorial revolved around the question of the war's place in local history and the urban landscape. Should a memorial stand in the city – the site of civilian, predominately female suffering and heroism during the war – or at the battlefront? Current residents, war veterans, survivors of the blockade, and architects (groups with considerable overlap) suggested a wide variety of possible locations that reflected competing conceptions of the memorial – a monument to the city connected to its imperial and revolutionary pasts, to the civilians who suffered through the blockade or worked in civil defense, or to military victory.

Blockade survivors, in particular, emphasized that any memorial must be a part of the city's everyday life. The most literal expression of this position came from letter writers who proposed new apartments for survivors as the best possible memorial to the blockade. In a letter addressed to Khrushchev, one group of survivors voiced the collective opinion that "the most effective memorial" to those who survived hunger and the blockade, won medals for the defense of Leningrad, and rebuilt the city would be to guarantee them "individual, modern, well-constructed apartments."[54] A letter accompanying a donation to the project began with Berggol'ts's "no one is forgotten," and charged that "many have been forgotten."

---

[53] I. A. Bartenev, *Monument geroicheskim zashchitnikam Leningrad v gody velikoi otechestvennoi voiny,* 2d ed. (Leningrad: Khudozhnik SSSR, 1981), 36. "Stenograficheskii otchet Soiuz Arkhitektorov Leningradskoe otdelenie" (16 November 1964), Tsentral'nyi Gosudarstvennyi Arkhiv Literatura i Iskusstva Sankt Peterburga (hereafter TsGALI SPb), f. 341, op. 1, d. 643, l. 4. "Dokumenty o vypolnenii resheniia Ispolkoma Lengorsoveta" (28 January 1974), TsGA SPb, f. 7384, op. 43, d. 445-V, l. 3.

[54] "Pis'ma – otkliki uchastnikov Velikoi Otechestvennoi voiny na proektirovanie i ustanovku pamiatnika v chest' geroichestkikh zashchitnikov Leningrada," TsGALI SPb, f. 341, op. 6, d. 1, l. 45; see also ll. 127–29.

The correspondent suggested that funds raised for the memorial should be used to build a "minidistrict" (*microraion*) called "Monument to the Defense of Leningrad" that would consist of new apartments for blokadniki. Khrushchev's plan to build prefabricated housing had made such minidistricts a common sight in Leningrad's suburbs, but many blokadniki remained in the communal apartments in which they had survived the war.[55]

Many Leningraders, as the numerous proposals for locating the memorial near the *Aurora* (the ship that famously fired on the Winter Palace during the Bolshevik takeover in October 1917) attest, tried to find ways to connect the war to the Revolution. One unsigned suggestion from a survivor of the blockade, which arrived on a postcard depicting the statue of Vladimir Lenin in front of the Finland Station, emphasized that the commemoration of the blockade must be closely associated with the words and experiences of women: "I think that the monument should immortalize the two women who spoke the suffering Truth about the Blockade – Ol'ga Berggol'ts and Ol'ga Matiushina."[56] While the writer called for a monument to two authors who presumably gave voice to his own memories of the "Truth about the Blockade," the card on which he sent his suggestion implicitly acknowledged the importance – at least to the people receiving his note – of linking the suffering of the blockade to another episode in local history, the glorious and heroic story of Lenin and the Revolution. He declined, however, to specify a location that might achieve this linkage.

Other letter writers suggested sites that highlighted the overlapping historical and personal associations of urban space. Proposing a monument on Nevskii Prospekt, one correspondent provided a precise description of the location he had in mind: near the statues of the generals from "the first Fatherland War" adjacent to Gostinyi Dvor, the landmark eighteenth-century arcade badly damaged by German air raids in the most

---

[55] "Pis'ma," TsGALI SPb, f. 341, op. 6, d. 6, l. 14. Ruble, *Leningrad*, 64–72. Geoffrey Barraclough, "Late Socialist Housing: Prefabricated Housing in Leningrad from Khrushchev to Gorbachev" (Ph.D. diss., University of California, Santa Barbara, 1997), 200–202. Natalia Korkonosenko, "Blokadnitsy," *Leningradskaia panorama*, 1991, no. 8: 28. Aleksei Oreshkin, "Khoroshie novosti: Dom veteranov stanovit'sia obitaemym," *Smena*, 8 September 1995. Steven E. Harris, "Moving to the Separate Apartment: Building, Distributing, Furnishing, and Living in Urban Housing in Soviet Russia, 1950s-1960s" (Ph.D. diss., University of Chicago, 2003), 210–11.

[56] TsGALI SPb f. 341, op. 6, d. 1, l. 69. See also "Pis'ma," TsGALI SPb f. 341, op. 6, d. 7, l. 124. I have inferred the letter writer's gender from the gender of the past tense verbs.

recent Fatherland War.[57] The precision with which the letter described the damage and the proposed location suggests a personal connection to the site – perhaps a scene witnessed firsthand during the blockade. Similarly, a female survivor, who emphasized the difficulty of coping with an alcoholic neighbor in her communal apartment, and deemed new housing the best way to honor blokadniki, proposed a location for a more traditional memorial. Her suggestion sounds very much like a personal memory. "Regarding a monument," she wrote, "I advise building it on the Field of Mars because during the blockade many of the dead were left there by relatives who were in no condition to get them to the cemetery."[58]

Leningraders recognized that the monument's location would shape the story it told. Advocates of honoring the thousands of predominantly young women who participated in local antiaircraft defense units (MPVO) imagined monuments within the city, where such units worked.[59] Those who hoped to emphasize the military aspects of the "Leningrad epic" called for monuments along the former front. One particularly catholic proposal suggested a series of monuments "at different ends of the city" capable of reflecting the site-specific "victories of sailors, infantrymen, pilots, tank drivers, and even the simple inhabitants of the city."[60] Away from the city center, "real" heroes – pilots, sailors, soldiers, tank crews – tended to overshadow the "simple inhabitants" of the city.

Expressing strong and varied opinions regarding where the monument should stand and what precisely it should commemorate, Leningraders turned out in droves to view the entries in the first round of competition. Sergei Speranskii, who chaired the public judging of the exhibition in November 1964 and who eventually became the chief architect on the project, noted that close to a thousand people a day had visited the exhibit.[61] Somewhat unusually for Soviet architectural competitions, amateurs submitted about half of the eighty-three entries.[62]

The inclusion of the projects by amateurs complicated the architects' efforts to judge the competition. The amateur projects purported to speak

[57] TsGALI SPb, f. 341, op. 6, d. 7, l. 22.

[58] TsGALI SPb, f. 341, op. 6, d. 6, l. 37.

[59] TsGALI SPb, f. 341, op. 6, d. 1, ll. 100–103. An MPVO commander asserted that women accounted for 80 percent of these units. TsGALI SPb, f. 341, op. 6, d. 6, l. 66. Published party documents do not break down MPVO volunteers by sex. A. R. Dzeniskevich, *Leningrad v osade: Sbornik dokumentov o geroicheskoi oborone Leningrade v gody Velikoi Otechestvennoi voiny* (St. Petersburg: Liki-Rossii, 1995).

[60] TsGALI SPb, f. 341, op. 6, d. 7, ll. 43–44.

[61] TsGALI SPb, f. 341, op. 1, d. 643, l. 2.

[62] Ibid., ll. 4–6.

for the people, and the architects affirmed their responsibility to listen to the public.[63] However, the professionals did not always like what they heard. It quickly became clear that most of the architects favored a site away from the city center that would anchor new postwar neighborhoods either in the western section of Vasil'evskii Island along the Gulf of Finland (twenty-nine proposals) or at the southern extreme of the city near the Pulkovo Heights, the front line during the blockade (eighteen proposals). The remaining thirty-six proposals (it is not clear how many of these were submitted by the amateurs) were spread around the city center, with the largest concentration on the Petrograd side in the vicinity of the *Aurora* (sixteen proposals). Popular opinion seemed to be on the side of these more central locations.[64]

At the public judging, advocates of a memorial in the city center presented arguments ranging from the practical to the symbolic. An engineer by the name of Goldshtein – the stenographic record of the public debate identified speakers by last name and sometimes by profession – objected to the Pulkovo Heights and the adjacent neighborhood of Sredniaia Rogatka on what he termed "utilitarian" grounds: "You know, no one goes there."[65] By contrast, sites in the city center would become stitched into the everyday fabric of city life, and would connect the blockade to the whole sweep of Petersburg–Leningrad's history. An architect advocating a location along the river noted that the "panoramas of the Neva present themselves as an enormous historical museum of our city," from the Decembrist Uprising of 1825 through Lenin's arrival at the Finland Station to the cruiser *Aurora*. The Neva embankments also had the advantage of being the places where Leningraders traditionally congregated on holidays.[66]

Perhaps the most impassioned plea for a monument in the city center came from an architect by the name of Popov, who emphasized the need to honor the unique experiences of the city during the war. He argued against locating the monument in Sredniaia Rogatka, the point at which the city met the front, because he believed that the front had no place in the city's memorial: "You know, this isn't a memorial to the troops.... This is a monument to the whole population of Leningrad and to the city as

[63] Ibid., l. 11.
[64] Ibid., ll. 6–7. For an assessment of public preferences, see ibid., ll. 14, 32.
[65] Ibid., l. 17.
[66] Ibid., l. 24; see also ll. 32, 58. On the embankments as gathering places, see TsGALI SPb, f. 341, op. 6, d. 7, l. 124.

a whole." Thus, he concluded, the monument should stand among the historic buildings and vistas that, for Leningraders and non-Leningraders alike, defined the city.[67]

On the other side, architects also claimed to be honoring the city as a whole, but they defined it less in terms of its past than its future. They objected to sites in the city center as too small. Only a memorial "complex," they argued, could both express the monumental events of the defense of Leningrad and accommodate the large gatherings anticipated on important anniversaries.[68] An advocate of locating the monument in a new, postwar section of the city on Vasil'evskii Island emphasized that the memorial "should rule out a funereal tone, the tone of the memorial cemetery, the tone of the eternal flame." Instead, it should stand among new houses and look toward the happy future: "We all want to live in new houses."[69] Placing the memorial among new apartments responded, at least in a token and symbolic way, to defenders of "old" Leningrad who hoped that their reward would be better living conditions. The new apartment buildings themselves constituted a means of representing national victory as something close to home – even if few blokadniki ended up living in them.

Focusing on the question of location, the initial planning largely avoided issues of representation. Yet the ultimate decision to place the memorial at the point were the city met the former front shaped the entries in the second round of competition (this time open only to professionals) that aimed to choose a design for the memorial. The winning site, dubbed "Victory Square," was an ellipse 350 meters wide and 380 meters long, a sort of glorified traffic island at the southern extreme of Moskovskii Prospekt, in the heart of a new residential district at Sredniaia Rogatka. This liminal location – the site of one of the temporary victory arches erected in 1945 – suggested that the memorial itself would bridge the experiences of the city and the front, of civilians and soldiers, of men and women.[70] The Sredniaia Rogatka location left open the possibility of at least a partially local, civilian-centered monument that would produce a vision of victory focused as much on state power as the good life in a new apartment. The location question settled, it was still almost a decade

[67] TsGALI SPb, f. 341, op. 1, d. 643, ll. 65, 32.

[68] Ibid., ll. 21, 29, 84.

[69] Ibid., ll. 60–62; see also ll. 29–31.

[70] A. K. Barutchev, "Arki Pobedy," *Arkhitektura i stroitel'stvo Leningrada: Sbornik*, June 1946, 1–2.

before construction began on a memorial at the imagined line between the city and the front in Leningrad.

The National and the Local: Celebrating Victory, Documenting Tragedy

In 1966, a competition to find a design for the monument produced no winners.[71] Three years later, a closed competition run by the Ministry of Culture of the USSR, together with the Executive Committee (Ispolkom) of the Leningrad city soviet likewise failed to recommend a design. In early 1970, the city soviet requested permission to have the most promising groups of architects submit revised proposals. By July 1970, the local government recommended the design proposed by a group of architects led by Sergei Speranskii. Future work on the project was entrusted to Speranskii, the architect Valentin Kamenskii, and the sculptor Anikushin, best known for his statue of the poet Aleksandr Pushkin in Arts Square.[72] In 1973, the local government took financial responsibility for completing the monument, and construction began in early 1974 for a planned opening on Victory Day 1975.[73]

The process that produced the memorial was thus largely closed to public involvement. However, the Leningrad branch of the Union of Architects did sponsor a public discussion of the designs submitted in 1966, as it had in 1964. The public debate on the proposals – as well as visitors' comments and letters to the local press – provide some insight into the difficulty of finding a design to honor the Soviet Union and the city, as well as the whole vast and varied array of people who "defended" the city front.

The responses of veterans and blockade survivors to the 1966 proposals often focused on the failure of designs to capture the "true [*istinnoi*] history of the defense of Leningrad."[74] One architect, who introduced himself as speaking less as an architect than as a survivor of the blockade, began his remarks by noting that the proposals lacked "Leningrad specificity." He suggested the need for a site-specific narrative that did

---

[71] For photographs of some of the entries from both 1964 and 1966, see "Konkursnyi proekty," TsGALI SPb, f. 341, op. 5, d. 96, T. 4.

[72] Ispolkom correspondence with USSR Ministry of Culture (1969, 1970), TsGA SPb, f. 7384, op. 43, d. 940, ll. 1, 4, 7, 15a.

[73] "Dokumenty o vypolnenii resheniia Ispolkoma Lengorsoveta" (29 January 1973), TsGA SPb, f. 7384, op. 43, d. 445-G, ll. 6–7. TsGA SPb, f. 7384, op. 43, d. 445-V, ll. 4–5. V. S. Speranskaia, "Sergei Speranskii," in Isachenko, *Zodchie Sankt-Peterburga*, 454–55.

[74] "Pis'ma," TsGALI SPb, f. 341, op. 6, d. 30, l. 54; see also ll. 13, 20, 26, 40, 76, 81.

not try to redeem trauma with overblown images of victory. Granting that "these monuments are well done," he complained that "they could stand in Belorussia, in Ukraine, outside Moscow." Above all, he objected to the "pomposity" of some of the projects: "This [the blockade] was difficult, and shouting 'hurrah' will not resolve this theme."[75] A large number of responses emphasized that the monument must tell the story of the blockade; many suggested including a museum.[76]

A number of architects focused on the need to fit any monument into the local landscape. Some emphasized the importance of formal elements in keeping with the architectural heritage of the city, by which they meant imperial St. Petersburg. The architect Raikhman, for example, called for a "vertical" element in the design that would transform Moskovskii Prospekt into a real Leningrad boulevard, "a second Nevskii."[77] The architect Otroshchenko agreed with the necessity of referencing Leningrad's unique architectural heritage, but emphasized that the monument had to do more than fit in with the local architecture: "The monument must express the spirit [*dukh*] of Leningrad, as a sort of Seventh Symphony in stone."[78] Somewhat incongruously, he deemed an international competition the best way to generate designs that captured the feeling of blockaded Leningrad in the way that Dmitrii Shostakovich's symphony had.

Given the association of victory with the heroism of male soldiers, it is not surprising that the question of how the memorial should represent women's wartime roles, while rarely framed quite this explicitly, generated much discussion. A construction engineer, Kostin, argued that the monument must "show our mothers and our fathers – the whole population of the city, beginning with the old people and ending with the children."[79] A woman by the name of Vinogradova, who identified herself as one of four children who survived the blockade after their parents' death, emphasized the importance of including the details of domestic life during the winter of 1941–42. She described herself as visiting the exhibit, expecting that "the monument projects would reflect hunger, the suffering of children, their mothers and even their grandmothers. But I didn't see this."[80] Indeed, only one project included the iconic image of

75 "Stenograficheskii otchet" (1966), TsGALI SPb, f. 341, op. 1, d. 700, ll. 76–77.
76 TsGALI SPb, f. 34, op. 6, d. 6, l. 47. TsGALI SPb, f. 341, op. 6, d. 1, ll. 58–59, 112, 166.
77 TsGALI SPb, f. 341, op. 1, d. 700, ll. 73, 101, 103, 113.
78 Ibid., l. 88.
79 Ibid., ll. 58, 110. TsGALI SPb, f. 341, op. 6, d. 1, l. 166.
80 TsGALI SPb, f. 341, op. 1, d. 700, ll. 125, 127.

the city during the blockade: a figure – perhaps a woman, wrapped in a scarf, the only visible feature oversize, lifeless eyes – pulling a sled with a smaller figure, probably her child, wrapped in a blanket or a sheet, a corpse. The judges did not place the project in the top category, and it received little attention at the public discussion.[81] However, visitors did respond positively to it, commenting that "here is reflected everything that people lived through during the 900 days of the blockade."[82]

Calls to show the truth about the blockade and to hold an international competition were not necessarily tantamount to calls for distorted, anguished figures in pain. Architects rejected a monument like Ossip Zadkine's expressive *The Destroyed City* in Rotterdam, along with the pompous allegories.[83] Moreover, some Leningraders objected to projects that privileged the civilian experience of the blockade, and deemed a monument to military victory both necessary and appropriate. A group of metalworkers from the Kirov Factory, who proudly identified themselves as veterans born and raised in Leningrad, favored a monument to victory over a memorial to the victims.[84]

Taking the emphasis on the state triumphant a step further, a few speakers advocated a more top-down notion of inclusiveness. Raikhman, who called for a vertical element, also argued for recognizing the "people who organized victory," by which he meant the party bigwigs, beginning with Andrei Zhdanov and including Aleksei Kosygin, who along with Leonid Brezhnev and Nikolai Podgornii had engineered Khrushchev's ouster in October 1964.[85] The poet Nikolai Tikhonov argued that the memorial ought to include the "image of Lenin." But his suggestion found no echo among the gathered architects.[86]

Perhaps not surprisingly, the competition failed to produce a winner. The public discussion and the visitors' comments exemplify the complications that may have prolonged the design process. Many veterans and survivors of the blockade – many of whom happened to be architects – were committed to a memorial that honored the city, all its inhabitants, and what most considered the unique Leningrad experience of the war. Their loyalty was to the *rodina* in the narrow sense of hometown, often

---

[81] TsGALI SPb, f. 341, op. 5, d. 96, T. 4, l. 170b.

[82] TsGALI SPb, f. 341, op. 6, d. 30, l. 175; see also ll. 13, 40, 54.

[83] TsGALI SPb, f. 341, op. 1, d. 700, l. 35. See also TsGALI SPb, f. 341, op. 1, d. 643, ll. 31, 60.

[84] "Pis'ma," TsGALI SPb, f. 341, op. 6, d. 33, l. 68.

[85] Brezhnev, alas, was not a Leningrader. TsGALI SPb, f. 341, op. 1, d. 700, l. 74.

[86] Ibid., l. 63.

embodied in Leningrad women, whose strength and determination got them through the blockade. However, others viewed the monument on "Victory Square" as primarily a celebration of the "heroic defense of Leningrad," a microcosm of the eventual Soviet triumph. Indeed, many architects seemed to relish the opportunity to add another victory monument to Leningrad–St. Petersburg's imperial cityscape. Such a monument could draw on the visual lexicon of the emerging war cult that included soldiers, pilots, sailors, and workers, along with obelisks and triumphal arches – often of imposing proportions. Of course, sailors, soldiers, and workers also contributed to the local Leningrad story. The difficulty was that transposing the local story into the monumental key of the national epic threatened to drive out the specificity of Leningrad's wartime experience, while a monument documenting the "true history" of the blockade might taint the celebration of victory. The Leningrad monument raised, in especially acute form, the problem of fixing in stone both local suffering – usually embodied as female – and national power – the triumphant male hero.

A Monument on Three Levels: Nothing Is Forgotten?

While the planning process that followed the inconclusive 1966 competition solicited less public input, the press continued to emphasize that the monument was a "people's" monument. It represented the designs exhibited in the early 1970s, the construction process itself, and the monument as finally completed in 1978 as historically and emotionally accurate, including and honoring everyone who "defended" Leningrad.[87] I would argue that the monument minimizes and forgets more than the press allowed – notably the horrors of battle, the extent of starvation, and the degree to which civil defense was women's and children's work.

Nonetheless, by creating both a grand public exterior oriented to the street and two increasingly enclosed, intimate spaces that contained increasingly local and personal images and finally artifacts, the designers found a way to create an expressly Leningrad memorial that commemorated suffering and struggle while obeying the war cult's injunction against the "image of a physically damaged but surviving figure" whose

---

[87] On the construction process see "V chest' velikoi pobedy," *Stroitel'stvo i arkhitektura Leningrada*, 1975, no. 1: 6. Bartenev, *Monument*, 9–10. The newspapers carried daily updates on the monument's progress, and comments from some of the twelve thousand volunteers.

24. Female metalworkers on the Monument to the Heroic Defenders of Leningrad. Photo by John K. Conway.

broken body suggests that victory does not heal all wounds.[88] Rather than combining monumental male embodiments of the "Victors" and female allegories of the suffering rodina, the memorial created discrete and distinct spaces for these competing images of the nation and the city. The result was a memorial that embedded local experience in Soviet military triumph – that at once honored and co-opted local stories and local loyalties.

From the beginning, the design team of Speranskii, Kamenskii, and Anikushin worked to include in the monument an impressive array of figures representing the city and the front. In 1972, *Leningradskaia pravda* emphasized the inclusiveness of one of their early designs. The plan situated more than thirty sculpted figures not on plinths but on the plaza itself, where visitors might walk among the heroes (Illustrations 24, 25, and 26). The figures included "emaciated women casting shells. A mother holding her child's stiff body in her outstretched arms.... Baltic sailors with automatic weapons going into a fierce attack.... A young nurse, almost a girl.... Three men carrying a heavy rail, stooping under the excessive

---

[88] Joan Pachner, "Zadkine and Gabo in Rotterdam," *Art Journal* 53, no. 4 (Winter 1994): 80.

25. Male soldiers and sailors on the Monument to the Heroic Defenders of Leningrad. Photo by John K. Conway.

26. "The Home Guard" on the Monument to the Heroic Defenders of Leningrad, which includes a young female medic. Photo by John K Conway.

27. A sniper and a girl embracing on the Monument to the Heroic Defenders of Leningrad. Photo by author.

weight – for a barricade that was constructed on the streets here, exactly here, where the monument will stand. The figures of paratroopers, snipers, partisans."[89] This was Soviet political correctness at its best.

The monument as built reduced somewhat the number of figures, and arranged them more hierarchically on pedestals placed on either side of a broad granite staircase, but retained the emphasis on inclusiveness and accuracy. Period details, including an out-of-style (for the 1940s) long coat that identified a man participating in building barricades as an intellectual and newly forged shells inscribed with insults directed at Hitler, "communicate," in the words of the critic V. A. Frolov, "realistic, lifelike, true [*pravdivye*] episodes from the blockade, and require long and attentive 'reading.'"[90] Even the most sentimental set piece – a sniper and a girl embracing (Illustration 27) – was, according to the sculptor Anikushin, based on a scene that he himself witnessed during the blockade.[91]

These realistic figures naturalized the myth of heroic defense. In an article published at the time of the opening of the monument, the sculptor

[89] O. Kolesova, ". . . Eto v serdtse bylo moem . . . ," *LP*, 10 March 1972.
[90] V. A. Frolov, "Monument na ploshchadi Pobedy (arkhitekturno-khudozhestvennyi analiz)," *Trudy gosudarstvennogo muzeia istorii Sankt-Peterburga*, vyp. 5 (2000): 301–2.
[91] Anikushin, "Bol' i muzhestvo," 19. Bartenev, *Monument*, 20, 18.

28. Leningraders building barricades and digging trenches on the Monument to the Heroic Defenders of Leningrad. Photo by author.

Anikushin wrote, "I would like to show Leningraders exactly as they were at that time.... These are ordinary people who accomplished this, who became legend." Nonetheless, the legend shaped the representation of the "ordinary people." When a photograph of the sculptures ran in the newspaper, Anikushin received a phone call from a woman who had dug antitank trenches during the war demanding to know why the woman digging trenches in the monument had bare feet (Illustration 28). "I myself dug trenches," she informed the sculptor, "and we had shoes." Anikushin tried to explain that "I sculpted the woman in that way because it seemed to me a sharper means of conveying the feeling of her defenselessness (combat above, cold and damp below). Yet all the same, she does not toss aside her shovel, all the same she fights to the death [*stoit nasmert'*]." The sculptor did not record the caller's response, and one wonders what she made of his effort to mythologize her war work: The fictional bare feet turned her into an exemplary soldier who had "fought to the death."[92]

The decision, made relatively late in the planning process, to replace a gilded "Motherland-Glory" with the forty-eight-meter obelisk and realistic representations of "The Victors" – a soldier and a worker

[92] Anikushin, "Bol' i muzhestvo," 19. See also Young, *Texture of Memory,* 159.

29. Obelisk and "The Victors" on the Monument to the Heroic Defenders of
Leningrad. Photo by John K. Conway.

(Illustration 29) – reflected the sculptor's conviction that in Leningrad,
"ordinary people" had become legend.[93] "The Victors," despite their size
(about twelve meters) and their symbolic role as personifications of the
"unity of the front and rear," were dressed, like the other figures, in period
clothes. The soldier and the worker were deities in everyday garb – at once
emblems of Soviet military and industrial power and "real" defenders on
the Leningrad front.

Declining to represent officers or political commissars, let alone the
party leadership, the sculptures maintained the myth of the "people's

---

[93] "Grafik," TsGA SPb, f. 7384, op. 43, d. 445-B, l. 13. Lezik, "Monument," 279. "V chest',"
6–8. *LP,* 19 January 1975. A mock-up published in January of 1974 still included the
"Motherland-Glory." "Nikto ne zabyt," 10, 11. *LP,* 26 August 1973.

30. The words "900 nights" and the broken ring at the Monument to the Heroic Defenders of Leningrad. Photo by John K. Conway.

war." They also maintained a speciously organic hierarchy of men fighting at the front and women supporting on the home front or as medics and nurses. Rather than an account of the city during the war, the sculptural groups that lined the monument's granite stairway offered a largely male story of military glory. The dates "1941–1945" visible on the obelisk that towers above the plaza marked this as a monument to the war, not the blockade, which ended in 1944.[94] The blockaded city and the women who "defended" it – most notably the women of the MPVO – were nowhere in sight.

The story shifted when the visitor descended a second broad staircase that led down, away from the traffic, into an open-air circular room. Breached by the stairway, the inner court was meant to symbolize the breaking of the ring of the blockade (Illustration 30). While the dates on the obelisk connected the monument to the war, the phrases "900 days" and "900 nights" clearly attached the courtyard to the experience of civilians. Paved with stones typical of prewar Leningrad streets, the

---

[94] A design from the 1960s (probably 1966) featured an obelisk with the dates "1941–1944." TsGALI SPb, f. 341, op. 5. d. 96, l. 100b. By contrast, a 1932 monument to V. I. Chapaev prominently featured a woman with a gun. *Iz bronzy,* 241.

31. "The Blockade" at the Monument to the Heroic Defenders of Leningrad. Photo by author.

floor of the central court evoked a concrete time and place. It also, in contrast to the triumphant mood of the expansive stairway and plaza, created a space for quiet reflection. The upper portion of the wall was decorated with a ring of eternal flames. Music added to the solemn mood and, along with the fire and gilt letters, turned the court into a secularized state shrine.[95]

Situated in the center of the room, just above the viewer's eye level and smaller in scale than the figures along the stairway (three rather than four meters), the six figures of "The Blockade" were, like the other figures on the monument, at once ordinary Leningraders and symbols (Illustration 31). The group included a woman whom a 1981 album of photographs of the monument described as "proud and inflexible despite her misfortune. She holds the sagging body of her child in her arms." According to Anikushin, this scene was also one that he himself witnessed during an artillery attack early in the blockade. A "courageous mother embracing her recumbent daughter and trying to shelter her" and a "soldier raising to her feet a woman who has collapsed of hunger" completed the

[95] Elena Hellberg-Hirn, *Soil and Soul: The Symbolic World of Russianness* (Aldershot, UK: Ashgate, 1998), 121. Tumarkin, *The Living and the Dead*, 126.

group.[96] According to *Stroitel'stvo i arkhitektura Leningrada*'s January 1975 review, the "sculptural group...narrates the most difficult ordeals of the blockade, the irreplaceable losses. But on the emaciated faces of the people there is no despair; they are stern [*surovy*], unbent."[97]

These "real" women thus functioned as symbols of the Motherland, in need of protection but naturally stoic, steadfast, and courageous. The weakest figure, largely hidden from view by the soldier who supports her, is cloaked in scarves, invisible except for subtly rendered skeletal hands. Her suffering is quiet – a far cry from the anguished scream of Zadkine's statue. In the case of the other two women, starvation has not obliterated the visible markers of womanhood – a painful loss noted by many survivors. The woman cradling her dead child can fairly be described as voluptuous, her nipples visible under her light garment. At first glance she appears to be bare breasted. The figures and their setting managed at once to recall the realities of the blockade and to sentimentalize suffering by turning it into allegory.[98]

In the subterranean museum that opened in 1978, the simultaneous expression of pain and courage that Anikushin deemed central to the purposes of the monument became even more pronounced. Walls faced in dark polished granite and the muted light of nine hundred lamps fashioned from empty 76 mm shell casings created an atmosphere of reverence and contemplation. The measured sound of the metronome that had been continuously broadcast on Leningrad radio during the blockade, occasionally interrupted by music and call signals from Radio Moscow, added to the sorrowful tone, but also insisted on the importance of documenting "how everything really happened."

The artifacts on display, including a violin used in the performance of Shostakovich's symphony, captured the material reality of the experience of the blockade. A shovel and a pail of sand represented the MPVO units that stood watch on rooftops to put out incendiary bombs. Such objects were likely to be especially evocative for survivors. Yet they also worked to soften the trauma and to efface the gender of the actors. The 125 gram bread ration, along with the "old weapons and blank shells" that the guidebook describes as "the silent witnesses of fierce fighting around

---

[96] Bartenev, *Monument*, 39, 26. The book includes some English text; I have used the English in the original. See also Anikushin, "Bol' i muzhestvo," 18.

[97] "V chest'," 8.

[98] Margaret Kelleher, "Hunger and History: Monuments to the Great Irish Famine," *Textual Practice* 16 (Summer 2002): 266–67. Eric Hobsbawm, "Man and Woman in Socialist Iconography," *History Workshop*, no. 6 (Autumn 1978): 127–29.

Leningrad," are suggestive and moving but hardly convey the extent of the human suffering within the city or on the front.[99]

The new high-rise buildings that came into view when the visitor left the museum and exited the ring of the blockade via the north staircase constituted the final piece of the monument to victory and a vital element of the myth of the hero city. The architects had conceived of the pair of twenty-two-story apartment buildings and the department store as a part of the memorial "ensemble."[100] Like the museum's newsreel showing Leningrad "today," the view of Moskovskii Prospekt was intended to make victory at once visible, local, and recuperative – "pleasure the son of misery."[101]

Nonetheless, the architects' and artists' insistence on embodying the myth of the hero city in "ordinary" Leningraders and actual artifacts facilitated multiple readings of the monument. Survivors might see the Motherland and national victory, their own mothers, their own personal tragedies, or all of these at once.[102] As Yitzhak Brudny has noted, the Soviet state's co-optation of the images and appeals of Russian nationalism in the 1960s and 1970s constituted an attempt to address the "decline of the mobilizational power of the official Marxist-Leninist ideology" and to enhance the regime's legitimacy.[103] Brudny does not connect this process to war memorials or gender, but the inclusion of images of the suffering rodina in the Leningrad monument – indeed at its very center – clearly added emotional legitimacy to the narrative of Soviet state power that constituted its façade. Moreover, in the Monument to the Heroic Defenders of Leningrad, the co-optation worked in two directions. While the state's effort to legitimize itself may have led it to adopt popular, national images, projections of national power offered a redemptive conclusion to the story of the blockade. The monument concretized the hopes of victory – a return to "normal" life that included a reinscription of "normal" gender boundaries – that had helped so many Leningraders to survive. Created, like Piskarevskoe, by people who had lived through the events

---

[99] Lezik, *Monument*, unpaginated. English in original.

[100] V. A. Vlasovskii, "Sooruzhaetsia muzei memoriala," *Stroitel'stvo i arkhitektura Leningrada*, 1977, no. 8: 11. TsGA SPb, f. 7384, op. 43, d. 445-V, l. 23. B. V. Murav'ev, "Doroga k ploshchadi pobedy," *Stroitel'stvo i arkhitektura Leningrada*, 1980, no. 5: 16–19.

[101] Primo Levi, *The Drowned and the Saved*, trans. Raymond Rosenthal (New York: Vintage International, 1989), 71.

[102] N. V. Voronov, *Sovetskaia monumental'naia skul'ptura* (Moscow: Znanie, 1976), 20.

[103] Yitzhak M. Brudny, *Reinventing Russia: Russian Nationalism and the Soviet State, 1953–1991* (Cambridge, MA: Harvard University Press, 1998), 60, 17.

commemorated and, at least in part, for them, the monument confounds efforts to separate state propaganda from survivors' identification with the Soviet cause, internalization of consoling myths, and efforts to speak memory in the visual language of the war cult.[104]

Ritual and the Persistence of Memory

Both Piskarevskoe Memorial Cemetery and the Monument to the Heroic Defenders of Leningrad became sites of rituals and even, as the museum guide cited in the epigraph notes, "gala events" – both political and personal, national and local. In post-Soviet Russia, both sites have retained their roles as venues for official functions. In April 2001, Russian President Vladimir Putin visited Piskarevskoe with German Chancellor Gerhard Schröder and a group of veterans from both Germany and Russia. In the leaders' joint press conference, Putin emphasized the national importance of the site. After the ceremony, the German and Russian veterans visited nearby Sologubovka Cemetery, opened in 2000, which contains the remains of almost eighty thousand German soldiers – the largest such cemetery in Europe.[105]

As in the Soviet period, visiting foreign dignities still pay their official respects to the fallen at one of the two places. To cite just two examples from a very long list: In 1996, U.S. President Bill Clinton used his visit to Piskarevskoe to honor the memories of the victims of both the Nazi blockade and of the Oklahoma City bombing in 1995.[106] In 1998, Nikolai Romanov, the great-great-grandson of Nicholas I and a distant cousin of Nicholas II, in town for the burial of the recently identified remains of the last tsar, visited Piskarevskoe Cemetery, noting "I am glad that I had the opportunity to thank the heroes who defended Leningrad."[107]

[104] Anna Krylova, "Soviet Modernity in Life and Fiction: The Generation of the 'New Soviet Person' in the 1930s" (Ph.D. diss., Johns Hopkins University, 2001), Chapter 1. Jochen Hellbeck, "Fashioning the Stalinist Soul: The Diary of Stepan Podlubnyi (1931–1939)," *Jahrbücher für Osteuropas* 44 (1996): 344–73.

[105] "President of the Russian Federation Vladimir Putin (sic) Remarks and Answers to Questions at Joint News Conference on Outcome of Russian-German Interstate Consultations, St. Petersburg, April 10, 2001," http://www.ln.mid.ru/bl.nsf/o/64bo9b4288cc3ce843256a31002ff53d?OpenDocument (accessed 17 February 2006).

[106] "Clinton Honors Russian World War II Dead," CNN, 19 April 1996, http://www.cnn.com/ALLPOLITICS/1996/news/9604/19/clinton.russia/index.shtml (accessed 17 February 2006).

[107] Alice Lagnado, "Attending Romanovs Bring Class, Clout to Burial," *St. Petersburg Times,* 17 July 1998, http://www.times.spb.ru/archive/times/382/news/attending.htm (accessed 5 July 2005).

The purposes and symbols of the state remain visible and important at Leningrad's war memorials.

The two memorials have also remained important sites of memory and ritual for Petersburgers. In post-Soviet Petersburg, as in Soviet Leningrad, veterans and blokadniki gather at the two memorials on important anniversaries related to the war and the blockade.[108] Formal wreath-laying ceremonies were also part of the city's celebration of its three hundreth anniversary in May 2003.[109] Since 1994, the Monument to the Heroic Defenders, a branch of the State Museum of the History of St. Petersburg, has hosted numerous commemorative events, including a performance by the women's choir of MPVO veterans founded in November 1942.[110] Newlyweds still stop by the monument with their small wedding parties to drink a toast, take videos, and leave flowers at the base of the "Blockade" sculpture.[111] These varied uses illustrate the degree to which memorials to the siege of Leningrad remain living, changing urban spaces. Clear embodiments of the Soviet war cult and the Leningrad epic, the memorials' continued importance in the ritual life of the city and the nation underscores the persistence and intertwining of the myth and memory of the blockade in post-Soviet St. Petersburg.

[108] A review of local newspapers on important dates makes clear the ritual importance of these two sites.

[109] See schedule of events at http://newsfromrussia.com/science/2003/05/24/47395.html (accessed 17 February 2006).

[110] Lezik, *Monument*. "Women's Choir Created in Blockaded Leningrad Turns 60," *Pravda. RU*, 2 November 2002, http://English.pravda.ru/culture/2002/11/02/39043_.html (accessed 17 February 2006). See also Galina Stolyarova, "German View of Both Siege Sides," *St. Petersburg Times*, 30 January 2004, http://www.sptimesrussia.com/archive/times/939/features/a_11519.htm (accessed 5 July 2005).

[111] "The Annals of the Great Patriotic War Reflected in War Memorials," http://www.vor.ru/55/Monument/Mon_eng.html (accessed 17 February 2006). Christel Lane, *The Rites of Rulers: Ritual in Industrial Society – The Soviet Case* (Cambridge: Cambridge University Press, 1981), 82. Christopher Binns, "The Changing Face of Power: Revolution and Accommodation in the Development of the Soviet Ceremonial System: Part II," *Man* 15 (March 1980): 177.

PART III

THE PERSISTENCE OF MEMORY

7

Speaking the Unspoken?

> A memory evoked too often, and expressed in the form of a story, tends to become fixed in stereotype, in a form tested by experience, crystallized, perfected, adorned, installing itself in the place of the raw memory and growing at its expense.
>
> Primo Levi[1]

Published in 1979 and expanded in 1982, Ales' Adamovich and Daniil Granin's collection of oral histories and diaries, *A Book of the Blockade* (Blokadnaia kniga), came as a revelation. Never before had the darker sides of the blockade been treated so fully and unflinchingly in print in the Soviet Union.[2] Still, in 1982 – five years before Mikhail Gorbachev's policies of glasnost and perestroika – much remained unspoken. A decade later, the editors recalled that the censor had "made over sixty removals in the first half of the book." Specifically, the censor objected to materials relating to "the facts of cannibalism and the postwar repression affecting the former defenders of the city."[3]

By 1992, both the censor and the Soviet Union had been consigned to the dustbin of history, and Adamovich and Granin considered filling in the blank spots. They had no compunctions about revealing the crimes of the former regime, but they expressed hesitation about publishing interviews that talked of cannibalism. Clearly willing to attack the pieties of the propaganda state, why did they question their "right to disclose" the

---

[1] Primo Levi, *The Drowned and the Saved,* trans. Raymond Rosenthal (New York: Vintage Books, 1989), 24.

[2] See Chapter 5.

[3] Ales' Adamovich and Daniil Granin, "Blokadnaia kniga: Glavy, kotorykh v knige ne bylo," *Zvezda,* 1992, no. 5–6: 8.

stories of cannibalism that survivors told them? The editors explained
that at the time of the book's original publication, they felt that "there
are things that shouldn't be told. They don't wound, but cripple the soul."
Thus "the censor simplified our problems and moral torment." As they
considered publishing the excised stories, their qualms returned. They
acknowledged that "the easiest thing is to close one's eyes: This didn't
happen, because if such things did happen, how is it possible to talk and
write about the heroism of the blockade, about the exceptional virtue
with which they held out and died in unbearable conditions, about the
high cultural level [*intelligentnosti*] of this city?"[4] The editors feared that
stories about cannibalism – but not about political repression – would
overshadow the story of Leningraders' heroism. Expressing their reservations about restoring the censor's expurgations, Adamovich and Granin
explicitly identified a tension that ran through many late- and post-Soviet
accounts of the siege.

One of the most striking elements of blockade stories from the late
1980s and 1990s is this often-simultaneous reverence for the myth
and contempt for the mythmaker. The desire "to talk and write about
the heroism of the blockade" complicated the impulse to tell the
full story of the blockade – to unmask lies, distortions, and omissions. Unlike the flood of memoirs and diaries that told the hidden
stories of the Stalinist terror and the camps, new accounts of the
blockade coexisted with a resonant myth that, while approved and
shaped by the state, effectively incorporated many individual stories.[5]
If state-enforced silence had denied survivors of the gulag a public language in which to tell their stories, the war cult provided well-worn
clichés, images, and anecdotes that proved difficult to avoid, let alone
subvert.

For survivors struggling to cope with painful memories and to endow
tragedy with meaning, the myth of the heroic city continued to offer a comforting frame for personal memory. If, as Saul Friedlander has observed
with regard to the Holocaust, "individual *common* memory, as well as
collective memory, tends to restore or establish coherence, closure, and
possibly a redemptive stance," it is not surprising that blockade survivors

---

4 Ibid., 8. See also Cynthia Simmons, "Lifting the Siege: Women's Voices on Leningrad
  (1941–1944)," *Canadian Slavonic Papers* 40 (March–June 1998): 49, n. 26.
5 Catherine Merridale, "Death and Memory in Modern Russia," *History Workshop Journal*, no. 42 (Autumn 1996): 12–13. Jehanne Gheith, "Dogs, Daughters, and Documents:
  Memory and the Gulag" (Paper delivered at the conference "Recontextualizing Russian
  Women's Studies," Harriman Institute, New York, April 2003).

internalized myths that offered just such a possibility of redemption.[6] Making a similar point, the radio journalist Lev Markhasev prefaced his 1991 reminiscences with the disclaimer that "memory has a strange character. It throws out gloom."[7] The official cult may have been "manifestly finished as an institution" by 1990, but the stories participants told about the war retained key features of the "bronzed saga."[8] Most fundamentally, the myth of the war affirmed the historical importance of personal, intimate stories of suffering and death.[9] In the post-Soviet period, the assertion of the meaningfulness of wartime sacrifices remained central to survivors' life stories and to their claims to respect – and material support – in a precarious and unfamiliar present.

Modes of Memory: Epic and Exposé

The openness sanctioned by glasnost led to an outpouring of blockade memoirs that told sometimes lurid tales of cannibalism, murder, deceit, war profiteering, and political repression. These revelations, so at odds with the mythical story of high-minded, disciplined, and valiant Soviet citizens inspired by the party's leadership, seemed to spell the end of the cult of the war. The unprecedented candor of these accounts clearly challenged Soviet myth. As in so many areas of Soviet life, openness, which was supposed to restore the party's credibility, ended up weakening the legitimizing myths upon which the regime depended.[10]

However, the exposé was not the only mode of memory encouraged by the reforms of the 1980s and 1990s. The economic and social uncertainties of the transitional period often bred nostalgic paeans to the generosity,

---

[6] Saul Friedlander, "Trauma, Memory, and Transference," in G. Hartman, ed., *Holocaust Remembrance: The Shapes of Memory* (Cambridge, MA: Blackwell, 1994), 254, emphasis in original. See also Peter Fritschze, "The Case of Modern Memory," *Journal of Modern History* 73 (March 2001): 117. James E. Young's description of the "ubiquitous twinning of martyrs and heroes in Israel's memorial iconography" of the Holocaust offers an interesting analogue to the Soviet myth of heroic defenders. Young, *The Texture of Memory: Holocaust Memorials and Meaning* (New Haven, CT: Yale University Press, 1993), 212–13.

[7] Lev Markhasev, "Po sravneniiu s nyneshnim—eto bylo chistoe vremia," *Anichkov most*, no. 4 (January 1991), 3.

[8] Nina Tumarkin, *The Living and the Dead: The Rise and Fall of the Cult of World War II in Russia* (New York: Basic Books, 1994), 190.

[9] Irina Paperno, "Personal Accounts of the Soviet Experience," *Kritika: Explorations in Russian and Eurasian History* 3 (Fall 2002): 577.

[10] John Gooding, "Lenin in Soviet Politics, 1985–1991," *Soviet Studies* 44 (1992): 413. Stephen Kotkin, *Armageddon Averted: The Soviet Collapse, 1970–2000* (New York: Oxford University Press, 2001), 67–73. Tumarkin, *The Living and the Dead,* 164–65.

heroism, and generally high moral tone of true Leningraders during the war. As the anthropologist Jennifer Dickinson found when interviewing survivors in the early 1990s, the graphic details of previously taboo topics could be enlisted in the cause of making the myth of heroic Leningrad more believable.[11] Even during the war, it had been clear that a truer, or at least darker, picture of the circumstances in Leningrad would throw the heroism into sharper relief.[12] Thus, Gorbachev's announcement in 1987 of the policy of openness about the Soviet past and present unleashed a flood of memoirs and previously unpublished letters and diaries from the blockade that alternately debunked and perpetuated the myth of heroic Leningrad.

Particularly in the early 1990s, the Soviet press published sometimes shocking memoirs that savaged official myths. Introducing two such memoirs, the journalist Mikhail Zolotonosov emphasized that "we have the information of eyewitnesses that destroys the official-propagandistic image of 'general heroism'" and unmasks the Soviet state's "propagandistic brokerage of tragedy."[13] One of the accounts presented by Zolotonosov, excerpts from Lidiia Slonimskaia's previously unpublished 1945 memoir, launched a frontal attack on the notion of the intelligentsia's steadfastness and heroism. In the excerpt published in *Chas pik*, Slonimskaia charged that Vera Ketlinskaia, the wartime head of the Leningrad Writers' Union, was "a robber, a bribe-taker, and a murderer."[14] Slonimskaia painted a grotesque picture of Ketlinskaia, who "had enough food not only for her family, but for drinking bouts and lovers."[15] Cynically providing food for her favorites while denying additional rations administered by the Union to those she disliked – the apparent source of Slonimskaia's murder charge – Ketlinskaia "and her whole clique carried themselves as if the defense of Leningrad depended on them." In Slonimskaia's account, those who did not retain "human dignity" passed themselves off as heroes, while the few who held on to their humanity – herself presumably among them – died or wept.

Slonimskaia's burning prose was perfectly in sync with the glasnost-era obsession with uncovering and publicizing crimes that the regime

---

[11] Jennifer Dickinson, "Building the Blockade: New Truths in Survival Narratives from Leningrad," *Anthropology of East Europe Review* 13, no. 2 (1995): 21.

[12] Cynthia Simmons and Nina Perlina, eds., *Writing the Siege of Leningrad: Women's Diaries, Memoirs, and Documentary Prose* (Pittsburgh, PA: University of Pittsburgh Press, 2002), 73.

[13] Mikhail Zolotonosov, "Osada cheloveka," *Chas pik*, 11 February 1991.

[14] Lidiia Slonimskaia, "'V eti mesiatsy strashnogo goloda . . . ,'" *Chas pik*, 11 February 1991.

[15] Ibid.

had kept hidden for half a century and more.[16] The introduction to the memoir emphasized that it was precisely the author's uncompromising denunciation of the state's lies that recommended her work for publication in the local press. Yet Slonimskaia's anger was directed less against the myth of heroic Leningrad than against corrupt individuals, who hypocritically ranked themselves among the steadfast. While denouncing certain egregious exceptions, she largely accepted the wartime myth of "true" Leningraders who retained their human dignity. Moreover, it is worth noting that while published for the first time during the era of glasnost, Slonimskaia's memoir had been written in the 1940s, fifteen years before the author's death. As a letter to the editor of *Chas pik* from Ketlinskaia's outraged family emphasized, these reminiscences were written at a time when "the nightmare of starvation still weighed heavily (and this is not her fault, of course)."[17] Her wounds – physical and psychological – were still fresh. Would she have told the same stories at a distance of fifty years? Would she, too, have thrown out some of the gloom?

Ideally suited to the temper of the times in which they were published, Slonimskaia's reminiscences should not be taken as a universally recognized new, "true" picture of the blockade. In accounts of their experiences, many survivors seemed ready to dispel the myth of high-minded, self-sacrificing party members and to accept the axiom that blame for the mass death of the blockade fell to both Josef Stalin and Adolf Hitler.[18] Likewise, many confirmed previously unmentionable rumors of cannibalism – a sensitive topic discussed in more detail in the next section. However, including previously taboo details did not necessarily imply a rejection of the Leningrad epic. Angry disclosures of thieving shop girls and crass self-interest were no more common than tales of generous strangers and powerful familial solidarity.

Stories of the blockade that promoted the myth of heroic Leningrad were just as rooted in the late-perestroika and early-post-Soviet context as revelations of crime and cannibalism. If digging up the past had become the rhetorical fashion of the moment, so had nostalgia for allegedly more

---

[16] Tumarkin, *The Living and the Dead*, 164–70. David Remnick, *Lenin's Tomb: The Last Days of the Soviet Empire* (New York: Random House, 1993), 36–51.

[17] S. A. Ketlinksii, S. A. Zonin, and V. A. Ketlinskii, "'Eto priamoe obvinenie i oskorblenie...,'" *Chas pik*, 1 April 1991.

[18] Simmons and Perlina, *Writing the Siege*, 139. Iakov Panovko, "Chashechka shokolada v blokadnuiu noch'," *Leningradskaia pravda* (hereafter *LP*), 29 August 1991. Elena Shul'gina, "V dvadtsat' let oni posedeli," *Smena*, 7 May 1995. Rimma Neratova, *V dni voiny: Semeinaia khronika* (St. Petersburg: Zhurnal "Zvezda," 1996), 34.

idealistic times. The mood of nostalgia intensified as the Soviet Union faded into history.[19] Nostalgia favored the mode of epic and tragedy, "in which the hero's power of action is greater than ours," not the ironic mode of exposé where "we have the sense of looking down on a scene of bondage, frustration, or absurdity."[20] Indeed, the revelations of the crimes of the 1930s added poignancy to the story of the war. Rimma Neratova was not alone in remembering "the whole time of the siege," particularly in contrast to the denunciations and arrests of the 1930s, as "the most happy, the most unforgettable time. Because we were together and needed one another."[21]

Like many survivors, Emma Kazakova began her story of "help and generosity" during the blockade with the present's incessant tug at memory. She noted that much as she would like to let memories of the blockade and the war "sink into oblivion... alas, our life constantly places us in situations where you involuntarily compare those unbearably difficult days with today."[22] The present did not hold up well in the comparison: "When I hear the malicious shouts of women standing in line, when I see the ferocious crowd of young folks, full of strength and ready for any feat for the sake of a bottle, holding everyone and everything in contempt... I more and more remember the person who saved my family from starving to death in the terrible December of 1941."

Having framed her story as a counterpoint to present "brutality," Kazakova nonetheless also incorporated stark images and assertions of Stalin's guilt. Eight at the start of the siege, Kazakova recalled that "at home or in the shelters, we children played only store and dining room. Mothers looked at us and cried." By the end of December, "hunger ruled not only the body, but the soul... a terrifying feeling that I still fear." Most of all, she remembered her mother's "despairing eyes." "What they lived through, our dear, unforgettable mothers?! Hitler, Stalin, and their

---

[19] Catherine Merridale, *Night of Stone: Death and Memory in Twentieth-Century Russia* (New York: Viking, 2000), 329. Yuri Levada et al., "Russia: Anxiously Surviving," in Vladimir Shlapentokh and Eric Shiraev, eds., *Fears in Post-Communist Societies: A Comparative Perspective* (New York: Palgrave, 2002), 13.

[20] Northrop Frye as quoted by Paul Fussell, *The Great War and Modern Memory* (New York: Oxford University Press, 1975), 311.

[21] Neratova, *V dni*, 51.

[22] Emma Kazakova, "Zhelanie pomoch' i shchedrost'," *Anichkov most*, no. 4 (January 1991), 3. See also Lotta Bogopol'skaia, "900 dnei, 900 rublei," *Nevskoe vremia* (hereafter *NV*), 26 January 1991. Nataliia Korkonosenko, "Blokadnitsy," *Leningradskaia panorama*, 1991, no. 8: 28–29. Iu. Nikatinskii, "Pis'ma blokadnikov," *NV*, 27 January 1994. A. Kalinichenko, "Pokolenie pobeditelei," *NV*, 7 May 1994.

ilk can never be forgiven for this suffering." Equating Hitler and Stalin, Kazakova's story is clearly marked as a product of glasnost.

Still, the core of Kazakova's story could have been told at the height of the war cult.[23] An unknown man had contacted Kazakova's mother's workplace, asking her to call on him. Mother and child made the hazardous trip across town, braving wind, cold, and snow. Exhausted, they arrived at midnight, meeting a man whom Kazakova's aunt had begged to bring food to her family. "Imagine! An emaciated, no-longer young man, coming on foot through the front, carrying in his rucksack a load for absolutely unknown people!" When they made ready to leave, he "ceremoniously" offered Kazakova's mother one more gift "as a sign of admiration for your courage, your unwomanly strength" – his own loaf of bread. "I was a child," concluded Kazakova, "but I was stunned by his nobility and lofty humanity. What a loaf of bread meant then?! Now there is no equivalent." And, she implied, there was little contemporary equivalent of the generosity and "high morals" of the "unknown Leningrader."

Nostalgia for the moral certainties and unity of the blockade sometimes came attached to apologies for the Soviet state, but mythic stories of heroic Leningrad could also serve more personal purposes. I would argue that it was their continuing personal resonance that made such stories politically powerful. As noted earlier, the journalist Markhasev, who got his start in radio during the blockade, recognized that his memories of the blockade were perhaps a bit too bright.[24] Affirming some of the primary clichés of the myth of Leningrad – the solidarity of the work collective, the solace taken in high culture, the optimistic faith in a "radiant future" – he ended with a challenge to the relevance, if not the truth, of revelations of the self-interest of party bosses. Because "we all grew up in circumstances of asceticism," Markhasev explained, "we were not interested in how the city leadership lived or in what they ate." Such an assertion flew in the face of contemporary accounts – such as those of Freidenberg and Slonimskaia – that documented and denounced the often deadly inequities in food distribution.[25]

---

[23] Compare Adamovich and Granin, *Blokadnaia kniga* (Moscow: Sovetskii pisatel', 1982), 123–36. Simmons, "Lifting the Siege," 64, n. 72. Barbara Alpern Engel, "Women Remember World War II," in Nurit Schleifman, ed., *Russia at a Crossroads: History, Memory, and Political Practice* (London: Frank Cass, 1998), 127.

[24] Markhasev, "Po sravneniiu s nyneshnim," 3.

[25] Ol'ga Freidenberg, "'Chelovecheskaia priroda otmenialas','" *Chas pik*, 11 February 1991. A fuller version of the memoir was published as Freidenberg, "Osada cheloveka," *Minuvshee*, 1987, no. 3: 7–44. A different excerpt from Freidenberg's diaries is included

Markhasev's more forgiving memory can be understood as a tool of politics – a means of dismissing attacks on the party as unrepresentative and anachronistic and of defending the system, or at least citizens' forbearance of the system. But for all its political implications, Markhasev's memoir is far from a political polemic. His fond memories of the "warmth and light" of his radio workplace and his nostalgia for the optimism engendered by the sight of cabbage growing amid the architectural grandeur of Catherine Square in the spring of 1942 suggest the personal importance, if not necessity, of throwing out the gloom. Markhasev's claim that the blockade years were "terrible, severe, pure times" at once called into question the purity of the era of reform and integrated the traumas of the siege into a story of heroism and virtue. He rejected raw accounts of the siege both because they denigrated an epoch of heroism and because they threatened the stories he had constructed from his own experiences.

Cannibalism and Culture

Stories of cannibalism constituted the most shocking revelations in accounts of the siege published in the 1980s and 1990s. Far from all accounts published in this period mentioned cannibalism, and those that did usually treated it only cursorily. Still, any discussion of cannibalism violated a long-standing taboo. The inclusion of stories of cannibalism no doubt stemmed in part from the calculation that such sensational disclosures "sold." Yet confirmations of rumors of cannibalism often functioned as more than mere sensation. Cannibals marked the limits of culture, a descent into barbarism. In many narratives, they functioned as dark reminders of how close all Leningraders had come to the abyss. Revealing incidents of cannibalism provided an opportunity for emphasizing that the majority of Leningraders managed to maintain cultural norms in the most unimaginable of circumstances. Cannibalism became the gruesome residue of heroism.

Adamovich and Granin began their lost chapter "On Cannibalism" with the assertion that the "terrible occurrence" about which they wrote was "the *necessary and inevitable* fellow traveler of any massive famine."[26] They allayed their own moral concerns about publishing

---

in Simmons and Perlina, *Writing the Siege*, 64–76. See also Germogen Germogenovich Ivanov, "38 dnei iz zhizni umiraiushchikh," *Smena*, 27 January 1994.

[26] Adamovich and Granin, "Blokadnaia kniga," 8, emphasis in original.

stories of cannibalism in part by underscoring its relatively limited scope. From this point of view, what was startling about blockaded Leningrad was that, comparatively speaking, cannibalism had been quite rare. Adamovich and Granin concluded that "our records and facts testify: the blockade of Leningrad is one of the examples in the history of mass starvation, when the incidence of cannibalism did not become as widespread as might be assumed based on the horror of the situation, in which a million people found themselves. And also the longest lasting – 900 days!"[27] (Here they exaggerated somewhat, as starvation conditions did not prevail during the entire blockade.) Thus limited, the fact of cannibalism was no less terrible, but it now pointed not to "general moral collapse," but instead to the remarkable strength of a city that, despite massive and long-term starvation, largely avoided its worst moral effects.[28]

Survivors who mentioned cannibalism often pictured it as one of the extrinsic disasters, along with freezing temperatures and German artillery, that befell the besieged city. Nikolai Gorshkov's diary provides an example of both the sensationalism that sometimes marked the publication of revelations from the Soviet past and the survivor's tendency to describe cannibalism as an inescapable fact of life in the starving city. Gorshkov's diary had been seized by the political police in December 1945, when he was arrested for "anti-Soviet agitation." In 1993, it was published as a "blockade diary found after fifty years in the secret archive of the KGB." Nonetheless, as the editor Nikolai Fedorov noted, it was a rather "dry" piece of writing, an account that noted the daily weather conditions but never used the word "I."[29] While Gorshkov's omission of personal responses may distinguish his diary, his characterization of cannibalism as a natural consequence of starvation and his clinical description of the circumstantial physical evidence have much in common with accounts of cannibalism found in memoirs and diaries that are generally far more emotional and reflective. His entry for 24 January 1942 compared cannibalism to the uncontrolled fires caused by German bombing. He substantiated these rumors with the account of an "eyewitness," who described seeing, along the Obvodnyi Canal, the "upper part of a female corpse" apparently butchered by cannibals.[30] Somewhat surprisingly for a diary whose

---

[27] Ibid., 8–9.
[28] The quotation comes from Freidenberg, in Simmons and Perlina, *Writing the Siege*, 74.
[29] N. P. Gorshkov, *Siloiu sveta v polsvechi: Blokadnyi dnevnik, naidennyi cherez 50 let v sekretnykh arkhivakh KGB* (St. Petersburg: BELL, 1993), 4–5.
[30] The quotation is from an excerpt published in the local press. *Sankt-Peterburgskie vedomosti* (hereafter *SPV*), 27 January 1994.

author was accused of anti-Soviet agitation, the discussion of cannibalism did not include an effort to blame the Soviet state for conditions in the besieged city.

The cultural historian Dmitrii Likhachev's account of the blockade – written in the 1950s and published in the 1990s – is far more intimate and thoughtful than Gorshkov's, but it too represented cannibalism as an inevitable horror of the blockade. Vague about time and place and about whether he was reporting things he himself saw, Likhachev wrote that the "soft parts were cut off corpses that had fallen in the streets. Cannibalism had begun! First the corpses were stripped, then sliced to the bone, but there was scarcely any flesh on them; these naked, dissected corpses were a terrible sight."[31] His use of the impersonal "Cannibalism had begun!" (*Nachalos' liudoedstvo*), suggests that cannibalism, like winter, was something that Leningraders had no power to stop. He described it in the detached language of scientific observation – "first the corpses were stripped..." Here, cannibalism seems to be something done to Leningraders, not by them. Moreover, Likhachev argued that "cannibalism can't be condemned out of hand.... Those who dissected the bodies seldom ate the flesh themselves, but either sold it without saying what it was or used it to feed their nearest and dearest [*blizkikh*] and keep them alive."[32]

Not surprisingly, "eyewitness" accounts of cannibalism remain extremely rare. Some, like that of Nina Abramova, eight years old when the siege began, mix rumor, fear, and ambiguous observation. Abramova recounted how the caretaker (*dvornik*) of her building spotted a pair of shoes belonging to one of the children along with a "suspicious bag" under the bed of a resident, who had asked her to come up and clean the floor. The caretaker "immediately made a statement to the police." Rather than doubting the plausibility of the story – why call the caretaker to the scene of the crime? – Abramova asserted her standing as eyewitness: "And then I saw it: two policemen came down the stairway with a

---

[31] I have used the translation in Dmitrii Likhachev, *Reflections on the Russian Soul*, trans. Bernard Adams (Budapest: Central European University Press, 2000), 234. Dmitrii Likhachev, "Kak my ostalis' zhivy," *Neva*, 1991, no. 1: 15.

[32] I have slightly altered the translation in Likhachev, *Reflections*, 234. See also Simmons and Perlina, *Writing the Siege*, 51, 173; interview with Viktor Koslov, quoted in Ed Vulliamy, "Orchestral manoeuvres (part one)," *The Observer*, 25 November 2001, http://observer.guardian.co.uk/life/story/0,6903,605454,00.html (accessed 17 February 2006); Ivanov, "38 dnei"; I. I. Zhilinskii, "Blokadnyi dnevnik," *Voprosy istorii*, 1996, no. 8: 6; Neratova, *V dni*, 59; Freidenberg, "'Chelovecheskaia priroda otmenialas'.'"

woman between them. The residents of the house said that she was going to be shot for cannibalism."[33]

In Abramova's reminiscences, this somewhat dubious eyewitness account set the stage for a more direct brush with cannibalism that established, paradoxically, not Leningraders' depravity but the solidity of family ties in the most fearful of times. Abramova related that "it was terrifying to walk outside. There were instances in which children were killed and eaten." Thus, her mother and the last remaining resident of their communal apartment, Aunt Liusia, constantly warned her to be vigilant. Abramova recounted her panic when, having been distracted for a moment, she realized that she had let go of her younger brother's hand. Unable to locate him in the entryway where she had lost him, she rushed into the neighboring fish store. There she found him "pressed up against the counter," held by the feet of a man who screened the child from view with long clothing. "By force I literally dragged Gena out from under the feet of the villain." Certain that she had saved her brother from death, Abramova resolved never to let him out of her sight again. Despite her own small size and emaciation, she took to carrying him in her arms whenever they left the house together. The story demonstrates less the reality of cannibalism than the eight-year-old's very real fear of it.[34] Overcoming her fear, she managed to save the last of her six siblings. Family loyalty triumphed, and the alleged cannibal was defeated.

By contrast, the eyewitness accounts of cannibalism presented by Adamovich and Granin focus not on family solidarity but on mothers forced to make desperate choices to keep their children or themselves alive. One of their interviewees reported asking a neighbor in her communal apartment, three-year-old Nina, where her older sister was. "We ate Galia," the girl replied. Understandably shocked, the neighbor went into the "frozen room" and found "a half-insane mother, and by the wall the frozen corpse of her older daughter. And she really ... She saved the younger one. Saved. But she herself died shortly thereafter."[35] Another interviewee, whom Adamovich and Granin deemed fully trustworthy, a

---

[33] Nina Vasil'evna Abramova, "Byla ia v detstve 'serebrianoi devochkoi.' A detstva u menia ne bylo," *Smena*, 19 January 1994. Cannibals were shot. Adamovich and Granin, "Blokadnaia kniga," 9. A. R. Dzeniskevich, *Leningrad v osade: Sbornik dokumentov o geroicheskoi oborone Leningrada v Velikoi Otechestvennoi voiny, 1941–1944* (St. Petersburg: Liki Rossii, 1995), 433–34.

[34] Stephen J. Ceci, "False Beliefs: Some Developmental and Clinical Considerations," in Daniel L. Schacter, ed., *Memory Distortion: How Minds, Brains, and Societies Reconstruct the Past* (Cambridge, MA: Harvard University Press, 1995), 99.

[35] Adamovich and Granin, "Blokadnaia kniga," 9, ellipses in original.

woman who worked for the local housing administration during the war, recounted visiting a family after a neighbor voiced concerns about their behavior. Remembering that there had been many children and seeing only two, Mariia Ivanovna asked about them. "They've all died," replied the mother. Unable to find the registration of the children's deaths, Mariia Ivanovna became suspicious. Her suspicions grew when she found meat – allegedly mutton – cooking on the stove. Opening the lid of the pot, she ladled up the soup and "dragged out a *hand*!!!" One of the women tried to explain: "We decided that rather than burying them in the earth, it would be better for us to eat." The adults – mother and daughter– were arrested.[36] In this case, the family was completely destroyed.

In Adamovich and Granin's work, the most difficult stories of the blockade, about which "it is best not to know – or hear, or take notes, or read," were those that illustrated the confusion, impairment, and destruction of fundamental moral obligations and of maternal care in particular.[37] Their examples involved a misshapen maternal instinct – a half-crazed mother trying to save one of her children – and an abdication of parental responsibilities in the name of self-preservation. Similarly linking "cannibalism" to a breakdown of the norms of maternal care, Likhachev recounted the story of a woman who took in orphans in order to appropriate their ration cards for herself. The children in her care "quietly died." Likhachev concluded that "what she did was also a form of cannibalism, the most terrible form."[38] In these stories, survivors connected the disintegration of cultured norms, epitomized by cannibalism, with the erosion of gender norms.

What also emerges in many survivors' accounts, however, is the stability and dependability of motherly love. If the cannibal – especially the cannibal/mother – embodied the abandonment of prewar morality, the self-sacrificing woman became the emblem of Leningraders' persistent virtue. By the 1990s, many of the surviving blokadniki had been children during the war, and like Kazakova, fondly remembered their "dear, unforgettable mothers." A collection of poems published in 1999 by the organization Young Participants in the Defense of Leningrad included a chapter devoted to celebrating "our mothers – holy blockade women."[39]

---

[36] Ibid., 11–13, emphasis in original.

[37] Ibid., 13.

[38] I have used the translation in Likhachev, *Reflections*, 241. Likhachev, "Kak my," 17–18.

[39] Iunye uchastniki oborony Leningrada, *Blokadnoi pamiati stranitsy: Poeticheskii sbornik* (St. Petersburg: OAO "VNIIG im. B. E. Vedeneeva," 1999), 59. See also Mezhdunarodnaia assotsiatsiia blokadnikov goroda-geroia Leningrada, *Deti blokada: Vospominaniia, fragmenty dnevnikov, svidetel'stva ochevidtsov, dokumental'nye materialy* (St. Petersburg: IPk "Vesti," 2000).

A poem by A. Molchanov asserted a well-known blockade aphorism: "Everyone who survived the blockade/Had a kind guardian angel." After listing a variety of possible saviors, the poet concluded,

> But most frequently the angel was mama –
> Holy Leningrad *mama*,
> Giving her bread up *mama*,
> Immortal blockade *mama*.[40]

In other accounts, selfless teachers became surrogate mothers, nursing orphans back to physical and psychological health.[41] Children kept alive in the kindergartens "do not remember the horrors of war." Instead, like Nina Rudnova, they recalled "how they gave us chocolate. I remember the love with which the adults related to us. Really, that love allowed us to survive."[42] Perhaps unsurprisingly, child survivors remembered the selfless maternal care as the norm in blockaded Leningrad.

Most vividly in the case of cannibalism, the mode of exposé did not displace but, on the contrary, stimulated memory in the epic mode and endowed it with renewed believability. In an article published as part of a series celebrating the fiftieth anniversary of the breaking of the blockade in 1994, Granin omitted stories of cannibalism (although he did mention it), preferring instead to make the theft of bread the emblem of desperation and depravity in the besieged city: "The picture of the destruction of the human organism and spirit was such that it was impossible to condemn people for stealing bread, even from their nearest and dearest." "Starvation," Granin concluded, "drove people to insanity." Striking as such stories were, he found that "this isn't amazing. What's amazing is that the overwhelming majority of Leningraders 'monitored themselves' [*sobliudali sebe*]." Repeating the theme of the savior that had been such an important element of the *Blokadnaia kniga*, Granin affirmed that "almost every blokadnik had stories of how someone helped him or someone near to him – leading him home when he fell in the street, sharing a crust of bread or a bowl of soup. This was typical in the blockaded city."[43]

Even allowing for the nostalgia typical of anniversary celebrations, Granin's summary of the tales told by blokadniki is remarkably uplifting. He used cases of stealing – and perhaps implicitly cannibalism, the

[40] Iunye uchastniki, *Blokadnoi pamiati*, 60, emphasis in original.

[41] Shul'gina, "V dvadtsat'." Elena Shul'gina, "Na risunkakh doshkoliat nashi vsegda bili nemtsev," *Smena*, 19 April 1995.

[42] Shul'gina, "V dvadtsat'."

[43] Daniil Granin, "Chelovek iz blokady," *SPV*, 5 January 1994. See also Vladimir Motov, "Gde ty, spasitel'?" *NV*, 7 February 1995; Vladimir Daev, *Pedagogi blokadnoi pory: Po arkhivakh leningradskikh uchrezhdenii* (St. Petersburg: Izdatel'stvo "Sudarynia," 1998).

"insanity" of hunger – to authenticate and magnify the "overwhelming" goodness of Leningraders. Where Freidenberg had written of the painful and deforming "siege of the person" (*osada cheloveka*), Granin emphasized the humanity of the "person of the blockade" (*chelovek iz blokady*). Rejecting the "victory without tragedy" that he claimed was portrayed in "official propaganda," he proposed that the "pure Leningrad spirituality" that accounted for the city's remarkable fortitude could only be understood in the context of profound suffering.

Numerous accounts took a similar approach, often evoking the legacy of the Petersburg intelligentsia as the key to Leningraders' ability to remain cultured in the face of brutalizing conditions. A. Mitrofanov, the vice president of the International Association of Blokadniki from the Hero City Leningrad, recalled a dramatic image from the first winter of the siege. A neighbor, "a soloist in the Philharmonic Symphony Orchestra, a trumpet player," who "due to malnutrition could hardly move, did not go down into the bomb shelter during air raids and artillery attacks. But he kept on playing. Even when the engines of fascist airplanes droned in the skies above Leningrad, the pure sounds of Chudnenko's trumpet drifted from the top floor."[44] In an interview in 1995, Ol'ga Grechina also affirmed the pervasive moral steadfastness of Leningraders: "But I wanted to say that even though it was so deadly cold, and almost everyone's windows were broken, even then not one Leningrader cut down a living tree. No one ever did that. Because we loved our city, and we could not deprive it of its greenery."[45] For many blokadniki, the ability to resist moral degradation became the mark of the Leningrader, who both established and lived up to the city's high cultural level, what Adamovich and Granin called Leningrad's *intelligentnost'*.

Attempting to explain their survival, many Leningraders suggested that "culture" – broadly defined to include not only high culture but also "monitoring oneself" and moral uprightness – sustained them. Cataloging the frequently evoked cultural pursuits of Leningraders, Granin argued that "people fell back on poetry, diaries, music, scholarly endeavors. Culture gave them new strength, supported them physically."[46] Elsewhere,

---

[44] A. Mitrofanov, "Blokada: Vsiu zhizn' stuchitsia v nashu pamiat' ee trevozhnyi metronom," *SPV*, 26 January 1994. See also E. P. Gruzdeva, "I golod, i kholod, i bomby, i pozhary – vse vynesli," in *Universitet v blokadnom i osazhdennom Leningrade 1941–1944: Sbornik ofitsial'nykh dokumentov, pisem, fotografii i drugogo fakticheskogo materiala* (St. Petersburg: TOO "Gippokrat," 1996), 108.

[45] Ol'ga Nikolaevna Grechina, "Interview, June 1995," in Simmons and Perlina, *Writing the Siege*, 111. See also ibid., 131, 35 (for an opposing view).

[46] Granin, "Chelovek iz blokady."

he emphasized that an ethos of selflessness increased one's chances of survival: "The people who were saved were those who saved others."[47] Vladimir Daev, whose essays on the blockade drew on both personal experience and archival research, expressed little patience for the myths of the siege and insisted that "the time has come to wipe off some of the syrup."[48] Nonetheless, he too argued that, in general, "the best" survived.[49] To Daev, "the person whose actions did not have a moral foundation more quickly gave in to depression.... Before others he collapsed in bed, his body swollen, and in the final analysis, he died earlier than active citizens supplied with the exact same ration."[50]

The rule that the cultured and selfless survived, or at least were more likely to survive, suggested, intentionally or not, the survivor-narrator's own moral worth. If, as Likhachev observed, some Leningraders "turned out to be marvelous, incomparable heroes, others – scoundrels, villains, murderers, cannibals," few of those who told their stories counted themselves among the scoundrels.[51] More broadly, blokadniki's diaries, memoirs, and oral histories rarely expressed a sense of shame in survival. For a few, however, the very fact of survival suggested moral weakness. Avgusta Saraeva-Bondar', who was sixteen when the war began, wrote in her 1993 memoir, that "native Leningraders... [u]nable to be unethical, dishonest, insolent, and cruel, not wanting to become shameless procurers of additional means of subsistence by looting abandoned apartments, they were the first to take leave of life." She left the corollary conclusion unspoken: She survived; therefore, she had been able to be unethical, dishonest, or shameless. She mourned the loss of that "genuine high culture [intelligentnost'] that corresponded not only to the spiritual life of our city, but to its external appearance as well – the architecture, avenues, embankments, gardens."[52]

---

47 Granin quoted in Marina Tokareva, "Mera velichiia. Mera viny...," *NV*, 27 January 1995. See also Simmons and Perlina, *Writing the Siege*, 118.
48 Vladimir Daev, *S distantsii poluveka: Ocherki blokadnogo Leningrada* (St. Petersburg: Sudarynia, 1998), 89.
49 The blokadniki's insistence on moral goodness as a predictor of survival stands in sharp contrast to Levi's conclusion that "[t]he worst survived, that is, the fittest; the best all died." Levi, *The Drowned and the Saved*, 82.
50 Daev, *S distantsii*, 85.
51 I have used the translation in Likhachev, *Reflections*, 244.
52 Avgusta Mikhailovna Saraeva-Bondar', "Silhouettes of Time," in Simmons and Perlina, *Writing the Siege*, 145. Her reminiscences of the siege are part of her memoir. A. M. Saraeva-Bondar', *Siluety vremeni* (St. Petersburg: Istoricheskaia illustratsiia, 1993), 56–61.

More commonly, the language of the Leningrad epic provided less painful answers to questions of survival. Abramova, who believed that she had saved her last remaining brother from cannibals, was, she noted in her reminiscences, her father's "silver girl." The "golden girl," her older sister, died early in the blockade. She appeared to agree with her father's assessment of their relative values: "Alia was beautiful. The whole school admired her. But I was silver, and that says it all." When she asked, "How did it happen that I remained alive at a time when children died one after the other?" she also seems to be asking why she was saved, while the "golden girl" was not. The answer, however, betrayed little of the guilt embedded in the question: A guardian angel, a neighbor who, behind her mother's back, gave her "a spoonful of soup with macaroni" saved her.[53] Sof'ia Buriakova credited not a guardian angel but her own stead-fastness and willingness to sacrifice. She admitted that "in the years fol-lowing the war, and even now, in old age, I have asked myself many times – where did I find the spiritual and physical strength to endure all the hardships that fell to my lot? The answer is simple. What played the decisive role was the feeling of civic patriotism, the realization of a patri-otic duty."[54] Here, she took for granted the fact that survival required "spiritual and physical strength," and answered the gnawing question of her own survival with the truisms of the story of heroic Leningrad.

By the early 1990s, the worst aspects of the siege, cannibalism in partic-ular, had come out of the shadows, but such revelations did not necessarily reshape blockade narratives. While blokadniki told stories in which can-nibals embodied the undeniable horrors of the war, they also honored the "holy blockade women," who represented the no-less-true spiritual, phys-ical, and cultural strength of the city. Survivors continued to explain their own survival in terms of steadfastness, patriotism, and intelligentnost'. The Leningrad myth remained largely intact.

Stalin's Crimes and the War on Leningrad

What is particularly striking about the epic narrative of the blockade is its persistence even in the face of the collapse of the state that did so much to construct and perpetuate it. Glasnost made it possible not only to speak about cannibalism and crime during the siege, but also

---

[53] Abramova, "Byla ia."
[54] Sof'ia Nikolaevna Buriakova, "A Half-Century Ago," in Simmons and Perlina, *Writing the Siege,* 98.

to question the myth of the Soviet Union's heroic victory over fascism – to blame both Hitler and Stalin for the horrors of war. New documents and previously silent participants testified to the ineptitude and failures of the Soviet response to the German invasion, to the fact that some Leningraders called for the surrender of the city, to the state's cover-up of the real extent of Soviet casualties, and to the leadership's contribution to the appallingly high numbers of Soviet dead. The Soviet authorities finally acknowledged and published the secret protocols of the 1939 Nazi-Soviet Pact that partitioned Poland, transferred the Baltic states to the Soviet Union, and opened the way for Hitler's invasion of Poland. In 1990, the Soviet government also admitted its role in the murder of Polish military officers at Katyn Forest in 1940.[55] Unlike Nikita Khrushchev's attacks on the myth of Stalin's military genius that had helped to stimulate the emergence of the war cult, the glasnost-era criticism of the war, and especially the equation of the two totalitarian states, posed a clear threat to the myth of a holy war that united people and party. In a very real sense, as Tumarkin emphasizes, these revelations tarnished the myth of the war. How, then, was it possible that the Leningrad epic and reverence for the war in general withstood this onslaught?

A good bit of the power of the war myth had stemmed from its ability to construct a grand narrative of suffering, struggle, and redemption out of the small, personal stories of individuals. The previous section illustrated how, even in the face of potentially devastating revelations of crime and cannibalism, survivors continued to employ the myth of heroic, virtuous Leningrad as a frame for their own stories. Here, I examine how attacks on the broader myth of the war affected their narratives and the meanings they attributed to their wartime experiences. With disclosures of the dark secrets of the Soviet state, the grand narrative faltered, but most survivors continued to insist in one way or another on the meaningfulness of their personal wartime losses and triumphs. As a 1994 headline marking the forty-ninth anniversary of victory noted: "The [Soviet] Union is no more – its heroes live on."[56]

None of which is to minimize the degree to which at least some of the accounts of the blockade published in the 1980s and 1990s challenged the image of the selfless struggle of Soviet citizens and the Soviet state. Written in the spring of 1942, but published locally only in 1991, Freidenberg's

---

[55] Tumarkin, *The Living and the Dead,* 174–81.
[56] Alla Malakhova, "Soiuza net – ego geroi zhivy," *Nezavisimaia gazeta* (hereafter *NG*), 7 May 1994.

account called into question the meaningfulness of sacrificing and dying for the Soviet cause. She blamed both Stalin and Hitler for the tragedies of the war, accusations that anticipated those published fifty years later, when the Nazi-Soviet Pact became a key marker of the impurity of the Soviet crusade against fascism.[57]

For Freidenberg, the Soviet state was not only responsible for the war, it was worse than war – an outlook that may explain her conviction that the city should have been surrendered. She argued that the daily horrors and humiliations of the blockade, which she cataloged in sometimes graphic detail, could not rival the ordinary workings of the Stalinist state. In one particularly unsettling passage, she provided a vivid picture of cannibalism. While "such things were talked of with horror, blanching and shuddering, I," Freidenberg averred, "felt no terror. Think about it, to cut up and sell a corpse! How much more horrifying was our reality, our Russian martyrdom of the living person, our NKVD [the political police], political repression [*ezhovshchiny*], moral scalpels and knives."[58] Leningraders suffered – but not in the name of a good cause, and no more than under the allegedly ordinary circumstances of Stalinist peacetime.

Freidenberg's memoir provides a clear illustration of how revelations of Stalin's crimes could destroy the myth of the holy war. Underlining the criminality and immortality of the Stalinist state, she rejected the mythic wartime language that provided the basis for the construction of the Leningrad epic. She saw the promotion of "beautiful patriotism" not as evidence of unity of purpose but as the party's patronizing means of "entertaining" the "crowd, the starving 'cattle' of humble and embittered slaves" that stood at the bottom of the rationing hierarchy. She dismissed the lofty language of myth as "pomposity and deception."[59]

However powerful and true such deconstructions of the myth appeared to journalists, historians, and especially the younger generation, they did not – perhaps could not – undermine heroic stories of the siege that many blokadniki had been telling themselves and others for fifty years. Even during the war, a clear understanding of the failures and crimes of the state could coexist with an acceptance of its myths. In his wartime

---

[57] Freidenberg, "Osada cheloveka," 16. Vitalii Tret'iakov, "Den' pobedy: Den' radosti, skorbi i voprosov, na kotorye net otveta," *NG*, 7 May 1991. Aleksandr Bangerskii, "Guntis Ulmanis: 'Nam etot den' ne prines svobodu,'" *NG*, 11 May 1995. Vitalii Tret'iakov, "Den' pobedy dlia nas: ne poteriannyi prazdnik poteriannoi strany," *NG*, 29 April 1995.

[58] Freidenberg, "Osada cheloveka," 20–21.

[59] Ibid., 34. See also Nina Perlina, *Ol'ga Freidenberg's Works and Days* (Bloomington, IN: Slavica, 2002), 184–87.

diary – published in 1994 – Germogen Ivanov, like Freidenberg, cataloged deadly inequities in food distribution. However, unlike Freidenberg, he not only accepted but also repeated the formulas of wartime propaganda, even when experience suggested their deceptiveness. In December 1941 he wrote: "Everyday life has become saturated with the heroic. . . . Become a hero or perish! – life tells each Leningrader, and the majority of citizens have become heroes. True, very many have also perished and are perishing." His own observations of mass death, a near riot in a bakery, and the theft of bread rations did not shake his belief that "war forms the moral character of the people."[60]

By the mid-1990s, blokadniki who also happened to be professional historians well acquainted with the sorts of revelations contained in Freidenberg's and Ivanov's diaries underscored that the story had become more complex, but continued to affirm the Leningrad epic. Writing in 1993, Gennadii Sobolev, one of the most prolific historians of the siege – and identified in his byline as "inhabitant of blockaded Leningrad, historian" – acknowledged the failures on the part of the Soviet leadership, but emphasized that new facts bore out the story of local heroism. Eschewing angry invective, Sobolev observed that "of course the leadership of the defense of Leningrad, headed by A. A. Zhdanov, carries direct responsibility for the fact that 2.5 million inhabitants remained in the blockaded city with negligible supplies of food." Positioning himself as a neutral historian, Sobolev added that "we would sin against truth [*istiny*] if we were to confirm that [the leadership] left the population at the mercy of fate and was concerned only about saving the party and Soviet nomenklatura." In this regard, he mentioned the evacuation of "nearly one million inhabitants" via the Road of Life.[61] While not exactly debunking the myth of

[60] Ivanov, "38 dnei."
[61] Gennadii Sobolev, "Eto gor'koe slovo 'blokada,'" *Sankt-Peterburgskaia panorama*, 1993, no. 8: 3. Scholarly work by Sobolev on the blockade includes "Blokada Leningrada v svete perestroiki istoricheskoi nauki," in I. A. Rosenko and G. L. Sobolev, eds., *Voprosy istorii i istoriografii Velikoi Otechestvennoi voiny: Mezhvuzovskii sbornik* (Leningrad: Izdatel'stvo Leningradskogo Universiteta, 1989), 64–81; and "Leningrad v Velikoi Otechestvennoi voine (nekotorye itogi i nereshenye voprosy)," *Vestnik Leningradskogo Universiteta: Seriia 2: Istoriia, iazykoznanie, literaturovedenie* 1989, vyp. 1, no. 2: 3–8. Other popular articles include Gennadii Sobolev, "Sobiralsia li Stalin sdavat' Leningrad?" *Leningradskaia panorama*, 1991, no. 6: 24–26; and "Tsena blokady," *Leningradskaia panorama*, 1991, no. 1: 18–21. Sobolev contributed to an important collection of documents on the blockade, Dzeniskevich, *Leningrad v osade*. A. R. Dzeniskevich, another survivor cum historian, was the project's primary editor. Like Sobolev, Dzeniskevich both distances himself from and embraces the Leningrad epic. Dzeniskevich, *Blokada i politika: Oborona Leningrada v politicheskoi kon"iunkture* (St. Petersburg: Nestor, 1998).

the party as the "organizer and inspirer of victory," Sobolev hardly gave it a ringing endorsement.

Questioning the Soviet leadership and implicating it in deepening the tragedy of the blockade, Sobolev's account both confirmed and subtly reformulated the Leningrad myth. He reminded his readers that, whatever the failings of the Soviet state, the death of "no less than one million civilians" in blockaded Leningrad "is one of the most vile crimes of German fascism." Moreover, the party leadership "relied not only on strict administrative means and ration dictatorship, but also on the population's understanding of its patriotic duty, its resolve to defend the city to the last breath." Substituting "collectivist psychology" (*kollektivist-skaia psikhologiia*) and "unity" (*splochennost'*) for the buzzwords of the war cult – heroism, steadfastness (*stoikost'*), and courage (*muzhestvo*) – Sobolev nonetheless reiterated many of the epic's central images and anecdotes. He described workers, weakened by starvation, who continued to repair ships, tanks, and artillery. He lauded the thousands of Komsomol "girls" who in early 1942 brought food, firewood, and water to neighbors on the verge of death. Emphasizing the maintenance of cultured norms, and also the predominance of impulses often regarded as sorely lacking in post-Soviet Russia, Sobolev focused on the "collectivism and unity of the defenders of Leningrad, their lofty moral spirit."[62]

Even during the years of the war cult, this sort of insistence on Leningrad's special status – its unique spirit and glory – had been a part of the blockade epic. With the end of the Soviet Union, the local emphasis became increasingly pronounced, but it did not diminish – indeed it may have enhanced – the wider significance of the Leningraders' stories. Particularly since the publication of *Blokadnaia kniga*, accounts of the siege had focused on ordinary "people with concrete fates and names."[63] Many of the diaries and reminiscences that appeared in the local Petersburg press in celebration of the fiftieth anniversaries of the end of the blockade (1994) and the end of the war (1995) – some of which have been cited here – told similar personal, family stories that often ignored the wider Soviet context. Fitted with headlines like "War and Peace, 1945–1995," "Impossible to Forget," or "We bow before those great years," small episodes

---

[62] Sobolev, "Eto gor'koe slovo," 3. On perceptions of the so-called New Russians, see Leslie Dayna Kaufman, "Building Castles in the Sky: The Domestication of Daily Life in Urban Russia" (Ph.D. diss., Columbia University, 2000), 155. See also the *Russian Review*'s forum on "The New Russians," *Russian Review* 62 (January 2003).

[63] Tokareva, "Mera velichiia."

claimed broad, if ambiguously defined, significance.[64] Detached from its Soviet foundations, the myth of heroic Leningrad could be attached to alternative overarching narratives.

The demise of the Soviet Union and the revelations of its crimes and failures required a rethinking, but not a rejection, of the blockade's relationship to a larger, meaningful story of struggle and triumph. Attentive to the survivors' need for meaning, Sobolev asked, "In whose name did Leningraders make such a sacrifice? Was their immense suffering and hardship justified? Why didn't Leningrad declare itself in open city, like Paris and other European capitals conquered by Hitler?" Such questions, he warned, "cannot become an object of the cynical and speculative discussion." Instead, he situated the blockade within the global "Second World War" – as opposed to the Soviet "Great Fatherland War" – and emphasized "Leningrad's contribution to saving European civilization." In the final analysis, "it is unworthy to call into question the fact that Leningraders fought and sacrificed in the name of the love of their Motherland [*Rodina*] and their city, in the name of their families and dear ones [*rodnykh i blizkikh*], the happy life of those who came after them. So let their memory be pure [or radiant, *svetlaia*]."[65] In language that emphasized emotional, local, and intimate ties – to rodina, hometown, and *rodnye* – Sobolev purged the Leningrad epic of the taint of Soviet power, while continuing to endow Leningraders' losses with world-historical significance. Leningraders had galvanized the whole Soviet people and saved European civilization.

From this perspective, the Soviet state often became yet another enemy faced by self-sacrificing Leningraders. While some survivors faulted Stalin and the Soviet leadership for failing to evacuate or feed Leningraders, and while the political police continued to operate in the blockaded city, many accounts of Stalin's war on Leningrad focused on the postwar purges – the so-called Leningrad Affair.[66] In the late 1980s, the drive to reestablish the Museum of the Defense of Leningrad – which had been organized during

---

[64] *NV*, 7 February 1995. *Smena*, 7 May 1995. *SPV*, 8 September 1995.

[65] Sobolev, "Eto gor'koe slovo," 3. See also A. Dzeniskevich, "Podvig i tragediia," *SPV*, 18 January 1994.

[66] Nikita Lomagin, *Neizvestnaia blokada* (St. Petersburg: Izdatel'stvo Dom "Neva," 2002). Likhachev, *Reflections*, 255–58. Simmons and Perlina, *Writing the Siege*, 37–38, 122–23. Freidenberg, "Osada cheloveka," 40. E. S. Kots, "'Na moiu doliu vypal schastlivyi lotereinyi bilet,'" *Istoricheskii arkhiv*, 1999, no. 3: 92–93, 89. Dzeniskevich, *Leningrad v osade*, 409–62. Irina Reznikova, "Repressionen Während der Leningrader Blockade," *1999: Zeitschrift für Sozialgeschichte des 20 und 21 Jahrhunderts* 15 (2000): 117–41.

the blockade, expanded in the postwar period, and shut down as a result of the Leningrad Affair – occasioned condemnations of the Stalinist state's attempt to obliterate the memory of Leningrad's wartime suffering and triumph.[67]

The second of Adamovich and Granin's censored chapters, which detailed the Leningrad Affair, effectively summarized the themes of many of the personal and scholarly accounts published in the 1980s and 1990s. "The heroism of the Leningrad blockade," they argued, "was perceived by the Stalinist milieu as a display of the freedom-loving spirit, the unruliness of the city, its excessive, and therefore threatening, independence [*samostoianie*]." As evidence, they cited the soon-to-be purged party leader A. A. Kuznetsov's preelection speech in January 1946: "How is it possible to not love such a city! How not love a city into which, since the moment of its foundation, no enemy has stepped foot! . . . The first city to stop the enemy, holding out during a twenty-nine month siege. . . . A city whose glory eclipsed the glory of Troy!" Since the memory of the blockade imbricated Leningraders' sense of independence, "the first wrath," the editors argued, of the postwar purge "was vented upon the museum" of the defense of Leningrad.[68]

Picturing Leningrad as the victim of the Soviet state made it possible to imagine the blockade as the heroic defense of St. Petersburg–Leningrad, the "freedom-loving" defender of "European civilization." "A city whose glory eclipsed the glory of Troy!" One of the distinguishing features of accounts of the blockade that emerged in the 1980s and 1990s was the degree to which the Leningrad epic – still presented as an event of national, if not global, significance – became a heroic defense of the ideals and traditions of St. Petersburg–Leningrad, rather than those of the Soviet state.

The Unspeakable

In the 1980s and 1990s, blokadniki began to speak the unspoken. At the same time, much remained not only unspoken but also, for reasons personal, social, and political, largely unspeakable. Revelations of

[67] V. Kutuzov, "Muzei oborony Leningrada," *Dialog*, 1988, no. 24: 21–27. "Pochta 'Dialog': Vosstanovim muzei oborony Leningrada!" *Dialog*, 1988, no. 35: 22–23. *Smena*, 9 September 1989, 17 September 1989, 7 January 1990. *Vechernii Leningrad*, 4 April 1990. NV, 30 April 1991. V. P. Kivisepp and N. P. Dobrotvorskii, "Muzei muzhestva, skorbi i slavy," *Leningradskaia panorama*, 1991, no. 8: 24–25. Gosudarstvennyi memorial'nyi muzei oborny i blokady Leningrada, *Muzei oborony i blokady Leningrada* (St. Petersburg: AGAT, 1998). Simmons and Perlina, *Writing the Siege*, 170–73.
[68] Adamovich and Granin, "Blokadnaia kniga," 17–18. See Chapter 4.

cannibalism and Stalin's crimes allowed for an increasingly complex and nuanced picture of the siege. However, as noted earlier, these new revelations scarcely affected the dominance of the epic mode of memory that emphasized the strength, dignity, and even heroism of most Leningraders. The next section addresses the question of the social stresses and political motives that shaped the ways in which blokadniki told their stories in the twilight years of the Soviet Union and in the early post-Soviet period. Here I want to focus on the individual and psychological foundations of mythic memory's resilience.

Primo Levi's argument, cited in the epigraph, regarding the tendency of oft-told tales to "crystallize," points to the importance of the act of telling stories in the process of making – testing, perfecting, adorning, installing – memories. The emphasis on narrative is particularly apt in the case of the blokadniki who, since practically the first days of the blockade, had been inundated with narratives that ostensibly reflected their own experiences, while framing them as part of an epoch-making struggle. The prefabricated stories provided by the state can be understood as providing narrative templates for structuring difficult, painful, and unprecedented experiences.[69] Consciously or not, individuals used stories provided by the state both to demarcate and reinforce the boundaries of the "unspeakable" and to integrate painful experiences into meaningful memory.[70]

The repetition of ritualized descriptions of the blockaded city illustrates how state-supplied narrative allowed survivors to quarantine the "unspeakable" aspects of their experiences, while incorporating such experiences into epic stories of the blockade. Survivors' accounts often deployed what the anthropologist Nancy Ries has described as "litany sequences of one-word elements" – some combination of "cold and hunger and bombs and rockets and fires" (*i kholod, i golod, i bomby, i snariady, i pozhary*). Ries observes that in the years of perestroika,

---

[69] Jerome Bruner, *Acts of Meaning* (Cambridge, MA: Harvard University Press, 1990), 108, 56. Soviet narratives can be understood as the sort of "misleading information" that, cognitive psychologists have found "can produce errors in what subjects report that they have seen." Elizabeth F. Loftus, Julie Feldman, and Richard Dashiell, "The Reality of Illusory Memories," in Schacter, *Memory Distortion*, 48. State-produced narratives can also be understood as a form of "linguistic encoding of post-traumatic emotions ... that provide access to traumatic information in a form that is less distressing [than emotional responses associated with the trauma]." John H. Krystal, Steven M. Southwick, and Dennis S. Charney, "Post Traumatic Stress Disorder: Psychobiological Mechanisms of Traumatic Remembrance," in ibid., 163.

[70] For a somewhat different analysis, which describes communist propaganda as a means of "tricking the mind," see Merridale, *Night of Stone*, 329.

"speaking in litanies seemed to be a sort of sacral act, one that shifted the discursive context, elevating any conversation to the epic plane of the universal Russian tale."[71] In the case of stories of the blockade, this strategy of epic storytelling functioned both to elevate personal tragedies and to block unspeakable sights from view.[72] "Hunger and cold and bombs" had long functioned as a standardized shorthand for the conditions in blockaded Leningrad, and survivors sometimes substituted it for more individual or idiosyncratic accounts of the first winter of the blockade. The ubiquity of litanies in all sorts of Russian talk during the perestroika years may have aggravated the blokadniki's frustrations with a younger generation that did not respect the sacrifices required by *real* hunger and cold.[73] But their own use of litanies could efface the specificity of the blockade's "hunger and cold," even as it sacralized them.

Survivors' accounts often used wartime poetry as another means of validating, ritualizing, universalizing, and avoiding personal stories. Many memoirs at some point reached for the appropriate verse, usually from Ol'ga Berggol'ts.[74] The appearance of Berggol'ts's poetry in reminiscences written in the 1980s and 1990s attests to the degree to which her work managed to combine a sense of the real, individual, personal, everyday, often housewifely details of the blockade with the epic language of glory and victory.[75] Her poetry had been an important part of the war cult's effort to revive the sense of shared purpose and civic engagement that had been such a notable feature of the war years. As the official war cult faded, her poetry, as well as that of other, usually female, siege poets, notably Vera Inber, remained evocative and authoritative and provided a way for survivors to link their small stories to the Leningrad epic.

In the collection of memoirs published in 1996 to commemorate the siege experiences of people associated with Leningrad State University, Berggol'ts's poetry, and to a lesser degree that of Inber, provided a

---

[71] Nancy Ries, *Russian Talk: Culture and Conversation during Perestroika* (Ithaca, NY: Cornell University Press, 1997), 86. Levada et al., "Russia," 18.

[72] Gruzdeva, "I kholod," 108. Simmons and Perlina, *Writing the Siege*, 90. Galina Gorbova (Veselova), "Moe detstvo – voina!" *Leningradskaia panorama*, 1991, no. 8: 26. *Blokadniki: Volgogradskoe oblastnoe dobrovol'noe obshchestvo "Zashchitniki i zhiteli blokadnogo Leningrad"* (Volgograd: Komitet po B70, 1996), 5.

[73] R. Zubova, "Pomnitsia eshche sil'nei," *Vechernii Leningrad*, 8 September 1987.

[74] See, for example, Zoia Fedorova, "Poklonimsia velikim tem godam," *SPV*, 8 September 1995; "Blokadnyi metronom," *SPV*, 18 January 1995; Z. Fedorova, "Stoi, potomok, ne slyshavshii groma blokadnykh orudii!" *SPV*, 8 September 1994; Sobolev, "Eto gor'koe slovo," 3.

[75] Katharine Hodgson, "Kitezh and the Commune: Recurrent Themes in the Work of Ol'ga Berggol'ts," *Slavonic and East European Review* 74 (January 1996): 6.

reservoir of shared images, memories, and interpretations. Anna Korol-eva, who started work at the university in 1941, began her account of "Blockade brotherhood under the thunder of bombs and missiles" with a piece of Berggol'ts's "Second conversation with a neighbor" that equated the blockaded city and the more traditional battlefront. For Koroleva, Berggol'ts "graphically expresses in verse my own blockade life, work, and activities, and that of so many other women," who made victory possible.[76]

Kira Golovan', only ten during the siege and later an engineer at the uni-versity, connected her personal memories of food during the siege with images found in Berggol'ts's verses. Golovan' remembered that "at our place, we had a small slab of carpenter's glue that we had found with father's tools.... Glue-jelly was very much enjoyed."[77] Immediately fol-lowing this recollection, Golovan' broke the flow of her narrative to quote Berggol'ts: "Yes, we make no secret of it – in those days/ We ate earth, glue, belts." The quotation both verifies and universalizes the childhood memory. Berggol'ts's poetry, with its sense of history and personal tragedy, offered a means of structuring "personal" memories of the siege that res-onated with historic significance.

Survivors' use of wartime poetry highlights the ways in which the rit-ualized, elevated language provided a means of fitting what Berggol'ts called "ordinary cares" – the housewife's domestic domain – into the Leningrad epic. This sort of language made it possible to talk about the war's disruption of family life and gender norms, to suggest intimate, per-sonal, and unspeakable memories, without specifying them. The poetry included by Golovan' allowed her to tell her own story in the first person plural – "we make no secret of it" – and to link her recollections to an epic moment – "in those days." Preserving some details of the story, the poetic interruption screened details that remained unspeakable. The verses with which Koroleva began her narrative are particularly telling in this respect, as they map the civilian and largely female experience of the blockade onto a more traditional, male military front. Broken windows have "left the ranks"; women fight "without relief" and take "anonymous heights" that cannot be found on any map. Women in the blockaded city thus

---

[76] A. A. Koroleva, "Blokadnoe bratstvo pod grokhom bomb i snariadov," in *Universitet*, 73. Ol'ga Berggol'ts, "Vtoroi razgovor s sosedkoi," *Sobranie sochinenii v trekh tomakh* (Leningrad: Khudozhestvennaia literatura, 1989), 2: 66.

[77] K. I. Golovan' (Liubomirova), "Nam ne zabyt' surovye gody fashistskoi voiny," in *Uni-versitet*, 125. A large number of the memoirs in this collection include excerpts from wartime poetry.

became heroes on a par with men at the front, but the specificity of their experiences and their losses largely evaporated. Including war poetry in their memoirs allowed blokadniki to allude to personal memory without speaking it, to submerge individual stories in the shared epic.[78]

For child survivors, the iconic story of Tania Savicheva functioned in ways analogous to Berggol'ts's poetry. In an oral history recorded in 1994, Natal'ia Stroganova, who was seven when the war began, recounted the deaths of five members of her family of nine. "After the war," she remembered, "my aunt, a doctor, said to me: 'Your family is like Tania Savicheva's,'" whose famous diary ended with the words "Everyone died, except Tania." Making the analogy a central feature of her own narrative, Stroganova related that "recently I transcribed all the data regarding my relatives during the siege." Her transcription clearly mimicked Tania's "diary," with its terse list of family members' names, ages, and dates of death. In one significant respect, Stroganova's log differed from Tania's. It included the 1943 arrest by the NKVD of her grandfather for "anti-Soviet activity under extreme circumstances" and his death "in transit to the site of detention and punishment." In a coda to her version of Tania's diary, Stroganova denied the validity of the charge, ending with the assertion that no one in her family, "not even a delirium," wished for the Nazis to enter the city.[79] By structuring her own experiences as parallel to Tania's, and by including her grandfather among the victims of the siege, Stroganova simplified her own story and turned it into part of the Leningrad myth.

The power of ritualized, crystallized narrative to displace unspeakable personal stories is nowhere clearer than in stories that touch the physical experience of the blockade – starvation's assault on the narrator's body. The use of the wartime euphemism "dystrophic," a term that soft-pedaled starvation by medicalizing it, and the characterization of starvation as both a physical and a moral problem made it possible to leave unspeakable memories of bodily injury unspoken while admitting starvation into an epic narrative of the triumph of culture.[80] E. P. Gruzdeva, a university

---

[78] Bruce M. Ross, *Remembering the Personal Past* (New York: Oxford University Press, 1991), 85.

[79] Natal'ia Vladimirovna Stroganova, "Oral history, recorded June 1994," in Simmons and Perlina, *Writing the Siege*, 130–31. In 1999, before telling me the story of her own siege childhood, a librarian at the Russian National Library made sure that I was familiar with the story of Tania Savicheva.

[80] Neratova, *V dni*, 55. See also Elena Kozhina, *Through the Burning Steppe: A Memoir of Wartime Russia, 1942–1943*, trans. Vadim Mahmoudov (New York: Riverhead Books, 2000), 122, 123. Freidenberg rejected this terminology. Perlina, *Ol'ga Freidenberg's Works*, 189.

administrator, described her own starvation in vague, impersonal terms. The difficult conditions of work on the city's defenses, she noted, led to her admission into the hospital "with the diagnosis 'DYSTROPHY.'" Borrowing the terms of the war cult, she emphasized not pain but "courage, steadfastness . . . we struggled, with our last strength, to do what we could to help the front."[81] Only the uppercase letters hint at the reality behind the rhetoric.

The epic narrative and the zone of the unspeakable reinforced each other. To renounce the formulas of the epic narrative, to remember the starving body, to speak the unspeakable threatened to destabilize not only the myth of heroic Leningrad but also survivors' stories that incorporated any components of that myth. The starving body's threat to the Leningrad epic emerges with particular clarity in the few accounts that attempted to tell of the war's assault on the body.[82] In reminiscences written in 1962 but published only in 1990, Berggol'ts focused on starvation's destruction of the female body, and her descriptions seemed to rule out compromises with the myth of shared struggle. Describing the scene at a Leningrad bathhouse in the spring of 1942, when warmer weather allowed survivors to take their first hot bath in months, she made the disappearance of the gendered body a measure of the degradation caused by war:

Then I looked at the women. . . . The blemished, stretched, rough skin of the women's bodies – no, not even women – they had ceased to resemble women. Their breasts had disappeared; their stomachs were shrunken; the purple and blue stains of scurvy had crawled across their skin. A few had horribly distended stomachs on top of skinny legs. . . . I repeat, torn off arms and legs are nothing compared to these bony bodies: You know, missing arms do not deform Venus. Here everything was in place and nothing was missing. One should sob, looking at the multitude of these women; one should be amazed, that they decided to bare in the light of day so profaned, emaciated, blemished, and spotted a body.[83]

The wounds she saw in the warmth and safety of the bathhouse were, Berggol'ts argued, more horrifying that the dismemberment of the soldier at the front.[84] The disfigured soldier, like Venus, might still embody godlike powers – heroism, bravery, and dedication. The starving woman projected only horror, shame, and despair.

[81] Gruzdeva, "I golod," 108, emphasis in original.
[82] See the discussion of Lidiia Ginzburg's *Blockade Diary* in Chapter 5.
[83] Ol'ga Berggol'ts, "Dnevnye zvezdy," *Ogonek*, no. 19 (5–12 May 1990): 16.
[84] Katharine Hodgson offers a similar reading of the bathhouse in "Under an Unwomanly Star: War in the Writing of Ol'ga Berggol'ts," in Rosalind Marsh, ed., *Women and Russian Culture: Projections and Self-Perceptions* (New York: Berghahn Books, 1998), 139.

Still, Berggol'ts, like other survivors who wrote less frankly about the starving body, hesitated to identify herself as among the wounded. Describing the women that she saw at the bath, Berggol'ts did not describe her own body, although there is every reason to believe that it too was "profaned, emaciated, blemished, and spotted."[85] Even as she described the effects of starvation and suggested its senselessness, she retained her silence about her own body, remained distanced from her own pain.

In her account of the bathhouse, Berggol'ts rejected the ritualized language and epic narrative that she had done so much to fashion and that continued to shape the stories of other survivors fifty years after the end of the war. I do not mean to suggest that this rejection of the myth of heroic Leningrad marks this narrative as her one "true" narrative of the siege. On the contrary, the point is that rejecting the crystallized narrative was tremendously costly – requiring the abandonment of the notion of meaningful suffering – and therefore tremendously difficult, if not impossible. The epic narrative may have grown at the expense of "raw" memory, but it was also nourished by survivors' desire or need for meaning and their own decisions – conscious or not – about the limits of the speakable. Like the soldier who, shortly after the war, told Berggol'ts that he wanted to read about "a real war that has heroism and brave deeds," not about the war as he remembered it, blokadniki most often wrote and spoke about the "real" blockade, not the unspeakable obscenities of war.[86]

Memory in Uncertain Times

By the late 1980s, the hardships and uncertainties currently faced by the war generation added political and social urgency to blokadniki's efforts to maintain and perpetuate the Leningrad epic. Economic reform and the eventual dissolution of the Soviet Union were particularly difficult for older Soviet citizens, both because they relied on small, fixed pensions and because the demise of a system that they had learned to negotiate, if not love, left them adrift, confused, vulnerable, and fearful.[87] Under

---

[85] Adamovich and Granin, *Blokadnaia kniga*, 329–32.

[86] Berggol'ts cited in Musya Glants, "Images of the War in Painting," in John Garrard and Carol Garrard, eds., *World War 2 and the Soviet People: Selected Papers from the Fourth World Congress for Soviet and East European Studies* (New York: St. Martin's Press, 1993), 111. See also Carin Tschöpl, *Die sowjetische Lyrik-Diskussion: Ol'ga Berggol'c' Leningrader Blockadedichtung als Paradigma* (Munich: Fink, 1988), 189, 193–94.

[87] Levada et al., "Russia," 16. "Kulturdugnad St. Petersburg," http://www.alien.no/ kulturdugnad/sider/january.html (accessed 17 February 2006).

these circumstances, their wartime heroism became a central component of claims to respect and social welfare.

In its last years, the Soviet state had taken some steps toward "improving the material circumstances and social and medical services provided to inhabitants of blockaded Leningrad."[88] In 1989, the party-dominated city government created a local award, Inhabitant of Blockaded Leningrad, for blokadniki who had not received the Soviet medal For the Defense of Leningrad, and petitioned the Soviet government to extend the same privileges to holders of both awards as to veterans of the war. In 1990, the Soviet government agreed to recognize the Inhabitant of Blockaded Leningrad award, and approximately four hundred and fifty thousand additional Leningraders were able to claim privileges ranging from reduced rents to free travel on the city's buses, trams, and subways. In 1994, Boris Yeltsin's government granted blokadniki privileges equivalent to those of war veterans. In post-Soviet Russia, not only war veterans and blokadniki but also heroes of Soviet labor and rehabilitated "enemies of the people" enjoyed similar, rather modest, privileges.[89] In the allocation of social welfare, the past still mattered.

Despite efforts to secure better housing and heath care for aging blokadniki, they continued to be represented in the press, and sometimes to represent themselves, as ignored by a society that neither guaranteed their material well-being nor respected their sacrifices and selflessness. In January 1991, the forty-seventh anniversary of the breaking of the blockade provided the occasion for a brief profile in the independent press of Anna Arkhipova, "an ordinary Russian woman with an ordinary fate." Married in 1934, widowed in 1942, having survived the siege along with her child, she now found herself in 1991 without savings, without even the "900 rubles I saved for my funeral." The journalist emphasized the "terrifying symbolism in that number . . . 900 days of the blockade – 900 funeral rubles," and concluded that current social transition, the "epoch of the war with the mafia," was particularly hard on women like Arkhipova.[90]

---

[88] "O merakh po dal'neishemu uluchsheniiu sotsial'nykh uslovii leningradtsev, perezhivshikh blokadku," *Biulleten' Ispolnitel'nogo komiteta Leningradskogo gorodskogo Soveta narodnykh deputatov*, no. 23 (December 1989): 14.

[89] N. Grichuk, "Leningradtsam, perezhivshii blokadu," *Vechernii Leningrad*, 5 May 1990. Lev Godovannik, "Kto imeet pravo na razlichnye l'goty?" *Smena*, 26 January 1994. N. Konovalova, "Sotsial'nye garantii zashchitnikam i zhiteliam blokadnogo Leningrada," *SPV*, 20 January 1994.

[90] Bogopol'skaia, "900 dnei." See also Tokareva, "Mera velichiia"; Korkonosenko, "Blokadnitsy," 28–29; "Russian Citizens View the Great Patriotic War as More Tragic Than Heroic," *Current Digest of the Post-Soviet Press* 55, no. 25 (2003): 13.

Her story was hardly unique. By 1994, more than one million of the city's five million inhabitants were retired, and according to one study, only 24 percent of the population lived above the poverty line. For senior citizens, the contrast with the Soviet past became a measure of real economic distress and a symbol of unanticipated, unpleasant changes. "Even in 1945," lamented a fifty-five-year-old woman in 1993, "it was not so dirty as it is now."[91]

The chronic housing shortage often stood at the heart of blokadniki's fears and complaints. In the 1990s, many blokadniki lived in the same communal apartments in which they had survived the war. In 1991, 63 percent of Leningrad's senior citizens lived in communal apartments, and "the percentage was even higher for blokadniki."[92] These rooms contained memories both of the war and of a time when factories and other enterprises maintained public housing. They functioned as emblems of the unfulfilled promises of both victory and the market. By the early 1990s, local factories and the city government often lacked the resources to undertake essential capital repairs, and much of the public housing stock, even apartments located in buildings officially designated as "historic," fell into disrepair.[93] In 1991, Liudmila Griaznevaia lived in the same communal apartment and slept "in the same place that I slept during the blockade." During the war, a rocket had come through the wall just above her head. However, she emphasized not wartime destruction but the building's recent deterioration. Whereas at some unspecified time in the past the "staircases were clean, the glass unbroken, the basements clean," now, in the room that she shared with her brother, there was "always dark, fetid, standing water." Similar stories could be heard four years later. As Daniil Granin concluded, "privileges have come too late."[94]

In 1994, the Russian Federation legalized the "privatization and sale of individual rooms in communal apartments." By 1998, "communal apartments comprised slightly more than 10 percent of the 1.6 million

[91] Jussi Simpura and Galina Eremitcheva, "Dirt: Symbolic and Practical Dimensions of Social Problems in St. Petersburg," *International Journal of Urban and Regional Research* 21 (1997): 472.

[92] Korkonosenko, "Blokadnitsy," 28. See also Aleksei Oreshkin, "Khoroshie novosti: Dom veteranov stanovit'sia obitaemym," *Smena*, 8 September 1995.

[93] Stephen Butler, Ritu Nayyar-Stone, and Sheila O'Leary, "The Law and Economics of Historic Preservation in St. Petersburg, Russia," *Review of Urban and Regional Development Studies* 11 (March 1999): 24, 30.

[94] "'Glavnoe – zimu etu perezhit','" *Chas pik*, 25 March 1991. Granin, "Chelovek iz blokady."

apartments in the city, down from nearly 16 percent in 1991." Still, 16 percent of the city's inhabitants lived in communal apartments, many in "less space than they are entitled to according to still-operational Soviet-era housing norms."[95] The gentrification of the central districts, where most communal apartments had been located, meant that many long-term residents could no longer afford to shop in local stores. However, the lack of adequate transportation, shops, and social services in outlying areas made a move to the periphery of the city unappealing.[96] More broadly, as Leslie Kaufman argues in her study of the Petersburg housing market in the 1990s, for many, the "mere existence" of a real estate market "threatened the structure through which they had structured their lives."[97] Pensioners, who constituted 28 percent of the population in one central Petersburg district in 2000, often expressed the deepest apprehensions about getting involved in the real estate market, even if such involvement would have allowed them to leave their communal apartments.[98]

At least as much as material hardships, blokadniki emphasized the younger generation's hurtful lack of respect. Mitrofanov, the vice president of the International Association of Blokadniki, feared that "we are raising a generation of people for whom nothing is holy."[99] In her 1994 memoir, Ol'ga Grechina emphasized the emotional pain both of remembering and of having her memories dismissed or disrespected by the younger generation. She feared that Leningraders were beginning not only to forget but to ignore the siege and to mock the blokadniki.[100]

The blokadniki's claims to social services and respect ultimately rested on their heroic sacrifices and their unimpeachable morality. Their claims, in other words, rested in large part on the perpetuation of the myth of

---

[95] James H. Bater and John R. Staples, "Planning for Change in Central St. Petersburg," *Post-Soviet Geography and Economics* 41, no. 2 (2000): 90, 87.

[96] Kaufman, "Building Castles," 157. Bater and Staples, "Planning," 89.

[97] Kaufman, "Building Castles," 141.

[98] Bater and Staples, "Planning," 94. Kaufman, "Building Castles," 183, 220–21. Jussi and Eremitcheva, "Dirt," 475. I. Dukeov et al., "Living Condition Index Measurements and Analysis in Saint Petersburg, Russia," *Total Quality Management* 12 (2001): 1035.

[99] Mitrofanov, "Vsiu zhizn'." See also "Pis'ma blokadnikov." On the role of blockade associations in shaping memory, see E. Martino, "Blokada: Mezhdu geroizmom i tragediei (k metodike izucheniia voprosa)," *Trudy gosudarstvennogo muzeia istorii Sankt-Peterburga*, vyp. 5 (St. Petersburg: Gosudarstvennyi muzei istorii Sankt-Peterburga, 2000), 267.

[100] Ol'ga Grechina, "Spasaius' spasaia: Chast I: Pogibel'naia zima (1941–1942 gg.)," *Neva*, 1994, no. 1: 212, 211, 224.

heroic Leningrad. In a 1994 interview, Mariia Buinitskaia, a retired meat processing worker, recalled that

those were terrible times. But how much that life taught us. The blockade and the war took all my relatives from me. Many of whom, like myself, were in the city. I have had sorrows and tears enough for several lifetimes. But, despite the cruel times, people were more amicable, more sincere. Today it's bitter to see that the city's inhabitants don't pity one another, that they offend old people.... And all of this in my beloved city, always renowned for its cultured human relations.... It's difficult for all of us to live now....I think that the state and the young must protect us [*vziat' nas pod zashchitu*]."[101]

Their high morals, their civic patriotism, their sacrifices, blokadniki argued, distinguished them from the postwar generation and entitled them to respect and protection.[102]

Despite the demise of the Soviet Union and the damage to the notion of a Soviet holy war, the Leningrad epic has remained personally and politically powerful. The following chapter examines how heroic Leningrad became part of broader political discourses. In large part, this was possible because both social and personal concerns worked to crystallize and perpetuate epic memory. For blockade survivors, the myth – the shared narrative – of the camaraderie, the generosity, the steadfastness of Leningraders during the war endowed wartime suffering with meaning. Often contrasted to the cruel realities of the emerging market economy, epic memories also provided the foundation for blokadniki's claims to respect and material support in the uncertain present. The Leningrad epic at once sanctified individual tragedies and provided a nostalgic critique of perestroika-era and post-Soviet life.

Ironically, the myth of the blockade remained politically powerful because it could be represented as the embodiment of all that was noble and pure and removed from crass politics. On the national level, liberal politicians were slow to incorporate the Great Victory into post-Soviet understandings of the nation. In the early 1990s, liberals emphasized not Soviet glories but Stalin's crimes and focused, for example, on returning – often to Germany – the World War II trophy art that the Soviet regime had long denied that it had expropriated and still possessed.[103] By contrast,

---

[101] T. Denisova, "Perezhit' takoe serdtse v sostoianii tol'ko raz," *SPV,* 20 January 1994.
[102] "Pis'ma blokadnikov."
[103] Kathleen E. Smith, *Mythmaking in the New Russia: Politics and Memory during the Yeltsin Era* (Ithaca, NY: Cornell University Press, 2002), 57–77. Anna Krylova, "Dancing on the Graves of the Dead: Building a World War II Memorial in Post-Soviet Russia," in Daniel J. Walkowitz and Lisa Maya Knauer, eds., *Memory and the Impact of Political Transformation in Public Space* (Durham, NC: Duke University Press, 2004): 91–97.

liberal politicians in Leningrad seem to have more readily grasped the tenacity of the Leningrad epic and to have learned the political advantages of endorsing some version of the mythic vision of the city's heroism, exceptional virtue, and special national – even international – mission. In May 1991, the liberal-dominated city government resolved to repair and maintain war graves and to create a "Book of Memory" with the names of all those who had died in the "heroic defense of Leningrad." The local liberals also sponsored a competition for a new statue of Marshal Georgii Zhukov, a particularly inspired choice inasmuch as the marshal was at once an architect of victory and, demoted to provincial commands after the war, a victim of Stalin's megalomania.[104] Anatolii Sobchak, the city's liberal mayor, supported the construction of apartment buildings for veterans and blokadniki.[105] In 1995, he facilitated the publication of an unexpurgated edition of *Blokadnaia kniga*. As Granin noted on the fiftieth anniversary of the end of the war, "up until now victory was enmeshed with lies." But revealing the lies, listening to so-called raw memory, did not necessarily undermine the power of the Leningrad epic. On the contrary, "Our Victory is greater and loftier, because it was a Victory in spite of" the lies, the cover-ups, the crimes.[106] In Leningrad–Petersburg, commitment to unmasking Soviet crimes coexisted with, even reinforced, respect for the wartime epic.

[104] "Ob uvekovechenii pamiati pogibshikh v gody Velikoi Otechestvennoi voiny i pri geroicheskoi oborone Leningrada i sozdanii leningradskoi Knigi Pamiati," *Vestnik Lensoveta*, no. 25 (August 1991): 56–57.
[105] Oreshkin, "Khoroshie novosti."
[106] Tat'iana Chesanova, "Daniil Granin: 'Nasha Pobeda bol'she i vyshe, potomu chto eto Pobeda vopreki...,'" *Chas pik*, 9 May 1995.

8

Mapping the Return of St. Petersburg

> If Petersburg is not the capital, then there is no Petersburg. Then its existence is merely imaginary.
>
> Andrei Belyi[1]

In 1991 the Soviet Union and the city of Leningrad disappeared from the map. The city's then-mayor, the liberal Anatolii Sobchak, remembered 1991 as the year that "we 'moved' [*pereekhali*] from one country to another, from one city, Leningrad, to a completely different one – St. Petersburg." For the usual metaphor of postcommunist transition (*perekhod*), Sobchak substituted relocation. In Leningrad–Petersburg, he suggested, the end of the Soviet Union required and facilitated the transformation of Soviet spaces – a transformation that itself was at once symbolized and accomplished by the return of prerevolutionary place names. Writing in 1999, he concluded that "today, all of us, from the smallest to the greatest, are completing a journey in time and space. More than that, in a historical instant, we found ourselves as if in another dimension."[2]

Sobchak's image of a "move" from Leningrad to St. Petersburg suggests the importance, if not the divisiveness, of urban space for the political struggles that characterized the transitional period and, more generally, for the human experience of the end of communism. The image of citizens leaving their rundown hometown and relocating to a new, post-Soviet city effectively captures the degree to which the transition reshaped familiar places and practices. But it minimizes the contests over the layers of

---

[1] Andrei Belyi, *St. Petersburg*, trans. John Cournos (New York: Grove Press, 1959), xxii.
[2] A. Sobchak, *Iz Leningrada v Peterburg: Puteshestvie vo vremeni i prostranstve* (St. Petersburg: Kontrfors, 1999): 5–6.

memory attached to the city's streets, squares, and buildings that could not be entirely left behind. Turning Leningrad into a "completely different" city required the rethinking of the multiple associations of Leningrad–St. Petersburg space. Beginning in the late 1980s, the issues of historic preservation and the return of historic place names became a particularly contentious and emotional locus of Leningraders' efforts to reimagine and remake both themselves and their city.

The debate over the city's name pitted those who identified themselves as "Leningraders" against those who identified themselves as "Petersburgers." The identities at stake were both national and local. What made the contest particularly vituperative was each side's contention that the other's self-representation was fundamentally illegitimate and deceptive.[3] Rejecting communist Leningrad, advocates of democratic change – those committed to some mix of civil liberties, representative government, and the free market – hoped to restore the town that Sobchak dubbed "the most democratic city in Russia" and the "only genuinely European city in Russia" to its rightful place as the symbolic center of a post-Soviet state.[4] For their opponents, this amounted to the "communist" sin of rewriting the past.[5] Defenders of Leningrad decried the abandonment of the ideals and the nation that had sanctified the city's wartime sacrifices.

The memory of the blockade constituted the most serious objection to efforts to begin anew by returning to the Petersburg of old. By restoring the names and places of "Petersburg," democrats ran the risk of forgetting "heroic Leningrad." Even Sobchak, who viewed the return of Petersburg as "one sign of the beginning of a new life," accepted that "everything connected with the blockade must preserve the Leningrad terminology."[6] The return of Petersburg thus highlights the complicated and contested process of mapping "the most democratic city in Russia" onto a landscape marked not only by the detritus of the Soviet regime but also by its still-potent legitimizing myths.

Back to the Future

In perestroika-era Leningrad, the cause of democracy was closely linked to efforts to preserve and reclaim urban space – to recover historic places and

---

[3] Michael Urban, "The Politics of Identity in Russia's Postcommunist Transition: The Nation against Itself," *Slavic Review* 53 (Fall 1994): 737, 738–39.
[4] Sobchak, *Iz Leningrada*, 111, 9–10.
[5] *Leningradskaia pravda* (hereafter *LP*), 25 May 1991.
[6] Sobchak, *Iz Leningrada*, 24, 25.

names and to protect "the city's history and character from the onslaught
of modern architecture."[7] Particularly for the young people involved
in the so-called informal organizations that blossomed after 1986, historic preservation offered the possibility of rehabilitating an alternative
usable past and thus provided the basis for imagining alternative futures.[8]
Unlike their fellow liberals in Moscow, who had little nostalgia for "old
Moscow," advocates of restoring historic place names in Leningrad hoped
to restore not just the symbols but something of the Western-orientation
of old St. Petersburg. This was nostalgia for "the unrealized dreams of
the past."[9]

The national program of democratization set in motion by Mikhail
Gorbachev in 1987 eventually gave Leningraders the opportunity to
undertake the biggest restoration project of all – the return of the city's
historic name. In March 1989, Soviet citizens participating in the first
nationwide democratic elections since 1917 chose representatives to the
new national legislature, the Supreme Soviet. The party stalwarts made
a poor showing. Nowhere did they fare worse than in Leningrad, where
the first secretary of the party committee suffered the embarrassment of
defeat. Local elections scheduled for March 1990 promised more than
embarrassment. Shortly before the election, the Supreme Soviet repealed
Article 6 of the Soviet Constitution, thus forfeiting the Communist Party's
monopoly on power. Party candidates who lost at the local level stood to
lose their jobs. Yet with little to offer save "hard-line retrenchment" – an
end to Gorbachev's reforms, the implementation of martial law – the party
again suffered electoral defeat.[10] In April 1990, the liberal opposition took
control of the Leningrad city soviet. Anatolii Sobchak, an erstwhile law
professor whose dynamic oratory as a member of the Supreme Soviet had
captured the imagination of Leningraders, became chair of the local soviet.
Almost immediately, he began working to establish an autonomous executive branch of the city government. The Russian Federation's decision to
hold a presidential election in June 1991 gave Sobchak the opportunity
to create – and run for – the post of mayor. The city soviet also used the

[7] Blair A. Ruble, *Leningrad: Shaping a Soviet City* (Berkeley: University of California Press, 1990), 93.

[8] Robert Orttung, *From Leningrad to St. Petersburg: Democratization in a Russian City* (New York: St. Martin's Press, 1995), 72–73. Hilary Pilkington, *Russia's Youth and Its Culture: A Nation's Constructors and Constructed* (London: Routledge, 1994), 120–21.

[9] On Moscow, see Kathleen E. Smith, *Mythmaking in the New Russia: Politics and Memory During the Yeltsin Era* (Ithaca, NY: Cornell University Press, 2002), 103. Sobchak, *Iz Leningrada*, 31, 43, 83. Svetlana Boym, *The Future of Nostalgia* (New York: Basic Books, 2001), xvi.

[10] Orttung, *From Leningrad*, 31, 68.

occasion of the June elections to put a nonbinding referendum question to the citizens of Leningrad: "Would you like our city to return to its original name – Saint Petersburg?"[11]

In the subsequent debates over the referendum, questions of civic and individual identity loomed larger than a desire to dethrone Lenin. That more Leningraders voted for the reform candidates for mayor and president – Sobchak and Boris Yeltsin – than for Petersburg suggests the divisiveness of these issues. With approximately two-thirds of the eligible voters participating, Yeltsin won about 67 percent of the vote in St. Petersburg, Sobchak, 66 percent, and the referendum only about 55 percent. Even those who agreed on specific reform measures clashed over issues of identity.[12]

On the pages of Leningrad's increasingly diverse and outspoken press in the spring of 1991, letter writers often identified themselves as party members, veterans, or blockade survivors. While a few party members expressed ambivalence or tepid support for Petersburg, veterans and survivors lent their moral authority to both sides in the form of emotional, personal letters and editorials. Writers without such wartime credentials tended to identify themselves primarily by place of residence, by profession, or not at all.

It is thus possible to trace a complicated range of public pronouncements on the question of returning Petersburg to the map. *Leningradskaia pravda* remained the mouthpiece of the party and steadfastly supported Leningrad, although it also published some interviews and letters in favor of St. Petersburg. At the other end of the political spectrum stood *Smena*, now independent despite its Komsomol affiliation. *Nevskoe vremia*, an independent paper founded in January 1991, had immediately established its liberal credentials with its strong opposition to the Soviet crackdown in Lithuania. A number of local, irregularly published, special-interest newspapers also carried articles and letters about the election. The relatively free Leningrad press in the first half of 1991 provides the basis for a reconstruction of the ways in which the public discussion

---

[11] Ibid., 126–35. Adrian Campbell, "Local Government Policymaking and Management in Russia: The Case of St. Petersburg (Leningrad)," *Policy Studies Journal* 21 (1993): 133–42. Alexander Vinnikov, "The End of Soviet Power in St. Petersburg: An Insider's View," *Europe-Asia Studies* 46 (1994): 1215–21. A facsimile of the ballot was published in *LP*, 11 June 1991.

[12] For a pre-election poll, see *Chas pik*, 10 June 1991. See also Smith, *Mythmaking*, 185, n. 2; "Sobytiia v zerkale pressy," *Leningradskaia panorama* 1991, no. 7: 15; Sobchak, *Iz Leningrada*, 22; Jussi Simpura and Galina Eremitcheva, "Dirt: Symbolic and Practical Dimensions of Social Problems in St. Petersburg," *International Journal of Urban and Regional Research* 21 (1997): 476.

of the return of Petersburg drew on Soviet myth as well as private memory and emotion.

An Attack on Lenin?

Some measure of iconoclasm inhered in the effort to remove Leningrad from the map. The notion that, as an editorial published just before the referendum expressed it, "Lenin was NO SAINT" constituted a basic premise for the advocates of St. Petersburg.[13] A letter to *Leningradskaia pravda* vividly expressed the distastefulness and absurdity of maintaining monuments to a failed system: "The scale of the October tragedy is equivalent to that of the Mongol invasion – are there 130 monuments to Batu in Moscow?"[14] (A grandson of Jenghiz Khan, Batu invaded Russia in 1236, initiating almost two hundred and fifty years of Mongol control.) For some, Lenin was the "greatest criminal of the twentieth century."[15] Others denied him any historical significance: "The most important affair in his life – the October armed uprising in Petrograd – was prepared without his direct participation, while he was in hiding."[16]

However, anti-Lenin rhetoric rarely dominated the debate, and advocates of St. Petersburg often disputed the charge that they in any way aimed to diminish or denigrate Lenin's memory.[17] Appealing to undecided voters in the week before the referendum, Sobchak claimed to have nothing against Lenin:

As is well known, no one has taken down monuments to Lenin. The name of the leader of the Revolution is preserved in the names of streets and enterprises, and no one is about to change them. As you see, the portrait of Lenin that my predecessors hung over thirty years ago continues to hang in my office. I do not consider the revival of the original name an act directed against Lenin. Just like a person, a city ought to carry the name given to it at birth.

---

[13] Vladimir Petrov, "'Chto v imeni tebe moem': Razmyshleniia o motivam golosovaniia," *Chas pik*, 10 June 1991, emphasis in original. See also "V chest' kakogo sviatogo Petra," *Novyi Peterburg*, 1991, no. 4: 1.

[14] *LP*, 29 September 1990.

[15] Petrov, "'Chto v imeni.'"

[16] *Smena*, 11 June 1991.

[17] A. Afanas'ev, "Sankt-Peterburg? Petrograd? Leningrad?" *LP*, 29 September 1990. *LP*, 11 September 1990. John Gooding, "Lenin in Soviet Politics, 1985–1991," *Soviet Studies* 44 (1992): 411. *Smena*, 11 June 1991. *Chas pik*, 3 June 1991. John Murray, *Politics and Place Names: Changing Names in the Late Soviet Period*, Birmingham Slavonic Studies, no. 32 (Birmingham: Centre for Russian and East European Studies, University of Birmingham, 2000), 137–49.

To further demonstrate his good will, Sobchak expressed his readiness to honor Lenin's wishes "to be buried in Petersburg, in Volkov cemetery, where the graves of his mother and sisters are located. We are prepared to fulfill the last will of this great person, and bury Lenin in our city. I consider it to be simply blasphemous that his last will remains unfulfilled."[18]

Here, Sobchak appears to be rather unabashedly playing politics. His generous offer to bury Lenin alongside his family cut two ways, disguising an attack on the Communists' holiest relic – Lenin's embalmed body in the mausoleum on Red Square – as a desire to fulfill the last wishes of a great man. He also neatly co-opted the Communists' central charge of "blasphemy." A story related by the American journalist David Remnick calls into question the sincerity of Sobchak's commitment to preserving monuments to Lenin. Shortly after the election, Remnick was surprised to find that the newly elected mayor "kept an enormous painting of Lenin hanging behind him." Sobchak's aide laughingly assured him, "We tried to take it down, but we found a huge stain on the wallpaper. We don't have money for new wallpaper."[19] Whether Sobchak had a postelection change of heart or was modulating his message to suit his audience remains unclear.

While Sobchak's avowals of respect for Lenin ring hollow, his argument in favor of Petersburg suggests a sincere conviction that the historical name had profound contemporary relevance. Sobchak linked the return of the historic name to the reclamation of the city's historic preeminence and its European orientation: "We are reviving the original name as a symbol of the city, which Peter founded as a window on Europe, as Russia's Western city. . . . That is why now, as we try to revive the meaning of the city as a window, or better, a wide-open door, to Europe we posed the question of the city's original name."[20] For Sobchak as for many other Leningraders, the issue was bigger – and more local – than Lenin.

The City as Hero and Martyr

Advocates of retaining the name Leningrad often labeled as "blasphemy" (*koshchunstvo*) the proposal to change the city's name. The choice of epithet had less to do with anger at the desacralization of Lenin's name – although this was clearly part of it – than with the notion that "precisely

---

[18] Anatolii Sobchak, "Kak i chelovek, gorod dolzhen nosit' imia, dannoe emu pri rozhdenii," *Nevskoe vremia* (hereafter *NV*), 8 June 1991. Gooding, "Lenin," 411.

[19] David Remnick, *Lenin's Tomb: The Last Days of the Soviet Empire* (New York: Random House, 1993), 309.

[20] Sobchak, "Kak i chelovek."

Leningrad, not St. Petersburg" had become, as a result of its wartime suffering, a sacred place.[21] While they praised Lenin's ideals, if not always his achievements, supporters of Leningrad did not make an appeal to Lenin's crumbling cult central to their appeal. By contrast, the regime's chief legitimizing myth, the Great Victory, at least in its local variant, remained potent. Thus, as Sobchak noted, his opponents accused him of trying to accomplish "what Hitler had failed to do: erasing the name Leningrad from the map of the earth [*ster imia Leningrada s karty mira*]."[22] Supporters of Leningrad emphasized the organic connection between the name "Leningrad" and the legendary status of the city and its inhabitants, their moral purity born of suffering, their special place in the nation.

One of the earliest articles on the possible return of St. Petersburg, carried prominently on the front page of *Leningradskaia pravda*, attempted to revitalize the symbolic power of the "city of Lenin" by enmeshing it in a complex web of individual memory, local pride, and national myth. Writing on the eve of the sixty-sixth anniversary of the declaration that turned Petrograd into Leningrad, V. Koshvanets, who as a child had been evacuated from besieged Leningrad, took what he called the "human" view of the issue, by which he meant that he wanted "to call myself a Leningrader." Koshvanets connected his pride in that designation directly to the experience of the war:

Probably the first time I savored the sweetness of that name [Leningrader] was in 1944 in Brianshchin, where my father came almost immediately after Leningrad was freed from the fascist blockade. I can still see the admiring eyes of my village peers, who knew that I was leaving for Leningrad. They looked at me as if I had borne all the tortures that had fallen to Leningraders' lot, as if I manifested all the signs of their courage, which the newspapers had already managed to communicate.

Everywhere receiving a warm reception because of his status as a Leningrader, Koshvanets eventually realized that Leningraders symbolized "in the eyes of other people some kind of special moral quality." The "legendary" status of the city and its inhabitants, Koshvanets emphasized, "was indebted not to St. Petersburg, Petersburg, or even Petrograd, but precisely to the city carrying Lenin's name."[23] For him, the word

[21] The phrase *imeno Leningrad, a ne Sankt-Peterburg,* or some variant of it, appears in many letters emphasizing the experience of the blockade. See *LP*, 23 May 1991, and A. F. Maiorov, "'Kogda my srazhalis' v lesakh, pereleskakh...,'" *LP*, 1 June 1991.

[22] Sobchak, *Iz Leningrada*, 28. *LP*, 1 June 1991, 12 May 1991.

[23] V. Koshvanets, "My – Leningradtsy! Davaite zadumaemsia!" *LP*, 26 January 1990.

"Leningrader" was magic: "I know that many doors and hearts were pushed open in front of me only because I was a Leningrader." Stripped of the name, his argument suggested, Leningrad and Leningraders would lose their "special moral quality."

While never explicitly defining Leningraders' "special" moral qualities, Koshvanets's description of the admiration of his peers draws on the notion that Leningraders – even evacuated Leningraders – are marked by their capacity to courageously endure. He defined Leningraders as, to borrow Nancy Ries's phrase, a "moral community created through shared suffering and difficulty."[24] Moreover, he told his readers, who in January 1990 faced empty stores and a precarious future, the very name Leningrad shaped and symbolized their valued civic identity. The trauma and misery condensed in the name Leningrad and epitomized by the blockade gave Leningraders their special moral status.

The defense of the memory of the heroes and victims of the blockade became the keynote of arguments in favor of Leningrad. Proponents of retaining the name Leningrad conceptualized the memory of the siege both as the sacred seed of communal identity and as the fulcrum of individual life histories. Placing the name Leningrad within a small field of holy places and objects that marked and preserved the memory of the siege, opponents of Petersburg equated the disappearance of the name with the destruction of the memory. Letters expressing support for Leningrad labeled the renaming of the city both blasphemous and insulting – as symbolic and psychic injury. Some letters emphasized the liberals' disrespect for core communist constituencies, namely, veterans and the war generation more generally. A group of deputies to the Supreme Soviet argued that those who attacked the name Leningrad "wounded those who wore the medal 'For the Defense of Leningrad' as their highest honor, those who survived the Leningrad blockade, those who fought on the Leningrad front."[25] Other letters pictured the attack on the name Leningrad as a threat to the sacred myth of the suffering and heroic city. The editors of *Leningradskaia pravda* noted that many of the letters they received viewed changing the city's name as a "blasphemous insult to the memory of those who fell at the walls of the city during the Great Fatherland War."[26]

---

[24] Nancy Ries, *Russian Talk: Culture and Conversation during Perestroika* (Ithaca, NY: Cornell University Press, 1997), 91.

[25] V. A. Almazov et al., "Imia goroda: Istoriia ne terpit suety," *LP*, 5 June 1991. See also the letter signed by forty-nine veterans, *LP*, 23 May 1991; *Smena*, 11 June 1991.

[26] *LP*, 5 June 1991. See also *LP*, 31 May 1991; *Smena*, 8 June 1991.

These charges of blasphemously insulting "those who fell at the walls" subsumed the largely female experience of the blockade under the rubric of "heroic defense," which was represented as the work of male soldiers. It is interesting that the opponents of Leningrad shared this tendency to erase the line between the experiences of actual soldiers and of "soldiers on the city front." The rhetorical blurring of the distinction between city and front carried on a long tradition of the Leningrad epic, which made civilian suffering part of the "heroic defense" of Leningrad and thereby both elevated and effaced the achievements and tragedies of Leningrad women. That both sides uncritically employed language that minimized women's unique and important contributions as civilians under siege, rather than honorary soldiers, suggests that neither viewed the marginalization of women's public roles as a problem. In other words, neither side's conception of reinvigorated or reformulated civic identities included an important public role for women, who remained important for both as allegories of suffering, not as political actors.

When they brought Lenin into the discussion, advocates of Leningrad emphasized his importance for the generation that had fought the war. The defense of Lenin's good name appears to have had more to do with honoring those who believed in Lenin, who sacrificed for the state he founded, than with honoring Lenin himself. Emphasizing less Lenin's achievements than the idealism he inspired, proponents of Leningrad linked the leader of the Revolution and the "just reconstruction of the world" for which he allegedly stood to the emotional core of their argument – the Leningraders who sacrificed, suffered, and died to defend their city.[27] "Ask any participant in the defense of Leningrad, any blokadnik," asserted an article in *Leningradskaia pravda,* "for which city did you fight – the answer will be the same." To illustrate the point, the author provided the answer offered by Ol'ga Berggol'ts's well-known wartime verses: "We are Leningraders."[28]

"Leningrader" denoted not simply someone who lived in Leningrad but a member of a "marked" community of the living and the dead, a local community of national significance. One could not, Elena Serebrovskaia argued, simply substitute "St. Petersburg" for "Leningrad" in the wartime poetry that had done so much to construct and perpetuate the myth of the hero city. She rewrote Berggol'ts's famous verse: "'I lived in Saint Petersburg in December of forty-one . . .' No, if you please, it

---

[27] A. Gordin, "Opiat' politicheskaia kon"iunktura," *LP,* 25 May 1991. See also *LP,* 23 May 1991, 31 May 1991, 1 June 1991, 6 June 1991, 8 June 1991.
[28] Gordin, "Opiat' politicheskaia kon"iunktura." Gordin mis-cites the first line of the poem, substituting "nego" for "tebia."

simply doesn't work."[29] Petersburg might suggest a point on the map, but Leningrad connoted a place with a vital connection to national, if not revolutionary, glory. It was a locality that literally had helped to make and define the Soviet nation. The national identity embedded in the name "Leningrad" sanctified Leningraders' suffering.[30] The myth of redemptive national victory transformed Leningraders into heroes and martyrs.

The City as Wonderworking Saint

Advocates of Petersburg, on the other hand, represented Leningraders as the victims of a criminally negligent, if not outright criminal, Soviet state. Like their opponents, advocates of St. Petersburg emphasized the city's special moral status, but they viewed the blockade as only one moment in a much longer history of saintly suffering. They emphasized the significance of local identities that predated, and were assaulted by, the Revolution. In these accounts, Leningraders appeared not as defenders of the "city of Lenin" but instead as victims of the Bolsheviks' war on them and the traditions of their beloved Petersburg. "Petersburg" offered an alternative vision of the city and its inhabitants, as well as an alternative capital of the nation.

Evoking the images and preoccupations of the Petersburg theme, some advocates of Petersburg traced the city's "spirit" or "personality" to the brutal act of genius that marked its foundation. Identifying himself as a "Petersburger," Oleg Asanov situated the current crisis in the long history of the Petersburg theme's vision of the beautiful and terrible city on the Neva. "The very foundation of the city on a swamp," he wrote shortly before the referendum, "was at once a creative act, and no less – and perhaps even more – an act of violence." This "original violent impulse" and its "dialectical negation," Asanov argued, shaped the city's subsequent history and left its inhabitants in a "perpetual state of bifurcation." In the classic fashion of the Petersburg theme, he linked the life of the city to one of its literary doubles, in this case Fedor Dostoevskii's *Crime and Punishment*: "We all have a bit of Raskol'nikov in us." He argued that the founding of the city shaped even its present residents. "Our fate and the fate of the city," Asanov contended, "are one and the same."[31]

[29] *LP*, 8 June 1991. The same issue featured a full page of Leningrad poetry, which gave pride of place to Berggol'ts.

[30] *LP*, 23 May 1991

[31] Oleg Asanov, "'Gorod – vymysel tvoi,'" *Novyi Peterburg*, 1991, no. 3: 4. See also Georgii Nikolaevich Shaglin, "Geroi Poltavy protiv 'geroia Oktiabria,'" *NV*, 1 June 1991; "Nevskii prospekt," *Novyi Peterburg*, 1991, no. 5: 1; Ol'ga Menakhina, "Za nashu i vashu svobodnuiu zonu," *Smena*, 25 May 1991.

While the river of blood running through the city's history could be traced back to Peter's cruel drive to build it, advocates of Petersburg focused more commonly on the twentieth century. They understood the blockade as just one of a series of tragedies endured by the city since 1917. Leningrad became not the exemplar of the best qualities of the Soviet people but the first and primary victim of an alien, Moscow-based regime that hijacked the ideals of the Revolution and laid waste its birthplace. A journalist in *Smena* emphasized the city's lost political and cultural character and status. Peter's postrevolutionary heirs obliterated his "splendid Western European city. . . . They boarded up the window on Europe."[32] From this point of view, the letter quoted earlier that equated the Bolshevik Revolution and the Mongol invasion can be understood as a particularly forceful statement of the idea that the Revolution was a foreign imposition on innocent Petersburg.[33]

Emphasizing the crimes of the Bolshevik "invaders," Leningrader Viktor Toporov, writing in Moscow's *Nezavisimaia gazeta,* went so far as to claim that

> it is impossible not to notice that all of the blows of Bolshevism and the regime that developed from it (with the exception, it is true, of collectivization) came down in the first instance and with special cruelty on Peter's burg [*grad Petrov*]. Here there were two famines, one of them the blockade. Here the red terror began, and here it ended just before Stalin's death. From here, they exiled the nobles, whom they had not managed to blow up on barges in the Neva or feed to the beasts of prey in the zoo. And here they shot workers demonstrating in support of the Constituent Assembly. Here they systematically exterminated and destroyed the intelligentsia.[34]

In this telling, the once-glorious capital and its inhabitants became the chief victims of Bolshevik terror. While collectivization and the ensuing famines constituted major exceptions to this rule, it was fairly accurate to describe the city as the epicenter of the purges in the 1930s and after the war. Still, by picturing the Bolshevik regime as destroying both the dreams of revolution and the dreamers, Toporov absolved the Petersburg

---

[32] Menakhina, "Za nashu." See also *Novyi Peterburg,* 1991, no. 4; *Chas pik,* 30 September 1991.

[33] *LP,* 29 September 1990. Sobchak also compared the Revolution to the Mongol invasion. Sobchak, *Iz Leningrada,* 69–70. On Leningrad as "the victim city," see Solomon Volkov, *St. Petersburg: A Cultural History,* trans. Antonina W. Bouis (New York: Free Press, 1995), 441.

[34] Viktor Toporov, "Reka, v kotoruiu resheno stupit' dvazhdy," *NG,* 30 May 1991. See also Sobchak, *Iz Leningrada,* 82.

intelligentsia of any responsibility for the Revolution's excesses – a stance that ignored the linkages between the two.[35] The blockade became one horror among many that established Petersburg's location atop the "hierarchy of victimization."[36] After cataloging further crimes against the Leningrad intelligentsia, Toporov concluded "and now Leningrad stands half-destroyed. And here, in the words of O. Mandelstam, we buried the sun."

The notion that the Bolsheviks, not the Nazis, had sought to destroy the city's essence, to figuratively wipe it from the map, found adherents primarily among the younger generation. Those who had not lived through the blockade were more likely to view the Bolsheviks as the real war criminals. I encountered no example of a member of the war generation going as far as Iulia Osipova, a twenty-three-year-old tour guide, who argued that "it seems to me necessary to distinguish Leningraders' victory in the days of the blockade from the fact of the degrading death of a million inhabitants for lack of a scrap of bread. If the former is properly admired, the latter, in my opinion, ought not to be a subject of historical pride, as speeches on the unprecedented nature of the event sometimes present it." Starvation during the blockade was instead "a terrible shame," a clear failure of the Communist Party, the self-described "organizer and inspirer of all our victories."[37]

While veterans and survivors of the blockade hesitated to reduce the war to just another Bolshevik crime, some did deny that "Leningrad" somehow embodied and sanctified the memory of the blockade. Andrei Mochalov, who identified himself as a "participant in the Great Patriotic War, inhabitant of blockaded Leningrad," explicitly linked the city's wartime suffering and postwar purges, thereby giving "Leningrad" a decidedly ambiguous moral valence: "Don't think that in Petersburg we will forget the 'Leningrad blockade' and the 'Leningrad Affair.'"[38]

Another veteran, Mikhail Konstantinovich Lebedev, asserted that the name "Leningrad" captured neither his own personal feelings for his hometown, nor its true character. He emphasized that "we defended our (!) native (!) city from the enemy! And trust me, I didn't consider whose name it then carried. For me (and I believe for most of the

[35] Katerina Clark, *Petersburg, Crucible of Cultural Revolution* (Cambridge, MA: Harvard University Press, 1995).
[36] Ries, *Russian Talk*, 105–10.
[37] *Smena*, 11 June 1991. See also *NV*, 8 June 1991; *Chas pik*, 10 June 1991.
[38] Andrei Mochalov, "Ostavliat' li partiinuiu klichku?" *NV*, 8 June 1991. See also *Smena*, 11 June 1991; *Chas pik*, 10 June 1991.

defenders of Leningrad) the name had no importance." What mattered during the war was defending "one's home, one's Fatherland." Leningrad was merely the city's name at that moment, not an essential part of the experience. Lebedev therefore concluded that in St. Petersburg his "For the Defense of Leningrad" medal would lose none of its meaning. He located the real essence of the city in its historic reputation: "We live in the Great City of Russia, always renowned for its beauty, culture, and the lofty morals of its inhabitants! Don't let it finally lose this quality. It's time to revive it!"[39]

The polls showed greater nostalgia for old St. Petersburg among the young, but the war generation was also capable of fanciful visions of the erstwhile capital. Certainly many older Leningraders, who, save for the occasional nonagenarian, had little firsthand experience of the old regime, derided it, as did E. Shmykova (born in 1912 and a member of the party since 1943), as a "city of 'princes' and 'counts.'"[40] Others, like A. Tsinzerling, who described himself as a "participant in the defense of Leningrad from beginning to end, a native of the city, whose forefathers lived here since the eighteenth century," imagined the old capital as a fairy-tale land. When the city carried its "true [*istnnogo*] name" it was "a sparkling, ecologically clean capital, with a well-fed [*sytym*] urban population living on a river whose water it was possible to drink, and in which, at the beginning of the century, great fish, even the Neva salmon, still swam."[41]

The campaign to restore the city's "true" name became attached to the notion of the name's wonderworking power to restore the city's essence – its beautiful buildings, its lovely squares, its high-minded populace. While not promising the return of the salmon, Tsinzerling predicted that the city's true name would strengthen it. Similarly, P. Kremlevskii, identifying himself as a professor, predicted that "the sooner the primordial name St. Petersburg is returned, the quicker cleanliness and order will be established in the city."[42] Stockbroker V. V. Ziuz'ko asserted that renaming the city "will give a push to the development of the stock exchange in the city."[43] Aleksandr Solzhenitsyn's rather idiosyncratic suggestion

---

[39] *Smena*, 11 June 1991.

[40] Ibid. A number of other letters in the same feature make the same point.

[41] Ibid.

[42] P. Kremlevskii, "Kesariu – kesarevo" *NV*, 8 June 1991.

[43] "Kuptsu milee Peterburg," *Novyi Peterburg*, 1991, no. 4: 1.

that the city take the "natural Russian form" of St. Petersburg – Sviato-Petrograd – took the faith in the transformative power of the name in a more explicitly religious and nationalist direction.[44] The notion that the city's name "shapes us, and our way of life" recurred often enough to prompt warnings that the name itself was unlikely to miraculously produce "clean streets, radiant houses, and polite speech."[45]

Such voices of reason notwithstanding, reliance on magical solutions was very much in the air. *Smena* repeated the "legend" that "when the scaffolding is removed from the [Church of the] Savior on the Blood, the end of Bolshevik power will come.... We have guessed why that marvelous church has been covered in scaffolding for a decade. Mysticism? Today all of us have 'turned' a little bit to mysticism." For the writer in *Smena,* the city's historic name had become a talisman: "We live in a city born under the protective name of Saint Peter. We want this name to return in order to save us from filth [*skverny*]."[46] The name Petersburg not only blotted out the immediate past – Soviet Leningrad. It also offered a means of conjuring the shimmering prerevolutionary capital.[47] The editors of the local newspaper *Novyi Peterburg* (New Petersburg), which began publishing in late 1990, chose the somewhat paradoxical name "in keeping with the dream of the renaissance of the city in all its former magnificence. The name, as it were, serves as a thread linking the present day with the best of days gone by."[48] Sobchak echoed such hopes, noting that the historic name embodied "an aspiration to return, to see, to revive Petersburg just as it was before it became first Petrograd and later Leningrad."[49]

The day before the referendum, both *Smena,* which endorsed St. Petersburg and *Leningradskaia pravda,* which opposed it, ran full-page posters that offered competing symbols of the city. Not surprisingly, the

---

[44] Aleksandr Solzhenitsyn, "K zhiteliam goroda na Neve," *Smena,* 30 April 1991. See also Volkov, *St. Petersburg,* 544.

[45] The "shapes us" remark was made by the artistic director of the Chamber Philharmonic. *Chas pik,* 10 June 1991. See also "... Gorod s chuzhim imenem obrechën," *Novyi Peterburg,* 1991, no. 4: 1; *NV,* 8 June 1991; "Razviazhut ruki?" *Novyi Peterburg,* 1991, no. 5: 1. The "polite speech" warning comes from the editors of *NV,* 25 May 1991. See also Toporov, "Reka," Menakhina, "Za nashu."

[46] *Smena,* 25 May 1991, ellipses in original. See also Marina Tokareva, "'Tvoi brat Petropol' umiraet...'?" *NV,* 8 January 1991.

[47] Ries, *Russian Talk,* 121.

[48] "Vozrashchaias' k istokam," *Novyi Peterburg,* 1990, no. 1: 1.

[49] Sobchak, *Iz Leningrada,* 6.

supporters of Leningrad chose a symbol of the blockade: the Mother-Motherland from Piskarevskoe Cemetery. The caption read simply "We Defend Leningrad!" (*Otstoim Leningrad!*).[50] Embodied in the image of its suffering, Leningrad once again required defenders against a treacherous enemy. The ballot, editors warned their readers, was designed to confuse, "asking you not if you want to keep Leningrad, but if you want to live in St. Petersburg!"[51] *Smena*'s editors chose as the emblem of the city not the Bronze Horseman but the angel atop the Alexander Column, whom they imagined expressing the fervent wish that "God grant that...those born in Leningrad will die in Petersburg."[52] Like their opponents, the advocates of Petersburg chose a war memorial – commemorating, in this case, the first Fatherland War against Napoleon – to represent their cause. Also like their opponents, they chose an image not of manly victory but of womanly, angelic respect for the fallen. Both sides eschewed the language of politics, deploying instead images that situated the community at the core of a national epic and evoked the city's suffering and endurance.

The referendum on the city's name was ultimately less about breaking communist icons than about the relationships among civic, individual, and national identities. What was the essence of the city? How did residents want to imagine themselves? Opponents of St. Petersburg sometimes argued that to call the dilapidated, filthy, sprawling city on the Neva "St. Petersburg" was nothing more than a laughable pretense. Until it bore more resemblance to its glittering imperial precursor, it did not deserve the name.[53] Advocates of Petersburg responded, as noted, with the claim that the name itself would restore the city's confidence, its "true" self, and speed its return to former glory. When opponents objected that the name change would cost 150 million rubles – the city soviet's own estimate – proponents of the new name countered that transformation required only eleven new signs: "at five railroad stations, on four main highways, at the airport and at the Mariinskii Palace [the seat of the city government] – that's it!"[54] No need to take down a single Lenin monument or reprint a

---

[50] *LP*, 11 June 1991.

[51] Ibid. After the election, the paper claimed to have received dozens of letters from distraught Leningraders who had misunderstood the ballot and therefore cast inadvertent votes for Petersburg. *LP*, 2 July 1991.

[52] *Smena*, 11 June 1991.

[53] "Sankt-Peterburg Ordena Lenina?" *Novyi Peterburg*, 1991, no. 5: 1. *LP*, 25 May 1991.

[54] Mikhail Chulaki, "Oni pugaiut – a nam strashno?" *Smena*, 6 June 1991. For typical objections to the cost, see *LP*, 14 May 1991, 15 May 1991, 23 May 1991; A. Soboleva, "Gde budem zhit', zemliaki?" *LP*, 30 May 1991.

single city form. The important change was in the mind of Petersburgers themselves.

Claiming the Streets

On 12 June 1991, Leningraders voted to restore the historic name of the city, but their preference had no legal standing as far as the national government was concerned.[55] By late August, however, the failed coup against Gorbachev and the resulting collapse of the Communist Party allowed Sobchak to seize the local party's assets, to install himself in its former headquarters – the famous Smol'nyi Institute from which the 1917 October Revolution had been directed – and to turn *Leningradskaia pravda,* which he renamed *Sankt-Peterburgskie vedomosti,* into the organ of the mayor's office.[56] The city's name change became official on 6 September 1991.

Unlike their peers in Moscow, reformers and Communists in Petersburg, within the space of just a few months after the August coup, had opportunities to reshape and rethink Soviet rituals relating to both the war and the Revolution.[57] On 8 September 1991, Petersburg commemorated the fiftieth anniversary of the beginning of the Leningrad blockade. Petersburgers also joined in the commemorations and anti-commemorations that took place on the seventy-fourth anniversary of the October Revolution. President Yeltsin's decision on the eve of the 7 November holiday to ban the Communist Party affected celebrations throughout the nation. In Petersburg, the mayor officially declared the day a celebration of the city's renaming.[58] In any event, the November festivities had clear local dimensions in Petersburg, where events could be commemorated, contested, or desacralized at the sites where they had occurred. The rituals surrounding the commemorations of the war and the Revolution provided particularly vivid illustrations of the connections between the reclamation of urban space and the reinterpretation of its layers of memory.

The public ceremonies and demonstrations surrounding the fiftieth anniversary of the beginning of the blockade constituted a departure from

---

[55] Ivan Titov, "My vernulis' v nash gorod, znakomyi do slez...," *Smena,* 20 June 1991. *LP,* 25 June 1991.

[56] Orttung, *From Leningrad,* 145, 199–200. *LP,* 27 August 1991, 28 August 1991. *Sankt-Peterburgskie vedomosti* (hereafter *SPV*) began publishing on 3 September 1991.

[57] On the 7 November 1991 holiday in Moscow, see Smith, *Mythmaking,* 80–82.

[58] *Smena,* 7 November 1991.

previous practice. In the years before perestroika, the anniversary of the closing of the blockade – 8 September – had not been an occasion for public commemoration. Even in the mid-1970s, at the height of the war cult, the date had passed unremarked in local newspapers. Given that the date marks one of the low points in the Soviet war, the silence is perhaps not very surprising. The January anniversaries of the partial break in the blockade in 1943 and its end in 1944 – dates that managed to balance mourning with the celebration of victory – had been the key local war anniversaries. However, the 1991 anniversary of the beginning of the blockade became a public event in the city. The commemorations may be related to the Soviet habit of making a fuss over round-numbered anniversaries.[59] The date also allowed for the public articulation of issues of memory and identity that had been central to the debate on renaming the city. The city's churches, streets, and war memorials offered sites for diverse interpretations of the blockade – as tragedy, as crime, as heroic defense, as some combination of all of these.

Liberal politicians in Petersburg attempted to solve what Kathleen Smith has identified as the problem of "how to adapt old patriotic rituals and myths to suit a new democratic Russia" by emphasizing the local meanings of the blockade.[60] The defense of native city had always been a piece of the official myth. In the liberal reworking of that myth, the local became preeminent. Distancing themselves from the state that fought the war, Sobchak and a representative of the city soviet, A. N. Beliaev, addressed an open letter to "Dear Leningraders, veterans of the Great Fatherland War, survivors of the blockade!" Sobchak and Beliaev asserted that "for Leningraders, this day – 8 September 1941 – the start of the 900-day blockade, is one of the cruelest pages of the wartime history of the city."[61] Sobchak himself participated in the anniversary ceremony most clearly linked to the city's unique wartime experiences. He placed flowers at the small war memorial on Nevskii Prospekt, a recreation of the wartime signs warning pedestrians that, in the event of an artillery attack, they stood on the dangerous side of the street.[62]

Sobchak and other reformers tried to contain and co-opt war memories by underscoring their connections to the city's suffering, its spirit,

---

[59] Christel Lane, *The Rites of Rulers: Ritual in Industrial Society – The Soviet Case* (Cambridge: Cambridge University Press, 1981), 144. Tumarkin, *The Living and the Dead*, 213.

[60] Smith, *Mythmaking*, 86.

[61] A. N. Beliaev and A. A. Sobchak, "K leningradtsam," *SPV*, 7 September 1991.

[62] *SPV*, 10 September 1991.

and its renewal. Omitting not only the party but also the larger national struggle, Sobchak and Beliaev's open letter emphasized the special qualities Leningraders manifested during the blockade, particularly their "civic patriotism and capacity for self-sacrifice in the name of the peaceful future of their beloved city." The letter linked the war generation's virtues to the city's "organization and unity" during the "difficult August days" just passed. "We appeal to you, dear Leningraders," they concluded, "to devote yourselves to the worthwhile cause of the quickest possible rebirth of the greatness of our own [*rodnogo*] city."[63] A writer in *Nevskoe vremia* made the connections between the trials of the blockade and the current crisis explicit: "September 8, 1941 went down in history as the beginning of a great courage, a great unity, and an enormous misfortune, the source of Leningraders' sorrows, which even today have not ended."[64] The liberals called on Leningraders who had triumphed over adversity during the war to apply their courage and steadfastness to the current struggle to remake the city – not necessarily the nation.

On the streets of Petersburg in September 1991, the commemoration of the blockade suggested both the limits and the possibilities of the liberals' emphasis on local memories and the city's rebirth. The public commemoration of 8 September was in and of itself a sort of victory for the liberals, who had long emphasized the need to tell the full story of the war.[65] The date, after all, marked a defeat that took almost three years to reverse. The diversity of ceremonies and the prominence of ordinary citizens, as opposed to party functionaries, marked a clear break with standard Soviet practice that liberals might applaud. However, few anniversary events took up Sobchak's call to focus exclusively on local history and local revival.

The inclusion of religious rites and leaders constituted an obvious departure from Soviet ritual. The anniversary happened to fall on a Sunday, and its commemoration began with "divine liturgies and the requiem for the victims of the blockade in all churches." While the church services signaled the breakdown of communist ideology, they also suggested that the liberals' preferred vision of change – the rebirth of the pluralist window on the West – might not be the sort of rebirth that many Leningraders had in mind. Metropolitan Ioann of St. Petersburg and Ladoga spoke at

---

[63] Beliaev and Sobchak, "K leningradtsam."
[64] Grigorii Brailovskii, "'Vam ne polozheno,'" *NV*, 7 September 1991.
[65] *SPV*, 14 September 1991. Donat Zherebov, "Tri dnia, reshivshie sud'bu blokady," *NV*, 7 September 1991.

the gathering at Palace Square with which the day's events ended. Evoking the city's saintliness, he sidestepped the question of its name: "Today, we who live in the Holy city on the Neva [*Sviatom grade na Neve*] do not forget those who sacrificed their lives for the salvation of their people, for the salvation of their Fatherland."[66] With its evocations of saintliness and national feeling, the metropolitan's speech suggested how Soviet nationalism and Soviet myths might be revived in religious language.[67] Indeed, the founder of the nationalist Orthodox Revival Party sponsored the construction of a so-called Blockade Cathedral (*Blokadnyi khram*), begun in 1996 and dedicated on the sixtieth anniversary of the beginning of the blockade, 8 September 2001 (Illustration 32).[68]

The myths and monuments of the Soviet cult of war that remained central to commemorations also worked against the purely local memory advocated by the liberals. As usual on anniversaries related to the war, thousands attended the wreath laying at Piskarevskoe Cemetery. The mayor stayed away, preferring to pay his respects on Nevskii Prospekt. But veterans continued to meet and mourn in the usual places. That Piskarevskoe and other Soviet monuments, notably the Monument to the Heroic Defenders of Leningrad, remained key commemorative sites suggests the continuing resonance of Soviet memorials and the tenacity of Soviet constructions of the memory of the war. True, the ceremony at Piskarevskoe indicated a reconfiguration, if not the demise, of Soviet practice. Instead of a series of speeches from local party officials, representatives of voluntary organizations of veterans and blockade survivors had pride of place. Also, clergy from "different confessions" participated in the ceremony. In its foregrounding of religious rites and its ecumenical nature, the commemorations at Piskarevskoe resembled the 24 August 1991 funerals for the three men who had died on the barricades in Moscow during the attempted coup.[69] But Piskarevskoe Cemetery and the Monument to the Heroic Defenders, unlike the unassuming

---

[66] *SPV*, 10 September 1991. See also *NV*, 5 September 1991.

[67] Ries, *Russian Talk*, 177.

[68] *NG*, 9 October 1991. Pavel Fel'gengauer, "Istoriia liuboi imperii – eto istoriia voin," *NG*, 22 June 1991. "Vozvedenie Khrama Uspeniia Presviatoi Bogorodintsy na maloi okhte," http://www.ost-west.ru/Russian/khram/xram.htm (accessed 20 February 2002). "The blockade cathedral," http://www.ost-west.ru/english/khram/blokada.htm (accessed 11 June 2003).

[69] *SPV*, 10 September 1991. Victoria E. Bonnell and Gregory Freidin, "Televorot: The Role of Television in Russia's August 1991 Coup," in Nancy Condee, ed., *Soviet Hieroglyphics: Visual Culture in Late Twentieth-Century Russia* (Bloomington: Indiana University Press, 1995), 43–44.

32. The Blockade Church, under construction in 2001. It stands on the site of a church closed in 1938 that became a site of mass graves during the blockade. Photo by author.

sign on Nevskii, honored the city's experience while situating it in a national narrative.

The war anniversary also included elements of a political demonstration, surely a first in the history of the Soviet war cult. In this case, a method associated with the liberals became a tool of those opposed to the "renewal" of St. Petersburg. The local paper's account noted that "veterans, blokadniki, and participants in the Great Fatherland War proceeded, without music, down Nevskii Prospekt. Many of them carried posters, expressing disagreement with the renaming of our city. Only the sound of the metronome accompanied the mournful procession."[70] The march

---

[70] *SPV,* 10 September 1991. See also Orttung, *From Leningrad,* 31.

ended at the city's symbolic center, Palace Square, where the participants observed a moment of silence. The living representatives of the spirit of Leningrad briefly reclaimed the streets of St. Petersburg.

Two months later, the mayor decreed that the 7 November holiday commemorating the Bolshevik victory become a celebration of the city's new identity as Petersburg. As *Nevskoe vremia* noted, the organizers of the Vivat, St. Petersburg festival "tried to convince us that seventy-four years ago in Peter, nothing in particular happened. It's not worth recalling." Freed from the hegemony of Revolution Day, Petersburgers constructed a wide array of demonstrations, celebrations, and commemorations linked to various monuments and memories throughout the city. Not everyone agreed that the Revolution should not be recalled. A small contingent of Communists met at the *Aurora*, the ship that fired the Russian Revolution's shot heard round the world. Some democrats observed a day in memory of the "victims of totalitarianism," and condemned the mayor's festival as "celebrating on bones." Lacking a site equivalent to the *Aurora*, those commemorating Josef Stalin's victims turned to religion for places and rituals antithetical to communism. Requiems were held at churches throughout the city. At the same time, a rock concert on Palace Square drew big crowds. Monarchists left flowers at the grave of Peter I. The day ended with fireworks, the likes of which, organizers claimed, the city had not seen since 1913 – the three hundredth anniversary of the Romanov dynasty.[71]

The Vivat, St. Petersburg festival is relevant to the discussion of the memory of the blockade because it throws into particularly sharp relief the multiple associations of space in Petrograd–Leningrad–St. Petersburg. In Leningrad, the traditional 7 November parade, the local version of the more famous Moscow affairs centered on Red Square, brought columns of marchers organized by party activists into Palace Square, where they saluted local bigwigs on the reviewing stand.[72] A fanciful cartoon of the 1991 holiday published in *Smena* presented an altogether more chaotic assemblage that illuminates the many possible meanings and uses of Palace Square. The drawing included a small column of goose-stepping

---

[71] Evgenii Uvarov and Viktoriia Robotnova, "Den' pliuralizma," *NV*, 9 November 1991. See also *SPV*, 9 November 1991; *Smena*, 9 November 1991. According to a poll conducted in late October and early November, a plurality of Petersburgers, 45 percent, considered the November holiday just another day off. Only 16 percent planned to celebrate the renaming of the city, 11 percent the October Revolution, and 6 percent the victims of Soviet repression. *Smena*, 7 November 1991.

[72] Yurchak, "Cynical Reason," 6–8.

Communists headed by a (presumably) red flag. They enter a square already full of, among other things, a group of followers being blessed by an Orthodox priest, a brass band, a rock band and enthusiastic rock fans, a man climbing a lamppost while holding a Russian tricolor, a couple snuggling on the steps of the Alexander Column, a would-be tsar addressing his would-be subjects from a balcony of the palace, a person hanging out of a palace window with the sign "All Power to the Soviets," two lone protestors – one holding a placard with the word "Yes," the other a placard with the word "No" – and a person capturing everything on video.[73] No longer dominated by the official parade, all the square's pasts – center of the monarchy, place of amusement, cherished local landmark, scene of Revolution and democratic protests – came alive at once. The mayor's holiday provided no single meaning to replace the commemoration of the Revolution. Instead, it allowed Leningraders–Petersburgers to reclaim the streets and squares, to memorialize or celebrate the many memories and meanings – personal and public – connected to the city's spaces.

[73] *Smena*, 7 November 1991. See also *NV*, 9 November 1991.

Epilogue

No One Is Forgotten?

If we agree that the symbols of the preceding epochs, including the Soviet epoch, must not be used at all, we will have to admit then that our mothers' and fathers' lives were useless and meaningless, that their lives were in vain. Neither in my head nor in my heart can I agree with this.

Vladimir Putin[1]

I think they don't remember enough today about the people who survived the siege. It's only because of this anniversary that they remembered about us and sent us congratulation cards.

Nina Konstantinovna, pensioner, twelve years old when the blockade began[2]

Things, events that occupy space yet come to an end when someone dies may make us stop in wonder.

Jorge Luis Borges[3]

Post-Soviet Petersburg remains a city in which multiple and contested memories, myths, and possible futures coexist. Successive waves of renamings have left eclectic traces on the map of St. Petersburg, where Palace Square exists alongside both the revolutionary [Jean Paul] Marat Street and the post-Soviet Academic [Andrei] Sakharov Square.[4] The Bronze

---

[1] Quoted in Patrick E. Tyler, "Soviet Hymn is Back, Creating Much Discord," *New York Times,* 6 December 2000, A1.

[2] Quoted in *St. Petersburg Times,* 27 January 2004. http://www.sptimes.ru/archive/times/938/news/n_11492.htm (accessed 25 June 2004).

[3] Jorge Luis Borges, "The Witness," in *Collected Fictions,* trans. Andrew Hurley (New York: Penguin Books, 1999), 306.

[4] The square in front of the library of the Russian Academy of Sciences on Vasil'evskii Island became Academic Sakharov Square in 1996. K. Gorbachevich and E. Khablo, eds., *Pochemu tak nazvany? O proiskhozhdenii nazvanii ulits, ploshchadei, ostrovov, rek i*

Horseman and Vladimir Lenin on an armored car continue to stand in salute on opposite sides of the Neva. The monument on the Field of Mars that commemorates the victims of the old regime has been joined by a quintessentially Petersburg monument to the victims of the Revolution: émigré sculptor Mikhail Chemiakin's pair of sphinx-skeletons. Distorted echoes of the ancient Egyptian sphinxes on the Academy of Arts embankment, the post-Soviet sphinxes erected in May 1995 stand, appropriately enough, on the Robespierre Embankment.[5]

The city's layered memoryscape is particularly visible on anniversaries related to the war, when, in order to honor the memory of the blockade, St. Petersburg officially becomes Leningrad.[6] Soviet memorials and rituals structured the city's post-Soviet celebrations of the fiftieth anniversary of the end of the blockade in January 1994 and the fiftieth anniversary of Victory in Europe in May 1995. However, on both occasions, the familiar rituals were – depending on one's point of view – polluted or purified by symbols of Petersburg's prerevolutionary past and its post-Soviet present. Many blokadniki and veterans turned out at the usual Soviet sites to lay wreaths, display their medals, and reunite with old comrades. They also participated in religious services that defied Soviet tradition and in political demonstrations that challenged the liberals who had taken charge of the old Soviet rituals. On 8 May 1995, the festive flotilla of battleships on the Neva for the first time included ships representing the members of the "anti-Hitler coalition" – Britain, the United States, France, Belgium, and the Netherlands – and constituted (again, depending on one's point of view) a welcome sign of better relations with former Cold War adversaries or a humiliating admission of the loss of superpower status.[7] As new

mostov Sankt-Peterburga, 5th ed. (St. Petersburg: "Norit," 1998), 16. *Gorodskie imena segodnia i vchera: Peterburgskaia toponimika: Spravochnik-putevoditel',* 2d ed. (St. Petersburg: Informatsionno-izdatel'skoe agentsvo "LIK," 1997), 10–17, 21.

[5] Chris Graeme and Alice Jondorf, "Riddle of the Sphinx Is Broken," *St. Petersburg Times,* 23–29 May 1995, http://www.chemiakinbooks.com/HTMLFILES/NEWS_htmlfiles/sphinx_riddle.htm (accessed 17 February 2006). Nadezhda Kozhevnikova, "Novye pamiatniki v starom Peterburge," *Nevskoe vremia* (hereafter NV), 29 April 1995. Svetlana Boym, *The Future of Nostalgia* (New York: Basic Books, 2001), 121, 143–44.

[6] Iu. I. Smirnov, ed., *Sankt-Peterburg XX vek: Chto? Gde? Kogda?* (St. Petersburg: Izdatel'stvo "Paritet," 2000), 17–18. "Saint-Petersburg Commemorates 60th Anniversary of Lifting of Siege of Leningrad," *Petersburg CITY/Guide to St. Petersburg Russia,* 26 January 2004, http://petersburgcity.com/news/city/2004/01/26/siege (accessed 17 February 2006).

[7] *Sankt-Peterburgskie vedomosti* (hereafter SPV), 11 May 1995. *Smena,* 11 May 1995. NV, 6 April 1995.

political parties sought new myths for a new Russia, heroic Leningrad emerged as durable, multivalent symbol.

In the media and in politicians' speeches, the blokadnik appeared as a powerful and ambiguous icon – of Petersburg, Russia, and the former Soviet Union. In January 1994, a spokesman for then-President Boris Yeltsin won a warm reception from a group of blokadniki and veterans when he linked the blockade to the spirit of the city, to local history and national pride: "Our city, since the time of its founding by Peter the Great, has served as a symbol of steadfastness, love for the Motherland, and the struggle for freedom. Loyalty to this tradition, which brought victory over fascism, in the future will further the glory and grandeur of Russia and St. Petersburg."[8] Belatedly grasping the "merits of encouraging a positive patriotism" that had long been clear to local democrats encouraging local patriotism, Yeltsin himself made a whirlwind one-day trip to Petersburg on 27 January 1994.[9] On the eve of his visit, Yeltsin emphasized that his reforms promised, at long last, to deliver the "happy future" for which Leningraders "fought and died."[10] During a reception for veterans at the Mariinskii Palace, the seat of the city government, Petersburg's liberal mayor Anatolii Sobchak more explicitly connected the "lessons of history" to the politics of postcommunist transition. He discounted the importance of the strong showing of nationalist and national-communist parties in the previous December's elections, noting that Leningraders, especially those who lived through the blockade, "understand particularly well that fascism, totalitarianism, and nationalism are the chief enemies of humanity."[11]

At the same time, the mayor and the local liberal press emphasized that the rejection of totalitarianism did not mean the rejection of the Soviet-era images, poetry, and monuments so closely connected to the war and its remembrance. In his official message to "dear comrades, the defenders and inhabitants of blockaded Leningrad, veterans of the Great Fatherland

---

[8] *SPV*, 26 January 1994.

[9] Kathleen Smith and Anna Krylova emphasize the new approach to Victory Day in 1995. The quotation is from Smith, *Mythmaking in the New Russia: Politics and Memory During the Yeltsin Era* (Ithaca, NY: Cornell University Press, 2002), 89. Anna Krylova, "Dancing on the Graves of the Dead: Building a World War II Memorial in Post-Soviet Russia," in Daniel J. Walkowitz and Lisa Maya Knauer, eds., *Memory and the Impact of Political Transformation in Public Space* (Durham, NC: Duke University Press, 2004), 96–97.

[10] *SPV*, 25 January 1994.

[11] *SPV*, 28 January 1994.

War," Sobchak underscored – as he did during the 1991 debate on the
city's name – the centrality of the blockade in shaping *local* history and
identity. Drawing freely on the clichés of the myth of heroic Leningrad, the
mayor declared, "History knows no examples of a victory like that of the
inhabitants and defenders of the city on the Neva. Overcoming hunger,
cold, and sickness, the inhabitants of the besieged city became an example to the world of unprecedented courage. The grandeur of the human
spirit prevailed over fascism."[12] On 27 January 1994, the front page of
Sankt-Peterburgskie vedomosti reproduced, without a hint of irony, the
emblems of the war cult. Ol'ga Berggol'ts's verse "No one is forgotten, and
nothing is forgotten" ran as the banner headline over an excerpt from her
poem "February Diary," the text of the 1944 announcement of the lifting
of the blockade, a quarter-page photograph of Piskarevskoe's Mother-
Motherland statue, and smaller photographs of the cemetery and the
Monument to the Heroic Defenders of Leningrad. The rest of Leningrad's
liberal press produced similar nostalgic spreads on the major war anniversaries – unlike Moscow's outspoken *Nezavisimaia gazeta,* which recognized the sanctity of the war in Russia while challenging both the purity
of the Soviet victory and the appropriateness of a Soviet-style military
parade through Red Square on Victory Day 1995.[13]

The liberals attempted to scrub the Soviet tarnish from the myth of
heroic Leningrad by recasting the heroic defenders as proto-reformers
struggling "for freedom" and for the liberals' "happy future" of democratic and market reforms. The respectful and, in the case of Yeltsin's
representative, "heartfelt" welcome given liberal politicians by blokadniki suggests that at least some embraced these post-Soviet readings of
the meaning of their sacrifices. The notion that the blockade had been a
moment of freedom constituted a recurrent motif in blockade memories,
and the liberals had been working since 1991 to connect this freedom-
loving blockade to a Western-oriented Petersburg identity. Indeed, Petersburg's liberals have achieved greater electoral success than their peers
nationwide in part because they have assiduously and consistently turned
local elections into "identity contests."[14] The difficulty for blokadniki

---

[12] *SPV,* 27 January 1994. For Sobchak's similarly locally focused remarks on the occasion
of Victory Day, see *Smena,* 7 May 1995.
[13] See, for example, *NV,* 11 May 1995; *Chas pik,* 11 May 1995; *Smena,* 7 May 1995;
Nezavisimaia gazeta (hereafter *NG*), 11 May 1995.
[14] Grigorii V. Golosov, "Identity Contests: Local History and Electoral Politics in St. Petersburg," in John J. Czaplicka and Blair A. Ruble, eds., *Composing Urban History and the
Constitution of Civic Identity* (Baltimore: Johns Hopkins University Press; Washington,

who might have been attracted to the liberals' version of the myth of the blockade was that market reforms caused extreme economic distress, not to mention a profound sense of personal dislocation, particularly for members of the war generation living on small, fixed pensions – below the poverty line, despite their heroic sacrifices.

Thus, commemorations of the blockade and the war, which had always been connected to politics, became in 1994 and 1995 occasions for overt political contests. Arriving at Petersburg's Pulkovo Airport on the morning of 27 January 1994, President Yeltsin told reporters, "Today I must be with Leningraders." Linking public commemoration of the blockade to the material well-being of blokadniki, he stressed that his government had undertaken "a series of measures to perpetuate the memory of those who perished, creating a number of new memorials in Petersburg and the Leningrad region. We have given privileges, social rights, and protections to blockade survivors, putting them on the same level as participants in the Great Fatherland War."[15] From the airport, the presidential motorcade sped to Piskarevskoe Cemetery. At the foot of the Mother-Motherland statue, Yeltsin, along with local officials, representatives from blockade and veterans' organizations, delegations from other hero cities and former Soviet republics, and foreign consuls general, participated in the traditional wreath-laying ceremony.

The president's co-optation of the Soviet ritual aroused the opposition of both communist and nationalist parties, whose leaders staged a joint protest meeting in central Petersburg in front of the Kazan Cathedral. They called on their followers to prevent Yeltsin's visit to the cemetery. The presence of the man who dissolved the Soviet Union on Soviet holy ground they deemed a "defilement of the graves." Appropriating the same rhetoric, Moscow's *Nezavisimaia gazeta* countered that, though unsuccessful, the "communists' efforts to turn holy ground, where the remains of thousands of citizens rest in peace, into a scene of scandal hardly needs comment."[16] Each side, in short, struggled to cast itself as the representative and heir of the "holy" losses of the blockade and the purity and simplicity of the survivors. Veterans and blokadniki could be found on both sides of the barricades.

DC: Woodrow Wilson Center Press, 2003), 117–39. See also Vladimir Kolossov, Dmitri Vizgalov, and Nadezhda Borodulina, "Voting Behavior in Russian Cities, 1995–2000," *Journal of Communist Studies and Transition Politics* 19, no. 4 (2003): 25–40.

[15] *SPV,* 28 January 1994. See also *NV,* 28 January 1994.

[16] Iuliia Kantor, "El'tsin na beregakh Nevy: Oppozitsiia trebovala ne puskat' ego na Piskarevskoe kladbishche," *NG,* 28 January 1994.

Similar confrontations marked the celebration of fifty years of victory in May 1995. Communists and nationalists joined – or, according to reports in the liberal press, disrupted and attempted to hijack – both a ceremony honoring Marshal Georgii Zhukov and the parade of blokadniki and veterans into Palace Square. The 7 May dedication of the monument to Zhukov attracted what one newspaper account described as "simple people [*prostye liudi*], veterans – warriors of the Leningrad front – blokadniki," who "cried, remembered, and complained" that the statue was not erected along the former line of defense or on the spot consecrated by the church for that purpose, but in the Moskovskii Victory Park, on a pedestal once meant for a statue of Stalin. The official ceremony included representatives from the army and the navy, the marshal's daughter Margarita Zhukova, as well as Sobchak, who took advantage of the opportunity to voice his support for an alternate location. A chorus of protestors singing the "Internationale" and agitating for a monument consecrated to Soviet (if not Stalinist) glory nearly drowned out the speakers. Once the official ceremony wrapped up, and "the city authorities hastily abandoned the park," the liberals' opponents, Communists with red flags and portraits of Stalin followed by nationalists carrying flags with a "black stripe" – probably the black, yellow, white tricolor favored by monarchists as well as radical nationalists – took over the site. As the correspondent for *Chas pik* ruefully noted, "That's why the simple people [*prostoi narod*], the veterans who ought to have been the main participants in this event, could be found around the pediment much later. People left flowers at the foot of the pedestal, crying, remembering. . . . Among the flowers on the stone steps someone laid an apple. Just as on the grave of a dear one on the day of remembrance."[17] The reporter emphasized the moral authority of blokadniki and veterans as real mourners – not political opportunists – but also seemed to be making a bid to turn them into emblems of the liberal cause. The apple, after all, was the symbol of the liberal Iabloka (Apple) Party.[18]

The newspaper similarly characterized the ranks of joyful blokadniki and veterans who, "like excited schoolchildren," marched down Nevskii to Palace Square as temporarily purifying the city center: "'New Russians' with fur coats, cell phones, and foreign brands, who have become a usual sight on Nevskii, were nowhere to be seen." The official ceremony

---

[17] *Chas pik*, 11 May 1995, ellipses in original. See also *NV*, 11 May 1995.
[18] The name came from the initials of the party's leaders, Grigorii Iavlinski, Iurii Boldyrev, and Vladimir Lukin. Smith, *Mythmaking*, 136.

made room for Soviet-era icons when they could be handled as objects of nostalgia or kitschy period pieces. Thus, musicians in Palace Square played "memorable Leningrad-Petersburg melodies," like the wartime songs "Holy War," "Victory Day," and the frontline soldiers' favorite, "Katiusha."[19] However, the "unexpected" appearance of a column of nationalists and communists, led by "half-dead Pioneers in shirts and red scarves, aged Komsomols" calling for Yeltsin to be brought to justice, silenced the happy throngs. According to *Chas pik,* "The audience's embarrassment gave rise not to sympathy but to disgusted hostility." Yet, as an accompanying photograph showing a veteran on Palace Square decked out in medals and holding a placard with Stalin's portrait made clear, these less-sympathetic old people might also have been blokadniki and veterans.[20]

The increasing prominence of religious rites further complicated these post-Soviet celebrations but did not necessarily clash with Soviet-era rhetoric. Indeed, the language of "holy war" and "holy ground" long associated with the war and Piskarevskoe Cemetery could be adopted wholesale by the church fathers – from whom the Communists had originally adopted it. Praying for blockade survivors in January 1994, Patriarch Aleksii II praised "Leningraders' steadfastness, which was above all the steadfastness of their spirit, overcoming the terror of daily artillery attacks" – an accolade clearly couched in the language of the myth of the hero city, if taking on new meanings when uttered by a clergyman. Where he struck a distinctly post-Soviet note was in his more earthbound call for Russian "government and society" to act on their "moral responsibility" to care for aging veterans and blokadniki struggling to survive in the current difficult economic times.[21] Such injunctions, of course, pointed more clearly to the shortfalls of the post-Soviet present than to the problems of the Soviet past.

The local and federal governments had, as Yeltsin noted, made some efforts to aid the war generation. Blokadniki who had been awarded the medal For the Defense of Leningrad, along with those who had been honored by post-Soviet Petersburg with the citation Inhabitant of Blockaded Leningrad, received monetary awards in January 1994 of 15,000

[19] *NV,* 11 May 1995. On the wartime popularity of such songs, see Richard Stites, *Russian Popular Culture: Entertainment and Society since 1900* (Cambridge: Cambridge University Press, 1992), 103–7.

[20] *Chas pik,* 11 May 1995.

[21] *NV,* 28 January 1994. See also *Chas pik,* 5 May 1995; *SPV,* 28 January 1994; *NV,* 7 May 1994, 28 January 1995.

and 10,000 rubles, respectively. At the then-current rate of exchange, the stipends amounted to about $9.75 and $6.50, at a time when the average Russian earned less than $100 per month, and rampant inflation meant that prices were quickly catching up with American levels.[22] Additional privileges accorded blokadniki included free travel on suburban trains and buses (although some complained that their right to travel was not honored), free concerts and movies on important anniversaries related to the war, and priority for new public housing.[23]

For their part, blokadniki drawing on the language of the myth of the blockade expressed the view that both material aid and respect were not only their due but also often insufficient. To obtain their monetary awards in January 1994, blokadniki and veterans complained, they had to wait in painfully long lines.[24] They appreciated the commemorative medal the city awarded them in honor of the fiftieth anniversary of victory, but felt "insulted" by the city's rather poor job of insuring that the district (*raion*) authorities responsible for handing them out did so in an appropriately solemn and celebratory manner. Recipients lamented the fact that the awards were distributed with no more ceremony than ration cards.[25] One woman bemoaning the difficulties of taking advantage of the privileges accorded to blokadniki concluded, "Earlier, when party or government resolutions were promulgated and published in the newspaper they were rigorously fulfilled. So it's strange that today they promulgate paper decrees."[26] Thus, the Soviet myth of the blockade and the Soviet state's (mythologized) respect for veterans and blokadniki could become the basis for negative assessments of current government programs that borrowed Soviet rhetoric but failed to deliver compelling results.

The blockade thus became a political commodity – and indeed an economic commodity used to sell soda and lure foreign tourists. Advertisements that made use of Soviet wartime images, like one for Herschi Cola that celebrated the Day of the Anti-Aircraft Forces, appeared in *Sankt-Peterburgskie vedomosti* in the run-up to Victory Day 1995. On the tourism front, the English-language Web site of the city's convention

---

[22] *SPV*, 18 January 1994. For historical currency conversions, see Finmarket, http://www.finmarket.ru/z/vlk/cbrfhist.asp (accessed 18 February 2006). Igor Birman, "Gloomy Prospects for the Russian Economy," *Europe-Asia Studies* 48 (July 1996): 740. By May 1995, similar awards would have been worth about $3 and $2, respectively.

[23] *SPV*, 26 January 1994, 27 January 1994, 10 February 1994, 7 May 1994, 18 January 1995. *NV*, 5 January 1995.

[24] *SPV*, 25 January 1994.

[25] *SPV*, 5 May 1995.

[26] *SPV*, 10 February 1994.

and visitors bureau lists "Soviet Memorials and Memorabilia," including the cruiser *Aurora,* the statue of Lenin in front of the Finland Station, Piskarevskoe Cemetery, and the Monument to the Heroic Defenders of Leningrad among the city's must-see sites.[27]

The blockade nonetheless remained, for those who lived through it, a profoundly personal memory. Blokadniki continued to remember "the blockade that I suffered" and to celebrate "my holiday" on anniversaries related to the war. In January 1994, Mikhail Kuraev, who had been evacuated, along with his mother and brother, across Lake Ladoga in February 1942, remembered that "we considered the day of the lifting of the blockade holy, just like 4 February, the day grandmother and [my infant brother] Boria died."[28] For Kuraev's family, 27 January had always been an occasion for "remembering our dear ones and relatives, those who lived and those who died." He recalled that "Mama always cried on that day. It was her holiday." She mourned not only for her mother and her infant son. She "always remembered" the four- or five-year-old child whom she had seen wandering through the snowdrifts along Malyi Prospekt in December 1941; with three children of her own, she had been unable to take him in. She was "unable to forget" the middle-aged "woman of the intelligentsia," motionless but alive, whom she saw loaded onto a truck full of corpses. Kuraev himself had not witnessed these horrible sights, but in memory of his mother, "I will now remember both that little boy and that woman. Perhaps [my brother] Sergei and I are the only ones left who do." For Kuraev, insuring that "no one is forgotten, and nothing is forgotten" was a personal and community obligation, a noble and painful task ultimately bound to fail. His notion of remembrance was a long way from Yeltsin's rather glib assurance that the Russian government was ready to fund new memorials as well as the renovations necessary to preserve Soviet monuments.

What meanings the state's memorials will hold when those who remember the blockade are gone remains an open question. The Monument to the Heroic Defenders of Leningrad seems unlikely to disappear from the Petersburg cityscape anytime soon, and newlyweds continue to visit

---

[27] See, for example, *SPV,* 8 April 1995; "All About St. Petersburg for Tourists," http://www.travel.spb.ru/theguide/museums8.html (accessed 17 February 2006); Theresa Sabonis-Chaffee, "Communism as Kitsch: Soviet Symbols in Post-Soviet Society," in Adele Marie Barker, ed., *Consuming Russia: Popular Culture, Sex, and Society since Gorbachev* (Durham, NC: Duke University Press, 1999), 368–82.

[28] Mikhail Kuraev, "Moi prazdnik ...," *NV,* 25 January 1994. See also Budumir Poliakov, "Zakonchilas' voina," *Chas pik,* 11 May 1995.

it – sometimes for the first time in their lives. Like the nineteen-year-old student interviewed on the sixtieth anniversary of the lifting of the blockade, young Petersburgers may know that the siege "lasted for 900 days and that people survived severe hunger." They may marvel or shake their heads at these heroic, patriotic, but, from the point of view of post-Soviet twenty-somethings, not very "pragmatic" Leningraders.[29] When the blokadniki and veterans cease to lay flowers on the graves at Piskarevskoe, it likely will still function as a solemn and politically potent backdrop for foreign dignitaries and Russian politicians. However, it will no longer be a place of remembrance, but rather a monument to the refusal to admit that "our mothers' and fathers' lives were useless and meaningless" – a place, perhaps, where "nostalgia flourishes" and a "has been country" finds in its "mythologized past...a source of strength to face the future."[30]

    With each passing anniversary, fewer and fewer blokadniki live in Petersburg. By one count, in January 2003 – the sixtieth anniversary of the breach of the siege – only about six hundred people who spent a few months in the besieged city and only fifty people who spent the entire war within the ring of the blockade still resided in the city.[31] Of course, many more survivors live in other parts of the former Soviet Union and abroad, and their memoirs, diaries, and poetry continue to be published. On war anniversaries, interviews appear in the press. Blokadniki continue to write and speak, often with the explicit aim of making sure that a generation that did not know the war knows the whole tragic, heroic story. That the blockade was tragic and heroic – a story of great suffering as well as moral and spiritual triumphs – has remained central to their narratives, even as Soviet-era constraints have disappeared. These stories may fundamentally shape popular understandings of the blockade, but efforts to preserve and pass on memory are by definition quixotic. Survivors – the people who were there – are, as Samuel Hynes has pointed out with regard to World War I veterans, the only people who can connect the mythic narratives

---

[29] *St. Petersburg Times*, 27 January 2004.

[30] Carina Perelli, "*Memoria de Sangre*: Fear, Hope, and Disenchantment in Argentina," in Jonathan Boyarin, ed., *Remapping Memory: The Politics of TimeSpace* (Minneapolis: University of Minnesota Press, 1994), 39. See also Gregory Guroff and Alexander Guroff, "The Paradox of Russian National Identity," in Roman Szporluck, ed., *National Identity and Ethnicity in Russia and the New States of Eurasia* (Armonk, NY: M. E. Sharpe, 1994), 88.

[31] The data are from the city Council of Veterans. "Sixtieth Anniversary of the Day When Blockade of Leningrad Was Broken Through," *Pravda.RU*, 18 January 2003, http://english.pravda.ru/region/2003/01/18/42216.html (accessed 17 February 2006).

"to actual memory."[32] With the death of the last witness, myth will cease to be tethered to memory.

Yet even if we can never know the "real meaning" of war for those who lived through it, even if we conceptualize memory more as imaginative construction than the retrieval of some proverbial "actual memory" that undergirds war stories but nonetheless remains ineffable, we can trace the fallout of war through survivors' long-term efforts as individuals and as a community to live with and make sense of their memories – in part by constructing and assimilating consoling myths, in part by adapting myths to the difficult circumstances of postwar and post-Soviet life. Those of us who were not there can find much of human and historic value in their stories if we seek "what they reveal about the protagonists' hearts, rather than their deeds."[33] The myths and monuments of the blockade do not encode the "real meaning" or the "actual memory" of the war. However, they provide a glimpse of real efforts – constrained, difficult, incomplete – to make peace with memory.

---

[32] Samuel Hynes, "Personal Narratives and Commemoration," in Jay Winter and Emmanuel Sivan, eds., *War and Remembrance in the Twentieth Century* (New York: Cambridge University Press, 1999), 220. See also Jay Winter and Emmanuel Sivan, "Setting the Framework," in ibid., 10.

[33] Salman Rushdie, *The Moor's Last Sigh* (1995; reprint, New York: Vintage International, 1997), 135.

Index